THE
MINNESOTA
ALMANAC
1988

Mary Ann Grossmann
Tom Thomsen
Editors

ISBN 0-942072-03-0

John L. Brekke and Sons, Publishers

i

First edition 1976 by Robert A. Jones

Second edition
Copyright © 1981 by John L. Brekke
Library of Congress Catalog Card Number 76-48553

Third edition 1987

John L. Brekke, Publisher
Rt. #1, Box 83
Taylors Falls, Minnesota 55084

Type Composition:
Nordell Graphic Communications
Staples, MN 56479

Printed in U.S.A.

Distributed By
Adventure Publications
P.O. Box 269
Cambridge, MN 55008

ACKNOWLEDGMENTS

In an effort to make this almanac useful, informative and above all accurate, many people in government and in the private sector had provided invaluable advice and encouragement and some have undertaken to write or edit sections in which they are expert. Here we wish to express our appreciation and gratitude.

Initially the Minnesota AFL-CIO, Minnesota Teamsters, Minnesota United Auto Workers, Minneapolis Central Labor Union, St. Paul Trades and Labor Assembly, the public relations departments of the Minnesota Fillies, North Stars, Twins, Vikings, and the State High School League and University of Minnesota sports information department. Also, Associated Press Minneapolis Bureau, KTCA-TV, Minneapolis Star and Tribune, Minnesota Newspaper Association, St. Paul Dispatch and Pioneer Press. Also these offices of the State of Minnesota: Council on the Economic Status of Women; Department of Agriculture; Department of Economic Development research division; Department of Military Affairs, office of the adjutant general; Department of Natural Resources; Department of Public Safety, Bureau of Criminal Apprehension; Department of Public Welfare; Department of Transportation; Department of Veteran's Affairs; Law Library staff; Legislative Reference Library staff; House of Representatives public information office; Senate Information Office; Office of the State Demographer; Secretary of State's office; State Planning Agency; Supreme Court, Court Information Office; Community College System; Department of Education; Private College Council; University of Minnesota, Department of University Relations. Also, the United States Census Office, United States Department of Agriculture, Norwegian Consul General; American Iron Ore Association, Corporate Report, Minnesota League of Women Voters, Minnesota Taxpayers Association, Fort Snelling Restoration and Historic Area, Minnesota Historical Society, Minnesota Zoological Garden, St. Paul Winter Carnival Association, University of Minnesota Center for Urban and Regional Development.

In addition to all those people who laid the groundwork for this edition of the almanac, the publisher wishes to acknowledge the contributions of others. . .with thanks and appreciation.

Ruth Aamot, Alice Brekke, Lillian Brekke, Ray Christensen, Jim Cordell, Nancy Gibson, Ann Ingvalson, Steve Kahlenbeck, Jack Miller, Cashie Nickelson, Les Norman, George Osland, meteorologist Bruce Watson, and the three people who gave so much of themselves, Mary Ann Grossmann, Tom Thomsen and David C. Nordell (Owner of Nordell Graphic Communications, Staples, Minnesota.)

Your comments and suggestions regarding this almanac are welcomed. Each succeeding almanac will try contain, to the greatest possible extent, the information you find useful and entertaining.

For the late
Bob Jones
whose vision brought
this book to life.

TABLE OF CONTENTS

History

Exploration and Territory 1654 - 1857

The earliest probable explorers to reach Minnesota were French traders Radisson and Groseilliers in 1654. In 1679 Daniel Greysolon Dulhut (Duluth) held a council with the Sioux (Dakota) near Mille Lacs Lake. He met Father Louis Hennepin at the Mississippi after traveling down the St. Croix River the following year. That same year, 1680, Father Hennepin, after being held captive in a village of the Mille Lacs Sioux, discovered the Falls of St. Anthony. On May 8, 1689, Nicholas Perrot, at Fort St. Antoine, on the Wisconsin shore of Lake Pepin, laid formal claim to the surrounding county for France. He also built a fort on the Minnesota shore of this lake, near its outlet. Between 1689 and 1736, the French continued to develop forts and settlements in Minnesota such as Isle Pelee in 1695, Fort L'Huillier in 1700, Fort Beauharnois near Frontenac in 1727 and Forts St. Pierre and St. Charles in extreme northern Minnesota established in 1731.

In 1745 the Chippewa won the most decisive battle in the war with the Sioux at the great Sioux village of Kathio on the western shore of Mille Lacs. The Sioux were eventually driven onto the western plains by the Chippewa.

The Versailles Treaty of 1763, following the French-Indian War, ceded the French territory east of the Mississippi River to England. France had ceded its area west of the Mississippi to Spain in 1762.

Following the Revolutionary War, the North West Company became important in the fur trade and Grand Portage became its headquarters in 1784. By 1797 the Minnesota area of the Northwest Territory had been mapped by North West trader David Thompson.

In 1803 President Thomas Jefferson purchased that part of Minnesota lying west of the Mississippi River, from Napoleon Bonaparte in the Louisiana Purchase.

During the War of 1812, the Sioux, Chippewa and Winnebago joined the English. Following the War of 1812, the United States established Fort St. Anthony (renamed Fort Snelling in 1825) in 1819 to protect the confluence of the Minnesota and Mississippi Rivers. The first steamboat arrived at Fort Snelling on May 10, 1823. In the same year American explorer Stephen H. Long visited the Minnesota River, the Red River, and the Northern frontier. In 1832 Henry R. Schoolcraft discovered the source of the Mississippi river and named it Lake Itasca. In 1836 after Michigan became a state, Minnesota became part of the territory of Wisconsin. The same year, Joseph N. Nicollet began his explorations into Minnesota.

In 1837, Governor Dodge of Wisconsin signed a treaty at Fort Snelling with the Chippewa, by which they ceded all their pine lands on the St. Croix and its tributaries. A treaty was also signed at Washington, D.C. with representatives of the Sioux for their lands east of the Mississippi. These treaties led the way to the first settlements within the area of Minnesota. The following year, Franklin Steele established a claim at the Falls of St. Anthony (Minneapolis) and Pierre Parrant built a shanty and settled on the present site of the city of St. Paul, then called "Pig's Eye", after that unsavory character.

The "Chapel of St. Paul" was built and consecrated in 1841, giving the name to the future capitol of the state.

On August 26, 1848, after the admission of Wisconsin to the Union, the "Stillwater Convention" adopted measures calling for a separate territorial organization, and asked that the new territory be named Minnesota. Two months later, on October 30, Henry Hastings Sibley was elected delegate to Congress.

In 1849 Minnesota was organized as a territory and the first territorial legislature assembled on September 3.

By 1850 commercial steamboating was inaugurated on the Minnesota River. The first U.S. census was taken in the Minnesota territory and recorded a population of 6,077 in 1850. In 1851 St. Paul, St. Anthony, and Stillwater were selected for the locations of capitol, university, and penitentiary.

During the 1850's a number of organizations were established to encourage the importation of blooded stock and the introduction of choice seeds, grain and fruit trees to the territory.

In 1853 W. A. Gorman was appointed governor and the first capitol was constructed. In 1854 commercial flour milling began in Minneapolis. Large scale immigration began in the mid 1850's and a real estate boom resulted. The first bridge to span the main channel of the Mississippi River anywhere along its length was opened in Minneapolis in 1855.

1857 saw the beginning of moves to establish the state government in Minnesota. The Minnesota Enabling Act was passed by Congress on February 26. Governor Samuel Medary, who had been appointed by President James Buchanan, arrived on April 22. The legislature passed a bill to move the state capitol to St. Peter, but since the bill was stolen before it was filed with the territorial secretary of state, the move to St. Peter never came about. On July 13 the Constitutional Convention assembled. There had been such a rift between Democrats and Republicans that two constitutions were adopted. The Constitution was adopted and the state officers elected on October 3, 1857. Minnesota had a population of 150,037 at this time. On May 11, 1858, Minnesota entered the Union as the 32nd state. At the time of its entry, Minnesota was the third largest state in the Union—only Texas and California were larger.

Early Statehood 1858 - 1898

At the beginning of the Civil War, Governor Alexander Ramsey wired Lt. Gov. Ignatius Donnelly to begin to organize volunteers from the state to fight in the war. On April 14, 1861, Ramsey offered President Lincoln 1,000 men giving Minnesota the distinction of being the first state to offer troops to the Union cause. The first Minnesota regiment left Fort Snelling on June 22, 1861.

On July 2, 1862, the first railroad was opened in Minnesota between Minneapolis and St. Paul. During the Sioux uprising in the late summer of 1862, a number of settlements were attacked. A military commission tried 392 Indians for murder, rape, and other charges, and 303 of them were condemned. On December 26, 1862, 38 Indians were hanged at Mankato.

At the battle of Gettysburg on July 2, 1862, the First Minnesota Regiment made its famous charge and within 15 minutes 215 of the 262 men were killed or wounded. On July 3, Chief Little Crow, Sioux leader of the Sioux Uprising, was killed near Hutchinson. At the close of the Civil and Indian Wars, the Minnesota troops totaled 21,982.

The University of Minnesota was opened in 1886 with William W. Folwell as its first president.

The development by Edmund N. LaCroix of the middlings purifier for flour helped expand the development of Minnesota, the Dakotas and western Canada.

The Legislative Amendment providing for biennial sessions was passed in 1877.

On March 1, 1881, the first state capitol burned. A second state capitol was built on the same spot. The legislature moved into the second capitol in January, 1883.

The first iron ore was shipped from Minnesota in 1884. The first mine was the Soudan mine on the Vermillion Range. Iron was first discovered on the Mesabi Range 6 years later in 1890 and that range shipped its first iron in 1892.

In 1893 the legislature appointed a Capitol Commission to select a site for and erect a new state capitol building.

Killer forest fires started on September 1, 1894, destroying over 400 sq. miles of area near Hinckley and Sandstone.

Three-fourths of the Red Lake Indian Reservation was opened for settlement in 1896.

The cornerstone on the new state capitol was laid on July 27, 1898. Minnesota was the first state to respond to the President's call for volunteers in the Spanish-American War. Minnesota supplied four regiments for service.

Growth and Development 1899 - 1950

During the late 19th and early 20th centuries the tide of immigration into the state swelled. The most notable origins of this movement were Germany, Sweden, Norway and Denmark. The other migrations from Southern and Eastern Europe contributed to a lesser degree to the state's population increase.

In 1909 President Theodore Roosevelt issued a proclamation establishing Superior National Forest. In 1911 the legislature ratified the proposed amendment to the U.S. Constitution allowing for the direct election of U.S. Senators.

Minnesota became the first state, in 1913, to adopt a non-partisan system of electing its legislators.

During World War I, Minnesota contributed 123,325 troops.

On October 12-13, 1918, forest fires spread over large parts of Carlton and southern St. Louis counties taking 432 lives.

In 1925 a general reorganization of the state government occurred.

In 1930 Minnesotan Frank B. Kellogg, U.S. Secretary of State, was awarded the 1929 Nobel Peace Prize for his work on the Kellogg-Briand Peace Pact signed in Paris in 1928. The purpose of the Pact was to outlaw war.

Floyd B. Olson was elected as the first Farmer-Labor governor of Minnesota in 1930. State population at this time was 2,563,953.

In 1931 Sinclair Lewis of Sauk Centre was awarded the Nobel Prize for Literature.

In the election of 1932 all nine of Minnesota's representatives were elected at large. In 1933 the legislature passed a Reapportionment Act, dividing the state into nine congressional districts.

As the depression worsened in 1933-34, federal and state projects were provided to assist the large numbers of unemployed. The Old Age Assistance Act became effective March 1, 1936.

In 1937, The Pipestone National Monument was established to protect the Indians' sacred quarry near Pipestone.

As a result of a special session of the legislature in 1944, persons in the armed forces were permitted to vote.

The 1946 value of crops in Minnesota was at a high of $683,000,000.

In 1948, for the first time, the value of manufactured products exceeded cash farm receipts in the state.

1951 - 1975

In 1951, Minnesota produced 82% of the nation's total iron ore output. That year Minnesota produced a new record—89,564,932 tons of iron ore.

A year long centennial celebration was held in 1958 marking the first 100 years of Minnesota statehood. Grand Portage National Monument was established to protect one of the nation's foremost inland centers of 18th and 19th century fur trading.

Oceanic trade began with the opening of the St. Lawrence Seaway in 1959. This significant event made Duluth accessible to ocean vessels from anywhere in the world.

In the state's closest race for governor, after more than four months of recounts, Karl F. Rolvaag was sworn in as governor on March 25, 1963. He was declared the winner by 91 votes.

Hubert H. Humphrey became the first Minnesotan to obtain national elective office when he was sworn in as President Lyndon B. Johnson's vice president on January 20, 1965.

The spring of 1965 saw the worst flooding in the state's history

Vice-President Hubert H. Humphrey, in 1968, became the first Minnesotan nominated by a major party for President of the United States.

The state noted in 1974 the death of Charles A. Lindbergh, Jr., a native of Little Falls, who was world renowned for being the first person to fly across the Atlantic Ocean alone.

The worst blizzard of the century swept through Minnesota on January 11, 1975, with the lowest barometric pressure reading ever recorded; spring and early summer flooding, especially in the Red River Valley, caused millions of dollars in crop damage. In early July the third known earthquake in state history was recorded in a large area of west-central Minnesota. The summer of 1976 brought the worst drought in 100 years to southwestern Minnesota.

1976-1982

Where blizzards, floods and windstorms dealt blows to the Minnesota economy in 1975, the state was plagued by an extensive drought and forest fires in 1976 and an energy emergency early in 1977.

Walter F. Mondale became the second Minnesotan to be elected to the nation's second highest office. Seventh district congressman Bob Bergland was appointed by President-elect Jimmy Carter to the post of secretary of agriculture.

On December 29, 1976, Gov. Wendell R. Anderson resigned midway through his second term and was succeeded by Lt. Gov. Rudy Perpich. The day after Perpich succeeded to the governorship, Mondale resigned his seat in the U.S. senate and Perpich appointed Anderson to succeed him.

National attention was focused on Minnesota in January of 1978 when Sen. Hubert H. Humphrey died. He was succeeded by his widow Muriel.

The Minnesota Zoological Garden opened in Apple Valley in May.

Concern over fuel shortages lasted throughout 1978, with Gov. Quie calling out the National Guard in June to protect tank trucks from possible violence during a shutdown by independent truckers protesting rising fuel prices.

After years of controversy and sometimes violent protest, a 436-mile power line from North Dakota to Minnesota was put into operation in July. The 400,000-volt line runs from Underwood, N.D., to Delano.

In 1980 Minnesotans, along with the rest of the nation, awaited word of the hostages held captive in Iran. Two Minnesotans were among the 52 -U.S. Charge d'Affairs Bruce Laingen, 57, of Odin, and Army Warrant Officer Joseph Hall, 31, Little Falls. (They were released with the other hostages in January of 1981.)

Concern about hazardous chemical wastes and where they are dumped spread throughout the state after residents of Spring Valley and Oakdale found that old dump sites in their areas posed a risk of contamination of wells.

The U.S. hockey team earned world attention at the Winter Olympics at Lake Placid, N.Y., defeating the Russians and winning a gold medal. Coach Herb Brooks and many of the players were from Minnesota.

A shortfall of $195 million in expected tax revenues forced Gov. Quie to order cuts in spending for state agencies, school districts and local governmental aids.

Minnesota's budget problems continued through 1981; by the end of the year the state had a revenue shortage of some $700 million. Gov. Al Quie called three special sessions during the year to resolve the cash shortfall problems and the state ran short of immediate cash, missing two payments to local govenments.

In the private sector housing construction fell to the lowest level since the Depression and layoffs were rampant in the Twin Cities, Duluth and the Iron Range.

More than 6,000 public school teachers in 36 districts struck for a total of 302 days in some three dozen teachers' strikes. And some 140,000 state workers, almost half of the state's employees, went on strike in July and returned to work August 11, ending the largest strike by public employees in state history.

Brighter news was made by Gerry Spiess of White Bear Lake who crossed the Pacific Ocean in his 10-foot sloop, Yankee Girl.

The last game was played at Metropolitan Stadium in Bloomington on December 20 and the Teflon-coated, fiberglass roof of the new Hubert H. Humphrey Metrodome was inflated in October.

In politics, Rudy Perpich won the governorship against Wheelock Whitney and Sen. David Durenberger withstood a well-financed challenge from Mark Dayton.

Other important 1982 events included the official opening of the Hubert H. Humphrey Metrodome in Minneapolis, trials of six members of the Cermak family of southern Minnesota accused of intra-familial abuse, a liver transplant at the University of Minnesota for 11-month-old Jamie Fiske of Massachusetts and the voyage of the Viking replica ship Hjemkomst, which sailed from its home port of Duluth to Norway.

1983 - Present

Grim economic news continued into 1983, with the unemployment rate at 15.7 in October in Minnesota's northeastern corner. The jobless rate was due to layoffs and shutdowns at Iron Range taconite mines, the largest employer in the region.

There was another record snowfall and cold weather during November and December of 1983.

In politics, Rudy Perpich was sworn in for a second term of office as governor and visited at least a dozen foreign countries and 21 states in his role as the state's leading salesman and booster.

The continuing story in most of 1984 was the presidential candidacy of native son Walter Mondale and his historic choice of Geraldine Ferraro as the nations's first female vice-presidential candidate.

About 6,300 nurses struck 16 Twin Cities hospitals for five weeks in a walkout that began on June 1, 1984 affected some 8,000 non-nursing employees. It was the largest nurses' strike in the nation's history.

In other 1984 developments, investors in Minnesota's first pari-mutual racetrack near Shakopee asked for controversial new financing; the sex abuse case that began in 1981 with the arrest of the Cermak family grew to implicate 35 adults in the Jordan area; C. Peter Magrath resigned after 10 years as president of the University of Minnesota to take a job at the University of Missouri; Calvin Griffith and his family ended a 65-year reign as owners of the Minnesota Twins when they sold the team to Minneapolis businessman Carl Pohlad and former Twins player Harmon Killebrew was voted into baseball's Hall of Fame.

Economic crisis for many of Minnesota's farmers, and its ripple effect on small town businesses and banks, were the top stories of 1985.

Ironically, it was also the year that Garrison Keiller put Minnesota on the map with publication of his best-selling book, "Lake Wobegon Days," which celebrates the state's rural heritage.

Minnesota lost 5,000 farms from June 1984 to June 1985; six rural banks failed, the most in any year since the Great Depression.

The state mourned for 70 people, most of them Minnesotans, who were killed in the crash of an airplane just south of Reno, Nev.

Bitterness swamped Austin as 1,500 meatpackers at the Geo. A. Hormel & Co. plant went on strike after a 10-month dispute.

In sports, Bud Grant returned as head coach of the Minnesota Vikings, University of Minnesota football head coach Lou Holtz became head coach at Notre Dame and the annual All-Star baseball game was played at the Metrodome in Minneapolis.

Other 1985 highlights included the opening of the $45 million Ordway Music Theatre in St. Paul and of the $70 million Canterbury Downs racetrack in Shakopee; the selection of Kenneth Keller as president of the University of Minnesota and implantation of an artificial heart in Mary Lund, the first woman to undergo the procedure.

The Hormel strike again dominated the news in January of 1986 when the plant reopened after a five-month strike and striking meatpackers ringed the plant, blocking entrances. Gov. Perpich called out the National Guard, which stayed until February.

In politics, legislators dealt with a $734 million budget shortfall, the legal drinking age was changed to 21 and Gov. Perpich was re-elected.

Will Steger's dogsled expedition reached the North Pole, making Sunfish Lake native Anne Bancroft the first woman to cross the ice to the pole.

After four years of intense negotiations and 200 years of disunity, three major Lutheran denominations agreed to merge into the new Evangelical Lutheran Church in America.

Military

TWENTY SIX year-old Lieutenant Zebulon Montgomery Pike arrived at the current site of Mendota on Sept. 21, 1806 and raised the Stars and Stripes, probably for the first time over Minnesota.

Under George Washington, the United States had developed and operated the "factor system," a chain of federal fur-trading posts and stores. Not motivated by profit, it was designed to serve as a deterrent to foreign traders, mostly English and Spanish, improve relations with the Indians, beef up frontier military muscle and protect the Indians from the fur traders.

Thomas Jefferson took a giant step in his dream to have America extend from the Atlantic to the Pacific when he engineered the Louisiana Purchase in 1803, buying nearly half a continent from Napoleon.

Military forts were set up in the new lands, and serious explorations conducted, with added facilities established where needed. Pike was given orders to find the headwaters of the Mississippi, conciliate the Indians, "attach them to the United States" and arrange for the construction of outposts and trading houses.

His discussion with the Sioux led to a treaty (ratified by the congress in 1808) which established the site of Fort Snelling. It has served the military interests of the country in the state since 1820.

History

The story of Fort Snelling is the story of the development of the Northwest (now called the Upper Midwest) from 1819 to the present.

Pre-1820. British fur traders from Canada continued effective control of the Northwest long after it became the United States' territory as a result of the Revolutionary War (1783) and the Louisiana Purchase (1803). The Chippewa and Eastern Sioux depended upon British trade goods to feed and clothe themselves. To obtain these manufactured necessities, they delivered millions of dollars worth of fur and allied themselves with the British in the War of 1812.

After the war, the United States developed a frontier policy to eliminate British influence in the Northwest. The goals of this policy were to keep out foreign traders, protect and regulate American traders, pacify and win the good will of the tribes and extend the frontier to the Great Lakes and the Mississippi. To carry out this policy, a chain of forts and Indian Agencies was built from Lake Michigan to the Missouri River. In 1819, the 5th Regiment of Infantry was ordered to build a post at the junction of the Mississippi and St. Peter's (Minnesota) Rivers. This post, called St. Anthony, was the northwestern link in the chain of forts. The river junction was chosen because it was the local fur trade depot, it lay between the lands of the Sioux and

Chippewa, it controlled traffic on both rivers and it had good water communications north, south and west.

1820-58. Fort St. Anthony was completed by 1825 and renamed to honor its builder and first commander, Colonel Josiah Snelling. The Indian Agent, Major Lawrence Taliaferro, established St. Peter's Agency beside the fort. Taliaferro was expected to lessen friction between the tribes and between the Indians and whites by drawing boundaries, making treaties, presenting gifts, providing missions, blacksmiths and model farms and by restraining the traders' most unscrupulous activities. The garrison of Fort Snelling was the force which could be used to keep settlers out of Indian Territory, to keep liquor out of the trade and to punish Indians and whites who broke the peace or violated the laws of the frontier. For almost 30 years, Snelling, Taliaferro and their successors acted as the only police and government for 90,000 square miles. The size and strength of the fort was the symbol of their power and authority. The soldiers, traders and Indians had no love for each other, but war was avoided by impartial enforcement of laws and a balance of restraint on both traders and Indians.

When the frontier of settlement reached the Mississippi in 1837, this balance was upset. Minnesota Territory was established in 1848 and soon the land-hungry farmers and speculators demanded the Sioux lands west of the river. By the treaties of 1851, the Sioux were confined to reservations and their land opened to settlement. Forts Ripley, Ridgely and Abercrombie were built to guard the new frontier further west. The Territorial government was established in St. Paul. Fort Snelling's frontier duty was over; it served as a supply depot until 1858, when, as Minnesota achieved statehood, it was turned over to the speculators who had bought it the year before.

1858-present. Although the military reservation was platted for a townsite, the City of Fort Snelling was never built. During the Civil War (1861-65) the state used the fort to train its volunteer troops, and after the war the regular army repossessed and used it as headquarters for Indian war campaigns in the Dakotas. Between 1870 and the early 1900s, many new brick barracks, officer's quarters, offices, shops and stables were built, while the old stone fort was allowed to decay and was gradually demolished. After serving as a recruiting and training center in two world wars, Fort Snelling was decommissioned in 1946 and turned over to the Veterans Administration and Army Reserve.

In 1956, the threat of a freeway through the heart of the old fort stimulated public efforts to save the remnants of the oldest buildings in Minnesota.

In 1960, Fort Snelling was designated Minnesota's first National Historic Landmark, and the following year the Legislature established Fort Snelling State Historical Park. Since 1963, the Legislature has appropriated funds to develop the 2,500 acre park and to rebuild the old fort. By the time all 18 buildings of the original fort are rebuilt, a staff acting as soldiers, cooks, laundresses, blacksmith, carpenter and armorer will show how men and women on the frontier lived and worked in the 1820s.

Fort Snelling Restoration is administered by the Minnesota Historical Society; phone 726-1171, Monday through Friday. It is located Northeast of the intersection of Interstate 494 and Highways 55, south of Minneapolis, north of the airport.

FORT SNELLING 1825-1835

This view shows the fort as it looked after completion but before major alterations were made in the 1840's; it also shows the fort as it will look when the restoration is complete.

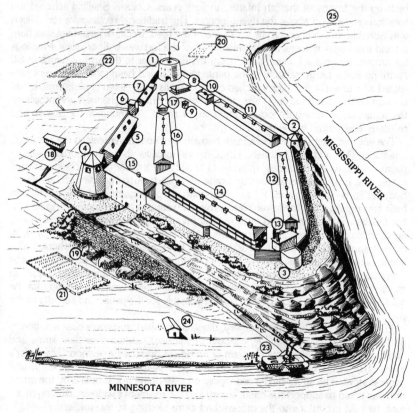

1. Round Tower*
2. Pentagonal Tower*
3. Semicircular Battery
4. Hexagonal Tower*
5. Shops
6. Gate House
7. Guard House*
8. Magazine*
9. Well*
10. Sutler's Store*
11. Short Barrack
12. Long Barrack
13. Commandant's House
14. Officers' Quarters
15. Commissary Warehouse
16. Hospital
17. School/Chapel*
18. Stable
19. Root Cellars
20. Cemetery
21. Gardens
22. Fields
23. Landing
24. Wash House
25. St. Anthony Falls—Sawmill Gristmill

*Restored by June, 1971

Description of the Fort
1820—1830

Fourteen stone and two wooden buildings and over 1500 feet of stone wall were built by the troops of the 5th Infantry in four years. Colonel Snelling selected the location on the bluff above the river junction. The traditional rectangular fort design was adapted to a diamond to fit the shape of the bluff. Because limestone was handy and there were masons in the ranks, most of the fort was built of stone. Pine logs for timbers and planks were floated from the Rum River to the army sawmill at St. Anthony Falls. Large cannon in the pentagonal (2) and hexagonal (4) towers protected all four walls. Sentries watched over the walls from elevated platforms. Small cannon on the round tower (1) were aimed over the prairie to the west and others on the semicircular battery (3) looked down on the rivers. Ammunition for cannon and muskets was stored in the magazine (8).

The enlisted men slept two in a bunk and ate their common meals in the barracks, one stone (11) and one wooden (12). Officers' families share the fourteen sets of rooms in the wooden officers' quarters (14) with the theater and bachelor officers' mess. The post commander set up home and headquarters in the commandant's house (13). In the post shops (5) the blacksmith, carpenter, armorer and wheelwright built and repaired the tools, vehicles, furniture, weapons and equipment needed on the frontier. The baker turned out the daily bread ration, eighteen ounces per man, aged or toasted before issue. Foodstuffs and supplies were stored in the four-story commissary warehouse (15): flour from the fort's gristmill at St. Anthony Falls, sugar, vinegar, uniforms, shoes, harness, blankets, nails, glass, paint, tents and everything else sent upriver annually from Philadelphia, Pittsburg and St. Louis. In the guardhouse (7) were cells for military and civilian prisoners, and quarters for the guard detail and the Officer of the Day, responsible for the peace and security of the post.

The hospital (16) included a surgery, dispensary, ward, surgeon's quarters, library and kitchen. In the school (17), children of the post worked over their sums and spelling, and on Sundays the chaplain or an officer preached a sermon. The sutler's store (10) was a combination post exchange, enlisted men's club, grocery, and general store. The sutler held a monopoly on everything not supplied by the army, but was taxed to support the band, library and the regiment's widows. Among much else, he sold provisions to the officers and extra clothing to the soldiers.

Everything needed by this community was located in the neighborhood. Down at the river landing (23) cargoes of food, supplies and firewood were unloaded from keelboats, flatboats, and steamboats, and hauled up the steep road to the fort. The wash house (24) stood handy to the river, because it was easier to carry clothes than water up the bluff. Vegetables grown in the gardens (21) on the river bottoms were stored in the cool cave-like root cellars (19) beneath the road. Fields (22) of corn, oats and wheat were fenced off on the prairie atop the bluff. Herds of beef cattle grazed in the prairie grass. The odors of manure, cowhides, hot fat and tar, woodsmoke, leather and hay filled the air around the stable (18). Draft horses and oxen drew carts loaded with wheat to the gristmill (25) at St. Anthony Falls and returned loaded with lumber from the sawmill or bricks and lime from the kilns. Occasionally a small procession marched slowly across the prairie to the cemetery (20), followed by a casket carried by soldiers with black armbands.

Garrison Life

Three to six companies of the regiment, 150 to 300 men, women and children, usually lived in the fort. Their daily routines were ordered by rank: officers and enlisted men. Officers were expected to inspect, supervise and report everything, everyone and every event. Still, they had the leisure to be gentlemen and sportsmen, and their tables were spread with varieties of game and fine wines. Officers and their families were assigned to private quarters, at least two rooms and a kitchen. Their wives organized the social life of the fort: teas, dances, dinners and concerts. By 1820, most young lieutenants were graduates of West Point and took their profession of arms seriously. After 30 years commanding a company on the frontier, they learned all about human failings, military forms and seniority and forgot nearly everything else. Most of them retired as middle-aged captains.

The life of the enlisted men was endless labor: building forts and roads, tending crops, cutting firewood and standing guard. Frontier duty made good farmers but rusty soldiers. Constant fatigue and guard details left no time for drill and ceremonies. They ate regulation rations of soup, bread and coffee, with vegetables from their gardens. Enlisted families shared 17 by 20 foot rooms in the barracks. Enlisted men's wives were chosen to follow the regiment to be cooks, laundresses and maids. No self-respecting man would enlist because the soldier was paid only $6.00 a month in comparison to the laborer's $25.00 and because rank distinctions were considered undemocratic. The ranks were filled with the ne'er-do-well, the shiftless and the troublesome. Some of the best recruits were immigrants wanting to learn English. Discipline was enforced by the cat-o-nine tails and solitary confinement on bread and water. Drunkenness and desertion were the common offenses: boredom and lethargy the common mood.

The Civil War

Night after night, Dred Scott sat in his basement quarters in officers' building No. 2 at Fort Snelling mulling over his plans to attain freeman status and little dreaming that his actions would bring about a Supreme Court decision which would, in turn, lead to the Civil War.

Scott, a slave owned by army surgeon Dr. John Sherman, had been taken by his master from Missouri, a slave state, to Illinois, a free state, and then to Minnesota territory in 1834, where slavery was prohibited by the Missouri Compromise. This was the result of a series of measures passed by congress to appease both the south and the north on the matter of slavery.

Scott married another slave at Fort Snelling and, after his master's death, sued the widow for his freedom. Scott's legal skirmishing ended up in the Supreme Court where Chief Justice Roger B. Taney handed down the controversial decision in favor of the widow Sherman, polarized the north (and the south), and resulted in the War between the States.

When the conflict started with the bombardment of Fort Sumter, Minnesota was only three years old and it was involved in it and, little more than a year later, a violent Sioux war. Minnesota Governor Ramsey by chance in Washington on April 3, 1861, learned about Fort Sumter and immediately went to Secretary of War Cameron to offer 1000 Minnesotans for federal service. President Lincoln accepted these men into federal armies, even in advance of his request for 75,000 volunteers from the entire north.

Quick to enter the fray, the First Minnesota Infantry Volunteers suffered heavy casualties in the battle of Bull Run on July 21.

All told, Minnesota provided 24,000 men—and this from a state whose total population was only 172,000. They made notable contributions at Corinth, Vicksburg, Gettysburg, Chickamauga, Chattanooga, Brice's Cross Roads and Nashville as well as clashes with the Sioux at home.

The Sioux War

Four young devil-may-care Wahpeton indians, Killing Ghost, Breaking Up, Runs Against Something When Crawling and Brown Wing, happened by the farm of Robinson Jones, whom they challenged to a friendly "turkey shoot." The friendly target practice unaccountably became violent and when the gunsmoke settled, five whites lay dead.

Learning of the incident, the outlying bands, seething because of their bad treatment at the hands of the whites, who, among other things, were late in their payments promised by treaty, gathered under Little Crow and mounted a series of surprise attacks against isolated farms, settlements and Fort Ridgeley. Drained of its fighting men by the Civil War, the state quickly trained available manpower and sent units out willy-nilly to trouble spots.

After two determined assaults on Fort Ridgeley and two on New Ulm were repulsed, the tide began to turn, and a militia of 1600 whites led by General Sibley brought the hostilities to an end. On September 26, his troops entered the Wood Lake Camp held by friendly Indians and were handed over 269 Sioux prisoners-107 whites and 162 half-breeds; the place is known in Sioux War history as *Camp Release*. It is estimated that in the widely scattered actions 486 white people were killed—360 civilians and 126 soldiers.

Captures of stray bands and voluntary surrenders brought the number of Sioux prisoners to 2,000, and a military commission sentenced 307 to death and 16 to imprisonment. President Lincoln reviewed the list and ordered Sibley to hang 39 (one of these was later reprieved) late in December in Mankato. A marker in that city indicates that spot where the 38 plunged to their deaths at the same instant on the day after Christmas.

The Spanish American War

By 1890, the dust of marching feet and battle had settled over Minnesota and the frontier forts closed. Ten years earlier, Fort Snelling was sold to one Franklin Steele, but he defaulted on his payments and later, at the urging of President Grant, Congress acted to reclaim the land and buildings, which was fortunate since they were needed to satisfy the needs of a national movement under way to re-activate a militia system. The state volunteer militia was moved into the National Guard, units of which were called out to handle state emergencies.

Meanwhile tensions were building between the United States and Spain and war broke out in the spring of 1898. Curiously, two Minnesotans were deeply involved; St. Paul's Archbishop Ireland, at the request of Pope Leo XII, had done his best to persuade President McKinley to avoid the conflict, but Senator Cushman K. Davis of St. Paul, chairman of the committee on foreign relations, steered a war resolution through the Senate.

Called by some a non-war that had been hatched by the yellow press of W. R. Hearst's *New York Journal* and Joseph Pulitzer's *New York World,* and the U.S. governments concern about the heavy losses of American investment in Cuba, it embroiled the nation.

Minnesota's adjutant general Herman Muehlberg proudly reported "The rapid mobilization resulted in our (Minnesota's) troops being the first volunteers mustered into the service of our country."

Altogether, 8,948 Minnesotans took part in the Cuban and Phillipine campaigns of the war.

World War I

Minnesota, like the rest of the U.S., was caught up in the great conflict, unprepared as usual. Imperialist, economic, territorial and nationalist rivalries lit the fuse.

A collection of amateurs, jerry-built into a disorganized system of National Guard units, formed a cadre for a monumental military machine composed of draftees and emotional volunteers dedicated to defeating the Kaiser and making the world "safe for democracy."

Minnesotans flocked to the colors with their customary enthusiasm and distinguished themselves in every branch of the service and theater of the war. A state contingent, the 1st Battalion, 151st Field Artillery, performed with distinction with the Famed Rainbow Division under Brig. Gen. George Leach, later mayor of Minneapolis.

Of the 127,578 Minnesotans in uniform, 887 died in battle, 1,251 died of wounds suffered in combat, 5,084 were wounded and 101 were taken prisoner.

World War II

On Sunday, Dec. 7, 1941, at 3:55 a.m. Hawaiian time, the U.S. Ward was on picket duty at the entrance to Pearl Harbor. Gun crew No. 3 opened fire on a Japanese submarine, sinking it—this, four hours before Japanese bombers struck in a surprise raid on Hickam Field and the harbored fleet. 2208 military personnel were killed and 1109 wounded, along with 68 civilian deaths. The U.S. was plunged into global war.

The Ward, formerly the Gopher, was manned entirely by a St. Paul Naval Reserve group that had trained in Duluth. Known as the "First Shotters," the survivors of the unit, mostly St. Paul residents, hold a reunion each December 7.

But the struggle was not limited to the Pacific. Minnesota's famous 34th "Red Bull" division held the distinction of being the first National Guard division shipped overseas. They fought their way across North Africa from the Kasserine Pass to the Mediterranean, up the boot of Italy, through Monte Cassino to the Po Valley, amassing the record for the greatest number of days in combat for any American division.

In these and battles on every continent, 4,399 North Star soldiers died in battle or of wounds, 302 were listed as missing and 382 died in prison camps.

Korean and Vietnam Wars

Many Minnesotans served their nation in the Korean war which lasted from June 25, 1950 until July 27, 1953. Eighteen years later, in 1961, they answered the call to fight in America's longest military involvement—the Vietnam conflict which dragged on until Jan. 27, 1973.

The final stories are yet to be written about the Korean "police action" and the unpopular Vietnam ordeal in relation to participation by natives of the North Star State, but official listings of veterans of those eras is impressive.

Veterans in Minnesota

As of March 31, 1980, there were about 31.1 million former servicemen and women living in the United States. Of these, an estimated 559,000 live in Minnesota. Approximately 190,000 Minnesota veterans had been in service during the Vietnam-era—that is, after Aug. 4, 1964. World War II veterans made up the largest group of veterans in the state, with an estimated 212,000. Approximately 88,000 veterans of the Korean conflict live in the state and there are 60,000 who saw military service between the Korean conflict and the Vietnam-era (Feb. 1, 1955—Aug. 4, 1964).

Approximately 12,000 World War I veterans live in Minnesota.

There are no surviving veterans of the Spanish-American War in the state.

Veterans Organizations

AMERICAN LEGION
Veterans Service Building
St. Paul, 55101
(612) 291-1800

The American Legion, Department of Minnesota, has a membership of 123,700. There are 602 posts in 584 communities. The oldest post is Theodor Petersen No. 1, Minneapolis. Richfield Post 435, with 5,351 members, is either the first or second largest post in the nation, vying for that honor with a unit in Lincoln, Neb. State Commander: Frank Fay.

VETERANS OF FOREIGN WARS
Veterans Service Building
St. Paul, 55101
(612) 291-1757

The VFW has 318 posts in 270 communities and a membership of 82,500. The oldest post in Minnesota is M.M. Carlton Post 5 which was chartered on April 18, 1902 and is still an active post. State Commander: Robert Larson.

DISABLED AMERICAN VETERANS
Veterans Service Building
St. Paul, 55101
(612) 291-1212

Organized in 1920-21, Disabled American Veterans has 10,672 members in 31 active posts. Department Commander: Hiram Fuller.

JEWISH WAR VETERANS
419 S. Cleveland Ave.
St. Paul, 55105

Jewish American War Veterans is the oldest veterans group in the state, organized in 1896. There are approximately 1,000 members in two Minneapolis posts and two St. Paul posts.

WORLD WAR I VETERANS

Organized in 1955, World War I Veterans has about 4,000 members in the state, who meet in 60 barracks (posts). State Commander: Andrew C. Hanson. The organization's national commander, William Fisher, is also from Minnesota and the Twin Cities will host the organization's national convention in September of 1981.

MILITARY ORDER OF THE PURPLE HEART
Veterans Service Building
St. Paul, 55101
(612) 227-4456

Military Order of the Purple Heart is a national organization composed for and of combat wounded veterans. The organization is founded upon the order issued by Gen. George Washington at Newburg, N.Y. on Aug. 7, 1782, during the Revolutionary War, when he established the Badge of Military Merit, in the figure of a heart, in purple, which he directed to be a permanent one. There are 475 members in Minnesota, where the organization's first chapter (post) was founded in 1935. Today there are eight chapters in the state.

Congressional Medal of Honor Winners
The Congressional Medal of Honor, established by a joint act of Congress on July 12, 1862, is awarded in the name of congress "to each person who while an officer or enlisted person of the army shall have distinguished himself or herself conspicuously by gallantry and intrepidity at the risk of his or her life above and beyond the call of duty in action involving actual conflict with the enemy."

The deed performed must have been of personal bravery or self-sacrifice so conspicuous as to clearly distinguish the individual for gallantry and intrepidity above his or her comrades and must have involved the risk of life."

Listed below are the Medal of Honor recipients from Minnesota:

(b) State of Birth   * Posthumous Award   † Second Award

Army-Air Force

Albee, George E.
1st Lt., 41st U.S. Inf.
(Owatonna)(b. N.H.)

Barrick, Jesse
Cpl., 3rd Minn. Inf.
(Rice Co.)(b. Ohio)

Bell, Harry
Capt., 36th Inf.,
U.S. Vol.
(Minneapolis)
(b. Wisc.)

*Bianchi, Willibald C.
1st Lt., 45th Inf.,
Philippine Scouts
(New Ulm)

Burger, Joseph
Pvt., 2nd Minn. Inf.
(Crystal Lake)
(b. Austria)

Burkard, Oscar
Pvt., Hosp. Corps,
U.S. Army,
(Hay Creek)
(b. Germany)

Cilley, Clinton A.
Capt., 2nd Minn. Inf.
(Sasioja)(b. N.H.)

Clark, Wm. A.
Cpl., 2nd Minn. Inf.
(Shelbyville)(b. Penn.)

Colalillo, Mike
Pfc., 100th Inf. Div.(Duluth)

†Cukela, Louis
Sgt., 5th Reg. USMC
(Minneapolis)(b. Austria)
(Also awarded Navy
Medal of Honor)

Flannigan, James
Pvt., 2nd Minn. Inf.
(Louisville)(b. Ohio)

Hanna, Milton
Cpl., 2nd Minn. Inf.
(Henderson)(b. Ohio)

Hawks, Lloyd C.
Pfc., 3rd Inf. Div.
(Park Rapids)

Army-Air Force

Holmes, Lovilo
1st Sgt., 2nd Minn. Inf.
(Mankato)(b. N.Y.)

Huggins, Eli L.
Capt., 2nd U.S. Cav.
(b. Ill.)

Johnson, John
Pvt., 2nd Wisc. Inf.
(Rochester)(b. Norway)

Lindbergh, Charles A.
Capt., A.C. Res.,
U.S. Army
(Little Falls)(b. Mich.)

Mallon, George H.
Capt., 33rd Div.
(Minneapolis)(b. Kans.)

Morgan, George H.
2nd Lt., 3rd U.S. Cav.
(Minneapolis)(b. Canada)

O'Brien, Henry D.
Cpl., 1st Minn. Inf.
(St. Anthony Falls)
(b. Maine)

*Olson, Kenneth L.
Spec. 4, 199th Inf. Brig.
(Paynesville)

*Page, John U.D.
Lt. Col., X Corps Arty.
(St. Paul)(b. Malahi
Island, Philippines)

Pay, Byron E.
Pvt., 2nd Minn. Inf.
(Mankato)(b. N.Y.)

Pickle, Alonzo H.
Sgt., 1st Minn. Inf.
(Dover)(b. Canada)

*Pruden, Robt. J.
S/Sgt., 75th Inf.,
Amer. Div.
(St. Paul)

*Rabel, Laszlo
S/Sgt., 173rd Airborne Brig.
(Minneapolis)(b. Hungary)

Reed, Axel H.
Sgt., 2nd Minn. Inf.
(Glencoe)(b. Maine)

Rudolph, Donald E.
2nd Lt., 6th Inf. Div.
(Minneapolis)

Sherman, Marshall
Pvt., 1st Minn. Inf.
(St. Paul)(b. Vt.)

Thorsness, Leo K.
Lt. Col., 357th Tact.
Fighter Sq.
(Walnut Grove)

Tracy, John
Pvt., 8th U.S. Cav.
(St. Paul)(b. Ireland)

Vale, John
Pvt., 2nd Minn. Inf.
(Rochester)(b. England)

*Wayrynen, Dale E.
Spec. 4,
101st Airborne Div.
(McGregor)

Welch, Charles H.
Sgt., 7th U.S. Cav.
(Ft. Snelling)(b. N.Y.)

Wilson, William O.
Cpl., 9th U.S. Cav.
(St. Paul)(b. Md.)

Wright, Samuel
Cpl., 2nd Minn. Inf.
(Swan Lake)(b. Ind.)

Navy-Marine Corps

Catlin, Albertus W.
Maj., USMC
(b. N.Y.)

*Courtney, Henry A. Jr.
Maj., USMC
(Duluth)

†Cukela, Louis
Sgt., 5th Reg., USMC
(Minneapolis)(b. Austria)
(Also awarded Army
Medal of Honor)

Dyer, Jesse F.
Capt., USMC
(St. Paul)

*Fleming, Richard E.
Capt., USMCR
(St. Paul)

*Hauge, Louis J. Jr.
Cpl., USMCR
(Ada)

*Kraus, Richard E.
Pfc., USMCR (b. Ill.)

*LaBelle, James D.
Pfc., USMCR
(Columbia Heights)

Nelson, Oscar F.
MMlc., U.S. Navy
(Minneapolis)

*Rud, George Wm.
CMM., U.S. Navy
(Minneapolis)

Sorenson, Richard K.
Pvt., USMCR
(Anoka)

Jewish War Vets Are Oldest

Jewish War Veterans of the USA is the oldest veterans group in the nation. On July 31, 1776, Frances Salvador, a plantation owner from South Carolina, was killed in a British incited Indian skirmish. He was the first Jew killed in the Revolutionary War. In 1896, 118 years later, a group of Jewish Civil War veterans organized the Hebrew Union Veterans, an organization that was later to become the Jewish War Veterans of the USA. A study of Jewish participation in the military during World War II indicated that the Jews served in the Armed Forces beyond their numerical proportion to the general population. They received more than 52,000 awards, including the Medal of Honor, the Air Medal, the Silver Star and the Purple Heart.

The Minnesota National Guard

There are 9,500 men and women in the Army and Air Force National Guard in the state. National Guard units are located in 69 Minnesota communities and there are two air units—one at Minneapolis-St. Paul International Airport and one at Duluth. The guard trains at the 53,000-acre Fort Ripley. Three state brigades were called to duty during the Spanish-American War, but only one saw combat, the 13th Minnesota volunteers. In January of 1951, during the Korean conflict, the 47th Infantry Division was activated but no units where shipped to Korea, although individuals served there. No units were activated during the Vietnam era.

VIETNAM VETERANS OF AMERICA
518 Russell Avenue North
Minneapolis, MN 55405
(612) 881-6744
(612) 374-5714

The Vietnam Veterans of America was founded nationally in 1978. The Minnesota organization was established about 1979. The VVA was chartered by Congress as a veteran's organization in 1986. It has about 800 members in 8 chapters and is busy forming about 15 other chapters. President of the Minnesota State Council is Randall Olson.

Cross-country Skiers at the Minnesota Zoological Garden.

Geography

LYING near the geographic center of North America, Minnesota is the northern-most of the continental United States, reaching latitude 49° 23' 50.28" north at the tip of the Northwest Angle, that portion of Minnesota not connected to the state by land. This unique area of land came into being by virtue of an international agreement that the common boundary between Canada and the United States was to follow the natural waterways into the "most northwestern point of the Lake of the Woods."

Much of the northern boundary is outlined by that lake, Rainy River, Pigeon River, Lake Superior and countless border lakes. The St. Louis, St. Croix and Mississippi rivers form most the eastern limits. The Red River of the North, and Big Stone and Traverse lakes mark the boundary on the west. Iowa lies to the south. Minnesota is a large state, the 12th in rank in size.

The longest distance across the state is from north to south, approximately 400 miles, from latitude 43 degrees 30' on the Iowa line to a point roughly 22 miles north of the 49th parallel. While the average width is 225 miles, the greatest width is 367 miles. The narrowest dimension is 175 miles, from Goose Creek north of Taylors Falls on the east to the south tip of Big Stone Lake on the west.

Minnesota covers an area of 84,068 square miles (53,803,520 acres), with 80,009 of these in land and 4,509 of water—the greatest water area of any state. The topography is largely level or gently sloping, with only a few regions of marked elevation. Both the lowest and highest points are in the northeastern part of the state; the level of Lake Superior is the lowest at 602 feet above sea level, and the highest is Eagle Mountain in the Misquah Hills a few miles inland at 2,301 feet above sea level. The highest town is Holland in southwestern Minnesota in Pipestone County situated at 1780 feet above sea level.

The land in the state is largely level and between 1000 and 1500 feet above sea level. Elevations above 1500 feet are limited to the northwest, a fairly large region in Itasca County and the Leaf Hills located in the southern part of Ottertail County.

The *Giant's Range* is a notable elevation 50 to 500 feet above the surrounding terrain. This 100 mile long granite ridge runs northeastward from near Grand Rapids into western Lake County. South of this formation lies the iron-bearing material of the Mesabi range.

This area is part of the vast, level Laurentian rocky platform which runs from northeastern Minnesota up into Canada. Some 2 billion years ago this became the first part of North America to be elevated on a permanent basis above the level of the sea, and here are to be found the oldest rocks on earth.

The Red River Lowland in northwestern Minnesota, was formed when the last of four enormous glaciers receded about 11,000 years ago, covering the area with a huge inland sea named *Glacial Lake Agassiz.* The lowest points in this basin extend from the Red River eastward to Koochiching County, with an average elevation today of about 760 feet.

The high and low areas of the state have been caused by stress and pressure from below and erosion by water and wind from above. These forces are of three types: 1. volcanism, a melting and eruption action; 2. diastrophism, a twisting, crumpling and uplifting of the earth's surface; and 3. gradation, a leveling-off in which high places are worn down and low places fill up by wind, water, ice and debris. Volcanism is evident along the north shore of Lake Superior where traces of the molten mineral that flowed out from fissures deep in the earth and hardened sheets of lava can be seen today.

Examination of rock layers reveals that the crumpling and tilting of sedimentary strata produced giant mountain ranges in Minnesota in the distant past. It is believed that earthquakes have had little or no effect on Minnesota — only three minor shocks have ever been noted.

The action of rivers and streams and even the waves produces erosion and deposition of particles, thus altering the earth's structure. Limestone rocks which are to be found in the state, are susceptible to erosion by ground water, thus producing underground caverns such as the *Mystery Caves* near Spring Valley.

The greatest sculptors of the state's surface have been the glaciers. These enormous ice masses developed during a long cold period and falling snow accumulated to a depth of many thousand feet. The lower layers, compacted into ice which spread out in all directions, gouged and scraped great quantities of soil and rock and incorporated them in its huge mass. Many of these glacial made basins can be seen in northern Minnesota. When the masses melted, the debris, or "drift" was strewn all over the land, in some cases forming high hilly configurations.

Rivers

Glacial activity brought about a vast water surface in Minnesota—one square mile of water to every twenty of land, and this does not include any portion of Lake Superior.

It also produced a number of massive drainage basins which gave rise to many flowing streams and rivers, the largest of which is the *"Father of waters"* the mighty Mississippi.

Henry Rowe Schoolcraft in 1832 discovered the source of the river and named the modest body of water Lake Itasca; it was an accomplishment that had eluded explorers Thompson, Pike, Cass and Beltrami before him.

The principal river of the United States, it flows in every point on the compass on its 2,552 mile journey to the Gulf of Mexico. It is second in length only to its main tributary, the Missouri, with which it combines to make up the third largest river system in the world after the Nile and the Amazon. Using all its tributaries, the river drains more than 1,322,000 acres of the mid-continental area, drawing from 31 states and two Canadian provinces.

Of major economic importance, it is navigable from St. Anthony Falls in Minneapolis to the ocean by means of a series of locks and dams. The U.S. Corps of Engineers maintains a nine foot channel from Minnesota to Vicksburg, Mississippi, where channel depths of up to 40 feet are provided downstream. Access to the St. Lawrence Seaway is made possible by the Illinois waterway.

Ever since 1811, when the first steamboats travelled the river, it has had a massive impact on opening up the new frontiers, and later, on distribution of untold tons of goods and materials necessary to a burgeoning commerce on a national and international level.

Water flows out of the state through seven different river valleys: the Mississippi, the Rainy, the Red River of the North, the Cedar, the Rock, the St. Louis and the Des Moines. No water enters the state boundaries. Many other rivers and streams never leave the state, but contribute their output to the above or into Lake Superior. In addition to the lengthy Minnesota, there are historic Minnehaha Falls made famous in Longfellow's poem *"Hiawatha"*, and colorful fast-flowing streams and falls such as Gooseberry, Temperance, Devil Track and Knife on the north shore.

Lakes

Lake Superior, the largest fresh water lake in the world, covers 31,820 square miles. At its largest dimensions, it is 351 miles long and 160 miles wide. It is also the highest (its surface elevation is 602 feet above sea level) and the deepest (1,302 ft.) of all the Great Lakes.

It receives water from many swift-flowing streams and rivers such as the Pigeon, St. Louis, Kaministikwia and the Nipigon. The irregular shore line is high and rocky, with many peninsulas, inlets and large bays.

Purer than the lower lakes, it has been only locally polluted—the largest contamination is attributed by many to the large taconite plant at Silver Bay which formerly discharged daily 67,000 tons of waste into its waters.

Commercial and sport fishing contribute significantly to the economy.

Since the St. Lawrence Seaway, an international waterway 2,342 miles long, was opened in 1959, Duluth, the principal Minnesota city on the lake and the furthest inland port in the world, operates a harbor visited by many large ocean-going vessels.

Probably discovered by the French explorer, Etienne Brule, the vast waters were visited by Pierre Radisson, sieur des Groseilleirs, Father Allouez and sieur Duluth, for whom the city was named, and A.M. Tracy, all hoping for deeds to increase the glory of France. The local Indians, the Algonquins, while they did accept most of the French terminology, rejected the name "Lake Tracy" and retained Superior, out of their reverence for its size and the great yield of fish.

Red Lake is the largest lake within the boundaries of the state; it covers 288,800 acres, has 123 miles of shoreline and a maximum depth of 31 feet. Other large lakes in their order of size are:

	Acres	Miles shoreline	Max. depth in feet
Mille Lacs	132,520	70	35
Leech Lake	122,610	154	150
Winnebegoshish	69,820	116	65
Vermillion	49,110	186	48
Cass	29,780	41	115
Kabetogoma	25,760	98	60
Pokegema	15,600	60	100

The most recent official count of the state's lakes (10 acres or more) is 15,291 but man, always tampering with the landscape, has drained 3,257 of these resulting in a net figure of 12,034.

Rock County, in the southwestern corner of the state, is the only one of the 87 counties that does not have a natural lake.

Land use in Minnesota

	Acres	%
Forested	18,400,000	34
Cultivated	23,750,000	43
Pasture and open	6,000,000	11
Water	3,300,000	6
Marsh	1,900,000	4
All other	1,300,000	3

Source: Minnesota Department of Natural Resources

Water Everywhere

Water is important to Minnesotans, for transportation and recreation. The state has 20,000 lakes, ponds and wetlands five acres or more. There are 12,034 lakes ten acres or more, and 25,000 miles of rivers and streams, as well as 90,000 miles of lake and river shoreline.

Minnesota Waterfalls

Name	River/Stream	Location	County
Outlet Falls	Rapid River	Mouth	L. of the Woods
Little Cascade	Little Fork River		St. Louis
Cascade	Vermillion River		St. Louis
Cascade	Vermillion River	Outlet Verm. Lake	St. Louis
Cascade	Vermillion River		St. Louis
Vermillion Dalles	Vermillion River	Inlet Crane L.	St. Louis
Cascade	Vermillion River		St. Louis
LaCroix Cascade	Border Water	Loon Lake Inlet	St. Louis
Bottle Falls	Bottle River B. W.	Bottle L. Portage	St. Louis
Curtain Falls	Crooked Lake B. W.	Outlet Crooked L.	St. Louis
Lwr Basswood Falls	Basswood River		Lake
Wheelbarrow Falls	Basswood River		Lake
Three Falls Cascade	North Kawishiwi		Lake
Two Lake Cascade	North Kawishiwi	Outlet Two Lake	Lake
Saganaga Falls	Border Water	Inlet Saganaga L.	Cook
Granite Cascade	Granite River B. W.	Outlet Granite L.	Cook
Sea Gull Falls	Sea Gull River	Outlet Sea Gull L.	Cook
Little Rock Falls	Pine River B. W.	Outlet Gunflint L.	Cook
Big (Pigeon River) Falls	Pigeon River		Cook
The Cascades	Pigeon River		Cook
Partridge Falls	Pigeon River		Cook

Minnesota Waterfalls

Name	River/Stream	Location	County
Reservation	Reservation River		Cook
	Kimball Creek		Cook
	Kadance Creek		Cook
	Arrowhead (Brule)		Cook
	Devil Track River		Cook
	Cascade River		Cook
	Poplar River		Cook
	Cross River		Cook
	Cross River	7 Falls in last 5 miles	Cook
	Temperance River	1 Mile N.W. Highway	Cook
	Two Island River	4 Falls total	Cook
Manitou Falls	Manitou River		Lake
Caribou Falls	Caribou River		Lake
Cascade (High) Falls	Baptism River		Lake
Gooseberry Falls	Gooseberry River		Lake
Gooseberry Cascade	Gooseberry River		Lake
Big Falls	Cloquet River		St. Louis
Lester Park	Lester River	Lester City Park	St. Louis
Minnehaha Falls	Minnehaha Creek	Minneapolis	Hennepin
Minneopa Falls	Minneopa Creek	Minneopa State Park	Blue Earth
Mound Falls	Mound Creek		Brown
Redwood Cascade	Redwood River	City Park	Redwood
Ramsey Falls	Ramsey Creek	City Park	Redwood
Pipestone Falls	Pipestone Creek	Pipestone	Pipestone

Minnesota Mentions in the Guinness Book of World Records

The greatest recorded distance ever swum was by Fred P. Newton of Clinton, Oklahoma. He swam from the Ford dam in the Mississippi to Carrollton Avenue in New Orleans July 6, to December 29, 1930, 1,826 miles.

One of the largest balls of string was amassed by Francis A. Johnson of Darwin, Minn.; 11 feet in Diameter and weighing five tons.

Sears Roebuck & Co. was founded by Richard W. Sears in the North Redwood, Minnesota railroad station in 1886. It is the largest general merchandising firm in the world, with net sales of $12,306,229,080 in the year ending Jan. 31, 1974.

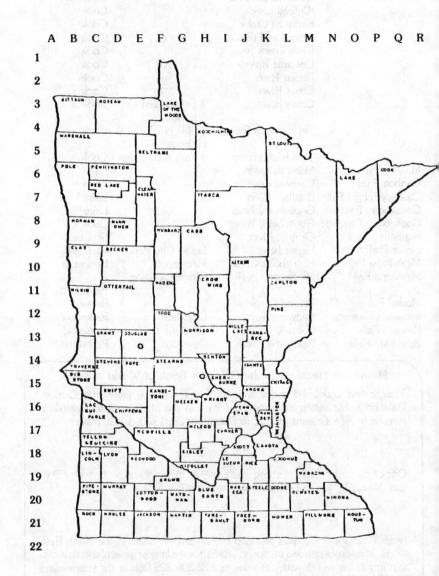

A B C D E F G H I J K L M N O P Q R

1
2
3
4
5
6
7
8
9
10
11
12
13
14
15
16
17
18
19
20
21
22

Minnesota's cities, towns and their population. Use grid letters and numbers to find community. County seats are capitalized, and MA indicates metropolitan area.

MINNESOTA INDEX TO CITIES

Population (1980 Census) 4,075,970   County Seats in Capital Letters

★ AIR

● BUS

■ RAIL

Minnesota's 87 Counties

Counties are governed by a board of commissioners and administrative officers elected by the people. State law allows alternative forms of government, chiefly to allow for an elected executive, a manager, or administrator, and the option to make administrative offices appointive.

During the decade of the seventies, the legislature has increased the responsibilities of county government. A county court system has been established; counties are developing shorelands management and solid waste management systems.

Counties have authority for planning and zoning, to establish housing and redevelopment authorities and to direct the assessing function (except in cities over 30,000 population) in addition to regular duties such as administration for the state of welfare, elections, vital statistics, tax levies, and highways.

County	County Seat	Acreage
Aitkin	Aitkin 56431	1,164,502
Anoka	Anoka 55303	273,735
Becker	Detroit Lakes 56501	837,688
Beltrami	Bemidji 56601	1,608,518
Benton	Foley 56329	257,798
Big Stone	Ortonville 56278	361,501
Blue Earth	Mankato 56001	477,158
Brown	New Ulm 56073	387,266
Carlton	Carlton 55718	550,092
Carver	Chaska 55318	226,810
Cass	Walker 56484	1,302,315
Chippewa	Montevideo 56265	370,269
Chisago	Center City 55012	269,369
Clay	Moorhead 56560	668,118
Clearwater	Bagley 56621	640,689
Cook	Grand Marais 55604	936,426
Cottonwood	Windom 56101	407,635
Crow Wing	Brainerd 56401	649,083
Dakota	Hastings 55033	365,190
Dodge	Mantorville 55955	280,638
Douglas	Alexandria 56309	401,477
Faribault	Blue Earth 56013	454,723
Fillmore	Preston 55965	553,101
Freeborn	Albert Lea 56007	449,241
Goodhue	Red Wing 55066	491,465
Grant	Elbow Lake 56531	348,226
Hennepin	Minneapolis 55487	354,225
Houston	Caledonia 55921	364,079
Hubbard	Park Rapids 56470	596,829
Isanti	Cambridge 55008	281,302
Itasca	Grand Rapids 55744	1,729,322
Jackson	Jackson 56143	446,068
Kanabec	Mora 55051	337,535
Kandiyohi	Willmar 56201	497,292

County	County Seat	Acreage
Kittson	Hallock 56728	700,372
Koochiching	International Falls 56649	1,989,188
La Qui Parle	Madison 56256	492,698
Lake	Two Harbors 55616	1,367,808
Lake of the Woods	Baudette 56623	833,821
Le Sueur	LeCenter 56057	283,692
Lincoln	Ivanhoe 56142	334,365
Lyon	Marshall 56258	453,072
McLeod	Glencoe 55336	311,488
Mahnomen	Mahnomen 56557	360,983
Marshall	Warren 56762	1,142,622
Martin	Fairmont 56031	450,521
Meeker	Litchfield 55355	382,891
Mille Lacs	Milaca 56353	365,472
Morrison	Little Falls 56345	719,593
Mower	Austin 55912	453,204
Murray	Slayton 56172	444,657
Nicollet	St. Peter 56082	280,866
Nobles	Worthington 56187	454,877
Norman	Ada 56510	558,689
Olmsted	Rochester 55901	422,400
Otter Tail	Fergus Falls 56537	1,267,003
Pennington	Thief River Falls 56701	391,606
Pine	Pine City 55063	906,366
Pipestone	Pipestone 56164	296,887
Polk	Cookston 56716	1,260,513
Pope	Glenwood 56334	426,102
Ramsey	St. Paul 55102	101,032
Red Lake	Red Lake Falls 56750	274,619
Redwood	Redwood Falls 56283	557,474
Renville	Olivia 56277	621,129
Rice	Faribault 55021	319,162
Rock	Luverne 56156	307,716
Roseau	Roseau 56751	1,073,344
St. Louis	Duluth 55802	4,043,532
Scott	Shakopee 55379	225,900
Sherburne	Elk River 55330	280,525
Sibley	Gaylord 55334	372,901
Stearns	St. Cloud 56301	864,521
Steele	Owatonna 55060	273,455
Stevens	Morris 56267	355,335
Swift	Benson 56215	475,592
Todd	Long Prairie 56347	604,286
Traverse	Wheaton 56296	363,462
Wabasha	Wabasha 55981	344,324
Wadena	Wadena 56482	341,126

County	County Seat	Acreage
Waseca	Waseca 56093	268,158
Washington	Stillwater 55082	254,868
Watonwan	St. James 56081	277,051
Wilkin	Breckenridge 56520	476,389
Winona	Winona 55987	406,320
Wright	Buffalo 55313	424,387
Yellow Medicine	Granite Falls 56241	481,686

Minerals of Minnesota

The minerals preceded by an asterisk are microscopic or rare and are not normally specimens for collectors.

*Acmite-augite, a pyroxene
*Actinolite, an amphibole
*Adularia, a feldspar
*Aegirine (acmite)
*Afwillite
Agate
Albite, a feldspar
*Allanite, an epidote
Almandite, a garnet
Alum
Amesite, a chlorite
Amethyst (purple quartz)
Amphibole group: actinolite, anthophyllite, asbestos, cummingtonite, glaucophane, grunerite, hornblende (green and brown), pargasite, riebeckite, tremolite, uralite
Analcime, a zeolite
*Anatase
*Andalusite
Anesine, a feldspar
Ankerite
Anorthoclase
Anthophyllite, an amphibole
*Antigorite, a serpentine
*Apatite
*Aragonite
*Arsenopyrite
Asbestos, an amphibole or serpentine
Augite (and titan-augite), a pyroxene
*Babingtonite, a pyroxene
Barite
*Bastite, a serpentine
Biotite, a mica
Bobierrite
Bornite
*Bowlingite
Braunite
Bronzite, a pyroxene
*Brookite
Bytownite, a feldspar
Cairngorm (smoky quartz)
Calcite
Carnelian

Catlinite, see pyrophyllite
*Ceylonite
Chalcedony (agate, carnelian, chert, flint, jasper sardonyx)
Chalocite
Chalcopyrite
Chert
Chlorite group: amesite, delessite, penninite, strigovite
*Chondrodite
*Chrysotile, see asbestos and serpentine
Clay mineral group: kaolinite, montmorillonite, pyrophylite, nontronite
*Clinoenstatite, a pyroxene
Cobalite
*Collophanite
*Columbite
Copper
*Cordierite
*Corundum
*Covelite
*Cristobalite
*Cummingtonite, an amphibole
*Cuprite
Cyanite, see Kyanite
Datolite
Delessite, a chlorite
Diallage, a pyroxene
*Diaspore
Diopside, a pyroxene
Dolomite
Enstatite, a pyroxene
Epidote group: allanite, clinozoisite, epidote, zoisite
Fayalite, an olivine
Feldspar group: adularia, albite, andesine, anorthoclase, bytownite, labradorite, microcline, orthoclase, perthite, plagioclase series, valencianite
Flint
Fluorite
*Fuchsite, a mica
*Galena

Garnet group: almandite, andradite, spessartite
Gibbsite (bauxite)
Glauconite
Goethite (limonite)
*Gold
Graphite
Greenalite
Groutite
*Grunerite, an amphibole
Gypsum
*Halite
Hematite
Heulandite, a zeolite
*Hisingerite
Hornblende, green and brown - an amphibole
Hortonolite, an olivine
Hypersthene, a pyroxene
Ice
*Iddingsite
Ilmenite
*Iolite (cordierite)
*Iron alloy (meteorite)
*Jarosite
Jasper
Kaolinite, a clay mineral
Kyanite
Labradorite, a feldspar
Laumonite, a zeolite
*Leucoxene
Limonite, see goethite
Lintonite, a zeolite
Magnetite
Malachite
*Malacon
Manganite
Manganosiderite
Marcasite
*Martite (hematite)
*Maskelynite (meteorite)
Mesotype, a zeolite
Mica group: biotite, fuchsite, muscovite, phlogopite, sericite
Microcline, a feldspar
Minnesotaite
*Molybdenite
*Monazite
Montmorillonite, a clay mineral (potash-montmorillonite)
Muscovite
*Nickel-iron (meteorite)
*Nontronite, a clay mineral
*Octahedrite (anatase)
Oligoclase, a feldspar
Olivine group: fayalite, hortonolite, olivine
*Orthite (allanite, an epidote)
Orthoclase, a feldspar
*Paraffin
*Pargasite, an amphibole
*Pectolite

Penninite, a chlorite
*Pentlandite
Perthite, a feldspar
*Phlogopite, a mica
Plagioclase, a feldspar
Prehnite
Psilomelane
Pyrite
Pyrolusite
Pyrophyllite, a clay mineral
Pyroxene group: acmite (aegirine), augite, babingtonite, bronzite, clinoenstatite, diallage, diopside, enstatite, hypersthene
Pyrrhotite
Quartz (amethyst, cairngorm, milky quartz, rock crystal, smoky quartz)
Rhodochrosite
*Rhodonite
*Riebeckite
Rock crystal (quartz)
*Rutile
Sanidine (soda sanidine)
Sardonyx
Selenite (gypsum)
Sericite, a mica
Serpentine group: antigorite, bastite, chrysotile (asbestos)
Siderite
*Sillimanite
Specularite (hematite)
*Spessartite, a garnet
*Sphalerite
*Sphene
*Spherosiderite
*Spinel
Staurolite
Stilbite, a zeolite
Stilpnomelane
Strigovite, a chlorite
*Talc
*Tantalite
Thomsonite, a zeolite
*Titanite (sphene)
*Topaz
*Tourmaline
*Tremolite, an amphibole
*Tridymite (meteorite)
*Troilite (meteorite)
Uralite, an amphibole
*Valencianite, a feldspar
*Vermiculite
Violarite
Vivianite
Xenotime
Xonotlite
Zeolite group: analcime, heulandite, laumontite (lintonite), mesotype, stilbite, thomsonite
*Zircon
*Zoisite, an epidote

Vital Statistics

State Seal

The Great Seal of the State of Minnesota is placed on all official state documents. Its design is similar to the design of the territorial seal which was used from 1849 until the adoption of a state seal in 1858. The picture on the seal is apparently a scene near St. Anthony Falls. A white man is plowing in the foreground while an Indian is riding into the sunset in the background. Henry H. Sibley, the first governor of Minnesota, is credited with selecting the motto which appears on the seal, "L'Etoile du Nord," which translated is "The North Star."

The Secretary of State is the custodian of the Great Seal of the State of Minnesota.

State Flag

The new Minnesota state flag was adopted by act of the 1957 legislature, replacing the old state flag which was adopted in 1893. The design on the old flag, though beautiful and artistic, was too expensive to reproduce by modern manufacturing methods.

The new flag retains the basic symbol of the 1893 flag—the state seal. Nineteen stars, which symbolized the fact that Minnesota was the nineteenth state to be admitted to the union after the original thirteen, were outside the center emblem on the 1893 flag. They are now included within the center emblem. The uppermost star is the largest and represents the North Star state.

The State Flower

The pink and white lady slipper, **Cypripedium reginae,** (the shoe of Venus, the queen) is Minnesota's state flower. Its common names are pink and white lady slipper and showy lady slipper.

In Minnesota the pink and white lady slipper grows best in the damp shady places provided by tamarack and spruce marshes. It cannot grow without the presence of a

tiny fungus which helps the flower's roots get food from the soil. The plant grows so slowly it takes from 10 to 20 years before it is old enough to bear blossoms. If it reaches full growth, from two to three feet tall, it may live to be 50 years old.

The pink and white lady slipper has become one of the state's rarest flowers, because the plant does not reproduce easily.

Courtesy of Dept. of Natural Resources

The State Tree

The Red Pine, **Pinus resinosa,** commonly known as the Norway Pine, a majestic evergreen was adopted as the official state tree in 1953 to symbolize Minnesota's history, background and physical characteristics.

It is easy to recognize. The lower two-thirds of its 60 to 140 foot straight trunk is bare of branches. Above, the branches grow straight out from the trunk and form a cone-shaped crown. The brownish red bark of the tree accounts for the origin of one of its names, the Red Pine.

The tree is disease-free and insect resistant, and often lives up to three hundred years.

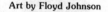

Art by Floyd Johnson

**Art by Dan Metz,
Courtesy of Dept. of Natural Resources**

The State Bird

No bird better typifies Minnesota lakes, woods and the northern wilderness than the loon, **Gavia Immer**, which knows no peer in swimming, diving or fishing. It was selected by the 1961 legislature.

Preferring the undisturbed isolation of the northern wilderness, it can be heard, if not often seen, throughout the northern lake country. The great northern diver, as it is called, is 32 inches long and bears distinctive black and white markings.

State Stone

The Lake Superior agate, a crypto-crystalline quartz, basically white with red bands, was selected by the 1969 legislature as the state gemstone.

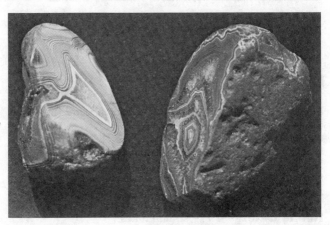

The State Fish

The Walleye, **Stizostedion v. vitreum**, is a fitting symbol of the cool and pleasant northland, and though found throughout Minnesota in lakes and rivers, is most at home in the larger clear cool lakes of Minnesota's northern forests.

Attaining a weight of nearly 17 pounds, it has flesh of the highest quality and is one of the most sought after fisherman's prizes. Nearly half of the state's fishing water is managed primarily for walleye fishing.

**Art by Dan Metz,
Courtesy of Dept. of Natural Resources**

Legal Holidays

January 1-New Year's Day
February-3rd Monday-Washington's and Lincoln's Birthday
May-Last Monday-Memorial Day
July 4-Independence Day
September-1st Monday-Labor Day
October-2nd Monday-Christopher Columbus Day
November 11-Veterans Day
November-4th Thursday-Thanksgiving Day
December 25-Christmas Day

Special Days

April-last Friday-Arbor Day
(up to one-half school day may be spent in observance, Minnesota Statutes 126.11)
February 15-Susan B. Anthony Day
May 11-Minnesota Day
September 28-Frances Willard Day
October 9-Leif Erickson Day
(one-half hour, school day, may be spent in "instruction and appropriate exercise relative to and in commemoration of the life and history of the respective persons and principles and ideals they fostered." Minnesota Statutes 126.09)

MINNESOTA IN PROFILE

Name—Derived from the Dakota Indian word "Minisota" meaning sky tinted waters.
Organized as Territory—March 3, 1849.
Entered union—May 11, 1858 (32nd state).
Motto—*L'Etoile du Nord (The North Star).*
Song—"Hail! Minnesota."
Area—84,068 square miles (12th largest state.).
Land area—79,289 square miles.
Inland waters—4,779 square miles.
Width—385 miles.
Length—405 miles, extending from 43°30' to 49°23'4''.
Population (1980 census)—4,077,148.
Density per square mile—48.0.
Largest cities—Minneapolis 370,091; St. Paul 268,248; Duluth 100,578; Bloomington 81,640; and Rochester 53,983.
Percent urban population—66.4.
Percent rural population—33.6.
Average mean altitude—1,200 feet.
Highest point—Eagle Mountain (Cook County), 2,301 feet.
Lowest point—Surface of Lake Superior, 602 feet.
Three major river systems—Mississippi, Minnesota, and Red River of the North; water flows from Minnesota in three directions—Hudson Bay, Atlantic Ocean, and Gulf of Mexico; no water flows into the state.
Number of lakes—15,291 larger than 10 acres.
Largest lake—Red Lake (451 square miles).
Average last spring freeze—April 30.*
Average first fall freeze—October 13.*
Annual precipitation—25.94 inches*; 30.26 inches +.
Annual snowfall—46.3 inches; 50.7 inches +.
January mean temperature—12.2°F.*; 5.5°F. +
July mean temperature—71.9°F*; 71.1°F. +
Average mean temperature—44.1°F.*; 44.2°F. +

* — *figures based on 30 year normals,* **Climatography of U.S.,** *#81, #60-20.*
+ — *figures taken as climatic data for 1978 for Minneapolis-St. Paul,* **Local Climatological Data, Annual Summary, Minneapolis-St. Paul,** *Environmental Data and Information Service, 1979.*
Sources: Minnesota Pocket Data Book, *Minnesota State Planning Agency, 1975;* **U.S. Fact Book,** *Grosset & Dunlap, 1975.*

MINNESOTA'S CHANGING POPULATION

by Hazel H. Reinhardt, *former Minnesota State Demographer*

Editor's note: In 1974 the Minnesota Legislature created within the State Planning Agency the position of state demographer, appointed by and serving under the supervision and control of the director of planning. Among the statutory duties of this agency are compiling an annual study of population estimates, reporting to the legislature annually an analysis of the implications of the population study, and providing maps of counties and certain municipalities prepared to scale and detail recommended by the federal bureau of the census. Hazel H. Reinhardt, appointed to the newly-created position in 1974, served as state demographer until January, 1979. On the eve of the eighties, Reinhardt examines for Minnesotans a major demographic theme she observed during the 1970's: a population growing older.

A transformation of Minnesota's society is in full swing. This transformation could affect nearly every facet of life. At its heart is a basic shift in Minnesota's age mix: fewer youngsters, more adults, and increased numbers of senior citizens.

Since 1959 a declining fertility rate has been laying the foundation for this change toward a larger proportion of elderly people and a smaller proportion of the young. In 1900 half of all Minnesotans were 22 years old or younger. Today the median age has reached 29. By 1981 it will have passed 30, and at the turn of the century half of Minnesota's population may be 35 or older.

Within the 1980s, if present trends continue, one out of five Minnesotans will be at least 55 years old. By 1980 for the first time in the state's history the number of people 55 and over will be larger than the school age population. As the population ages, the proportion of people over 18 will increase. During this aging process it is unlikely that any aspect of life—economy, employment, politics, medical-legal practices, education—will remain unchanged.

During the 1970s the number of teenagers and young people exceeded any other single age group. These young people were born in increasingly large numbers every year from the end of World War II (1945) until 1959, when births in Minnesota peaked at 88,000.

In response to growing numbers of pupils, elementary schools sprouted in most districts. As these young people leave high school and college classrooms, their impact in the labor market and housing market is seen. This population bulge has had an impact on society at every stage, and it will have new and different consequences as the generation moves through the age structure of the state's population.

At the dawn of the 1980s the aging of Minnesota's population is becoming apparent. The decline in births during the 1970s is reflected in the decline in child and youth populations. The preschool population (under 5 years) has declined by 58,000 or 18%, since 1970. The youth population (5 to 14 years) has decreased by 92,000, or 11%. These declines are not of equal magnitude everywhere in Minnesota. For example, the decline in the number of children under 5 years is greater in the Twin Cities metropolitan area than in the balance of the state, 26% compared with 8%.

The movement of the 1945-1959 "baby-boom" population into adulthood is reflected in rapid growth of the population 25 to 44 years old by 159,000 or 19% since 1970. In contrast, the 45 to 64 year-olds, many of whom were born during the low birth years of the 1920s and 1930s, increased by only 2%. The number of older Minnesotans, those 65 years and over, increased by 45,000 or 11%.

A dependency ratio is a way of expressing the change in age structure. This measure compares the size of the economically productive population (18 to 64 year-olds) to the size of the dependent population (those under 18 years and those 65 years and older). Between 1940 and 1970 the dependency ratio increased steadily. In 1970 Minnesota had 89 young and old for every 100 persons aged 18 to 64. By 1977 the dependency ratio had declined (75 young and old for every 100 persons aged 18 to 64). Looking toward the future, the elderly dependent ratio is expected to increase while the youth dependency ratio remains constant or continues to decline.

The changing age structure has had a visible impact in Minnesota on households, families, educational attainment, the labor force, and income. Some examples of this trend will be examined in the following sections.

HOUSEHOLDS AND FAMILIES

Housing needs are influenced by population trends. Generally, housing needs follow a lifecycle pattern. Young adults move from their parents' homes and establish their own households. As their family lifecycle stage changes, so may the type of housing which they occupy. The impact of changing age structure is clearly seen in housing in Minnesota in the 1970s. The number of year-round housing units in Minnesota increased by 16%.

Two-thirds to three-quarters of the growth in households resulting from the maturation of this population group will have occurred by 1985.

Although the number of housing units and households increased by 16%, the population living in households grew by only 4% since 1970. The faster growth of housing units reflects the movement of the population boom generation into adulthood and the increasing numbers of elderly. The result is a decline in number of persons per household. In addition, diverse social factors—trends toward smaller families, postponement of marriage, increases in the number of divorced and elderly living alone—also contributed to the decline in persons per household (3.20 to 2.88). For example, 47% of one-person households are maintained by persons 65 years old or more.

Accompanying the change in age structure and the growth in housing units has come an increasing number of households maintained by single (never married) persons (from 10% to 12%). This change is apparently related to an increasing tendency for young adults either to marry at later ages or perhaps not to marry at all. During the 1970s the proportion of 20 to 24 year-old men and women who are single increased from 57% to 68% for men and from 41% to 47% for women. Most of these men and women may marry eventually, but the fact that a corresponding increase in singleness occurred since 1970 among those 24 to 34 years old suggests that more young adults are pursuing alternatives to marriage for longer periods of time.

During the 1970s the proportion of households maintained by divorced or separated persons rose from 6.5% to 8% of all households. The proportion of women 25 to 34 years old who are divorced (not remarried) increased from 6% in 1970 to 9% in 1977. Both the delay in marriage and the higher incidence of divorced persons are found primarily in the Twin Cities metropolitan area.

Although the increase in unmarried persons living along contributed to the rapid growth in households, three of every four households are family households. Husband-wife households account for 67% of all households. Family households maintained by a woman with no husband present comprise 7% of all households.

The 1970s marked changes in household mix in Minnesota which correspond to national changes, although they are less pronounced. Female-headed families grew more rapidly in the United States than in Minnesota, 37% compared with 23%, and account for a larger share of households, 10% compared with 7%. Nonfamily households grew more rapidly nation wide, 48% compared with 35%, although such households comprise the same share of all households—24% in the United States and in Minnesota.

Another indicator pointing to change in households is the increase in Minnesota families with no children under 18 years at home. Forty-five percent of all families have no children under 18 years at home. The decline in the presence of children is found in husband-wife families, not in female-headed families.

The proportion of children under 18 years living with one parent only rose 10% in Minnesota in 1977 but remained below the 16% observed nationally. In the Twin Cities metropolitan area the porportion of children living with one parent only is close to the national average, 15%.

EDUCATIONAL ATTAINMENT

Aside from a high proportion of the population being age 65 or more, many of the changes resulting from a shifting age structure were noticed in the last half of the 1970s or will occur during the first half of the 1980s. For example, elementary and secondary school enrollment will reach its low point by 1985. Post-secondary school enrollment will peak in the early 1980s and then start to decline.

Also affected by the changing age structure, the level of educational attainment in Minnesota is rising as a larger proportion of each generation graduates from high school and college.

In 1977 70% of all persons 25 years or older were high school graduates, compared with 58% in 1970 and 44% in 1960. The proportion of persons with college degrees has more than doubled since 1960 from 8% to 17% in 1977. Conversely, the number of persons 25 years and over who have completed less than nine years of school has declined by 43% since 1960. The number completing only nine to eleven years of school has declined by 14%; in contrast the number of college graduates has increased by 167%.

Changes in educational attainment since 1970 differ for men and women. Since 1970 the number of women college graduates increased by 73% compared with a 62% increase among men. Despite these changes, differences in the levels of educational attainment between men and women remain.

Educational attainment in Minnesota will continue to rise because school attendance has reached new highs. In 1977 99% of the 6 to 15 year-olds and 95% of the 16 to 17 year-olds were enrolled in public or private schools. Since 1965 about 94% of 17 to 18 year-olds have graduated from high school. However, the decline in births since 1960 will produce a continued decline in the number enrolled in school through 1990.

Minnesota's young adults have a higher level of educational attainment than their fellow Americans. Among 25 to 34 year-old males, 93% of Minnesotans have completed at least 12 years of school, compared with 85% nationwide. Among women of the same age, 93% in Minnesota are high school graduates, compared with 82% nationally. National educational attainment surpasses Minnesota only in the proportion of males 65 and over with 12 or more years of school, 36% national versus 29% in Minnesota.

THE LABOR FORCE* AND LABOR FORCE PARTICIPATION

The Minnesota labor force increased by 320,000 (21%) between 1970 and 1977. This compares with an increase of 254,000 in the entire decade of the 1960s. Significant shifts in the composition of the labor force have accompanied this rapid increase.

Young adults accounted for 87% of the increase. In 1977 51% of the labor force was under 35 years old, compared with 43% in 1970. Women accounted for 60% of the increase, and married women with children accounted for over 25% of the increase. Women increased their share of the labor force from 38% in 1970 to 42% in 1977. Over 60% of the increase occurred outside the Twin Cities metropolitan area.

Labor force participation varies by sex, by age, and—for women—by marital status, the presence of children, and educational attainment. Over-all, participation rates for men have changed little. However, the rate for young males (16 to 24 year-olds) has increased while the rate for males 65 years and over has decreased, thus resulting in a total male participation rate that has been relatively constant since 1960.

The greatest change in participation rates has occurred among women 25 to 34 years old which has more than doubled from 30% in 1960 to 70% in 1977. The rate of women 35 to 44 years old rose to 60% in 1977; the rate of women 45 to 64 years old appears to have stabilized at over 50%.

Over half of all married women were in the labor force in 1977 compared with 41% in 1970. The increase has been most marked among young married women with children under 18, however women are less likely to work or seek work if they have children under 6 years than if their children are between 6 and 17 years. Marriage has little effect upon the participation rates of young women with no children under 18; their participation rate is nearly that of males of the same age.

all employed persons and unemployed persons actively seeking work.

INCOME

The income of families is another important characteristic of population because income is a measure of economic well-being. The median money income of families in Minnesota rose by 48% from $9,931 in 1969 to $14,730 in 1976. Husband-wife family income grew from $10,408 in 1969 to $15,560 in 1976, an increase of 49%.

Despite the limitations in interpreting the meaning of money income, the median money income of families by county in Minnesota is instructive. Considering husband-wife families only, the difference in income among counties is great. County median incomes of husband-wife families range from $7,871 in Clearwater County to $19,342 in Washington County. In only ten counties is the median income of husband-wife families above the state median; seven of these counties are in the Twin Cities metropolitan area.

FOR REFERENCE:
• *Minnesota Population Projections: 1970-2000*, Office of State Demographer, State Planning Agency, November, 1975.
• *Housing in Minnesota, 1977*, Office of State Demographer, State Planning Agency, June, 1978.
• *Educational Attainment in Minnesota, 1977*, Office of State Demographer, State Planning Agency, October, 1978.

•*Minnesota Household Characteristics, 1977*, Office of State Demographer, State Planning Agency, November, 1978.

•*Median Income Estimates for Minnesota Counties, 1976*, Office of State Demographer, State Planning Agency, November, 1978.

•*Minnesota Age Estimates, April, 1977*, Office of State Demographer, State Planning Agency, December, 1979.

•*Minnesota Labor Force, 1977*, Office of State Demographer, State Planning Agency, February, 1979.

From Legislative Manual, 1979-1980.

"Milk Carton" races at the Minneapolis Aquatennial.

MARRIAGES OCCURRING IN MINNESOTA
BY AGE OF BRIDE AND GROOM, 1978

Groom's Age

Bride's Age	Total	Under 18	18-19	20	21-24	25-29	30-34	35-39	40-44	45-49	50-54	55-59	60-64	65 & Over	Un-known*
Total	33,480	8	2,774	2,736	12,430	8,065	3,108	1,462	817	523	497	353	249	440	18
Under 18	1,088	1	541	189	293	53	7	3	—	—	—	—	—	1	—
18-19	6,672	1	1,742	1,384	2,829	610	74	19	9	2	1	—	—	—	1
20	3,936	2	291	678	2,210	625	91	29	7	—	2	—	1	—	—
21-24	11,286	2	171	427	6,119	3,520	762	191	50	25	6	8	1	1	3
25-29	5,539	—	15	47	830	2,730	1,269	426	129	45	29	11	3	1	4
30-34	2,013	1	10	7	116	429	693	434	203	67	32	15	4	1	1
35-39	930	—	3	2	17	72	155	256	212	117	70	16	8	1	1
40-44	537	—	1	—	2	13	44	81	133	116	85	39	11	11	1
45-49	412	—	—	—	2	4	11	15	58	98	122	55	25	21	1
50-54	336	—	—	—	—	1	1	7	10	41	105	92	60	19	—
55-59	248	1	—	—	—	2	—	—	6	12	29	86	57	54	1
60-64	196	—	—	1	1	—	—	—	—	—	10	26	60	98	—
65 & Over	262	—	—	—	1	—	1	1	—	—	4	4	19	231	1
Unknown*	25	—	—	1	10	6	—	—	—	—	2	1	—	1	4

*Includes age specified as legal
Source: *Minn. Health Statistics 1978* (Minn. Dept. of Health, Nov. 1979)

DIVORCES AND ANNULMENTS BY AGE OF HUSBAND AND WIFE
MINNESOTA, 1978

Husband's Age

Wife's Age	Total	15-19	20-24	25-29	30-34	35-39	40-44	45-49	50-54	55-59	60-64	65 & Over	Un-known
Total	14,393	68	1,889	3,420	2,733	1,900	1,283	866	648	348	176	229	833
15-19	336	39	234	43	10	4	4	—	—	—	—	1	1
20-24	3,043	23	1,448	1,223	244	71	16	4	—	2	—	1	11
25-29	3,446	2	167	1,883	1,073	220	59	21	6	2	1	—	12
30-34	2,415	2	26	221	1,207	692	172	48	32	9	—	1	5
35-39	1,699	—	6	31	149	782	507	136	59	16	6	—	7
40-44	1,038	1	1	8	26	95	433	331	102	28	5	4	4
45-49	643	1	—	1	12	22	67	260	197	55	18	10	—
50-54	460	—	1	—	5	7	18	55	188	125	41	19	1
55-59	238	—	1	1	—	1	6	7	46	81	56	39	—
60-64	129	—	—	—	—	—	—	3	11	22	33	60	—
65 & Over	122	—	—	—	—	—	—	—	6	7	14	94	1
Unknown	824	—	5	9	7	6	1	1	1	1	2	—	791

Source: *Min.. Health Statistics 1978* (Minn. Dept. of Health, Nov. 1979)

LIVE BIRTHS BY AGE OF MOTHER AND LIVE BIRTH ORDER
MINNESOTA RESIDENTS, 1978

Age of Mother

Live Birth Order	Total Births	Under 15 Years	15-19 Years	20-24 Years	25-29 Years	30-34 Years	35-39 Years	40-44 Years	45 & Over Years	Age Not Stated
First	25,030	55	5,560	10,557	7,055	1,556	216	24	—	7
Second	19,904	1	993	7,204	8,240	3,046	389	31	—	—
Third	9,553	—	79	1,856	4,360	2,718	499	39	2	—
Fourth	3,496	—	6	333	1,318	1,305	479	53	2	—
Fifth	1,253	—	—	39	330	507	317	58	2	—
Sixth	592	—	—	8	94	221	214	52	3	—
Seventh	263	—	—	—	17	88	121	32	5	—
Eight or Over	373	—	—	4	19	59	169	107	15	—
Not Stated	1,513	4	181	482	565	227	44	6	1	3
TOTAL	61,977	60	6,819	20,483	21,998	9,727	2,448	402	30	10
Percent	100.0	0.1	11.0	33.0	35.5	15.7	3.9	0.6	—	—

Source: *Minn. Health Statistics 1978* (Minn. Dept. of Health, Nov. 1979)

Population Characteristics By Age, 1970 and 1977

Age and Sex	Population		Minnesota Percent Distribution		Change 1970-77	
	1970	1977	1970	1977	Number	Percent
Age						
All Ages	3,804,971	3,962,000	100.0	100.0	157,029	4.1
Under 5 years	331,771	273,793	8.7	6.9	-57,978	-17.5
5 to 14 years	819,318	727,249	21.5	18.4	-92,069	-11.2
15 to 24 years	665,442	753,523	17.5	19.0	88,081	13.2
25 to 44 years	851,858	1,011,027	22.4	25.5	159,169	18.7
45 to 64 years	729,325	744,468	19.1	18.8	15,143	2.1
65 years and over	407,257	451,940	10.7	11.4	44,683	11.0
Under 18 years	1,383,149	1,247,503	36.4	31.5	-135,646	-9.8
18 to 64 years	2,014,565	2,262,557	52.9	57.1	247,992	12.3
65 years and over	407,257	451,940	10.7	11.4	44,683	11.0
Dependency Ratio[a]	88.9	75.1	—	—	—	—
Child Dependency Ratio[b]	68.7	55.1	—	—	—	—
Aged Dependency Ratio[c]	20.2	20.0	—	—	—	—
Sex						
Male	1,863,810	1,940,483	49.0	49.0	76,673	4.1
Female	1,941,161	2,021,517	51.0	51.0	80,356	4.1

a. Population under 18 and 65 and over per 100 population 18 to 64.
b. Population under 18 per 100 population 18 to 64.
c. Population 65 and over per 100 population 18 to 64.

Source: Office of State Demographer.

How 87 counties stack up

County	1980 Pop.	1970 Pop.	% change	1980 Housing Units	1970 Housing Units	% change
Aitkin	13,395	11,403	+17.5	11,108	7,798	+42.4
Anoka	195,462	154,712	+26.3	62,770.	40,857	+53.6
Becker	29,238	24,372	+20.0	15,407	10,912	+41.2
Beltrami	30,815	26,373	+16.8	13,006	9,590	+35.6
Benton	24,901	20,841	+19.5	8,694	6,018	+44.5
Big Stone	7,718	7,941	-2.8	3,483	3,024	+15.2
Blue Earth	52,302	52,322	same	19,357	15,767	+22.8
Brown	28,629	28,887	-0.9	10,462	9,070	+15.3
Carlton	29,898	28,072	+2.9	11,772	9,044	+30.2
Carver	36,924	28,331	+30.3	12,569	8,266	+52.1
Cass	21,104	17,323	+21.8	17,378	11,004	+57.9
Chippewa	14,962	15,109	-1.0	6,114	5,308	+15.2
Chisago	25,608	17,492	+46.4	9,535	6,430	+48.3
Clay	49,250	46,608	+5.7	17,783	13,950	+27.5
Clearwater	8,700	8,013	+8.6	3,809	3,167	+20.3
Cook	4,072	3,423	+19.0	3,442	2,360	+45.8
Cottonwood	14,838	14,887	-0.3	5,792	5,130	+12.9
Crow Wing	41,633	34,826	+19.5	25,660	19,799	+29.6
Dakota	194,252	139,808	+38.9	66,871	39,224	+70.5
Dodge	14,709	13,037	+12.8	5,507	4,128	+33.4
Douglas	27,898	22,910	+21.8	13,178	9,073	+45.2
Faribault	19,713	20,896	-5.7	7,948	7,232	+9.9
Fillmore	21,974	21,916	+0.3	8,442	7,637	+10.5
Freeborn	36,298	38,064	-4.6	13,812	12,142	+11.3
Goodhue	38,735	34,808	+11.3	14,360	11,436	+25.6
Grant	7,182	7,462	-3.8	3,175	2,908	+9.2
Hennepin	939,550	960,080	-2.1	379,020	320,479	+18.3
Houston	19,458	17,556	+10.8	7,062	5,486	+28.7
Hubbard	14,072	10,583	+33.0	9,040	6,062	+49.0
Isanti	23,431	16,560	+41.5	8,340	5,574	+49.6
Itasca	43,178	35,530	+21.5	21,221	14,944	+42.0
Jackson	13,669	14,372	-4.8	5,513	4,918	+12.1
Kanabec	12,095	9,775	+23.7	5,484	3,735	+46.8
Kandiyohi	36,704	30,548	+20.2	15,081	11,109	+35.8
Kittson	6,679	6,853	-2.5	3,011	2,747	+9.6
Koochiching	17,447	17,131	+1.8	7,158	6,277	+14.0
Lac qui Parle	10,591	11,164	-5.1	4,272	3,984	+7.2
Lake	13,018	13,351	-2.5	6,093	4,952	+23.0
Lake of the Woods	3,764	3,987	-5.6	2,710	1,730	+56.6
Le Sueur	23,450	21,332	+9.9	9,514	7,672	+24.0
Lincoln	8,207	8,143	+0.8	3,292	2,882	+44.2
Lyon	25,254	24,273	+4.0	9,185	7,526	+22.0
Mahnomen	5,536	5,638	-1.8	2,406	2,148	+12.0
Marshall	13,031	13,060	-0.2	5,245	4,660	+12.6
Martin	24,669	24,312	+1.5	9,762	8,451	+15.5
McLeod	29,590	27,662	+7.0	10,893	8,767	+24.3
Meeker	20,577	18,387	+11.9	8,530	6,598	+29.3
Mille Lacs	18,418	15,703	+17.3	8,291	6,055	+36.9

County	1980 Pop.	1970 Pop.	% change	1980 Housing Units	1970 Housing Units	% change
Morrison	29,294	26,949	+8.7	11,609	9,055	+28.2
Mower	40,336	44,919	-10.2	15,662	14,364	+9.0
Murray	11,401	12,508	-8.9	4,628	4,236	+9.3
Nicollet	26,926	24,518	+9.8	8,959	6,843	+30.9
Nobles	21,698	23,208	-6.5	8,141	7,386	+10.2
Norman	9,396	10,008	-6.1	4,016	3,722	+7.9
Olmsted	91,793	84,104	+9.1	34,292	26,639	+28.7
Otter Tail	51,903	46,097	+12.6	26,909	20,486	+31.4
Pennington	15,212	13,266	+14.7	5,959	4,451	+33.9
Pine	19,881	16,821	+18.2	10,300	7,102	+45.0
Pipestone	11,704	12,791	-8.5	4,636	4,286	+8.2
Polk	34,565	34,435	+0.4	14,645	12,343	+18.7
Pope	11,612	11,107	+4.6	5,651	4,500	+25.6
Ramsey	457,429	476,255	-4.0	176,289	153,623	+14.8
Red Lake	5,471	5,388	+1.5	2,042	1,675	+21.9
Redwood	19,328	20,024	-3.5	7,361	6,718	+9.6
Renville	20,347	21,139	-3.7	7,891	7,190	+9.7
Rice	46,081	41,582	+10.8	15,672	12,330	+27.1
Rock	10,717	11,346	-5.5	4,096	3,680	+11.1
Roseau	12,550	11,569	+8.5	5,034	3,983	+26.4
St. Louis	221,724	220,693	+0.5	95,046	80,859	+17.5
Scott	43,581	32,423	+34.4	14,132	8,789	+60.8
Sherburne	29,808	18,344	+62.5	10,349	6,448	+60.5
Sibley	16,452	15,845	+2.5	5,619	4,991	+12.6
Stearns	107,855	95,400	+13.1	35,899	26,089	+37.6
Steele	30,330	26,931	+12.6	11,258	8,758	+28.5
Stevens	11,312	11,218	+0.8	4,216	3,594	+17.3
Swift	12,937	13,177	-1.8	5,183	4,717	+9.9
Todd	24,929	22,114	+12.7	10,673	8,253	+29.3
Traverse	5,544	6,254	-11.4	2,402	2,298	+4.5
Wabasha	19,345	17,224	+12.3	7,607	5,827	+30.5
Wadena	14,174	12,412	+14.2	5,423	4,280	+26.7
Waseca	18,450	16,663	+10.7	6,880	5,406	+27.3
Washington	113,720	83,003	+37.0	37,140	22,765	+63.1
Watonwan	12,328	13,298	-7.3	4,929	4,583	+7.5
Wilkin	8,449	9,389	-10.0	3,276	3,041	+7.7
Winona	46,230	44,409	+4.1	16,445	13,682	+20.2
Wright	58,780	38,933	+51.0	21,888	14,238	+53.7
Yellow Medicine	13,663	14,523	-5.9	5,383	5,032	+7.0
Total	**4,068,856**	**3,806,103**	**+6.9**	**1,610,097**	**1,276,552**	**+26.1**

Source: Preliminary 1980 Cenusus Data (Dec. 1980)

Changes in county population

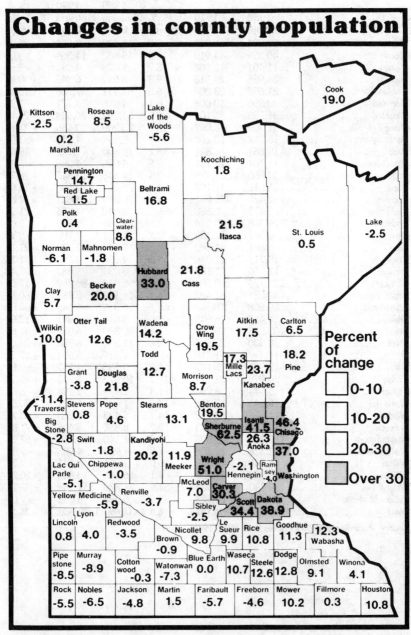

Here is how Minnesota Counties' populations changed after release of 1980 preliminary census figures.

Reprinted with permission from the Minneapolis Tribune.

Minnesota County Population Projections:
1990-2000

County	1990	Projections: 1995	2000
Aitkin	14,600	15,100	15,400
Anoka	260,300	282,300	305,900
Becker	30,800	31,400	31,800
Beltrami	35,500	37,100	38,400
Benton	27,000	28,600	29,700
Big Stone	7,500	7,300	7,000
Blue Earth	54,200	54,900	55,500
Brown	30,600	30,800	30,700
Carlton	32,200	32,400	32,100
Carver	43,600	45,900	47,800
Cass	24,300	25,100	25,800
Chippewa	15,900	15,600	15,200
Chisago	34,400	39,800	44,900
Clay	52,400	53,400	54,000
Clearwater	9,700	9,700	9,500
Cook	4,800	4,800	4,900
Cottonwood	15,900	15,700	15,200
Crow Wing	46,200	48,500	50,600
Dakota	249,300	272,400	293,300
Dodge	13,600	13,600	13,400
Douglas	30,500	32,300	34,100
Faribault	18,700	18,100	17,300
Fillmore	21,200	20,800	20,400
Freeborn	37,900	37,600	36,800
Goodhue	44,500	46,600	48,600
Grant	7,200	7,000	6,600
Hennepin	886,000	882,500	880,000
Houston	19,200	19,500	19,900
Hubbard	15,800	16,800	17,500
Isanti	29,000	33,000	37,000
Itasca	47,000	47,300	46,500
Jackson	14,000	13,700	13,200
Kanabec	14,000	15,300	16,500
Kandiyohi	37,400	38,400	39,100
Kittson	6,700	6,500	6,200
Koochiching	18,400	18,300	17,800
Lac Qui Parle	10,900	10,700	10,400
Lake	15,100	15,000	14,700
Lake of the Woods	4,300	4,300	4,200
Le Sueur	23,000	23,300	23,500
Lincoln	8,200	8,100	7,900
Lyon	26,700	27,200	27,600
McLeod	33,800	35,400	37,400
Mahnomen	5,800	5,600	5,400

County	1990	1995	2000
Marshall	13,800	13,700	13,400
Martin	25,100	24,700	24,300
Meeker	21,700	22,100	22,300
Mille Lacs	22,000	22,900	23,500
Morrison	29,100	29,100	28,700
Mower	43,400	43,100	41,900
Murray	12,500	12,200	11,700
Nicollet	26,600	27,000	27,300
Nobles	23,900	23,700	23,100
Norman	10,200	10,000	9,600
Olmsted	112,200	119,500	125,500
Otter Tail	52,000	52,200	51,700
Pennington	17,300	18,000	18,600
Pine	21,200	21,800	22,200
Pipestone	11,700	11,500	11,100
Polk	37,600	37,300	36,500
Pope	11,600	11,500	11,400
Ramsey	444,500	443,000	442,000
Red Lake	5,200	5,200	5,100
Redwood	19,500	19,100	18,500
Renville	21,500	21,200	20,800
Rice	49,100	50,500	51,700
Rock	11,600	11,500	11,300
Roseau	13,700	13,800	13,700
St. Louis	229,900	232,100	234,000
Scott	51,700	55,500	58,700
Sherburne	41,200	43,900	45,300
Sibley	16,000	16,000	15,800
Stearns	121,100	125,600	129,300
Steele	32,000	32,500	32,700
Stevens	10,900	10,800	10,700
Swift	13,000	12,800	12,400
Todd	26,200	26,600	26,700
Traverse	5,900	5,700	5,500
Wabasha	20,000	20,100	20,100
Wadena	14,200	14,100	13,900
Waseca	19,100	19,400	19,500
Washington	141,900	153,900	163,500
Watonwan	11,800	11,600	11,300
Wilkin	8,600	8,400	8,100
Winona	46,000	46,100	46,200
Wright	71,100	79,100	87,000
Yellow Medicine	14,100	13,900	13,500
STATE	**4,329,700**	**4,440,400**	**4,529,600**

Source: Office of State Demographer

Minnesota's Ethnic Roots

When Senator Stephen Douglas introduced the bill to Congress in 1849 to create the Territory of Minnesota, thirty years had passed since the first permanent white settlement at Fort Snelling. At that time, he told his colleagues that eight to ten thousand settlers lived in the territory.* Most of this population was located within the protective shadow of Fort Snelling at Mendota, a few miles downstream from Mendota in the emerging village of St. Paul, or a few miles upstream at the Falls of St. Anthony. The few remaining people were scattered in small clusters along the lower St. Croix and Mississippi Rivers. Later in that same year, Governor Alexander Ramsey, addressing the first territorial legislature, estimated the Indian population at 25,000, while the 1849 census counted 5,000.* The Indians were spread across what is now Minnesota and the Dakotas east of the Missouri River.

By 1860, two years after statehood and establishment of Minnesota's western border at the Red River, the population had grown and spread, reaching some 172,000. From those early numbers the total population of the state rose to 2 million by 1910 and 4 million today, virtually all the result of immigration and subsequent natural increase of the immigrants.

Meanwhile, geographical differences in the ethnic character of the population evolved rapidly as immigrants entered the state, spread across the land, multiplied, and migrated again. Native American Indians were concentrated on a few reservations as treaty cessions opened most of the land to white settlement in the mid-nineteenth century.

Immigration to Minnesota was first dominated by western Europeans who established themselves on the state's best agricultural lands. Western European immigration slowed and eastern and southern European immigration increased toward the end of the nineteenth century and into the early twentieth century. These people settled on the remaining and poorer agricultural lands, on the state's iron ranges, and in the Twin Cities area. In the mid-twentieth century, black migrants from the southern United States arrived along with a second wave of eastern European immigrants. More recently newcomers to Minnesota have included those from Mexico and Indochina in particular.

Less colorful but at least equally important have been Minnesota's internal population shifts. Geographical concentrations of young and elderly have evolved as people have migrated in large numbers in response to changing economic and social conditions. There are accompanying large differences in wealth, income, unemployment rates, health care, disease, housing, crime, life expectancy, and needs for welfare aids across the state. Minnesotans have adapted themselves to changing conditions and opportunities. One response is seen in the network of social organization and technology; another in the attention given to health and education — the basic requisites to guiding change.

THE EUROPEAN STOCK

The Minnesotas' first white settlers were New England Yankees of English, Scottish, and Irish stock who cut the trees, established the lumber mills and later the flour mills, became the early managers and professionals, and assumed political leadership in the mid-nineteenth century.

*William Watts Folwell, *A History of Minnesota.* Minnesota Historical Society: St. Paul, 1956, Vol. 1, pp. 244, 254, 316.

Foreign Born Population⅓

	1970			1930			1890		
	Number	Percent of Total Population	Percent of Foreign Born Population	Number	Percent of Total Population	Percent of Foreign Born Population	Number	Percent of Total Population	Percent of Foreign Born Population
Total State Population	3,804,971	100.00		2,563,953	100.00		1,310,283	100.00	
Foreign Born	98,056	2.58	100.00	390,790	15.07	100.00	467,356	35.67	100.00
British Isles[a]	5,871	0.15	6.0	18,769	0.72	4.8	49,541	3.78	10.6
Germany and Austria	14,058	0.37	14.3	67,281	2.59	17.2	122,123	9.32	26.1
Norway	9,800	0.26	10.0	71,562	2.76	18.3	101,169	7.72	21.6
Sweden	12,978	0.34	13.2	90,623	3.49	23.2	99,913	7.63	21.4
Finland	4,628	0.12	4.7	24,360	0.94	6.2	d	d	d
USSR[b]	6,160	0.16	6.3	13,470	0.52	3.4	7,233[e]	0.55	1.5
Eastern Europe	9,734[f]	0.26	9.9	40,056[f]	1.54	10.3	18,414[g]	1.41	3.9
Other Europe[c]	10,434	0.27	10.6	33,303	1.28	8.5	24,451	1.87	5.2
Canada	9,815	0.26	10.0	27,264	1.05	7.0	43,580	3.33	9.3
Asia[c]	5,295	0.13	5.4	1,371	0.05	0.4	282	0.02	0.0
Other	9,283	0.24	9.5	2,731	0.11	0.7	650	0.05	0.0

a) England, Scotland, Wales, Ireland, Northern Ireland.
b) Includes Latvia, Lithuania, and Estonia.
c) All of Turkey counted in Asia.
d) Included with USSR (Russia).
e) Russia.
f) Poland, Yugoslavia, Czechoslovakia, Hungary, Rumania, Bulgaria.
g) Poland, Bohemia, Hungary.
Source: U.S. Censuses of Population.

The accelerating population growth in the state in the 1860s, 70s, and 80s consisted largely of non-English-speaking European immigrants who clustered in areas of the state that were opening for settlement when they arrived. Germans, Minnesota's largest ethnic group, settled in the Lower Mississippi valley beginning in the 1850s, moving up the Mississippi and Minnesota valleys in large concentrations to within 80-100 miles of the Twin Cities area. The Swedes, Minnesota's second largest ethnic group, first arrived in Minnesota at about the same time as the Germans, eventually filling almost solidly several counties immediately north of the Twin Cities area and several smaller areas in west-central and western Minnesota. Norwegians, the third largest group in Minnesota, settled first in Fillmore County at about the same time and gradually moved across the southern counties toward the west and northwest and are now the dominant ethnic group in western Minnesota and the Red River valley.

Arriving slightly later, in smaller numbers and filling the gaps were French Canadians, Bohemians, Irish, Dutch, Flemish, Polish, Danish, Welsh, Swiss, Luxemburgers, and Icelanders. With most of the good agricultural lands in Minnesota already claimed, immigrant groups arriving around the turn of the century came to the cities or were attracted by employment opportunities in the Twin Cities and on the Iron Ranges. These groups included Finnish, Russian, Austrian, Cornish, Italian, Slovakian, Moravian, Serbian, Croatian, Hungarian, Romanian, and Greek, with important Jewish immigration from several European countries. Many of these groups were concentrated in small areas.

Wherever immigrant groups settled, they brought with them their churches which served important social and cultural, as well as religious functions.

In the nineteenth and early twentieth century, these differences in European cultural heritage were reflected in well-known regional variations in language, farming practices, and social or business affiliations. Large variations in the architecture of church buildings and size of church membership today bear witness to that important aspect of the state's historical geography. Today a number of festivals, restorations, and commercial enterprises display a continuing or revived interest in embellishing the legacy.

RACIAL MINORITIES
AMERICAN INDIANS

Before white settlement, the Sioux occupied most of Minnesota, but were concentrated in the woodland areas. Pressure from whites in eastern North America pushed the Chippewa westward. They in turn gradually pushed the Sioux from Minnesota's woodlands onto the prairie. The horse, introduced by the Spanish, and adapted and bred by the Indians, provided the Sioux with the mobility to pursue the abundant wildlife of the grasslands. In 1970, the Bureau of the Census recorded 23,000 Indian people living in Minnesota. This has been generally regarded as an understatement: tribal rolls alone exceeded that number by more than 50 percent. According to estimates, 45,000 Indians resided in Minnesota in 1975, about 24 percent living on the state's eleven reservations. The seven largest reservations are

Chippewa, while the four smallest are Sioux. The largest reservation is Leech Lake with over 2,800 residents; the Red Lake and White Earth reservations are just slightly smaller. The four reservations in southern Minnesota have a total population of slightly over 300 Dakota Sioux. At the present time, at least 90 percent of Minnesota's Indian population is Chippewa; most of the remainder are Sioux.

Non-reservation American Indians in the Twin Cities area numbered about 18,600 in 1975, accounting for 41 percent of the state's total. About two-thirds of that number lived within the city of Minneapolis and were most concentrated on the city's near south side.

*Minnesota Department of Education, *Minorities in Minnesota,* State of Minnesota: St. Paul, 1976, pp 4-5 and Table B.

**American Indian Reference Book.* The Earth Co.: Portage, Michigan, 1976, p. 36.

BLACKS

A few black persons had come to Minnesota as free people before the Civil War. Following the Civil War, employment opportunities attracted an additional small number. Most clustered together and were segregated in areas of low cost housing in Minneapolis and St. Paul at locations easily accessible to employment opportunities by public transportation.

Following World War II, there was an unprecedented migration of rural southern blacks to the urban north. The Twin Cities area shared in that growth, usually as a second or third residence after Kansas City, Saint Louis, Chicago, or smaller metropolitan areas in the Lower Midwest.

Minnesota's present black population is dominantly urban and highly concentrated. An estimated 46,300 blacks were living in Minnesota in 1975, 92 percent in the Twin Cities area.* The black population in the Twin Cities area represents about 2.1 percent of the metropolitan population, one of the lowest proportions among major metropolitan areas in the United States. More than 90 percent of Twin City blacks are concentrated in three neighborhoods. The largest, with about 13,000 population, is the Summit-University area, just west of downtown St. Paul. Two slightly smaller black communities of about equal size are in Minneapolis, one on the near north side, the other in the south-central area of the city. Though Minnesota's black population is highly concentrated in these three neighborhoods, the population is inter-mixed, with very few blocks in the core cities being entirely black. Most of the state's remaining 3,500 blacks are located in Duluth, Rochester, St. Cloud, or other similar communities.

CHICANO-LATINOS

Minnesota's largest minority group is the Chicano-Latino population, numbering some 49,500 persons in 1975.* This population includes persons of Spanish heritage identified by surname, language, or place of birth. Minnesota's Hispanic population first arrived as migrant farm laborers, assisting with the vegetable production operations of southern Minnesota. With expansion of sugar beet production in the Red River valley, and the availability of summer-long employment, an increasing proportion of migrant laborers have sought year-round residence and employment in Minnesota.

*Minnesota Department of Education, *Minorities in Minnesota,* State of Minnesota: St. Paul, 1976, Table B.

*Minnesota Department of Public Welfare, Office of Indochinese Resettlement.

The Census has recorded 37,300 persons of Spanish heritage living in Minnesota in 1970. It is generally agreed that this figure represents some undercounting, though not at the rate of the American Indian population. There was an increasing migration of Chicano-Latinos to Minnesota between 1970 and 1975 and this trend has continued since that time. About two thirds of Minnesota's Hispanic population lived in the seven county Twin Cities area in 1975, with the others more widely scattered across the state than either the black or Indian populations. The single largest concentration of Chicano-Latinos was on the west side of St. Paul. Of the remaining third, about half lived in the vegetable growing areas of southern Minnesota or the sugar beet growing areas of the Red River Valley.

ASIANS

Several thousand persons of Chinese, Japanese, and Filipino stock have lived in Minnesota—primarily in the Twin Cities area—for many years. Important Asian immigrant groups arriving since world War II have included Korean and Indochinese. The Indochinese were estimated to number about 10 thousand in the state in early 1980.**

THE SETTLEMENT PROCESS

From its beginning in the southeastern part of the state, Minnesota's white population gradually pushed westward and northward, during the 1850s, following the stream valleys which served as means of transportation and provided wood for building materials and fuel.

DISPLACEMENT OF INDIANS; DEVELOPMENT OF RAIL PATTERN

Railroad development beginning in the 1860s joined together the existing settlements and triggered the sweep of white settlement across the state. White settlement gradually displaced the native Chippewa and Sioux populations and confined their reduced numbers to reservation lands. In recent years, nearly half the Indian population has shifted from these reservations to the Twin Cities area, particularly Minneapolis.

Until about the time of World War I, both the state's population and rail network advanced, then thickened in density. This was the era of resource acquisition and development. Settlers spread out to cultivate the land, harvest the timber and later to settle the Iron Ranges and dig the rich, natural ores. Towns and cities sprang up and grew to serve these economic activities, to assemble and process their output, and feed it into the mainstream of the national economy.

TRACTOR-AUTO AGE

Since the Depression and World War II, the economy of the state has become more noticeably diversified, providing a great range of services in areas like finance, education, medicine, law, business, and government. These changes in Minnesota's economy coincided with improvements in personal mobility and new machinery that allowed greater production with fewer workers. This resulted in a steady increase in farm size and a decline in farm population at the same time that employment opportunities were expanding in the urban areas of the state.

Population shifts reduced rural densities and contributed to growth in the state's cities. These urbanization trends were inhibited during the 1930s by economic stagnation and by the national emergency in the early 1940s. Beginning in the late 1940s, urbanization resumed with new vigor after being restrained for more than a

**Minnesota Department of Public Welfare, Office of Indochinese Resettlement.

decade and a half.

During the 1950s, urban growth in Minnesota, as throughout the nation, was almost explosive. Concurrently, 279,000 persons left Minnesota's farms, as the number of farms decreased and the average farm size increased rapidly. The remaining farms produced more food than ever. And the more affluent and mobile farm population was able to travel greater distances to the larger trade centers, contributing to their growth and dominance, while the smallest towns struggled to survive the competition.

The shift from natural ore mining to taconite processing on the Mesabi Range during the 1950s resulted in the emergence of several completely new communities in northeastern Minnesota.

During the 1950s, Minnesota's population incrased by 431,400 persons with the urban counties increasing most rapidly in both number and percent. Meanwhile, the predominantly rural counties of the state (those without major trade centers), experienced losses in population. Notwithstanding the large urban population growth, there was a net outmigration of 98,000 persons from Minnesota, a large share of whom moved to urban centers in other states, particularly on the West Coast.

FLUCTUATION IN BIRTH RATE AND MIGRATION

Minnesota's overall population growth during the 1950s was the result of natural increase—the excess of births over deaths. Birth rates in Minnesota, as throughout the country, experienced a continual increase during the 1950s, reaching a peak in 1959.

During the 1960s, Minnesota increased in population by 391,100 persons, while net outmigration declined to 0.7 percent of the 1960 population. Birth rates dropped steadily. The state's urban population continued to shift outward from the centers of employment toward the accessible countryside areas of lakes, trees, and hills. Population increased in the metropolitan fringe counties and in certain counties in the central part of the state with physical amenities. During the 1960s, farm size increased and off-farm migration continued. Many farmers located within commuting distance of alternative employment opportunities converted to part-time farming. Other farms were purchased by exurbanites and converted to recreational, hobby, or retirement farms. But in those agricultural areas of the state which were not easily accessible to expanding employment opportunities, farmers did not have the option of securing supplemental income. The choices for many middle-aged farmers on small holdings were limited to selling out or struggling to survive—and as a result pockets of rural poverty became evident in some areas of the state.

The cities, too, were affected by the shifting patterns of population. Two-parent middle class families with children made up most of the population spreading from the cities into suburban and nearby countryside areas. This left behind a population that was less able or less inclined to pursue the suburban lifestyle. They included the elderly, minority groups, and the socially and psychologically alienated. Certain older urban neighborhoods continued to attract transient, upwardly mobile, young adults who were seeking jobs, education, and social contacts. These population groups brought new social problems and increasing costs to the cities, and even more families left. Some persons felt trapped by their environments and unable to participate in the opportunities available to others; this brought waves of violence to American cities, including Minneapolis and St. Paul in the late 1960s.

Source: *Atlas of Minnesota Resources & Settlement, 1980.*

INDIANS

Northwest Ordinance
Act of Congress, July 13, 1787
Section 14, Article III

"Religion, morality and knowledge being necessary to good government and the happiness of mankind, schools and the means of education shall forever be encouraged. The utmost good faith shall always be observed towards the Indians; their lands and property shall never be taken from them without their consent; and in their property, rights and liberty they never shall be invaded or disturbed, unless in just and lawful wars authorized by Congress; but laws founded in justice and humanity shall, from time to time be made for preventing wrongs being done to them, and for preserving peace and friendship with them."

Minnesota's Indian Reservations

The following Chippewa and Sioux Indian Reservations are located in the State of Minnesota: Fond du Lac, Grand Portage, Bois Forte (Nett Lake), Leech Lake, Mille Lacs, and White Earth. These six Chippewa reservations are organized and known as the Minnesota Chippewa Tribe. The following Sioux reservations are located in the southern portion of the State; Prairie Island, Lower Sioux, Upper Sioux, and some small scattered tracts of land north of Prior Lake which are sometimes referred to as the Prior Lake Reservation.

The only other Indian reservation in Minnesota is the Red Lake Chippewa Reservation in northern Minnesota. As the only "closed" reservation in the state, Red Lake maintains its own court system and police force.

Indian Facts

There is no general legislative or judicial definition of "an Indian" that can be used to identify a person as an Indian. For census purposes, an Indian has been identified on a self-declaration basis. If an individual did not declare his race, the enumerator has counted him as an Indian if he appeared to be a full-blooded American Indian - or if of mixed and white blood - was enrolled or was regarded as an Indian in the community in which he lived.

The Congress on June 2, 1924, extended American citizenship to all Indians born in the territorial limits of the United States. They vote on the same basis as other citizens.

There is no automatic payment to a person because he is an Indian. Payments may be made to Indian tribes or individuals for losses which resulted from treaty violations or encroachments upon lands or interests reserved to the tribe by the Government. Tribes or individuals may receive Government checks for income from their land and resources, but only because the assets are held in trust by the Secretary of the Interior and payment for the use of the Indian resources has been collected by the Federal Government. Contrary to popular belief, Indians **do not** receive regular monthly payments from the government.

They pay local, state and federal taxes the same as other citizens unless a treaty, agreement or statute exempts them. Most tax exemptions which have been granted apply to lands held in trust for them and to income from such land.

In addition to the aforementioned, Minnesota has seen many others - Algonquin, Oto, Omaha, Iowa, Mandan, Cheyenne, Sauk, Fox, Ottowa, Potawatomie, Cree and Menomonie, some of which still reside here in small numbers.

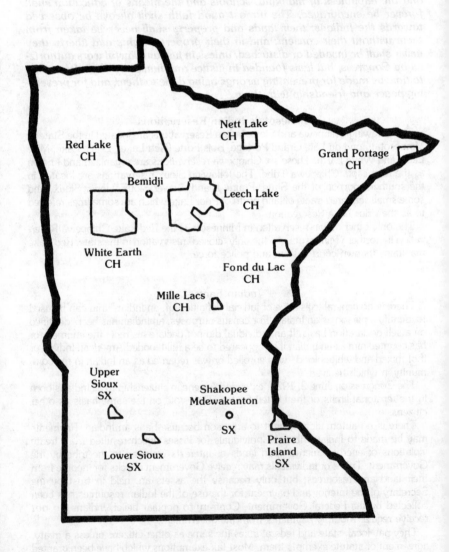

CH - Chippewa   SX - Sioux

Where to Apply For a Certified Copy of Birth or Death Records

Copies of records of births and deaths which occurred in any years **after** 1870 **within the city limits** of the cities of Duluth, Minneapolis or St. Paul, should be ordered from the City Health Department of the city concerned. In Minneapolis, the request should be sent to the City Health Department, Room 235, 250 South 4th Street, Minneapolis, Minnesota 55401. Checks should be made payable to the City treasurer.

Copies of records of births and deaths which occurred elsewhere in Minnesota **in any year** should be ordered from the clerk of District Court of the county where the event occurred. Checks should be made payable to the Clerk of District Court of that county.

Copies of records of births and deaths which occurred anywhere within the State of Minnesota **since 1900** may also be ordered from the Minnesota State Department of Health, Vital Statistics Department, 717 Delaware Street Southeast, Minneapolis, Minnesota 55440. The fee for a search of its files is $2.00. One search fee pays for one certified copy. Additional copies of the same certificate are $2.00 each. Checks should be made payable to Treasurer, State of Minnesota, and mailed directly to the Minnesota Department of Health with your request for the record.

For birth records, the following information is required: name of child, date of birth, location of birth and mother's and father's names.

For death records, the following information is required: name of descendent, date of death and location of death.

For marriage records, the following information is required: name of each party, date of marriage and place where application was made for the license. Records would be kept in the county seat where original application was made. Send requests to the Clerk of District Court of the county. The fee is $2.00.

Requirements of Applicants for a Marriage License
in the State of Minnesota

The residence of the man is immaterial, but if the woman resides in the State, the application for the license must be made in the County of her residence and the ceremony may take place anywhere within the State. If she is a non-resident of Minnesota, the application for the license may be made in any County in the State, and the ceremony may take place anywhere within the State.

The statute requires that one of the parties to contemplated marriage appear in person before the Director and make the application, and five days thereafter the license is issued; the marriage may take place immediately. The waiting period may be waived by a Judge of the District Court, but this is a matter between the applicants and the Judge, and when an Order is issued waiving the waiting period, authority is given the Director to issue the license as soon as the application has been made and the marriage may take place immediately.

The man must be eighteen years of age and the woman eighteen. If either party has been divorced, or had a previous marriage annulled, the decree must have been final six months prior to the application for the license. This also applies to non-residents of the State. A certified copy of the divorce decree is necessary.

The statute further provides that no nearer of kin than second cousins may marry, and that neither party is imbecile, feeble-minded or afflicted with insanity. A Medical certificate is not required. The license fee is $10.00.

Passports

With a few exceptions, all U.S. citizens need a passport to depart from or enter the United States and to enter most foreign countries. The exceptions generally relate to travel between the United State and countries in North, South and Central America and the Carribean, except Cuba. However, some of these countries require a passport or other travel document for admission. For information, contact the embassy or consulate of the country to be visited or consult the Passport Office publication M-264, "Visa Requirements of Foreign Governments."

For your first passport, you must personally present a completed Passport Application (Form DSP-11) at any Federal or State court of record accepting applications; or at a post office designated by the Postmaster General.

If you have had a previous passport, you may be eligible to apply for a passport by mail.

What do you need to obtain a passport?

* A properly completed passport application.
* A Birth Certificate must be presented if you were born in the United States.
* A Certificate of Naturalization shall be submitted if you claim Citizenship by naturalization.
* A Certificate of Citizenship issued by the Immigration and Naturalization Service shall be submitted if citizenship was acquired through naturalization of a parent or parents. If such certificae is not available, your parent's (s') certificate (s) of naturalization and your foreign birth certificate and evidence of admission to the United States shall be submitted with the application.
* A Report of Birth Abroad of a Citizen of the United States of America (Form FS-240), A Certificate of Birth (Form FS-545 or DS-1350), or a Certificate of Citizenship should be submitted if Citizenship was acquired by birth abroad to a U.S. citizen parent or parents.
* Two Photographs.
* FEES - the fee for a passport is $10.00
* PROOF OF IDENTIFICATION

The following persons may normally be included in your passport:

Your husband/wife

Any minor children including your stepchildren and adopted children;

Any minor brothers or sisters.

Animals may not be included in your passport even though they might be traveling with you.

Entering Canada

Minnesotans can cross the U.S. - Canada border either way, usually without difficulty or delay. They do not require passports or visas. Naturalized U.S. citizens should carry a naturalization certificate or some other evidence of citizenship, in case they are asked for it. Permanent residents of the United States who are not American citizens are advised to have their Alien Registration Receipt Card (U.S. Form I-151).

Recreational Equipment

Visitors may bring into Canada sporting outfits and other equipment, for their own use, by declaring them at entry. These can include fishing tackle, portable boats, outboard motors, ice boats, motorized toboggans, snowmobiles, etc., equipment for camping, golf, tennis and other games, radios and portable or table-model television sets used for the reception of sound broadcasting and television programs, musical instruments, typewriters and cameras (with a reasonable amount of film and flashbulbs) in their possession on arrival. Although not a requirement, it may facilitate entry if visitors have a list (in duplicate) of all durable items carried, with a description of each item, including serial numbers, where possible. All such articles must be identified and reported when leaving Canada.

While such items are normally admitted free of duty and tax, a deposit may be requested to ensure exportation. This deposit will be forwarded to the non-resident's home address by check on proof of exportation of the goods.

Dogs may be brought into Canada if they are accompanied by a rabies vaccination certificate. There are no restrictions on cats.

Minnesotans entering Canada from three locations, the Duluth airport, Grand Portage and International Falls, may purchase spirits free of any federal and state taxes if they are taken directly across the border. Many visitors feel the saving, despite the duty and tax imposed by Canadian customs on anything over 1.1 liters of liquor, is still worthwhile.

CB RADIO OWNERS, PLEASE NOTE: You must have a special permit to transmit in Canada. This can be obtained by writing to the Canadian Consulate, 15 S. 5th St., Minneapolis—two weeks in advance. Any unit transmitting in Canada without a permit is subject to confiscation.

Minnesota Population, 1860-1978

Year	Population in Thousands	Percent in Seven County Twin Cities Area
1860	172	30
1870	440	25
1880	781	24
1890	1310	31
1900	1751	28
1910	2076	31
1920	2387	32
1930	2564	36
1940	2792	36
1950	2982	40
1960	3414	45
1970	3805	49
1978	4008	49

Sources: U. S. Censuses of Population; Minnesota State Demographer (1978).

You may see anything during a Minnesota winter.

Government

United States Senator

Constitution provides: to qualify as senator a person must be thirty years old, citizen of the United States nine years, resident of the state. Each state is allowed two senators.

Term: six years.   **Salary:** $89,500.

Senator Dave Durenberger
(Independent-Republican)

Minnesota address:	Capitol address:
1020 Plymouth Bldg.	154 Russell Senate Office Bldg.
12 S. 6th St.	Washington, D.C. 20510
Minneapolis, MN 55402	(202) 224-3244
(612) 370-3382	
MN toll-free 1-800-752-4226	

Biography: Minneapolis. Born August 19, 1934, St. Cloud; education: St. John's Preparatory School, St. John's University (B.S. cum laude, 1955), University of Minnesota Law School (J.D., 1959); wife: Penny, sons: Charles, David, Michael, Daniel.

Committees: Finance; Environment and Public Works; Aging.

Subcommittiees: (of Finance): Health, Trade, Social Security and Family Planning: (of Environment & Public Works): Hazardous Wastes & Toxic Substances, Environmental Protection, and Water Resources, Transportation & Infrastructure.

Elected: Special Election November 7, 1978, 1982.

Term Expires: January, 1989.

Senator Rudy Boschwitz
(Independent-Republican)

Minnesota address:
210 Bremer Bldg.
419 N. Robert St.
St. Paul, MN 55101
(612) 221-0904

Capitol address:
506 Hart Office Bldg.
Washington, D.C. 20510
(202) 224-6541

Biography: Plymouth. Born 1930, Berlin, Germany; education: New York University (B.S. 1950, LL.B. 1953); U.S. Army Signal Corps (1954-55); founder and chair, Plywood Minnesota, Inc.; Republican National Committee; wife: Ellen, children: Gerry, Ken, Tom, Dan.

Committees: Agriculture; Budget, Foreign Relations, Small Business.

Subcommittees: (of Ag.) Agricultural Credit, Domestic & Foreign Marketing, Nutrition & Investigations; (of Foreign Relations) Near Eastern & South Asian Affairs, European Affairs; (of Small Business) Export Expansion, Rural Economy & Family Farming.

Elected: 1978, 1984.

Term Expires: January, 1991.

United States Representative

Constitution provides: to qualify as representative a person must be twenty-five years old, citizen of the United States seven years, resident of the state, and elected by the people. Representation is based upon population; Minnesota is divided into eight districts with one representative for each district.

Term: two years.   **Salary:** $89,500.

Minnesota Representatives in the 100th Congress

Congressional District 1

Representative Tim Penny
(Democratic-Farmer-Labor)

Minnesota address:
Park Towers
22 N. Broadway
Rochester, MN 55904
(507) 281-6053

410 5th St. S.
Mankato, MN 56001
(507) 625-6921

Capitol address:
436 Cannon HOB
Washington, D.C. 20515
(202) 225-2472

Biography: Born in Freeborn County, MN November 19, 1951; 1969 graduate of Keister High School; 1974 honor graduate from Winona State University; graduate work in Public Affairs at the University of Minnesota; elected to the Minnesota State Senate in 1976; reelected in 1980; Waseca PALS, Waseca County Association of Retarded Citizens; married the former Barb Christianson, 1975; four children: Jamison, Joseph, Molly, and Marcus; elected to the 98th Congress, November 2, 1982; reelected to each succeeding Congress.

Committees: Agriculture, Education & Labor, Veteran's Affairs, Select Committee on Hunger (International Task Force).

Subcommittees: (of Agricultural) Conservation, Credit and Rural Development; Wheat, Soybeans, and Feed Grains; (of Education & Labor) Labor Standards; (of Veteran's Affairs) Hospitals & Health Care; Compensation, Pension & Insurance, Congressional Commission: Canada-U.S. Interparliamentary Group.

Elected: 1982, 1984, 1986.

Term expires: January 1989.

Congressional District 2

Representative Vin Weber
(Independent-Republican)

Minnesota addresses:

919 1st St. S.
Willmar, MN 56201
(612) 235-6820

1212 E. College Dr.
P.O. Box 1294
Marshall, MN 56258
(507) 532-9611

Capitol address:

106 Cannon HOB
Washington, D.C. 20515
(202) 225-2331

Biography: Slayton. Education: University of Minnesota (1974, political science); staff, Minnesota Independent-Republican Chair Bob Brown (1973-74); state board member: Minnesota Citizens Concerned for Life (1973-74); married Jeanie Lorenz of Waseca.

Committees: Appropriations

Subcommittees: Agriculture, Rural Development & Related Agencies; Labor/Health and Human Services/Education.

Elected 1980, 1982, 1984, 1986.

Term expires: Jan., 1989.

MINNESOTA CONGRESSIONAL DISTRICTS

The United States District Court for the District of Minnesota ordered a reapportionment of Minnesota's eight congressional districts on March 11, 1982. The population goal was 509,496 for each district with an average deviation of 9.5.

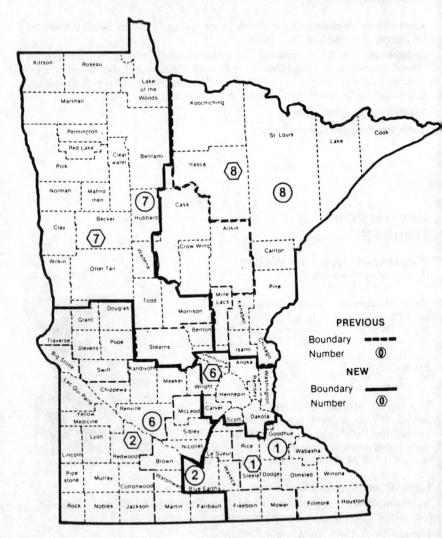

PREVIOUS

Boundary ▬ ▬ ▬

Number ⓪

NEW

Boundary ▬▬▬▬

Number ⓪

Congressional District 3

Representative Bill Frenzel
(Independent-Republican)

Minnesota address:
8120 Penn Ave. S.
Bloomington, MN 55431
(612) 881-4600

Capitol address:
1026 Longworth Office Bldg.
Washington, D.C. 20515
(202) 225-2871

Biography: Golden Valley. Born July 31, 1928, St. Paul; education: elementary and secondary, St. Paul, Dartmouth College (B.A., 1950; M.B.A., 1951); Minnesota House of Representatives (1963-70); married Ruth Purdy, three daughters.

Committees: House Administration, Ways and Means.

Subcommittees: (of House Admin.) Elections, Libraries & Memorials; (of Ways & Means) Oversight, Public Assistance & Unemployment Compensation, Trade.

Elected: 1970, 1972, 1974, 1976, 1978, 1980, 1982, 1984, 1986.

Term Expires: Jan., 1989.

Congressional District 4
Representative Bruce F. Vento
(Democratic-Farmer-Labor)

Minnesota address:
American Nat'l Bank Bldg.
5th & Minnesota
Suite 905
St. Paul, MN 55101
(612) 224-4503

Capitol address:
2304 Rayburn HOB
Washington, D.C. 20515
(202) 225-6631

Biography: St. Paul. Born October 7, 1940, St. Paul; education: Johnson High School (1958), Wisconsin State University (B.S. with honors, 1965); teacher, Minneapolis; Minnesota House of Representatives (1971-76); assistant majority leader (1974-76); married Mary Jean Moore; sons: Michael, Peter, John.

Committees: Banking, Finance & Urban Affairs; Interior & Insular Affairs.

Subcommittees: (of House Banking): Economic Stabilization; Financial Institutions Supervision; Regulation and Insurance; Housing and Community Development; (of Interior & Insular Affairs): Insular & International Affairs, National Parks & Public Lands (chairman).

Elected: 1976, 1978, 1980, 1982, 1984, 1986.

Term expires: Jan., 1989.

Congressional
District 5

Representative Martin Olav Sabo
(Democratic-Farmer-Labor)

Minnesota address:	Capitol address:
462 Fed. Courts Bldg.	2201 Rayburn HOB
110 So. 4th St.	Washington, D.C. 20515
Minneapolis, MN 55401	(202) 225-4755
(612) 348-1649	
FTS 787-5110	

Biography: Minneapolis. Born February 28, 1938; education: Augsburg College (B.A.); Minnesota House of Representatives (1961-78), minority leader (1969-72), speaker of the house (1973-78); former president, National Conference of State Legislatures; wife: Sylvia, daughters: Karin, Julie.

Committees: Appropriations, Democratic Steering & Policy.

Subcommittees: (of Appropriations) Defense, Transportation, and Dist. of Columbia.

Elected: 1978, 1980, 1982, 1984, 1986.

Term expires: January, 1989.

Congressional
District 6

Representative Gerry Sikorski
(Democratic-Farmer-Labor)

Minnesota address:	Capitol address:
8060 University Ave. NE	414 Cannon HOB
Fridley, MN 55432	Washington, D.C. 20515
(612) 780-5801	(202) 225-2271

Biography: Stillwater. Born April 26, 1948; education: University of Minnesota (J.D. magna cum laude, 1973); Minnesota State Senate (1977-82); senate majority whip (1981-82); married Susan Erkel, daughter: Anne.

Committees: Energy and Commerce, Post Office and Civil Service.

Select Committee: Children, Youth & Families.

Subcommittees: (of Energy & Commerce) Oversight & Investigations; Health & the Environment; and Transportation, Tourism & Hazardous Material; (of Post Office and Civil Service) Human Resources (chairman), and Census and Population.

Elected: 1982, 1984, 1986.

Term expires: Jan., 1989.

METROPOLITAN AREA
CONGRESSIONAL DISTRICTS

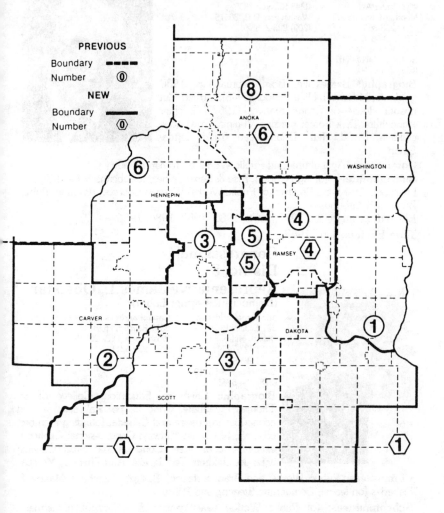

Congressional District 7
Representative Arlan Stangeland
(Independent-Republican)

Minnesota address:
403 Center Ave.
Moorhead, MN 56560
(218) 233-8631
FTS 783-5616
720 Mall Germain
St. Cloud, MN 56301
(612) 251-0740

Capitol address:
2245 Rayburn HOB
Washington, D.C. 20515
(202) 225-2165

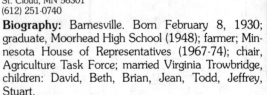

Biography: Barnesville. Born February 8, 1930; graduate, Moorhead High School (1948); farmer; Minnesota House of Representatives (1967-74); chair, Agriculture Task Force; married Virginia Trowbridge, children: David, Beth, Brian, Jean, Todd, Jeffrey, Stuart.

Committees: Agriculture, and Public Works of Transportation.

Subcommittees: (of Ag.) Cotton, Rice & Sugar; Wheat, Soybeans & Feed Grains; Livestock, Dairy and Poultry; (of Public Works) Water Resources, Aviation, Public Building & Grounds.

Elected: February 22, 1977, 1978, 1980, 1982, 1984, 1986.

Term Expires: Jan., 1989.

Congressional District 8
Representative James L. Oberstar
(Democratic-Farmer-Labor)

Minnesota address:
231 Federal Bldg.
Duluth, MN 55802
(218) 727-7474
316 Lake St.
Chisholm, MN 55719
(218) 254-5761

Capitol address:
2351 Rayburn HOB
Washington, D.C. 20515
(202) 225-6211

Biography: Chisholm. Education: College of St. Thomas, graduate work in political science and economics in Europe and Canada; founding member, co-chair, Northeast Midwest Congressional Coalition; executive committee. Congressional Steel Caucus; wife: Jo, children: Ted, Noelle, Ann-Therese, Monica.

Committees: Public Works and Transportation, Budget, Merchant Marine & Fisheries (on leave), Democratic Steering and Policy.

Subcommittees: (of Public Works) Investigations & Oversight (Chairman), Economic Development, Water Resources.

Elected: 1974, 1976, 1978, 1980, 1982, 1984, 1986.

Term expires: January, 1989.

STATE CONSTITUTIONAL OFFICERS

The Minnesota constitution defines three branches of state government: legislative, executive, and judicial. Article V establishes a six-member executive branch consisting of governor, lieutenant governor, secretary of state, auditor, treasurer, and attorney general. These constitutional officers are nominated with political party designation and elected by statewide ballot.

OFFICE OF THE GOVERNOR

Rudy Perpich
State Capitol
St. Paul 55155
(612) 296-3391

Constitution provides: that to qualify as governor a person must be 25 years old, resident of the state one year, citizen of the United States, and elected by the people (Article V).

Term: four years.　　　　　　　**Salary:** $95,118

Rudy Perpich
(Democratic-Farmer-Labor)

Born on June 27, 1928, in the small mining town of Carson Lake, near Hibbing, Minnesota; graduated from Hibbing High School in 1946 and Hibbing State Junior College in 1950; received a Doctor of Dental Surgery Degree from Marquette University in 1954; served on the Hibbing School Board (1956-62); Minnesota Senator (62-70); Lt. Governor (70-76), and served as Minnesota's 34th governor (76-78); three years as trade representative for Control Data Corp.; elected as Minnesota's 36th governor in 1982, and reelected in 1986; he has served longer as Governor of Minnesota than anyone in history; served as the chairman of the Committee on International Trade and Foreign Relations of the National Governors' Association.

Elected: 1982, 1986.
Term expires: Jan., 1991.

Powers:
　The governor has the responsibility of informing the legislature about the general condition of the state. This is done by means of his inaugural message delivered to a joint legislative session immediately after he takes his oath of office and by a "state of the state" address at the beginning of the second half of each term in office.
　The financial needs of state government for the next two fiscal years are submit-

ted to the legislature in the governor's proposed budget within three weeks after the governor's inauguration and again in the second half of his term for the following biennium.

The governor also sends a special messages to the legislature on subjects that he feels warrant particular emphasis and attention.

The governor must review all laws passed by the legislature. The governor may approve a bill by signing it, or he may veto a bill by returning it to the legislature stating his objections. A two-thirds vote in each legislative body is required to pass a bill over the governor's veto. When the governor does not sign a bill passed on the final three days of a session within 14 days after adjournment, he exercises a pocket veto, and the bill does not become law.

Functions:

Judicial appointments: The governor fills vacancies which occur in municipal, district, and supreme court judgeships. These appointments do not require confirmation by the senate.

Extradition and civil rights power: The governor issues extradition papers and restores civil rights to felons.

Commissions notaries public: The governor commissions notaries public. Approximately 5,500 commissions are issued during each fiscal year.

Commander-in-chief of military forces: The governor is commander-in-chief of the military forces in Minnesota. He may call out such forces to execute the laws, suppress insurrections, and repel invasion, and for such other emergencies as he may determine.

Planning: The governor as state planning officer prepares comprehensive long range plans for the orderly coordinated growth of the state. He reports with recommendations to the legislature for the implementation of such plans.

Ex officio membership: The governor is an ex officio member of the state pardon board, the executive council, the state board of investment, and the land exchange board; presiding officer of the legislative advisory commission.

Minnesota's 87 Counties

Counties are governed by a board of commissioners and administrative officers elected by the people. State law allows alternative forms of government, chiefly to allow for an elected executive, a manager, or administrator, and the option to make administrative offices appointive.

During the decade of the seventies, the legislature increased the responsibilities of county government. A county court system has been established; counties are developing shorelands management and solid waste management systems.

Counties have the responsibilities of tax assessment, tax administration, elections, record keeping, transportation, planning and zoning, environment, parks and water management, law enforcement, courts, and health and welfare.

OFFICE OF THE LIEUTENANT GOVERNOR

Marlene Johnson
122 State Capitol
St. Paul 55155
(612) 296-2374

Constitution provides: that to qualify as lieutenant governor a person must be 25 years old, resident of the state one year, citizen of the United States, and elected by the people jointly with the governor by a single vote applying to both offices (Article V).

Term: four years.   **Salary:** $52,317

Marlene Johnson
(Democratic-Farmer-Labor)

Biography: Born January 11, 1946, Braham. Macalester College (B.A., political science, 1968); founder and president, Split Infinitive, Inc., St. Paul advertising and public relations firm (1970-82); member, Minnesota High Technology Council; founder and immediate past chair, National Leadership Conference for Women Executives in State Government; past president, National Association of Women Business Owners (NAWBO); founder, Minnesota chapter, NAWBO; vice chair, Minnesota Task Force on Small Business (1978); chair, DFL Small Business Task Force; co-chair, Minnesota delegation, White House Conference on Small Business (1980); former membership director, National Women's Political Caucus; former chair, Minnesota Women's Political Caucus, Macalester College Distinguished Citizen Citation (1982); Minnesota Jaycees Ten Outstanding Young Minnesotans, U.S. Women Jaycees Ten Outstanding Women in Government (1983).

Elected: 1982, 1986.
Term Expires: Jan., 1991.

The lieutenant governor serves as an extension of the governor. He is first in line when a vacancy occurs in the office of the governor. The lieutenant governor represents the governor and state of Minnesota within the state, nationally, and internationally.

In order to make the office of lieutenant governor more meaningful and productive, a bill was enacted in 1971 enabling the governor to delegate to the lieutenant governor such powers, duties, responsibilities, and functions as are prescribed by law to be performed by the governor, subject to his control, by filing a written order specifying such delegation with the secretary of state; provided, however, that no power, duty, responsibility, or function imposed upon the governor by the constitution shall be delegated by such written order or otherwise.

Formerly, the lieutenant governor presided over the Minnesota senate. A constitutional amendment ratified in November, 1972, permitted the senate to choose its own presiding officer. Consequently, the duties of the lieutenant governor were changed, and he became a full time official of the executive branch.

Functions:

The lieutenant governor has the statutory responsibility of serving as chairman of the Capitol Area Architectural and Planning Board. He is a member of the Executive Council. The governor, by executive order, has delegated the following responsibilities to the lieutenant governor: coordination and direction of the legislative process between the office of the governor and both houses of legislature; development and coordination of a systematic program to preserve and enhance the relationship between the state and local units of government and between the state and business, industry, and labor; assisting the governor in preparation, revision, implementation, and analysis of the biennial budget; advising the governor on matters of policy and personnel; representing the governor at public presentations and public events as designated. Further, the lieutenant governor has been appointed to serve as a member of/or governor's liaison to the following boards and commissions:

- Minnesota State Retirement System
- Legislative Commission on Minnesota Resources
- State Employee Suggestion Board
- Credit Union Advisory Council
- Upper Great Lakes Regional Commission
- Mississippi River Parkway Commission
- Minnesota-Wisconsin Boundary Area Commission
- Upper Mississippi River Basin Commission
- Iron Range Resources and Rehabilitation Board
- Great Lakes Commission
- Public Employees Retirement Association
- Teachers Retirement Association
- Highway Patrolmen's Retirement Association
- Rural Development Council

Services:

The lieutenant governor's office often serves constituents who call or come to the office with inquiries and concerns. Either directly or by referral to legislators and agencies and/or commissions, the lieutenant governor assists citizens in finding answers to their questions and problems.

OFFICE OF THE SECRETARY OF STATE

Joan Anderson Growe
180 State Office Bldg.
St. Paul 55155
(612) 296-3266

Constitution provides: that the secretary of state is an officer in the executive department; to qualify as secretary of state a person must be a qualified voter, 21 years old, and elected by the people (Article V; Minnesota Statutes, Chapter 5).

Term: 4 years.   **Salary:** $52,317

Joan Anderson Growe
(Democratic-Farmer-Labor)

Biography: Minneapolis, Born September 28, 1935, Minneapolis; education: St. Cloud State University (B.S.), University of Minnesota (special education certificate), Kennedy School of Government Executive Management Program, Harvard University (1979); Minnesota House of Representatives (1973-74); president, National Assn. of Secretaries of State (1979-80); advisory board, Federal Election Commission; recipient: MEA School Bell Award, YWCA Outstanding Achievement Award for Government Politics, St. Cloud University Distinguished Alumni Award; active in AAUW, Minnesota Women's Network, St. Paul BPW, Citizens League, Common Cause, Minnesota Assn. for Retarded Citizens, League of Women Voters, Minnesota Shares for Hunger, Women's Economic Roundtable, Minnesota Women's Political Caucus, NOW, Urban Concerns, YWCA, Zonta, MN Nuclear Freeze.

Elected: 1974, 1978, 1982, 1986.

Term Expires: Jan., 1991

DIVISIONS OF THE OFFICE OF THE SECRETARY OF STATE

Corporations — files information about corporations of Minnesota and other states.

Fiscal Operations — administers receipts and budget matters.

Uniform Commercial Code — files information on finances of Minnesota businesses.

Election — administers elections and open appointments functions; publishes *Legislative Manual.*

Election Law Recodification Task Force (appointed by the secretary of state in 1978 to study and recommend a reordering and rewriting of the election laws to simplify and clarify the language and intent of the statutes. The task force completed a recodification of five chapters which was submitted to the legislature. The task force will make recommendations to the secretary of state on substantive changes in the election laws).

Voting Machine Advisory Committee (appointed by the secretary of state to aid in examining and reporting on new voting machines.

The secretary of state serves with the other constitutional officers on special policy boards for decision-making which affects the entire state: the Executive Council and the State Board of Investment.

In order of gubernatorial succession, the secretary of state is fourth after lieutenant governor, president of the senate, and speaker of the house.

As chair of the state canvassing board, the secretary of state certifies the election of candidates.

As keeper of the great seal of the state of Minnesota, the secretary of state certifies the authenticity of official records, documents, proclamations and executive orders of the governor, and acts of the legislature.

Functions and services:

State law has designated this office as custodian of many official records of the state.

All records and documents on file in the secretary of state's office are open and available to the public. Certified copies of corporate records and commercial financial records may be purchased. Three million pieces of paper are filed in the office including 150,000 articles of incorporation, copies of rules and regulations for all state agencies, and a wide array of election data. The secretary of state annually issues over 5,000 certificates for new businesses and collects more than $1,000,000 annually in revenue for the state. Over 40,000 commercial statements are filed annually, with revenue exceeding $100,000.

The election responsibilities of the secretary of state are outlined in the constitution and in statute. As commissioner of voter registration for the state, the secretary of state assists county auditors and other local election officials in administering voter registration in Minnesota. Precinct maps of all Minnesota cities are filed in this office, with new maps submitted when boundaries are changed.

Candidates for statewide office and for multi-county legislative, congressional, and judicial district offices file with the secretary of state. Candidates for federal office are required to file financial reports with the federal election commission and send copies to the secretary of state.

The secretary of state prepares the format to be used by counties in reporting returns of primary, general, and special elections. These returns are filed in this office and compiled for public information. State election laws (compiled by the attorney general) are published by this office biennially, following the close of the second year of each legislative session.

Each biennium, the Secretary of State publishes and distributes *The Minnesota Legislative Manual* to legislators and their staffs, state agencies, schools, libraries, and the public.

The secretary of state administers the open appointments process (enacted in 1978); informs the public of vacancies existing in multi-member state agencies; accepts applications for appointment; forwards the applications to the agencies' appointing authority.

OFFICE OF THE STATE AUDITOR

Arne H. Carlson
555 Park Street
St. Paul 55103
(612) 296-2551

Constitution Provides: that the state auditor is an officer in the executive department; to qualify as state auditor a person must be a qualified voter, 21 years old, and elected by the people (Article V; Minnesota Statutes, Chapter 6).

Term: four years.   **Salary:** $57,076

Arne H. Carlson
(Independent-Republican)

Biography: Shoreview. Born in New York City; attended public schools and awarded scholarship to Williams College: graduate school, University of Minnesot; awarded Bush Foundation Leadership Fellowship (1971); co-authored Legislative Reform Report (1974); Minneapolis city council, majority leader (1965-67); Minnesota House of Representatives (1972-79); minority whip (1974-78).

Elected: 1978, 1982, 1986.
Term expires: Jan., 1991

Created by the Minnesota Constitution in 1858, the office of the state auditor performed simple bookkeeping functions and monitored the administration of the financial affairs of the state. The first state auditor, William F. Dunbar, coordinated local government audits across the state within the confines of the horse and buggy.

Today, the office is moving into an era of computerized audits and data collection involving on-going training for a complement of up to 111 employees operating continually in all parts of the state.

Audited data from counties, school districts, municipalities, townships, metropolitan agencies, and regional development authorities is collected and standardized by the state auditor's municipal reporting unit which provides the information for state aids and federal revenue sharing.

All audit reports are submitted to the proper governmental authorities to make certain that all units of government operate in compliance with state law and maintain financial records which conform to generally accepted accounting principles. In addition, audit reports are available to the news media and the public.

The state auditor's office works with local governmental units to improve financial management and provides training workshops for local officials.

OFFICE OF THE STATE TREASURER

Mike McGrath
303 State Administration Bldg.
St. Paul 55155
(612) 296-7091

Constitution provides: that the state treasurer is an officer in the executive department; to qualify as state treasurer a person must be a qualified voter, 21 years old, and elected by the people (Article V; Minnesota Statutes 7.01-7.20).

Term: four years.   **Salary:** $49,493.

Mike McGrath
(Democratic-Farmer-Labor)

Biography: born in Trenton, N.J 1942; graduated from high school, 1961; joined the Air Force for a four year hitch, 1962-66, followed by two years in the reserve; in the service he was assigned to accounting and finance offices in Mississippi and Turkey; enrolled at Stetson University in DeLand, Florida where he earned a Bachelor of Arts degree in American Studies; graduated from Stetson in 1969 and moved to Minnesota where he enrolled in the University of Minnesota graduate program for American Studies; before completing the graduate course, McGrath joined the First Trust Company in St. Paul; in 1986, he founded M/M Policy Advisors to consult businesses in franchise services and employment practices; during his campaign for Minnesota State Treasurer, McGrath also owned and operated a taxi with Suburban Taxi Company; He served as Treasurer for the Third Congressional District DFL and Chair of Senate District 41. He was co-chair of the 1984 DFL State Convention Endorsements Committee, a member of the State Central Committee for the DFL and is past president of the Bloomington DFL Club; served as a member of both the Minneapolis and Bloomington Charter commissions, former Board Chair for Urban Concerns Workshop, Chair of the Bloomington Human Rights Commission and Secretary and Director of the League of Minnesota Human Rights Commissions. Mike and his wife of twenty years, Marsha, live with their three children in Bloomington.

Elected: 1986

Term Expires: January, 1991

By law, the state treasurer shall receive and receipt for all monies paid into the state treasury and safely keep the same until lawfully dispersed. The treasurer therefore handles over $5.5 billion in bank transactions annually.

The treasurer's office maintains careful control over the amount of money the state holds in non-interest bearing bank accounts, keeping those accounts constantly updated so that the maximum of state funds can be turned over for investment by the State Board of Investment.

The state treasurer is a member of the State Board of Investment, which is responsible for the formulation of state investment policies and the purchase and sale of securities of various funds.

The treasurer's office acts as the agent through which all security transactions are channeled. The treasurer is custodian of nearly $3 billion worth of securities.

As the state's paymaster, the treasurer sends out and then redeems over 4 million warrants (checks annually.)

When the state borrows through bonding, the treasurer's office pays off that debt by redeeming bonds at maturity and paying interest as it falls due on outside issues.

The state treasurer by law attempts to find owners to certain unclaimed property, and if unsuccessful, disposes of that property pursuant to Minnesota Statutes, Chapter 345. This abandoned property comes in the form of volumes of contents of bank safety deposit boxes which have remained idle over seven years, personal checking and savings accounts which have been abandoned over seven years, and other abandoned property held by banking and financial institutions, life insurance corporations, business associations, state courts, public officers and agencies.

The state treasurer's office receives and distributes funds under the fiscal disparities law.

The state treasurer approves the acceptance of gifts to the state.

The state treasurer is a member of the Executive Council, which among other duties, approves or disapproves peat and mineral leases (taconite, copper-nickel leases), the extension of timber permits, and the sale and disposal of certain state lands. He is treasurer ex officio of the Department of Economic Security, Metropolitan Airports Commission, State Retirement System, and Public Employees Retirement Association.

The state treasurer reports biennially the condition of the treasury and of the public funds.

OFFICE OF THE ATTORNEY GENERAL

Hubert H. Humphrey III
(Democratic-Farmer-Labor)

Biography: New Hope. Born June 26, 1942. Education: Shattuck School, Faribault, American University, Washington, D.C. (B.A., 1965), University of Minnesota (J.D., 1969); state senator, district 44 (1972-1983); attorney, twelve years private practice, Minneapolis; member: Hennepin County Bar Assn., Minnesota Bar Assn., American Bar Assn.; community activities: board of management, Northwest Branch YMCA, board of trustees, Minneapolis Society of Fine Arts; wife: Nancy Lee, children: Lorie, Pam, Hubert H. "Bucky" IV.

Elected: 1982, 1986.   **Term:** four years.   **Salary:** $74,308.
Term expires: January, 1991

Hubert H. Humphrey III
102 State Capitol
St. Paul 55155
(612) 296-6196

Constitution provides: that the attorney general is an officer in the executive department; to qualify as attorney general a person must be a qualified voter, 21 years old, and elected by the people (Articles V, VII; Minnesota Statutes, Chapter 8).

The attorney general is the chief legal officer for the state and is the legal advisor to the governor and all of the constitutional officers. Every board, commission, and agency of the state receives its legal advice from the attorney general. His opinions have the force and effect of law as they apply to tax and education matters. In addition, his opinions are generally sought and followed by the attorneys for the cities, counties, and townships of the state. The attorney general's duties stem from the state constitution, statutes, and common law.

Functions:

The attorney general appears for the state in all cases in the supreme and federal courts, in all civil cases in the district courts, and, upon request of the governor or any county attorney, in any criminal case in the district courts.

The attorney general prosecutes all actions against persons who claim an interest adverse to the state, as well as claims of the state against the federal government. He may institute, conduct, and maintain any action or proceeding he deems necessary for the enforcement of the laws of the state, the preservation of order, and the protection of public rights. The attorney general may inquire into the affairs of charitable corporations and, if necessary, may take action to terminate their corporate existence where it appears that they are not operating in the public interest. He may also apply for injunctions against violators of the law governing solicitation of charitable funds.

The attorney general possesses authority to enforce compliance with the state's antitrust and consumer laws.

The attorney general provides legal services to the Departments of Administration, Agriculture, Commerce, Corrections, Economic Security, Education, Health, Labor and Industry, Natural Resources, Public Safety, Public Welfare, Revenue, and Transportation, as well as the various other agencies, boards, and commissions of the state.

Services:

The attorney general assists in the legislative process. He and the members of his staff assist members of the legislature in drafting new legislation or amendments to existing laws. The governor, before signing or vetoing bills, consults with the attorney general and is provided with his analysis and advice with respect to the effect of a given bill. Administrative rules and regulations must be submitted to the attorney general for approval as to form and legality.

The attorney general attempts to provide information and solve problems for citizens.

The attorney general is a member of the State Executive Council, the State Board of Investment, the Board of Pardons, and the Land Exchange Board, as well as other boards and commissions.

(See Law & Crime Chapter for judicial branch.)

EXECUTIVE DEPARTMENTS AND AGENCIES

Article V of the Minnesota Constitution defines in broad outline the dimensions of the executive branch. Action by the legislature over the last 121 years has supplied details about administration and finances. Each biennium the legislature reviews budget requests as departments and agencies identify goals and services.

Numerous state boards, committees, commissions, councils, task forces, and similar multi-member agencies with statewide jurisdiction are located within the executive branch.

Nomenclature: The legislature has adopted a system of nomenclatur to encourage uniformity in naming agencies and easier identification by the public. The following is the system of name designations by type:

advisory task force —	advisory agency created to study a single topic and scheduled to expire within two years or less;
authority	— agency other than a department whose primary purpose is to issue bonds for financing, ownership, and development;
board	— agency other than a department having rule-making, license-granting, adjudicatory, or other administrative powers;
commission	— generally, agency composed of legislators (except certain agencies such as those created by interstate compact);
committee	— advisory agency:
council	— advisory agency with at least one-half of its members from specified occupations, political subdivisions, or other groupings of person;
governor's	— agency created by executive order to advise or assist on matters relating to state laws; such agencies are named beginning with the prefix "governor's task force on", "governor's council on", or "governor's committee on".

Expiration: Laws 1975, Chapter 315, placed the common expiration date of June 30, 1983, on advisory councils and committees created by statute unless they are extended by specific laws. All advisory task forces have a maximum two-year life.

Appointment process: The appointing authority for multi-member agencies is either the governor or the department head or state agency being advised by the council, committee, or task force. The advice and consent of the senate is required for appointments to administrative boards with the exception of examining and licensing boards. Minnesota's open appointments act (1978) requires the secretary of state to notify the public of vacancies occurring in multi-member state agencies and accept applications from any member of the public wishing to apply for appointment to the position. The secretary submits all applications to the appointing authority charged with filling the vacancy.

LEGISLATIVE BRANCH

A total of 120 session days may be used for each biennium (*two year session*) as 201 legislators examine public policy and the laws which establish a measure of the quality of life in the North Star State. Citizens participate in discussions during the session and in the interim months of recess between the odd year session and even year session as each house maintains an active calendar of hearings and meetings.

THE MINNESOTA LEGISLATURE

Senate Office
231 State Capitol
St. Paul 55155
(612) 296-2343

House Information
175 State Office Bldg.
St. Paul 55155
(612) 296-2146

Constitution provides: to be elected a member of the State Senate or House of Representatives, a person must be a qualified voter, 21 years old, a resident of Minnesota for one year, and a resident of the legislative district for six months immediately preceding the election (Article IV).

Term: State Senator — 4 years; State Representative — 2 years.

Compensation: $24,174 annually; round trips between home and state capital; per diem allowance for living expenses during session.

Membership and apportionment: The state of Minnesota is divided into sixty-seven senate districts, each of which is divided into two of the one hundred and thirty-four house districts. Each senate district is entitled to elect one senator and each house district is entitled to elect one representative.

The United States district court for the district of Minnesota ordered a reapportionment of the legislative districts on March 11, 1982. The population goal for each senate district was 60,835. The court ordered that no future elections could be conducted under any apportionment plan except that adopted by the court or a constitutional plan adopted after that date by the state of Minnesota.

Laws of Minnesota 1983, Chapter 191 adapted the court reapportionment plan.

Presiding officers:

Senate members elect the president of the Senate from among their ranks. The president presides over the Senate and shares with the Speaker the chairmanship of the Legislative Coordinating Commission.

The Speaker of the House is both a voting member of the House of Representatives and the presiding officer. The Speaker also presides over joint sessions of the House and Senate.

Committees:

Due to the tied House in 1979-80, the Speaker and the Rules Committee Chairman acted jointly to appoint committee chairmen and members. In the Senate, the chairman of the Committee on Rules and Administration, normally the leader of the majority group, has similar power. The Senate Committee on Committees names the committee members and chairmen.

The committee system is a vital component of the legislative machinery. The volume of legislation pending before a single session is too great to permit all legislators to work closely with all proposals. It is at the committee level that the public may testify for or against a bill. Committees hear testimony from proponents and opponents of legislation before they make recommendations to the full legislature.

A committee may decide the fate of any legislative proposal. After study, hearing, research, and deliberation, a committee may amend, recommend passage, re-refer to another committee, or table a bill.

The number of committees in each house and the number of members serving on each committee varies from session to session as state concerns and problems dictate. During the 1987 session the Senate had eighteen standing committees and the House twenty-one.

In addition to the standing committees which operate during each session, some committees continue to study specific problems during the legislative interim to report findings to the next legislative session.

Each legislative body has a Rules Committee which directs the operating procedures of the legislature. The rules the two houses adopt, their joint rules, Minnesota Statutes, and the state constitution provide the guidelines under which the legislature conducts legislative business.

Regular sessions:

The Minnesota legislature convenes in regular session each odd-numbered year on the first Tuesday after the first Monday in January. The 1972 flexible session amendment to Article IV of the Constitution authorized the legislature to meet in regular session in both years of the biennium, for a total of 120 legislative days.

Bills which have not become law or been defeated by legislative action or vetoed by the end of the first half of the session are still available for possible action in the second half of the session. This means standing committees may hear such bills in the interim recess and make recommendations on their passage.

Special sessions:

The legislature may be called into special session at any time by the governor. Special sessions become necessary when legislative action is needed to meet emergencies or when legislative work is unfinished at the end of a regular session. The governor is the only official empowered to call a special session. The governor does not have the power to limit the length or scope of the session.

Functions and powers:

The principal legal task of the legislature is to make law by which public policy is established. Legislative acitivity affects a wide range of state programs and resources including agriculture, conservation, crime prevention, contracts, education, economic development, consumer protection, elections, environment, finance, forestry, health, highways, human rights, insurance, labor relations, natural resources, property, pollution control, recreation, safety, taxation, transportation, utilities, unemployment compensation, veterans' affairs, workmen's compensation, and other matters that may necessitate state action.

Additional legislative functions include proposing amendments to the state constitution for approval by the electorate, electing regents of the University of Minnesota, confirming certain gubernatorial appointments (Senate), and performing legislative oversight or review.

The legislature possesses a judicial function: judges the election and qualifications of its members, may punish or expel members for contempt or disorderly behavior, and may impeach or remove from office members of the executive and judicial branches.

"The style of all laws of this state shall be: 'Be it enacted by the legislature of the state of Minnesota.' "
—Minnesota Constitution, Article IV, Section 22

How are laws passed?

All revenue (**tax measures**) must originate in the House. All other matters may originate in either the House or the Senate.

How long does it take to pass a bill?

There is no stated time schedule; speed is often related directly to the legislative support a proposal gathers.

- In 1971, the legislature ratified the 26th amendment to the U.S. Consitution lowering the voting age to eighteen in a time shorter than one committee hearing on a more controversial matter.
- The Campaign Finance Reform legislation required all of the 1973 and 1974 halves of the session for its hearings, debates, and final passage.

What is the public's role in passing laws?

Committee meetings are open to the public, and anyone wishing to speak for or against proposals being considered is given a chance to be heard.

Where can the public get copies of bills?

The House and Senate index offices in the capitol keep a file of bills by number, and anyone may visit these offices to request and receive a copy of a bill without charge.

A Bill for an Act. . . .

. . . is an idea for a new law or an idea to change or abolish an existing law. Ideas follow ten steps on their way to become Minnesota laws:

1. The Idea
Anyone can propose an idea for a bill — an individual, a consumer group, corporation, professional association, a govermental unit, the governor — but most frequently ideas come from members of the legislature.

2. The chief author
Each bill must have a legislator to introduce it in the legislature as chief author. The chief author's name appears on the bill with the bill's file number as identification while it moves through the legislative process.

3. Other authors
The chief author of a bill, under legislative rules, may select other authors, but no more than a total of five in the House and five in the Senate. These authors' names also appear on the bill.

4. The revisor of statutes
The revisor puts the idea into the proper legal form as a bill for introduction into the House of Representatives or the Senate, usually both. The revisor also updates **Minnesota Statutes** to include all new laws after the legislative session.

5. Introduction
When introduced in the House of Representatives, a bill receives a House File number (**H.F. 2312, for example**); in the Senate, a Senate File number (**S.F. 503, for example**). These numbers indicate the bill's choronological order of introduction in each body.

6. Committee consideration
Next the bill has its first reading (**the Minnesota constitution requires three readings for all bills — on three separate days**), and the presiding officer of the House or Senate refers it to an appropriate standing committee.
All committee meetings are open to the public. A committee may:
• recommend passage of a bill in its original form.
• recommend passage after amendment by the committee.
• make no recommendation, in which case a bill may die when the session ends.
• refer a bill to another committee (**one requiring funds to the appropriation or finance committee, for example**).
After acting on a bill, the committee sends a report to the House or Senate, stating its actions and recommendations.

7. General Orders
After adoption of the committee report in the House and Senate, the bill has its second reading and goes onto General Orders of the Day. In Committee of the Whole legislators discuss bills on General Orders; they may debate the issues, adopt amendments, present arguments on the bills, and they may vote to recommend:
• that a bill "do pass".

- that a bill not pass.
- postponement.
- further committee action.

8. The calendar

The calendar is a list of bills the Committee of the Whole recommends to pass. At this point:
- a bill has its third reading.
- amendments to the bill must have the unanimous consent of the entire body.
- legislators vote on it for the final time.

By committee recommendation, bills of a noncontroversial nature can by-pass General Orders and go directly onto a "consent calendar," usually passing without debate.

Every bill requires a majority vote of the full membership of the House and Senate to pass.

Voice votes may be used in House and Senate votes until the bill is being voted on in final passage. That final vote and vote on any amendments are roll call or recorded votes.

9. Conference Committee

When the House and the Senate both pass the same version of a bill, that bill goes to the governor for his approval or disapproval. If the House and Senate do not agree, a conference committee, with members of both houses, meets to reach an agreement. It both bodies then pass the bill in compromise form, it goes to the governor.

10. The governor

When a bill arrives, the governor may:
- sign it and the bill becomes law.
- veto it (*return it with a "veto message" stating objections*) to the body where it originated.
- pocket veto the bill (*after final adjournment of the legislature*).
- exercise the right to line veto portions of appropriations bills.

If the governor does not sign or veto a bill within three days after receiving it, while the legislature is in session, the bill becomes a law.

Minnesota Senate 1987-88

Leadership

Roger D. Moe
Majority Leader

William P. Luther
Assistant Majority Leader

Duane D. Benson
Minority Leader

Senate Members

District

ADKINS, Betty A. (DFL)   22
550 Central Ave. E.
St. Michael 55376

ANDERSON, Don (IR)   12
703 S. Jefferson
Wadena 56482

BECKMAN, Tracy L. (DFL)   29
Box 37
Bricelyn 56014

BELANGER, William V., Jr. (IR)   41
10716 Beard Ave. S.
Bloomington 55431

BENSON, Duane D. (IR)   32
RR 2
Lanesboro 55949

BERG, Charles A. (DFL)   11
Chokio 56221

BERGLIN, Linda (DFL)   60
2309 Clinton Ave. S.
Minneapolis 55404

BERNHAGEN, John (IR)   21
RR 1, Box 122
Hutchinson 55350

BERTRAM, Joe, Sr. (DFL)   16
887 Flanders Dr.
Paynesville 56362

BRANDL, John E. (DFL)   62
310 W. Elmwood Pl.
Minneapolis 55419

BRATAAS, Nancy (IR)   33
839 10½ St. S.W.
Rochester 55902

CHMIELEWSKI, Florian (DFL)   14
Sturgeon Lake 55783

COHEN, Richard J. (DFL)   64
591 S. Cretin Ave.
St. Paul 55116

DAHL, Gregory L. (DFL)   50
942 120th Ln. N.W.
Coon Rapids 55433

DAVIS, Charles R. (DFL)   18
RR 2, Box 132
Princeton 55371

DeCRAMER, Gary M. (DFL)   27
Ghent 56239

DICKLICH, Ronald R. (DFL)   5
1522 E. 25th St.
Hibbing 55746

DIESSNER, A.W. "Bill" (DFL)   56
3191 Pennington Ave.
S. Afton 55001

FRANK, Don (DFL)   51
517 Manor Dr. N.E.
Spring Lake Park 55432

FREDERICK, Mel (IR)   30
611 W. Holly
Owatonna 55060

FREDERICKSON, David J. (DFL) 20
RR 1, Box 102
Murdock 56271

FREDERICKSON, Dennis R. (IR) 23
RR 1, Box 49
Morgan 56266

FREEMAN, Michael O. (DFL)   40
7115 16th Ave. S.
Richfield 55423

GUSTAFSON, Jim (IR)   8
1936 Woodhaven Ln.
Duluth 55803

HUGHES, Jerome M. (DFL)   54
1978 Payne Ave.
Maplewood 55117

JOHNSON, Dean E. (IR)   15
910 11th St. S.W.
Willmar 56201

JOHNSON, Douglas J. (DFL)   6
Box 395
Cook 55723

JUDE, Tad (DFL)   48
14803 78th Ave. N.
Maple Grove 55369

KNAAK, Fritz (IR)   53
4248 Oakmede Ln.
White Bear Lake 55110

KNUTSON, Howard A. (IR)   38
1907 Woods Lane
Burnsville 55337

KROENING, Carl A. (DFL)   57
4329 Webber Pkwy.
Minneapolis 55412

LAIDIG, Gary W. (IR)   55
504 S. Greeley St.
Stillwater 55082

LANGSETH, Keith (DFL)   9
RR 2
Glyndon 56547

LANTRY, Marilyn M. (DFL)   67
2169 Beech St.
St. Paul 55119

LARSON, Cal (IR)   10
316 E. Cherry
Fergus Falls 56537

LESSARD, Bob (DFL)   3
RR 8, Box 432
International Falls 56649

LUTHER, William P. (DFL)   47
6809 Shingle Creek Dr.
Brooklyn Park 55445

MARTY, John J. (DFL)   63
2478 Lydia
Roseville 55113

McQUAID, Phyllis W. (IR)   44
4130 Yosemite Ave. S.
St. Louis Park 55416

MEHRKENS, Lyle G. (IR)   26
1505 Woodland Dr.
Red Wing 55066

MERRIAM, Gene (DFL)   49
10451 Avocet St. N.W.
Coon Rapids 55433

METZEN, James (DFL)   39
312 Deerwood Ct.
South St. Paul 55075

MOE, Donald M. (DFL)   65
110 Virginia St.
St. Paul 55102

MOE, Roger D. (DFL)   2
RR 3, Box 86A
Erskine 56535

MORSE, Steven (DFL)   34
410 River St.
Dakota 55925

NOVACK, Steven G. (DFL)   52
747 Redwood Ln.
New Brighton 55112

OLSON, Gen (IR)   43
6750 County Rd. 110 W.
Mound 55364

PEHLER, James C. (DFL)   17
734 14th Ave. S.
St. Cloud 56301

PETERSON, Donna C. (DFL)   61
2824 38th Ave. S.
Minneapolis 55406

PETERSON, Randoph W. (DFL) 19
155 Collen St.
Wyoming 55092

PIPER, Pat (DFL)   **31**
301 D 4th Ave. N.E.
Austin 55912

POGEMILLER, Lawrence J.(DFL) **58**
201 University Ave. N.E.
Minneapolis 55413

PURFEERST, Clarence M. (DFL) **25**
RR 1
Faribault 55021

RAMSTAD, Jim (IR)   **45**
2618 Crosby Rd.
Minnetonka 55391

REICHGOTT, Ember D. (DFL)   **46**
7701 48th Ave. N.
New Hope 55428

RENNEKE, Earl W. (IR)   **35**
RR 2
LeSueur 56058

SAMUELSON, Don (DFL)   **13**
1018 Portland Ave.
Brainerd 56401

SCHMITZ, Robert J. (DFL)   **36**
6730 Old Highway 169 Blvd.
Jordan 55352

SOLON, Sam G. (DFL)   **7**
616 W. Third St.
Duluth 55806

SPEAR, Allan H. (DFL)   **59**
2429 Colfax Ave. S.
Minneapolis 55405

STORM, Donald A. (IR)   **42**
5109 Grove St.
Edina 55436

STUMPF, LeRoy A. (DFL)   **1**
RR1, Box 47
Plummer 56748

TAYLOR, Glen (IR)   **24**
134 Ridgley Rd.
Mankato 56001

VICKERMAN, Jim M. (DFL)   **28**
Tracy 56175

WALDORF, Gene (DFL)   **66**
1176 Orange Ave. E.
St. Paul 55106

WEGSCHEID, Darril (DFL)   **37**
14085 Guthrie Ave.
Apple Valley 55124

WILLET, Gerald L. (DFL)   **4**
207 Mill Rd.
Park Rapids 56470

Senate Committee Assignments

AGRICULTURE
Chairman: Davis
Vice Chairman: Frederickson, DJ

Anderson	Beckman
Berg	Bertram
Brandl	Davis
DeCramer	Frederickson, DJ
Frederickson, DR	Freeman
Larson	Morse
Renneke	Stumpf
Vickerman	

COMMERCE
Chairman: Solon
Vice Chairman: Metzen

Adkins	Anderson
Belanger	Benson
Cohen	Dahl
Frederick	Freeman
Kroening	Luther
McQuaid	Peterson, DC
Purfeerst	Samuelson
Spear	Wegscheid

ECONOMIC DEVELOPMENT AND HOUSING

Chairman: Frank
Vice Chairman: Beckman

Bernhagen	Cohen
Dahl	Dicklich
Gustafson	Knaak
Kroening	Morse
Reichgott	
Storm	

EDUCATION

Chairman: Pehler
Vice Chairman: Reichgott

Beckman	Dahl
DeCramer	Dicklich
Frederickson, DJ	Hughes
Knaak	Knutson
Langseth	Larson
Mehrkens	Morse
Olson	Peterson, DC
Peterson, RW	Pogemiller
Ramstad	Stumpf
Wegscheid	

ELECTIONS AND ETHICS

Chairman: Hughs
Vice Chairman: Morse

Johnson, DE	Johnson, DJ
Laidig	Luther
McQuaid	Moe, RD
Peterson, DC	Samuelson
Willet	

EMPLOYMENT

Chairman: Chmielewski
Vice Chairman: Piper

Adkins	Beckman
Brataas	Diessner
Frank	Gustafson
Kroening	Pehler
Ramstad	

ENVIRONMENT AND NATURAL RESOURCES

Chairman: Willet
Vice Chairman: Dahl

Berg	Bernhagen
Davis	Frederickson, DR
Knaak	Laidig
Larson	Lessard

Marty	Merriam
Morse	Novak
Olson	Peterson, RW
Stumpf	Wegscheid

FINANCE

Chairman: Merriam
Vice Chairman: Freeman

Brataas	Dahl
DeCramer	Dicklich
Frederickson, DR	Hughes
Johnson, DE	Knutson
Kroening	Langseth
Lantry	Lessard
Luther	Mehrkens
Metzen	Moe, DM
Piper	Purfeerst
Ramstad	Renneke
Samuelson	Solon
Spear	Taylor
Waldorf	Willet

GENERAL LEGISLATION AND PUBLIC GAMING

Chairman: Lessard
Vice Chairman: Berg

Bertram	Davis
Diessner	Frederickson, DR
Johnson, DE	Lantry
McQuaid	Samuelson

GOVERNMENTAL OPERATIONS

Chairman: Moe, DM
Vice Chairman: Wegscheid

Benson	Frederickson, DJ
Frederickson, DR	Freeman
Jude	Marty
Pogemiller	Renneke
Waldorf	

HEALTH AND HUMAN SERVICES

Chairman: Berglin
Vice Chairman: Vickerman

Adkins	Anderson
Benson	Brandl
Brataas	Chmielewski
Diessner	Knutson
Lantry	Piper
Solon	Storm
Waldorf	

JUDICIARY
Chairman: Spear
Vice Chairman: Cohen

Berglin	Jude
Luther	Marty
Merriam	Moe, DM
Peterson, DC	Peterson, RW
Pogemiller	Belanger
Knaak	Laidig
Ramstad	Storm
Reichgott	

LOCAL AND URBAN GOVERNMENT COMMITTEE
Chairman: Schmitz
Vice Chairman: Adkins

Bertram	Frederickson, DJ
McQuiad	Metzen
Olson	Renneke
Vickerman	Wegscheid

PUBLIC UTILITIES AND ENERGY
Chairman: Dicklich
Vice Chairman: Marty

Brandl	Frank
Gustafson	Johnson, DE
Johnson, DJ	Jude
Novak	Olson
Piper	Storm
Waldorf	

RULES AND ADMINISTRATION
Chairman: Moe, RD
Vice Chairman: Luther

Belanger	Berglin
Bernhagen	Bertram
Chmielewski	Davis
Dicklich	Frank

Frederick	Hughes
Johnson, DE	Johnson, DJ
Knutson	Laidig
Lessard	Luther
Merriam	Moe, DM
Novak	Pehler
Peterson, R.W.	Purfeerst
Renneke	Schmitz
Solon	Spear
Taylor	Willet
Benson	

TAXES AND TAX LAWS
Chairman: Johnson, DJ

Anderson	Belanger
Benson	Berg
Berglin	Bernhagen
Bertram	Chmielewski
Cohen	Davis
Diessner	Frank
Frederick	Gustafson
Jude	Laidig
Novak	Pehler
Peterson, D	Peterson, R
Pogemiller	Reichgott
Schmitz	Stumpf

TRANSPORTATION
Chairman: Purfeerst
Vice Chairman: DeCramer

Bernhagen	Frederick
Langseth	Lantry
McQuaid	Mehrkens
Metzen	Novak
Schmitz	Vickerman

VETERANS AND MILITARY AFFAIRS
Chairman: Bertram
Vice Chairman: Diessner

Beckman	Laidig
Langseth	Larson
Lessard	Mehrkens
Schmitz	

LEGISLATIVE DISTRICT MAPS

LEGEND

— Senate and House District Boundaries

--- House District Boundaries

-- Counties

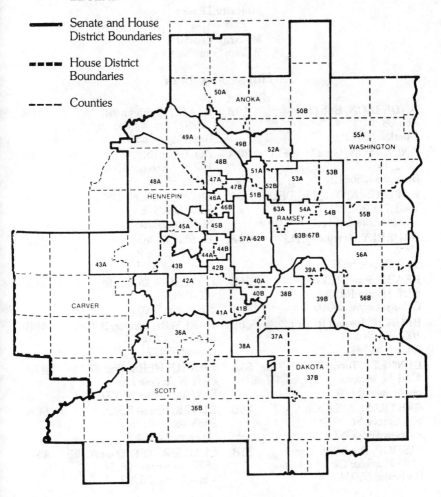

LEGEND

Senate and House
District Boundaries

House District
Boundaries

Counties

1987 MINNESOTA
HOUSE OF REPRESENTATIVES

House Leadership

Speaker
Robert E. Vanasek*

Majority Leader
Ann Wynia

Minority Leader
William Schreiber

House Members

District

ANDERSON, Bob (IR)   **10B**
Box 28
Ottertail 56571

ANDERSON, Glen H. (DFL)   **20A**
RR 1, Box 9
Bellingham 56212

BATTAGLIA, David P. (DFL)   **6A**
1803 7th Ave.
Two Harbors 55616

BAUERLY, Jerry J. (DFL)   **18B**
RR 2
Sauk Rapids 56379

BEARD, Pat (DFL)   **56B**
8236 Hames Rd.
Cottage Grove 55016

BEGICH, Joseph R. (DFL)   **6B**
1001 W. 2nd St.
Eveleth 55734

BENNETT, Tony (IR)   **53A**
4131 N. Victoria
Shoreview 55126

BERTRAM, Jeff (DFL)   **16B**
662 Spruce St.
Paynesville 56362

BISHOP, Dave (IR)   **33B**
1185 Plummer Cir.
Rochester 55902

BLATZ, Kathleen (IR)   **41B**
11040 Glen Wilding Ln.
Bloomington 55431

BOO, Ben (IR)   **8B**
102 E. Arrowhead Rd.
Duluth 55803

BROWN, Chuck (DFL)   **11A**
RR 3, Box 108
Appleton 56208

BURGER, John (IR)   **43A**
3750 Bayside Rd.
Long Lake 55356

CARLSON, Doug (IR)   **14B**
430 Division St.
Sandstone 55072

CARLSON, Lyndon R. (DFL)   **46B**
8216 35th Ave. N.
Crystal 55427

CARRUTHERS, Phil (DFL)   **47B**
6931 N. Willow Ln.
Brooklyn Center 55430

CLARK, Karen (DFL)   **60A**
2633 18th Ave. S.
Minneapolis 55407

CLAUSNITZER, Dale A. (IR)   **48A**
6577 Forestview Ln. N.
Maple Grove 55369

Footnote on House Speaker

*Fred C. Norton resigned as Speaker of the House when Gov. Perpich appointed him to the Minnesota Court of Appeals. A special election was called for 3 November 1987 to fill his seat in District 65A.

COOPER, Roger (DFL)   **21B**
260 S. 6th St.
Bird Island 55310

DAUNER, Marvin (DFL)   **9B**
RR 2
Hawley 56549

DeBLIECK, Norman (DFL)   **27A**
RR 1, Box 121
Milroy 56263

DEMPSEY, Terry (IR)   **23A**
309 S. Minnesota St.
New Ulm 56073

DILLE, Steve (IR)   **21A**
RR 2, Box 73
Dassel 55325

DORN, John (DFL)   **24A**
1021 Orchard Rd.
Mankato 56001

FORSYTHE, Mary (IR)   **42B**
5308 Brookview Ave.
Edina 55424

FREDERICK, Marcel"Sal"(IR) **24B**
RR 6, Box 25
Mankato 56001

FRERICHS, Don L. (IR)   **32A**
2233 Brook Ln. S.W.
Rochester 55902

GREENFIELD, Lee (DFL)   **61A**
2308 32nd Ave. S.
Minneapolis, MN 55406

GRUENES, Dave (IR)   **17B**
234 Danora Pl.
St. Cloud 56301

GUTKNECHT, Gil (IR)   **33A**
3812 16th Ave. N.W.
Rochester 55901

HARTLE, Dean (IR)   **30A**
RR 4, Box 14
Owatonna 55060

HAUKOOS, Bob (IR)   **31A**
1502 S. Broadway
Albert Lea 56007

HEAP, Jim (IR)   **45B**
4030 Cottonwood Ln.
Plymouth 55441

HIMLE, John (IR)   **41A**
9254 Hyland Creek Rd.
Bloomington 55437

HUGOSON, Gene (IR)   **29A**
RR 2, Box 218
Granada 56039

JACOBS, Joel (DFL)   **49B**
2608 116th Ln. N.W.
Coon Rapids 55433

JAROS, Mike (DFL)   **7B**
1014 W. 3rd St.
Duluth 55806

JEFFERSON, Richard H. (DFL) **57B**
1314 Washburn Ave. N.
Minneapolis 55411

JENNINGS, Loren G. (DFL)   **19B**
Box 27
Rush City 55069

JENSEN, Bob (DFL)   **36B**
17995 Flagstaff Ave.
Lakeville 55024

JOHNSON, Alice (DFL)   **51A**
801 Ballantyne Ln. N.E.
Spring Lake Park 55432

JOHNSON, Bob (DFL)   **4A**
RR 2, Box 145
Bemidji 56601

JOHNSON, Virgil J. (IR)   **34A**
RR 2, Box 88
Caledonia 55921

KAHN, Phyllis (DFL   **58B**
100 Malcolm Ave. S.E.
Minneapolis 55414

KALIS, Henry J. (DFL)   **29B**
RR 1, Box 55
Walters 56092

KELLY, Randy C. (DFL)   **67A**
1630 David St.
St. Paul 55119

KELSO, Becky (DFL)   **36A**
151 S. Shannon Dr.
Shakopee 55379

KINKEL,Anthony"Tony"(DFL) **4B**
315 Front St.
Park Rapids 56470

KLUDT, Kenneth J. (DFL) **9A**
2408 Fairway Dr.
Moorhead 56560

KNICKERBOCKER, Jerry (IR) **43B**
5312 Rogers Dr.
Hopkins 55343

KNUTH, Dan (DFL) **52B**
1106 Rockstone Ln.
New Brighton 55112

KOSTOHRYZ, Dick (DFL) **54B**
2478 E. Indian Way
North St. Paul 55109

KRUEGER, Richard (DFL) **12B**
  "Rick"
524 N. 6th St.
Staples 56479

LARSEN, Ernest (DFL) **50A**
7229 153rd Ln. N.W.
Ramsey 55303

LASLEY, Harold (DFL) **19A**
RR 2, Box 870DD
Cambridge 55008

LIEDER, Bernie (DFL) **2A**
911 Thorndale St.
Crookston 56716

LONG, Dee (DFL) **59A**
2409 Humboldt Ave. S.
Minneapolis 55405

MARSH, Marcus (IR) **17A**
1172 8th Ave. N.
Sauk Rapids 56379

McDONALD, K.J. (IR) **35B**
301 Carter St.
Watertown 55388

McEACHERN, Bob (DFL) **22A**
601 Walnut Ave. N.
St. Michael 55376

McKASY, Bert J. (IR) **39A**
716 Round Hill Rd.
Mendota Heights 55118

McLAUGHLIN, Peter (DFL) **60B**
3440 Longfellow Ave. S.
Minneapolis 55407

McPHERSON, Harriet (IR) **55B**
2398 Stagecoach Tr. N.
Stillwater 55082

MILBERT, Robert P. (DFL) **39B**
308 Deerwood Ct.
South St. Paul 55075

MILLER, Howard (IR) **20B**
504 Elm St.
Redwood Falls 56283

MINNE, Lona (DFL) **5B**
RR 1, Box 74
Hibbing 55746

MORRISON, Connie (IR) **38A**
909 W. 155th St.
Burnsville 55337

MUNGER, Willard (DFL) **7A**
1121 S. 70th Ave. W.
Duluth 55807

MURPHY, Mary (DFL) **8A**
6794 Arrowhead Rd.
Hermantown 55811

NELSON, Clair (DFL) **11B**
Lake St.
Barrett 56311

NELSON, Darby (DFL) **49A**
1013 Vera St.
Champlin 55316

NELSON, Ken (DFL) **62A**
4201 Garfield Ave. S.
Minneapolis 55409

NEUENSCHWANDER, (DFL) **3A**
  Bob
200 2nd Ave.
International Falls 56649

O'CONNOR, Rich (DFL) **66B**
657 Case St.
St. Paul 55106

OGREN, Paul Anders (DFL) **14A**
Box 113, Fleming Rt.
Aitkin 56431

OLSEN, Sally (IR) **44A**
3307 Decatur Ln.
St. Louis Park 55426

OLSON, Edgar L. (DFL) **2B**
RR 3, Box 99
Fosston 56542

OLSON, Katy (DFL) **28B**
RR 2, Box 115
Sherburn 56171

OMANN, Jr., Bernie (IR)   **16A**
RR 1
St. Joseph 56374

ONNEN, Tony (IR)   **22B**
RR 2, Box 211
Cokato 55321

ORENSTEIN, Howard (DFL)   **64B**
1284 Watson
St. Paul 55116

OSTHOFF, Tom (DFL)   **66A**
766   Maryland   Ave.   W.
St. Paul 55117

OTIS, Todd (DFL)   **59B**
4152 Colfax
Minneapolis 55409

OZMENT, Dennis (IR)   **37B**
3275 145th St. E.
Rosemount 55068

PAPPAS, Sandy (DFL)   **65B**
182 Prospect Blvd.
St. Paul 55107

PAULY, Sidney (IR)   **42A**
17450 W. 78th St.
Eden Prairie 55344

PELOWSKI, Jr., Gene (DFL)   **34B**
257 Wilson
Winona 55987

PETERSON, Jerome (DFL)   **18A**
 "J.P."
306 6th Ave. S.
Princeton 55371

POPPENHAGEN, Dennis (IR)   **10A**
RR 4, Box 51
Detroit Lakes 56501

PRICE, Len (DFL)   **56A**
6264 Applewood Rd.
Woodbury 55125

QUINN, Joe (DFL)   **50B**
650 121st Ave. N.W.
Coon Rapids 55433

QUIST, Allen (IR)   **23B**
RR 3, Box 33
St. Peter 56082

REDALEN, Elton R. (IR)   **32B**
Box 110
Fountain 55935

REDING, Leo J. (DFL)   **31B**
709 12th Ave. N.W.
Austin 55912

REST, Ann H. (DFL)   **46A**
9332 Northwood Pkwy.
New Hope 55427

RICE, James I. (DFL)   **57A**
2220 Vincent Ave. N.
Minneapolis 55411

RICHTER, Don (IR)   **12A**
RR 2, Box 220
Wadena, 56482

RIVENESS, Phillip J. (DFL)   **40B**
2209 E. Old Shakopee Rd.
Bloomington 55420

RODOSOVICH, Peter (DFL)   **25B**
614 S.E. 1st St.
Faribault 55021

ROSE, John (IR)   **63A**
2500 Fernwood
Roseville 55113

RUKAVINA, Thomas (DFL)   **5A**
Star Rt., Box 2207
Virginia 55792

SARNA, John J. (DFL)   **58A**
2837 Ulysses St. N.E.
Minneapolis 55418

SCHAFER, Gary (IR)   **35A**
Box 51
Gibbon 55335

SCHEID, Linda (DFL)   **47A**
6625 81st Ave. N.
Brooklyn Park 55445

SCHOENFELD, Jerry (DFL)   **30B**
518 2nd Ave. N.W.
Waseca 56093

SCHREIBER, Bill (IR)   **48B**
10001 Zane Ave. N.
Brooklyn Park 55443

SEABERG, Art (IR)   **38B**
3146 Farnum Dr.
Eagan 55121

SEGAL, Gloria (DFL)   **44B**
2221 S. Hill Ln.
St. Louis Park 55416

SHAVER, Craig (IR) **45A**
250 Peavey Ln., Box 61
Wayzata 55391

SIMONEAU, Wayne (DFL) **51B**
465 N.E. 57th Pl.
Fridley 55432

SKOGLUND, Wesley J. (DFL) **61B**
"Wes"
4915 31st Ave. S.
Minneapolis 55417

SOLBERG, Loren A. (DFL) **3B**
Box 61, 115 5th Ave.
Bovey 55709

SPARBY, Wallace "Wally" (DFL)**1B**
RR 4
Thief River Falls 56701

STANIUS, Brad (IR) **53B**
4160 Myrle Ave.
White Bear Lake 55110

STEENSMA, Andy (DFL) **27B**
RR 1, Box 46
Luverne 56156

SVIGGUM, Steven (IR) **26A**
RR 3
Kenyon 55946

SWENSON, Douglas G. (IR) **55A**
9429 Jewel Ln. Ct.
Forest Lake 55025

THIEDE, Paul M. "T.D." (IR) **13A**
RR 1, Box 52
Pequot Lakes 56472

TJORNHOM, Chris (IR) **40A**
6218 Portland Ave. S.
Richfield 55423

TOMPKINS, Eileen (IR) **37A**
14217 Genesee Ave.
Apple Valley 55124

TRIMBLE, Steve (DFL) **67B**
77 Maria Ave.
St. Paul 55106

TUNHEIM, Jim (DFL) **1A**
Box 66
Kennedy 56733

UPHUS, Sylvester (IR) **15A**
RR 1, Box 182A
Sauk Centre 56378

VALENTO, Don (IR) **54A**
636 LaBore Rd.
Little Canada 55117

VANASEK, Robert E. (DFL) **25A**
706 Highland Dr.
New Prague 56071

VELLENGA, Kathleen (DFL) **64A**
2224 Goodrich
St. Paul 55105

VOSS, Gordon O. (DFL) **52A**
11120 N.E. 7th St.
Blaine 55434

WAGENIUS, Jean (DFL) **62B**
4804 11th Ave. S.
Minneapolis 55417

WALTMAN, Bob (IR) **26B**
Box N
Elgin 55932

WELLE, Alan W. (DFL) **15B**
RR 4, Box 319D
Willmar 56201

WENZEL, Stephen G. (DFL) **13B**
312 3rd St. S.E.
Little Falls 56345

WINTER, Ted (DFL) **28A**
RR 2, Box 23
Fulda 56131

WYNIA, Ann (DFL) **63B**
1550 Branston
St. Paul 55108

Minnesota House of Representatives
1987-88 Committees

AGRICULTURE

Chair: Wenzel
Vice Chair: Nelson, C.

Bauerly	Bertram
Brown	Cooper
Dauner	DeBlieck
Dille	Frederick
Hugoson	Kahn
Kalis	Krueger
McDonald	McPherson
Olson, E.	Olson, K.
Omann	Quist
Redalen	Richter
Riveness	Schoenfeld
Sparby	Steensma
Tunheim	Uphus
Waltman	Winter

APPROPRIATIONS

Chair: Anderson, G.
Vice Chair: Knuth

Anderson, R.	Battaglia
Bishop	Boo
Carlson, D.	Carlson, L.
Dom	Forsythe
Greenfield	Haukoos
Jennings	Johnson, V.
Kahn	Kalis
Krueger	Lieder
Miller	Munger
Murphy	Nelson, D.
Orenstein	Pappas
Poppenhagen	Price
Rice	Riveness
Rodosovich	Rose
Sarna	Schoenfeld
Seaberg	Sparby
Stanius	Steensma
Wynia	

COMMERCE

Chair: Sarna
Vice Chair: Milbert

Andersen, R.	Beard
Bennett	Bishop
Burger	Forsythe
Hartle	Jacobs
Jaros	Kinkel
McDonald	McEacherm

McKasy	Murphy
Nelson, C.	O'Connor
Pelowski	Peterson
Price	Richter
Solberg	Sparby

ECONOMIC DEVELOPMENT AND HOUSING

Chair: Otis
Vice Chair: Lasley

Burger	Carlson, L.
Clark	Dille
Frerichs	Himle
Hugoson	Jefferson
Kelso	Knickerbocker
Knuth	McLaughlin
McPherson	Murphy
Nelson, C.	Neuenschwander
Ogren	Olson, K.
Peterson	Poppenhagen
Riveness	Rukavina
Schafer	Sparby
Thiede	Tjornhom
Cooper	

EDUCATION

Chair: McEachern
Vice Chair: Olson, K.

Bauerly	Beard
Gruenes	Hartle
Hugoson	Johnson, A.
Kelso	Kinkel
Kostohryz	McDonald
McPherson	Nelson C.
Nelson, K.	Olsen, S.
Olson, E.	Otis
Ozment	Pelowski
Quinn	Richter
Schafer	Segal
Swenson	Thiede
Tompkins	Trimble
Tunheim	Vellenga
Wagenius	Wenzel

ENVIRONMENT AND NATURAL RESOURCES

Chair: Munger
Vice Chair: Wagenius

Battaglia	Begich
Carlson, D.	Himle

Hugoson
Johnson, A.
Kahn
Larsen
Marsh
Nelson, D.
Ogren
Reding
Rukavina
Shaver
Skoglund
Trimble

Jennings
Johnson, R.
Knuth
Long
McPherson
Neuenschwander
Pauly
Rose
Schafer
Simoneau
Thiede
Waltman

FINANCIAL INSTITUTIONS AND INSURANCE

Chair: Skoglund
Vice Chair: Bertram

Anderson, G.
Boo
Carruthers
Frederick
Knickerbocker
Milbert
Olsen, S.
Otis
Poppenhagen
Rodosovich
Uphus
Wenzel
Wynia

Blatz
Carlson, L.
Clausnitzer
Hartle
McKasy
Neuenschwander
Osthoff
Peterson
Quinn
Scheid
Voss
Winter

FUTURE AND TECHNOLOGY

Chair: Reding
Vice Chair: Pelowski

Bauerly
Frederick
Gruenes
Himle
Kelso
Krueger
Morrison
Price
Rest
Rose
Shaver

Dorn
Frerichs
Haukoos
Kahn
Knuth
Larsen
Peterson
Quist
Riveness
Rukavina
Trimble

GENERAL LEGISLATION, VETERANS AFFAIRS AND GAMING

Chair: Kostohryz
Vice Chair: Quinn

Bennett
Brown

Boo
Gutknecht

Jensen
Knickerbocker
Orenstein
Price
Redalen
Scheid
Steensma

Kludt
Minne
Osthoff
Quist
Reding
Shaver
Sviggum

GOVERNMENTAL OPERATIONS

Chair: Simoneau
Vice Chair: Larsen

Bertram
Carruthers
Cooper
Dille
Heap
Jensen
Kludt
Lasley
Morrison
Omann
Rukavina
Tjornhom
Waltman

Burger
Clark
DeBlieck
Gutknecht
Jefferson
Johnson, R.
Knickerbocker
Milbert
O'Connor
Reding
Shaver
Uphus
Winter

HEALTH AND HUMAN SERVICES

Chair: Greenfield
Vice Chair: Kelso

Anderson, G.
Clausnitzer
Dauner
Gruenes
McLaughlin
Orenstein
Quist
Segal
Sviggum
Tompkins
Welle

Clark
Cooper
Dom
Jefferson
Onnen
Ozment
Rodosovich
Stanius
Swenson
Vellenga
Wynia

HIGHER EDUCATION

Chair: Jaros
Vice Chair: Johnson, R.

Boo
Gruenes
Johnson, V.
Kludt
Lasley
Omann
Ozment
Reding
Tompkins

Forsythe
Heap
Kinkel
Larsen
Nelson, K.
Otis
Pelowski
Rukavina
Trimble

JUDICIARY

Chair: Kelly
Vice Chair: Kludt

Bishop	Blatz
Brown	Carruthers
Clausnitzer	Dempsey
Forsythe	Greenfield
Kalis	Long
Marsh	McKasy
Milbert	Miller
Nelson, D.	Orenstein
Pappas	Quist
Rest	Schoenfeld
Seaberg	Solberg
Swenson	Vellenga
Wagenius	Welle

LABOR-MANAGEMENT RELATIONS

Chair: Begich
Vice Chair: Beard

Battaglia	Clausnitzer
Dille	Gutknecht
Hartle	Heap
Johnson, A.	McPherson
Miller	Murphy
O'Connor	Pappas
Rice	Sarna
Scheid	Simoneau
Solberg	Sviggum
Wenzel	

LOCAL AND URBAN AFFAIRS

Chair: Battaglia
Vice Chair: Winter

Anderson, R	Bauerly
Bertram	DeBlieck
Dom	Frederick
Haukoos	Jacobs
Jennings	Johnson, V.
Kinkel	Krueger
Lieder	Morrison
O'Connor	Olson, E.
Omann	Onnen
Pauly	Rice
Richter	Sarna
Segal	Tompkins
Tunheim	Valento

METROPOLITAN AFFAIRS

Chair: Osthoff
Vice Chair: Jefferson

Blatz	Carruthers
Clausnitzer	Johnson, A.
Kelly	Kostohryz
Long	McLaughlin
Morrison	Nelson, D.
Ozment	Pappas
Pauly	Rest
Simoneau	Skoglund
Stanius	Swenson
Tjornhom	Valento
Wagenius	

REGULATED INDUSTRIES

Chair: Jacobs
Vice Chair: McLaughlin

Beard	Bennett
Clark	Gruenes
Hartle	Jaros
Jennings	Jensen
Lieder	Minne
Ogren	Olsen, S.
Osthoff	Poppenhagen
Quinn	Redalen
Rodosovich	Rose
Scheid	Stanius
Tjornhom	

RULES AND LEGISLATIVE ADMINISTRATION

Chair: Vanasek
Vice Chair: Riveness

Anderson, G.	Blatz
Himle	Jacobs
Knickerbocker	Long
Minne	Munger
Nelson, K.	Norton
Otis	Pappas
Redalen	Reding
Rice	Schoenfeld
Schreiber	Simoneau
Thiede	Valento
Voss	

TAXES

Chair: Voss
Vice Chair: Rest

Begich	Bennett
Blatz	Brown
Dauner	Dempsey
Frerichs	Himle
Jacobs	Jaros
Kelly	Long
Marsh	McKasy

McLaughlin
Nelson, K.
Norton
Onnen
Pauly
Redalen
Schreiber
Sviggum
Vanasek

Minne
Neuenschwander
Ogren
Osthoff
Peterson
Scheid
Skoglund
Valento
Welle

McDonald
Olson, E.
Richter
Segal
Tunheim
Waltman
Johnson, A.

McEacherm
Olson, K.
Seaberg
Steensma
Valento
Welle

TRANSPORTATION

Chair: Kalis
Vice Chair: Jensen

Begich
Carlson, D.
DeBlieck
Frerichs
Johnson, R.
Lasley

Brown
Dauner
Dempsey
Haukoos
Johnson, V.
Lieder

WAYS AND MEANS

Chair: Norton

Anderson, G.
Carlson, L.
Forsythe
Long
Minne
Olsen, S.
Schreiber
Voss

Carlson, D.
Dempsey
Kahn
McEacherm
Nelson, K.
Rice
Vanasek
Wynia

A center for the study of media ethics and the law was created in August, 1984, at the University of Minnesota, thanks to a gift of $350,000 from Otto A. Silha, retired chairman of the board of Cowles Media Co., and his wife Helen. Silha's contribution was augmented by a $100,000 grant from The Minneapolis Star and Tribune Foundation. Prof. Donald M. Gillmore, a communications law scholar, is the first director of The Silha Center. Silha, who graduated in 1940 from the university's school of journalism and mass communications, said of media ethics and the law, "They go to the heart and core of both the profession of journalism and the business."

Due to a confusion in the wording of the enabling act which opened the way for Minnesota's statehood, the first state legislature met in December, 1857, passed hundreds of laws, and adjourned before statehood had become official (on May 11, 1858).

Early Minnesota photo honoring the Voyageurs.

Although the name, "Hiawatha," has become firmly embedded in Minnesota culture, the name itself is Iroquois and eastern in origin. Minnesota's Ojibwa Indians knew of the hero, but called him **Manabozho**.

In 1700 Pierre Charles le Sueur, the French explorer built a fort on the Blue Earth River in order to mine what he thought was copper ore (hence the name). He was mistaken.

The first church in Minnesota was the Mission of St. Michael the Archangel near Fort Beauharnois on the Minnesota side of Lake Pepin. It was built by two Jesuit priests in 1727.

The first land purchase by white men in Minnesota was in 1819, when the land on which Fort Snelling stands was bought for the U.S. Government by Zebulon M. Pike.

Explorer Henry R. Schoolcraft found the source of the Mississippi River in 1832. He took the name, "Itasca" from the Latin, **Veritas Caput,** or "True Source."

The first official U.S. Post Office in Minnesota was established at Fort Snelling in 1827.

The first institution of higher learning in Minnesota was Hamline University, established in Red Wing in 1854. It was re-established in St. Paul in 1880.

Law, Courts & Crime

A PROFILE OF THE JUDICIAL BRANCH

Introduction. For the average citizen the court system is probably the most remote and least understood branch of government. Though his attention may be drawn to the court proceedings on television, his personal involvement with the courts is likely limited to a traffic violation, a divorce proceeding or the settlement of a deceased relative's estate.

What may not be readily apparent to him is the tremendous variety and volume of business transacted in our court system. At one time or another almost every aspect of life is touched by the courts. Aside from the duty to try persons accused of criminal violations, the courts must decide civil disputes between private citizens ranging from the routine collection of an overdue charge account to the complex adjudication of an antitrust case involving many millions of dollars and months or even years of costly litigation. The courts also must act as referees between the citizens and their government by deciding what are the permissible limits of governmental power and the extent of an individual's rights and responsibilities.

A judicial system which strives for fairness and justice must be capable of first finding the truth and then deciding disputes under the rule of law. Thus, the courts are the places in which the facts are determined and the rules regulating conduct are interpreted and applied.

WHERE DOES "THE LAW" COME FROM?

Judges rely on several sources of the law in making their decisions. First and foremost is the **United States Constitution,** as well as the **Constitution of the State of Minnesota.** Secondly, the courts rely on the **statutes** passed by the legislatures - the Minnesota legislature, the Congress, ordinances passed by city governments, and **regulations** made by any agencies of government, such as the Internal Revenue Service and others. Another source of the law is previous **cases.** Under our legal system, **precedents** are set by the decisions of high courts, such as the Supreme Court, and these are used as models in deciding later cases. All of the decisions of appeals courts may be found in legal books, and it is these cases that are generally referred to in briefs that lawyers write.

Source: *The Minnesota Courts*
       (Court Info. Office of the Minn. Supreme Court, 1979)

How well the judicial branch performs the tasks we assign it depends a great deal on its organization and structure. In recent years many citizens, lawyers, legislators and judges have complained that the judicial process has become so expensive and time-consuming that justice is denied to many citizens.

Supreme Court

Jurisdiction:
The Minnesota Judicial system is headed by the supreme court, the state's court of last resort. The court consists of one chief justice and six to eight associate justices. Vacancies on the court are filled by governor's appointment.

To the supreme court may be taken appeals from decisions of the state's district court. In some cases, matters may be presented directly to the supreme court without having been heard previously by a lower court.

The chief justice of the supreme court is required to supervise and coordinate work of the state's district courts. In order to carry out these additional duties, the supreme court may provide by rule that the chief justice not be required to write opinions as a member of the court. This same law permits the court to provide by rule to hear cases in divisions, rather than have all members present at the hearing of a case.

Pursuant to law, the supreme court each court term has appointed a judge of district court to act as a justice of the court in hearing and deciding cases.

Terms:
The supreme court has one court term each year beginning the first Tuesday after the first Monday in January. This term generally continues until the end of the calendar year, with recesses at the discretion of the court.

Election:
Justices are elected by the voters of the state for six-year terms. Under the law, a candidate seeking election to the supreme court must specify that the candidate is filing for a specific justice's office which would otherwise become vacant. Justices are nominated and elected without party designation.

Court of Appeals

Jurisdiction: the court of appeals has jurisdiction of appeals from all final decisions of trial courts other than conciliation courts except for appeals in legislative contest convictions of murder in the first degree, and appeals from the workers compensation court of appeals and the tax court.

Judges: the court of appeals has twelve judges; after 1987 the number of judges may increase or decrease depending on the number of appeals. Judges are elected by the voters to six-year terms; vacancies are filled by governor's appointment. Judges are elected without party designation and candidates file for specific seat. All judges of the court of appeals are subject to statewide election, but one seat on the court is designated for each congressional district. One year's residence in the district is required for appointment or election to a congressional district seat. The governor designates one of the judges as chief judge, who, subject to the authority of the chief justice, has administrative authority for the court.

District Court

Jurisdiction:

There is one district court for the state of Minnesota, divided into ten judicial districts. The chief justice of the supreme court has the power to assign judges from one district to serve in another district.

The constitution provides that the district court shall have original jurisdiction in all civil and criminal cases and shall have such appellate jurisdiction as may be prescribed by law. At present the law provides for appeals from county court, probate court, and municipal courts.

In Ramsey and Hennepin counties the district courts have jurisdiction of juvenile court matters.

Election:

Judges are elected by the voters of their respective districts for six-year terms. Candidates file for a specific judgeship, and this information is stated on the ballot. Judges are nominated and elected without party designation.

County Court

Jurisdiction:

The county court system combines probate, municipal, and justice courts into one court and in some instances combines two or more counties into single county court district. Hennepin and Ramsey counties are excluded from the county court law.

The county court is divided into three divisions, civil and criminal, family court, and probate. The county court has civil jurisdiction where the amount in controversy does not exceed $5,000 exclusive of interest and costs. The county court has criminal jurisdiction over misdemeanor, petty misdemeanor, and preliminary hearing cases. The family court division includes all cases arising under the juvenile court act over which the county court has original exclusive jurisdiction and all cases arising out of or affecting the family relationship including civil commitments. The county court has concurrent jurisdiction with the district court over actions for divorce, separate maintenance, adoption, and change of name. The probate division hears all cases in law and in equity for the administration of estates of deceased persons and all guardianship and incompetency proceedings. In addition the county court may establish a traffic violations bureau and a conciliation court within the civil and criminal division.

Election:

Judges are elected by the voters of their respective county court districts for six-year terms. Candidates file for a specific judgeship, and this information is stated on the ballot. Judges are nominated and elected without party designation.

Municipal Court

Jurisdiction:

The only separate municipal courts in Minnesota are in Hennepin and Ramsey counties.

Designated as Hennepin County Municipal Court and Ramsey County Municipal Court, these courts have jurisdiction in civil matters where the amount in controversy does not exceed $6,000. Each county has a conciliation court with jurisdiction limited to civil actions involving $1,000 or less.

Election:
Municipal court judges are elected by voters of Hennepin and Ramsey counties for six-year terms.

Probate Court

Jurisdiction:
Probate court jurisdiction is incorporated into the county court except in Hennepin and Ramsey counties which have a separate probate court with judges elected for six-year terms. The probate court has unlimited original jurisdiction in law and equity for the administration of the estates of deceased persons and all guardianship and incompetency proceedings.

Justices of the peace were abolished Minnesota as of July 1, 1977.
Source: Minn. Legislative Manual, 1985-86.

SUPREME COURT

State Capitol
St. Paul 55155
(612) 296-2581

Constitution provides: one chief justice and six to eight associate justices elected by the people; vacancies are filled by governor's appointment; state court administrator, clerk of supreme court, supreme court reporter, and state law librarian are appointed by the court to serve at its pleasure (Article VI; Minnesota Statutes, Sections 480.09; 480.15).

Term: six years.   **Salary:** $82,902 chief justice; $76,940 associate justice.

CHIEF JUSTICE
Douglas K. Amdahl

Biography: Minneapolis. Born Mabel, 1919; Mabel schools, University of Minnesota (B.B.A.), William Mitchell College of Law (J.D.); private practice (1951-55); assistant county attorney (1955-61); municipal court judge, Minneapolis (1961-62); district court judge (1962-80); supreme court (1980-81); wife: Phyllis. Appointed chief justice December 18, 1981.

Elected: 1984

Term Expires: January, 1991

ASSOCIATE JUSTICE
M. Jeanne Coyne

Biography: Edina. Born December 7, 1926, Minneapolis; University of Minnesota (BS.L., 1955; J.D., 1957); member: American and Minnesota Bar Assns., National Assn. of Women Judges, National Assn. of Women Lawyers. Appointed September 1, 1982.

Elected: 1984

Term Expires: January, 1991

ASSOCIATE JUSTICE
Glenn E. Kelley

Biography: Woodbury. Born April 25, 1921; Northern State College (B.S., 1944), University of Michigan Law School (LL.B., 1948); private practice (1948-69); district judge (1969-81); wife: Margaret, three children. Appointed December 18, 1981.

Elected: 1984

Term Expires: January, 1991

ASSOCIATE JUSTICE
Peter S. Popovich

Biography: St. Mary's Point. Born November 27, 1920; University of Minnesota (B.A.), St. Paul College of Law; admitted to practice, 1947; Minnesota House of Representatives (1953-63); four children. Appointed November 1, 1983, elected 1984 Chief Judge to Court of Appeals; appointed to Supreme Court in August, 1987.

ASSOCIATE JUSTICE
John E. Simonett

Biography: Little Falls. Born July 12, 1924, Mankato; education: St. John's University (B.A., 1948), University of Minnesota (LL.B., 1951); practiced law, Little Falls (1951-80); married Doris Bogut, six children. Appointed September 8, 1980.

Elected: 1982

Term Expires: January, 1989

ASSOCIATE JUSTICE
Rosalie E. Wahl*

Biography: Lake Elmo. Education: University of Kansas (B.A., 1946), William Mitchell College of Law (J.D., 1967); assistant state public defender (1967-73); professor of law, William Mitchell College of Law (1973-77); five children. Appointed October 3, 1977.

Elected: 1978, 1984

Term Expires: January, 1991

ASSOCIATE JUSTICE
Lawrence R. Yetka

Biography: Maplewood. Born, raised, practiced law in Cloquet; education: Cloquet public schools, University of Minnesota and its law school; former lawyer, legislator

Justice Wahl is the first woman ever to serve on the Minnesota Supreme Court.

(10 years); chair, Judicial Planning Committee; wife: Ellen, sons: Frank Barry, Lawrence George, Christopher Hubert. Appointed July 3, 1973.
Elected: 1974, 1980, 1986.
Term Expires: January, 1993

COURT OF APPEALS

Chambers
1300 Amhoist Tower
4th and St. Peter
St. Paul 55102
(612) 297-1000

Salary: $74,015 chief judge; $70,978 judges

CHIEF JUDGE
Daniel Donald (D.D.) Wozniak

Biography: St. Paul. Born 1922, Silver Lake; College of St. Thomas (B.A., 1943, cum laude), University of Minnesota (J.D., 1948); naval aviator (WWII); Minnesota House of Representatives (1951-67), Minnesota state department, private practice (1948-83); married, four children. Appointed November 2, 1983, elected 1984.

Judges

Gary Lee Crippen, Mendota Heights. Born 1936, Worthington; University of Minnesota (J.D., 1960); private practice, Worthington (1960-74), Nobles county attorney (1966-74), trial judge (1974-84); married, seven children. Appointed April 2, 1984.

Daniel F. Foley, Rochester. Born October 9, 1921, Wabasha; College of St. Thomas (B.A.), Fordham University (LL.B.), Mexican Academy of International Law (LL.D., 1964); private practice (1948-66); district judge (1966-83); married, five sons. Appointed November 2, 1983, elected 1984.

Thomas G. Forsberg, Fridley, Born 1927, Appleton; University of Minnesota (LL.B., 1952; law review); private practice (1952-68), municipal judge (1968-72), district judge (1972-84); married, four children. Appointed April 2, 1984.

Doris Ohlsen Huspeni, Minneapolis. University of Minnesota (B.A., 1964) William Mitchell College of Law (J.D., 1970); municipal judge (1980-82), district judge (1982-84); married, five children. Appointed April 2, 1984.

Thomas J. Kalitowski, Denmark Township. Born 1946. University of Minnesota Law School (1973); assistant attorney general (1975-1977); chairman of Minnesota Water Planning Board (1977-1983); chairman of Minnesota Environmental Quality Board (1983-1984); head of Minnesota Pollution Control Agency (1984-1987). Appointed Aug. 26, 1987.

Harriet Lansing, St. Paul. Born May 19, 1945; Macalester College (B.A. 1967), University of Minnesota Law School (J.D., 1970); private practice (1973-76), city attorney (1976-78), municipal judge (1978-83); married, one child. Appoined November 1, 1983, elected 1984.

Roger J. Nierengarten, Sartell. Born 1925; St. John's University (B.A., 1948), Marquette University Law School (J.D., 1951); private practice (1956-84), Stearns county attorney (1962-66), special attorney general (1972-76), U.S. Army Paratroops (1943-46). Appointed March 2, 1984.

Fred C. Norton, St. Paul. Born 1928; education: Wesleyan University (B.A.), University of Minnesota (LL.B); assistant attorney general (10 years); board member: Legal Assistance of Southern Minnesota; Minnesota House of Representatives (1966-80); Speaker of the House (1980-87); married, three children. Appointed by Gov. Perpich at the time of publication.

Edward James Parker, Minneapolis. Born November 2, 1927, Detroit, MI; University of Minnesota (B.A., 1952; LL.B., 1955); Minneapolis municipal court (1963), district judge (1966); married, five children. Appointed November 1, 1983, elected 1984.

R.A. (Jim) Randall, Hibbing. Born August 31, 1940, Little Falls; Gonzaga University (B.A., 1962), University of Minnesota (J.D., 1967); private practice (1967-84); asst. public defender (1967-84); married Monica Eichton, three children. Appointed April 1, 1984.

Robert H. Schumacher, Eden Prairie. Born 1936. St. Thomas College, (1957); William Mitchell College of Law, (1962); private practice, (1962-1974); Hennepin County Municipal Court (1974-1984); Hennepin County District Court and chief judge (1984-1987). Appointed Aug. 26, 1987.

Susanne C. Sedgwick, Excelsior. Born June 10, 1931, Minneapolis; University of Minnesota, William Mitchell College of Law (1956, cum laude); asst. Hennepin county attorney (1968-70); municipal judge (1970-74); district judge (1974-84); married, four children. Appointed November 1, 1983, elected 1984.

DISTRICT COURT

Judges: Three or more judges in each district.

Term: Judges are elected for six years; terms expire first Monday in January; vacancies are filled by governor's appointment.

Salary: $68,054

COUNTY COURT

Judges: In 1971 when the county court system was established, former probate judges had the option of becoming county court judges or judicial officers. All new county court judges must be learned in the law.

Term: Judges are elected for six years; terms expire first Monday in January; vacancies are filled by governor's appointment.

Salary: $68,054

ADMINISTRATIVE AGENCIES

Board of Judicial Standards
202 Minnesota State Bank Bldg.
200 S. Robert St.
St. Paul 55107
(612) 296-3999

Law provides: that the board has ten members representing the courts, lawyers and the public. Appointed to four-year terms by the governor and confirmed by the senate.

Function: Recommends to the supreme court the retirement of a judge when disability interferes with performance of duties. Recommends censure of judges for incompetence or disreputable conduct affecting judicial office.

Executive Secretary: Richard E. Aretz

Lawyers Professional Responsibility Board
444 Lafayette Rd.
4th Floor
St. Paul 55101
(612) 296-3952

Law provides: that the board is established by the supreme court and funded by lawyers' registration fees; board has twelve lawyer members, nine nonlawyer members, and a chairman; members serve three-year terms.

Function: the board investigates complaints of misconduct and disability involving lawyers. Provides educational programs on standards of conduct for attorneys to the public and members of the bar.

Director: Michael J. Hoover

State Board of Law Examiners
310 Minnesota State Bank Bldg.
200 S. Robert St.
St. Paul 55107
(612) 297-1800

Law provides: that the board is composed of nine members, seven lawyers and two lay people appointed by the supreme court for three years. (Rules of the Supreme Court).

Function: to process and review applications of persons seeking to practice law in Minnesota; to administer the bar examination; to provide research and counsel on requirements for admission.

Director: Marcia L. Proctor

State Board of Public Defense
State Public Defender
95 Subplaza
University of Minnesota Law School
Minneapolis 55455
(612) 373-5798

Law provides: for governor's appointment of a seven member board to appoint the state and district public defenders and to distribute funds to selected legal defense corporations. The public defender has responsibility for criminal cases on appeal, post-conviction cases, parole revocation proceedings for juveniles and adults, civil and prison disciplinary proceedings for inmates, and law student clinical work.

Chair: Judge Kevin Burke
Public Defender: C. Paul Jones

MINNESOTA ARREST INFORMATION

Arrest information for Minnesota in 1986 is presented with a state total concerning age, sex, and race factors. Data has also been tabulated for the specific kinds of narcotic arrests and the individuals involved.

The total number of arrests involving criminal offenses in the state in 1986 was 153,751*, with 122,931 males and 30,820 females arrested. Compared with 144,550* total arrests (116,905 males and 27,645 females) for 1985, the 1986 figures represent a 6.4 percent increase in total arrests. Arrests of males increased 5.2 percent and female arrests increased 11.5 percent from 1985 to 1986.

There are several significant factors to consider when arrest data is evaluated. One arrest situation is counted for each time an individual is arrested whether it be several times a year for one type of offense or for different offenses.

Another factor to consider is that an arrest can be reported for an offense that occurred during a previous reporting period and thus can reflect an arrest picture not totally consistent with the total actual offenses for that period. In some extreme cases arrests may outnumber offenses, which in large measure is a result of this factor.

As stated previously, an arrest situation constitutes a form of detention for uniform crime reporting purposes. Because police arrest activities often vary, especially with relation to juveniles, the reporting agencies are instructed to count one arrest each time a person is taken into custody for committing a specific crime. The FBI's instructions state that:

"A juvenile is counted as a person arrested when he commits an offense and the circumstances are such that if the offender were an adult an arrest would be made."[1]

*Based on detailed arrest information received by the BCA.
[1]*Crime in the United States*—Uniform Crime Reports, 1986 Annual FBI, Washington, D.C.

Source: *1986 Minnesota Annual Report on Crime, Missing Children, and Bureau of Criminal Apprehension Activities. Bureau of Criminal Apprehension, Criminal Justice Information Systems Section. July 1, 1987.*

Three of Minnesota's sons achieved eminence in the field of law. Pierce Butler, who was born in Dakota county, was appointed Associate Justice of the Supreme Court in 1923 by President Harding. He was generally considered a conservative.

Criminal Process in a Felony Case

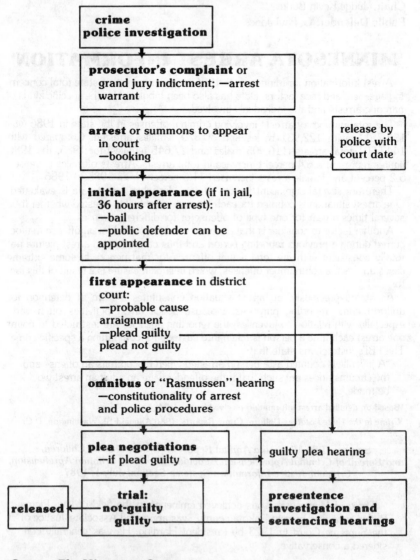

Source: The Minnesota Courts

(Court Information Office of the Minnesota Supreme Court, 1979)

Anatomy of a Jury Trial

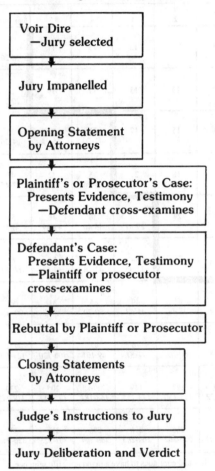

Voir Dire
—Jury selected

↓

Jury Impanelled

↓

Opening Statement
by Attorneys

↓

Plaintiff's or Prosecutor's Case:
Presents Evidence, Testimony
—Defendant cross-examines

↓

Defendant's Case:
Presents Evidence, Testimony
—Plaintiff or prosecutor
cross-examines

↓

Rebuttal by Plaintiff or Prosecutor

↓

Closing Statements
by Attorneys

↓

Judge's Instructions to Jury

↓

Jury Deliberation and Verdict

Process in A Civil Case

Dispute develops
↓
Complaint by plaintiff
Served with summons on
defendant
↘
Default by defendant;
Plaintiff can proceed to
judgment
↙
Answer by defendant
Counterclaim by defendant
↓
Discovery
(interrogatories, deposition, etc.)
↓
Motions
↓
Negotiations ⟶
↘
Settlement
↓
Pre-Trial Conference
↓
Trial
↓
Verdict
(Judgment)

SENTENCING GUIDELINES GRID

Presumptive Sentence Lengths in Months

Italicized numbers within the grid denote the range within which a judge may sentence without the sentence being deemed a departure.

Offenders with nonimprisonment felony sentences are subject to jail time according to law.

SEVERITY LEVELS OF CONVICTION OFFENSE		CRIMINAL HISTORY SCORE						
		0	1	2	3	4	5	6 or more
Unauthorized Use of Motor Vehicle Possession of Marijuana	I	12*	12*	12*	13	15	17	19 *18-20*
Theft Related Crimes ($2500 or less) Check Forgery ($200-$2500)	II	12*	12*	13	15	17	19	21 *20-22*
Theft Crimes ($2500 or less)	III	12*	13	15	17	19 *18-20*	22 *21-23*	25 *24-26*
Nonresidential Burglary Theft Crimes (over $2500)	IV	12*	15	18	21	25 *24-26*	32 *30-34*	41 *37-45*
Residential Burglary Simple Robbery	V	18	23	27	30 *29-31*	38 *36-40*	46 *43-49*	54 *50-58*
Criminal Sexual Conduct, 2nd Degree (a) & (b)	VI	21	26	30	34 *33-35*	44 *42-46*	54 *50-58*	65 *60-70*
Aggravated Robbery	VII	24 *23-25*	32 *30-34*	41 *38-44*	49 *45-53*	65 *60-70*	81 *75-87*	97 *90-104*
Criminal Sexual Conduct 1st Degree Assault, 1st Degree	VIII	43 *41-45*	54 *50-58*	65 *60-70*	76 *71-81*	95 *89-101*	113 *106-120*	132 *124-140*
Murder, 3rd Degree Murder, 2nd Degree (felony murder)	IX	105 *102-108*	119 *116-122*	127 *124-130*	149 *143-155*	176 *168-184*	205 *195-215*	230 *218-242*
Murder, 2nd Degree (with intent)	X	216 *212-220*	236 *231-241*	256 *250-262*	276 *269-283*	296 *288-304*	316 *307-325*	336 *326-346*

1st Degree Murder is excluded from the guidelines by law and continues to have a mandatory life sentence.

☐ At the discretion of the judge, up to a year in jail and/or other non-jail sanctions can be imposed as conditions of probation.

☐ Presumptive commitment to state imprisonment.

*one year and one day

Source: *Minnesota Sentencing Guidelines and Comentary*, Rev., Aug. 1, 1987.

TOTAL ARRESTS BY AGE IN MINNESOTA FOR 1986

Offense and Sex		Under 10	10-12	13-14	15	16	17	17 and Under Juvenile	18	19	20	21	22	23	24	25-29	30-34	35-39	40-44	45-49	50-54	55-59	60-64	65 and Over	18 and Over Adult	Total for State
Murder	T			3	2	2	3	10	8	4	6	9	5	5	2	11	8	8	4	6		2		1	80	90
	M			3	2	2	3	10	6	4	5	8	4	5	2	10	7	7	4	4	1	2		1	70	80
	F								2		1	1	1			1	1	1		2	1				10	10
Negligent Manslaughter	T			1	2			3	1				1	2		1			1						6	9
	M			1	2			2	1				1	2		1			1						6	8
	F							1																		1
Rape	T	1	4	17	18	14	11	65	17	17	30	21	15	18	23	86	57	42	31	13	4	10	1	5	390	455
	M	1	3	17	18	14	11	64	17	17	29	21	15	18	23	85	55	42	31	13	4	10	1	5	386	450
	F		1					1			1					1	2								4	5
Robbery	T	3	17	64	51	60	80	275	80	49	60	54	51	39	47	152	90	39	16	6	3		1	1	688	963
	M	3	17	61	40	53	72	246	73	43	52	50	49	36	42	136	87	35	15	6	3		1	1	629	875
	F			3	11	7	8	29	7	6	8	4	2	3	5	16	3	4	1						59	88
Aggravated Assault	T	19	37	148	100	122	185	611	111	133	119	136	108	98	130	525	364	227	117	80	40	22	9	11	2,230	2,841
	M	16	32	121	85	100	165	519	100	116	99	117	101	88	110	459	322	199	103	76	33	19	9	11	1,962	2,481
	F	3	5	27	15	22	20	92	11	17	20	19	7	10	20	66	42	28	14	4	7	3			268	360
Burglary	T	70	209	550	465	468	482	2,244	423	368	276	207	189	167	134	426	176	83	37	27	10	5		3	2,531	4,775
	M	65	187	506	443	427	445	2,073	405	357	268	198	179	162	127	414	170	80	35	26	9	4		3	2,437	4,510
	F	5	22	44	22	41	37	171	18	11	8	9	10	5	7	12	6	3	2	1	1				94	265
Larceny	T	555	1,702	3,246	2,108	2,177	2,049	11,837	1,390	1,139	870	721	665	597	573	2,318	1,631	1,234	731	500	376	323	276	508	13,852	25,689
	M	447	1,269	2,192	1,416	1,528	1,443	8,295	1,022	813	578	461	395	385	411	1,470	1,073	832	446	309	232	185	168	292	9,072	17,367
	F	108	433	1,054	692	649	606	3,542	368	326	292	260	270	212	162	848	558	402	285	191	144	138	108	216	4,780	8,322
Auto Theft	T	3	57	414	416	447	388	1,725	216	182	148	85	69	79	64	204	80	41	25	8	4	2	2	1	1,210	2,935
	M	2	44	335	355	391	349	1,476	202	169	141	81	63	76	57	180	74	40	23	7	4	2	2	1	1,122	2,598
	F	1	13	79	61	56	39	249	14	13	7	4	6	3	7	24	6	1	2	1					88	337
Arson	T	21	23	46	23	7	15	135	18	10	6	8	15	4	3	18	15	7	8	4	6	2		4	128	263
	M	20	23	37	22	5	13	120	16	8	5	7	15	4	2	16	14	7	5	4	5	1		3	112	232
	F	1		9	1	2	2	15	2	2	1	1			1	2	1		3		1	1		1	16	31
Part I Total	T	672	2,049	4,489	3,185	3,297	3,213	16,905	2,264	1,902	1,515	1,241	1,118	1,009	976	3,741	2,421	1,681	970	644	444	366	289	534	21,115	38,020
	M	554	1,575	3,272	2,383	2,520	2,501	12,805	1,842	1,527	1,177	943	822	776	774	2,771	1,802	1,242	663	445	291	223	181	317	15,796	28,601
	F	118	474	1,217	802	777	712	4,100	422	375	338	298	296	233	202	970	619	439	307	199	153	143	108	217	5,319	9,419
Other Assaults	T	46	191	513	336	354	430	1,870	289	344	405	384	420	459	480	2,074	1,376	876	480	282	171	71	55	60	8,226	10,096
	M	40	163	360	256	261	335	1,415	250	301	355	332	370	410	435	1,887	1,259	786	438	256	161	65	51	55	7,411	8,826
	F	6	28	153	80	93	95	455	39	43	50	52	50	49	45	187	117	90	42	26	10	6	4	5	815	1,270
Forgery/Counterfeiting	T	3	22	81	108	140	187	541	155	142	143	94	102	97	80	281	182	131	58	25	10	2	1	5	1,508	2,049
	M	2	16	41	92	92	109	329	92	98	93	60	53	53	60	195	119	95	43	21	10	1	1	4	998	1,327
	F	1	6	40	70	48	78	212	63	44	50	34	49	44	20	86	63	36	15	4		1		1	510	722

Offense and Sex	Under 10	10-12	13-14	15	16	17	17 and Under Juvenile	18	19	20	21	22	23	24	25-29	30-34	35-39	40-44	45-49	50-54	55-59	60-64	65 and Over	18 and Over Adult	Total for State
Fraud T	—	8	21	24	62	88	203	217	281	313	303	314	374	285	1,330	839	620	415	241	99	57	15	167	5,870	6,073
M	—	7	16	21	44	62	150	116	130	155	183	208	204	153	719	442	373	244	144	78	40	9	79	3,277	3,427
F	—	1	5	3	18	26	53	101	151	158	120	106	170	132	611	397	247	171	97	21	17	6	88	2,593	2,646
Embezzlement T																								5	5
M																								3	3
F																								2	2
Stolen Property T	2	39	149	125	135	143	593	156	126	100	78	87	59	64	184	80	58	32	23	8	4	4	—	1,063	1,656
M	2	37	133	114	113	133	532	140	107	89	70	76	52	54	143	66	44	28	21	5	4	4	—	903	1,435
F	—	2	16	11	22	10	61	16	19	11	8	11	7	10	41	14	14	4	2	3	—	—	—	160	221
Vandalism T	163	468	816	556	550	539	3,092	381	309	296	165	181	157	120	487	228	127	61	39	19	12	5	14	2,601	5,693
M	155	426	743	502	506	492	2,824	360	294	280	150	165	136	112	444	199	117	56	36	13	12	3	11	2,388	5,212
F	8	42	73	54	44	47	268	21	15	16	15	16	21	8	43	29	10	5	3	6	—	2	3	213	481
Weapons T	11	58	149	94	83	108	503	82	74	64	50	44	67	51	193	143	81	47	19	20	8	6	4	953	1,456
M	10	56	144	93	79	100	482	80	67	60	47	42	64	49	178	130	74	46	19	18	8	6	4	892	1,374
F	1	2	5	1	4	8	21	2	7	4	3	2	3	2	15	13	7	1	—	2	—	—	—	61	82
Prostitution T	—	1	11	13	21	33	79	35	70	66	67	53	53	48	232	90	54	43	26	13	11	4	9	874	953
M	—	1	7	5	6	11	29	6	7	7	13	9	12	11	62	43	35	34	21	13	10	4	8	295	324
F	—	—	4	8	15	22	50	29	63	59	54	44	41	37	170	47	19	9	5	—	1	—	1	579	629
Other Sex T	15	37	115	59	57	61	344	46	49	61	43	49	42	53	218	178	123	99	39	29	24	24	44	1,121	1,465
M	15	35	105	58	56	61	330	43	49	60	40	48	42	47	211	172	120	99	39	28	24	24	44	1,090	1,420
F	—	2	10	1	1	—	14	3	—	1	1	1	—	6	7	6	3	—	—	1	—	—	—	31	45
Narcotics T	1	10	97	109	185	302	704	378	320	302	279	312	290	262	1,074	606	252	97	27	11	5	2	3	4,219	4,923
M	1	6	76	86	162	268	599	353	291	263	248	287	253	244	953	547	222	85	19	10	3	1	2	3,781	4,380
F	—	4	21	23	23	34	105	25	29	39	31	25	37	18	121	59	30	12	8	1	2	1	1	438	543
Gambling T	—	—	—	1	1	1	3	—	—	—	1	—	—	—	3	3	1	3	4	6	1	—	—	22	25
M	—	—	—	1	—	1	2	—	—	—	1	—	—	—	3	3	—	3	4	5	1	—	—	20	22
F	—	—	—	—	1	—	1	—	—	—	—	—	—	—	—	—	1	—	—	1	—	—	—	2	3
Family/Children T	1	—	3	1	5	1	11	24	28	23	24	13	18	11	43	44	32	19	4	7	—	—	3	293	304
M	1	—	1	1	4	1	8	22	24	16	18	11	12	9	35	34	24	16	2	6	—	—	3	232	240
F	—	—	2	—	1	—	3	2	4	7	6	2	6	2	8	10	8	3	2	1	—	—	—	61	64
Driving Under Influence T	5	1	2	27	254	546	835	1,151	1,813	2,002	2,070	2,115	2,040	2,006	8,295	5,002	3,316	2,098	1,274	857	631	397	448	35,555	36,390
M	4	1	2	22	205	443	677	981	1,507	1,667	1,727	1,809	1,709	1,628	7,093	4,256	2,833	1,788	1,071	752	564	366	408	30,159	30,836
F	1	—	—	5	49	103	158	170	306	335	343	346	331	378	1,202	746	483	310	203	105	67	31	40	5,396	5,554
Liquor Laws T	9	15	240	472	983	1,325	3,044	2,399	594	295	244	177	166	115	428	287	227	115	84	57	50	15	14	5,267	8,311
M	8	8	135	304	730	1,031	2,216	1,935	485	249	206	158	146	99	372	248	205	106	79	52	45	15	14	4,414	6,630
F	1	7	105	168	253	294	828	464	109	46	38	19	20	16	56	39	22	9	5	5	5	—	—	853	1,681

Offense and Sex	Under 10	10-12	13-14	15	16	17	17 and Under Juvenile	18	19	20	21	22	23	24	25-29	30-34	35-39	40-44	45-49	50-54	55-59	60-64	65 and Over	18 and Over Adult	Total for State
Disorderly T	20	83	299	260	282	378	1,322	510	618	606	586	496	494	381	1,506	879	572	323	177	123	73	29	45	7,418	8,740
M	16	69	227	206	239	312	1,069	445	538	505	515	447	423	337	1,296	775	506	268	145	112	64	25	38	6,439	7,508
F	4	14	72	54	43	66	253	65	80	101	71	49	71	44	210	104	66	55	32	11	9	4	7	979	1,232
Vagrancy T	—	—	1	—	—	—	1	—	1	—	1	—	—	—	—	—	1	—	—	—	1	—	—	4	5
M	—	—	—	—	—	—	—	—	1	—	1	—	—	—	—	—	1	—	—	—	1	—	—	4	5
F	—	—	—	—	—	—	—	—	—	—	—	—	—	—	—	—	—	—	—	—	—	—	—	—	1
Other Except Traffic T	127	191	698	700	830	937	3,483	1,114	1,200	1,165	1,256	1,241	1,233	1,132	4,197	2,626	1,628	929	540	325	230	124	135	19,075	22,558
M	85	149	529	552	650	767	2,732	944	1,004	987	1,064	1,061	1,051	959	3,539	2,210	1,381	751	427	250	198	95	110	16,031	18,763
F	42	42	169	148	180	170	751	170	196	178	192	180	182	173	658	416	247	178	113	75	32	29	25	3,044	3,795
Part II Total T	403	1,124	3,195	2,885	3,942	5,079	16,628	6,937	5,968	5,841	5,645	5,644	5,549	5,089	20,546	12,564	8,099	4,820	2,804	1,756	1,180	681	951	94,074	110,702
M	338	973	2,520	2,290	3,148	4,126	13,396	5,767	4,902	4,786	4,675	4,744	4,567	4,197	17,130	10,504	6,816	4,006	2,304	1,514	1,040	605	780	78,337	91,732
F	65	151	675	595	794	953	3,233	1,170	1,066	1,055	970	900	982	892	3,416	2,060	1,283	814	500	242	140	76	171	15,737	18,970
Curfew/Loitering T	12	87	467	502	533	472	2,073	—	—	—	—	—	—	—	—	—	—	—	—	—	—	—	—	—	2,073
M	9	62	289	329	389	321	1,399	—	—	—	—	—	—	—	—	—	—	—	—	—	—	—	—	—	1,399
F	3	25	178	173	144	151	674	—	—	—	—	—	—	—	—	—	—	—	—	—	—	—	—	—	674
Runaways T	13	188	1,007	771	632	345	2,956	—	—	—	—	—	—	—	—	—	—	—	—	—	—	—	—	—	2,956
M	10	91	376	296	253	173	1,199	—	—	—	—	—	—	—	—	—	—	—	—	—	—	—	—	—	1,199
F	3	97	631	475	379	172	1,757	—	—	—	—	—	—	—	—	—	—	—	—	—	—	—	—	—	1,757
Grand Total for State T	1,100	3,448	9,158	7,343	8,404	9,109	38,562	9,201	7,870	7,356	6,886	6,792	6,558	6,065	24,287	14,985	9,780	5,790	3,448	2,200	1,546	970	1,485	115,189	153,751
M	911	2,701	6,457	5,298	6,310	7,121	28,798	7,609	6,429	5,963	5,618	5,566	5,343	4,971	19,901	12,306	8,058	4,669	2,749	1,805	1,263	786	1,097	94,133	122,931
F	189	747	2,701	2,045	2,094	1,988	9,764	1,592	1,441	1,393	1,268	1,196	1,215	1,094	4,386	2,679	1,722	1,121	699	395	283	184	388	21,056	30,820

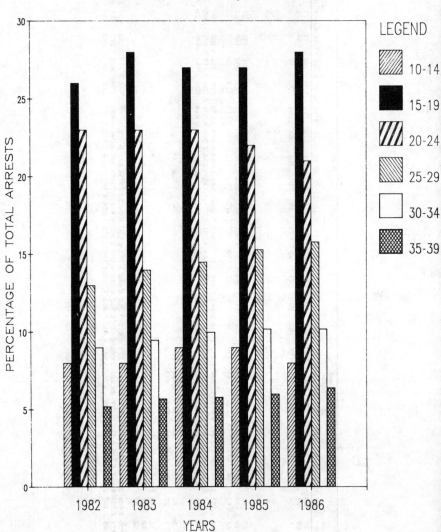

PERCENTAGE OF PERSONS ARRESTED
BY AGE GROUPS, 1982-1986

PERCENT OF TYPES OF NARCOTICS ARRESTS IN MINNESOTA FOR 1986

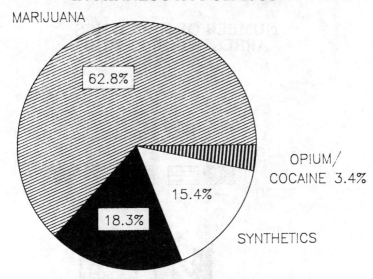

MARIJUANA

62.8%

OPIUM/ COCAINE 3.4%

15.4%

18.3%

SYNTHETICS

OTHER DANGEROUS DRUGS

TOTAL NARCOTICS ARRESTS = 4,923

IF YOU ARE THE VICTIM OF A CRIME. . .

. . . you may be eligible for compensation from the state of Minnesota.

It is the purpose of the Minnesota Crime Victims Reparations Law *"to provide innocent victims of violent crime with compensation for loss of earning or support and out-of-pocket loss for injuries sustained as a direct result of a crime committed against their person. Out-of-pocket loss means reasonable medical care or other services necessary as a result of injury. In the event of the death of a victim, reasonable medical care plus reasonable expenses incurred by a legal representative of decreased for funeral, burial or creamation."*

Eligible is the innocent victim of a violent crime against his or her person and the dependent or legal representative of an innocent victim who has met death as a result of a violent crime. Loss of personal property is not covered.

Categories of claims submitted include arson, assault, hit and run, homicide, mugging and rape.

The reparations law is funded from state general revenues. There are 27 such programs in the United States; Minnesota was the 13th to pass this legislation in 1974.

For full information, contact the Minnesota Crime Victims Reparations Board. 1(800)247-0390.

NUMBER OF NARCOTICS ARRESTS FOR PERIOD 1977-1986

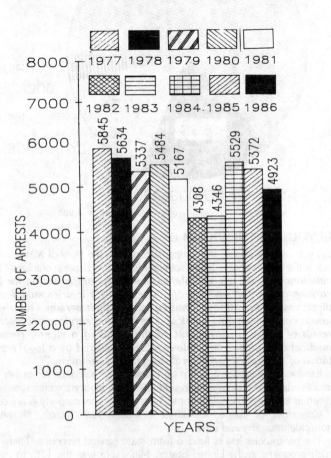

Politics

CATO, the great Roman political philosopher, couldn't have had Minnesota in mind in the year 194 B.C. when he said, "Some have said it is not the business of private men to meddle with government,—a bold and dishonest saying, which is fit to come from no mouth but that of a tyrant or a slave. To say that private men have nothing to do with government is to say private men have nothing to do with their own happiness or misery; that people ought not to concern themselves whether they be naked or clothed, fed or starved, deceived or instructed, protected or destroyed."

Certainly not many, if any, Minnesota pioneers had time to read and absorb Cato's wisdom. As private citizens however, concerned with their government, they shared the great Roman's political philosophy. Today this great state can look back on 123 years and challenge any of the 50 states in the Union to match its records of vigorous and socially productive politics.

Both the Republican and Democratic parties and later the Farmer-Labor and Democratic-Farmer-Labor parties (the Democrats and Farmer-Labor fused in 1944) have experienced control of the state's political offices. Not, however, without confrontations with a strong tradition of reformist protest. The political mix has produced many major protest groups—the Grange, the Greenbackers, the Anti-Monopolists, the Farmers' Alliance, the Populists, the Prohibitionists, and the Nonpartisan League. This "mix" provided the original impetus to, and eventual implementation into law of, the numerous reforms that the more conservative parties enacted when the time for their acceptance by the public arrived.

Minnesota's constitution is one of the oldest in the nation. In fundamental principle and framework it hasn't changed much since it was first ratified by Congress in 1858 when Minnesota joined the Union as the thirty-second state. While conservative in its governmental institutions, at times the people of Minnesota have often been liberal, occasionally radical, in their politics, as has been pointed out previously. It presents a study in contrasts equalled by few other states. Over the years the reform movements initiated have undergone frequent rebirths, all attesting to the prolonged distress that came along with the transition from a simple frontier community to a complex, interdependent economy. Agriculture—Minnesota's mainstay—was the dominant factor in the state's maturing. If farm prices were depressed—farmers took to the warpath. Populism, which represented the strong protests of Minnesota wheat farmers, grew strong and felt no decline until wheat prices began to climb after McKinley was elected President in 1896. However, profitable years were the exception and farmers eked out a living and some kept even with their debts. Farmers' woes were blamed on the railroads, the banks and terminal grain elevators. Not without some justification, as these firms did exact a disproportionate tribute for their services. The wheat farmers never diversified, insisting on raising wheat exclusively, when the times called for diversification.

Many of the farmers were forced by poor wheat crops to adjust their operations to include livestock raising and dairying which eventually brought a modicum of success—never for long, however.

Third parties in Minnesota didn't always confine their interests to farmers' welfare exclusively. The prohibition party in 1872 came out for women's suffrage. "Give women the vote," was their battle cry. In 1879 the Greenbackers advocated a graduated and equitable income tax and a vociferously worded platform plank for the outright end to employment of children under fourteen. In 1888 the Farm and Labor party made demands for the Australian ballot, the eight-hour work day, employer liability for workmen injured on the job and a sizeable number of other reforms.

Thirty four men have occupied the governor's chair since Henry Sibley, a Democrat, was the first to be elected in 1858. Twenty five of those were Republicans, four were Democrats, two were Farmer-Laborites and four belonged to the hyphenated Democratic-Farmer-Labor party.

One fact stands out in going over the political annals of Minnesota— Minnesotans don't like to be bossed—they have inherited a stiff independence from sturdy forebears of various stocks. Attempts to crank up political machines have never worked out. Leaders with that thought in mind were quickly shunted aside. It became harder to build a working political organization at the turn of the century, all party lines were wiped out except for state and congressional offices. With civil service laws much of the incentive for doing grass roots political work vanished—there were no more "spoils" to be dished out.

Minnesota has produced a number of public figures who attained national status. They were Ignatius Donnelly, John Lind, John A. Johnson, Arthur C. Townley, Frank B. Kellogg, Floyd B. Olson, Harold Stassen, Hubert H. Humphrey, Eugene J. McCarthy and Walter F. Mondale. While obscured by the exploits of his son, Charles Jr., Charles A. Lindbergh, Sr., as a Congressman played a significant role in the development of Minnesota and American political reforms.

Ignatius Donnelly was one of the most colorful personalities associated with third parties in Minnesota. He was brilliant, cantankerous and a man of wide-ranging interests in social and literary pursuits. He was often referred to as the "universal genius of the prairies." While he initially led the People's Party (commonly known as the "Populists") he was eventually elected lieutenant governor and to the U.S. House of Representatives as a Republican. In his later years Donnelly spent much of his time as an editor and his last public office was as a member of the legislature in 1897. His fame rests more on his literary achievements than on his political successes. He was too much of a "loner."

John Lind was the state's outstanding Democrat at the turn of the century. He had served a term in Congress as a Republican but crossed swords with that party over the tariff and quit as a Representative. Lind was a deadly serious man and his dour dignity was taken by many as a sign of ability and rectitude. Scandinavian voters preferred stuffiness in their candidates and frowned on levity in a public man. Lind's stern bearing accommodated them. Lind held the distinction of being the only one-armed man ever to enter the United States Army. He was given a commission in the Minnesota National Guard when the Spanish-American war broke out. He served one term as governor, refusing to run a second time. Named personal representative by President Woodrow Wilson, he was assigned to go to Vera Cruz, Mexico and observe the country's internal problems. He once said that Pancho Villa was the hope of Mexico. It was not John Lind's recommendation that U.S. Army and General John J. Pershing march across the border to capture Villa—an incident that never happened. Villa died in bed, unfettered and uncaught, years later.

John A. Johnson, editor of the St. Peter Herald, the Democratic governor from 1904 to 1910 was the embodiment of the "rags to riches" tradition in a Horatio Alger era. Born on a farm near St. Peter, Johnson's early life was a struggle. His alcoholic father deserted the family, forcing his mother to take in washing. He was thirteen at the time and took various jobs to supplement the family's income. Successful as a journalist (he was elected president of the Minnesota Newspaper Association at age 32) Johnson won his first political victory in 1898 when he was voted in as a senator in the state legislature. His political acumen and vigorous Compaigning attracted the attention of state Democratic leaders and he became their gubernatorial candidate in 1904. A "reform" governor, he drew strength from Minnesota's liberal third parties. He was a devoted conservationist, went after the railroads for their abuses, protected the public against utility privileges and never failed to defend the exploited and downtrodden. He was responsible for enacted codes to regulate insurance companies. Inheritance taxes were tightened, railroads prohibited from giving free passes to office holders, and cities were empowered to own and operate public utilities.

Johnson's achievements eventually brought him a national reputation. He was the first Minnesotan to receive serious consideration for Presidency. To Democrats who thought William Jennings Bryan was too radical, Johnson seemed an attractive alternative. Several Johnson-for-President clubs sprang up around the country but by the time of the national Democratic convention Bryan had most of the delegates sewed up. Then in 1909, following abdominal surgery for a cancer, he died. A statue of John A. Johnson looks down on the capitol plaza in St. Paul. It is a fitting tribute to one of the best loved men in Minnesota history.

Arthur C. Townley and his lieutenants descended on Minnesota in 1917 bringing the gospel of the Nonpartisan League. Specially trained organizers came in droves to canvas rural areas under the direction of local farmers' committees. Townley preached public ownership of certain essential farm services and facilities—flour mills, packing houses and grain terminal elevators. "Nonpartisan" in principle, the League was originally not another political party but was to work for its chosen candidates within the established parties. Nevertheless, despite its neutral sounding name the Nonpartisan League played a big part in politics, first in its own way and finally as the "father" of the Farmer-Labor Party in 1920. Towneley gained national prominence and certainly gave the solidly entrenched Republicans in Minnesota some uneasy moments.

Frank B. Kellogg was an outstanding Minnesota lawyer but not much of a politician. Elected to the U.S. Senate in 1922, he lasted only one term. However, from the ashes of political defeat he went on to become ambassador to Great Britain, secretary of state, a judge in the World Court, and gave his name to the Kellogg-Briand treaty which gave an illusive promise of lasting universal peace. He was a friendly, folksy person with an extremely nervous manner. His Washington nickname was "Nervous Nellie."

Floyd B. Olson first came into prominence in Minnesota when he led the old Non-partisan League and labor unions to a victory that set the Farmer-Labor Party in a seat of political power for eight turbulent years. He was a political genius with a gift for taming the party's "wild men." He had a winning personality and a saving sense of humor. He headed a one-state party, but if he had lived, he certainly would have represented Minnesota in the U.S. Senate and been a national figure with Presidential possibilities. Olson was headed for Tom Schall's senate seat. They were destined, it was thought, to meet in heads-on clash in 1936—both were loaded for bear. However, Schall, who was blind, was killed by an automobile just before Christmas in Washington, and the battle-of-the-century never came off. Olson died the following August in Rochester as the result of an inoperable cancer. To all intents and purposes the Farmer-Labor party died with him. In 1938 Harold Stassen was elected governor by the sweeping majority of almost 300,000 votes.

Minnesota was ripe for a change when Harold E. Stassen, a young South St. Paul attorney, 31 years old, took over the governor's office. He went in with a program to reorganize state government, centralize responsibility and to install a civil service system. The legislature backed him. Although Stassen was a three term governor, he had served only four months of his third term when he resigned and accepted a commission in the U.S. Navy. After VJ day Stassen became a delegate to the United Nations' conference in San Francisco.

Harold E. Stassen made a greater impact on national affairs than any previous son of Minnesota. He was a contender for the Republican Presidential nomination making his first serious bid in 1948. He lost out to Tom Dewey. he spent the next four years as president of the University of Pennsylvania. From the national platform such a position afforded, he prepared for the 1952 Republican convention. He couldn't contend with the power of war hero, Dwight D. Eisenhower, however, and his second bid for the nomination floundered when his own Minnesota delegation switched allegiance from him to Eisenhower. He finally lost his Minnesota image as the "boy wonder" but continued to serve in a cabinet-ranked post in the Eisenhower administration. He never made a political comeback and the Administration never made the most of his talents.

By far Minnesota's top vote-getter and most prominent political personality was Hubert H. Humphrey. In 1943 he was 32 years old and lost his first bid for political office when he was defeated in the Minneapolis mayoralty race. Undaunted, he came back and ran again in 1945 and was elected. An effective administrator, he proved to be a strong mayor and cracked down on vice, gambling and corruption. He used citizens' volunteer committees to study and make recommendations on housing, veterans' affairs, fair employment practices and law enforcement. He was aided in the latter by an outstanding police chief, Ed Ryan. In 1948 he took on Joe Ball for the United States Senate as the first Democratic-Farmer-Labor candidate and won after a masterful campaign. He received nearly 60 percent of the Minnesota vote.

Humphrey first captured national attention while mayor of Minneapolis when he established the city's 'Fair Employment Practices Commission. At the 1948 Democratic convention he was accorded national acclaim for his civil rights stand.

"To those who say that this civil rights program is an infringement on states' rights," Humphrey asserted, "I say this. The time has arrived in America for the Democratic party to get out of the shadow of states' rights and to walk forthrightly into the bright sunshine of human rights."

After Humphrey was elected to a second term in the Senate in 1954 he became a powerful and controversial member of the Senate's inner council. His legislative activities and interests were wide-ranging—foreign policy, social welfare, agriculture and government reform.

His nimble mind and articulate tongue, his tremendous energy and unbridled ambition coupled with great personal warmth made him a formidable candidate in any political campaign and a continuing force on the national political scene. He proved this contention in 1964 when he was elected Vice President and again in 1968 when as the Democratic nominee for President he lost in a whisker finish to Richard M. Nixon. He almost swung it but the spector of riots at the Chicago Democratic convention and the lackluster support he received from other highly ranked Democrats put him in the loser's corner for the second time in his political career. He was reelected to the Senate and died in 1978.

Other Minnesotans who have etched their names high on the political wall are Eugene McCarthy, member of the House of Representatives and U.S. Senate, a Presidential contender in 1968, and an independent candidate for president in several states in 1976. Also, Walter F. Mondale, former Minnesota Attorney General and Minnesota's senior senator since 1966—he was appointed to the Senate in 1964 and elected in 1966 and 1972. With a distinguished liberal record he was encouraged to enter the presidential race for 1976 but "after considerable thought and study" declined to run in order to devote full time to his Senate responsibilities. But when Jimmy Carter offered him the opportunity to be his Vice Presidential running mate he accepted. Orville Freeman, another Minnesotan in politics, was elected governor in 1954 and went on to become Secretary of Agriculture in John F. Kennedy's administration.

Source: Minnesota Legislative Manual.

ELECTIONS

Where do elections begin?

Constitutions and charters provide the basic framework for elections by defining the qualifications for voting and the offices to be elected and the qualifications and terms for each.

Statutes, ordinances, and rules spell out details for administering these elections.

In Minnesota, statutes define political parties and regulate the conduct of primary elections for partisan and nonpartisan offices.

Who is eligible to vote?

Any citizen of the United States who will be eighteen years old by the date of the next election, who has resided in Minnesota for twenty days, and who is registered to vote is eligible.

Who is not eligible to vote?

The following are not eligible to vote in Minnesota: anyone who is convicted of treason or a felony and not yet restored to civil rights; anyone under guardianship over her/his person; anyone adjudcicated mentally incompetent; anyone not properly registered.

REGISTRATION

All voters are required to register before they can vote. Registration in areas where pre-registration is allowed will be accepted at all times except 20 days before an election. In areas that do not have pre-registration, registration will only be accepted on election day. You may also register as you vote on election day at all polling places in Minnesota. Should you decide to register on election day you will be asked to prove your residency by producing a valid drivers license, a non-qualification card, or have a registered voter of your precinct swear to your residency. Your registration is permanent once you register providing you vote at least once every four years. You may register by mail by requesting a registration form from your county auditor. You must cancel any previous registration if you change your address and register in a new community.

If you will be away from your voting residence on election day you may still participate in the election process by casting an absentee ballot. Your county auditor will provide you with a form to apply for an absentee ballot. Application must be made not more than 45 days nor less than one day before an election.

Members of the armed forces may request ballots from their county auditor. All servicemen who are not already registered will be required to register before they will be allowed to vote. When a serviceman applies for an absentee ballot, if he is not registered, an application for registration will accompany his ballot. He may return the registration form in the same envelope as his absentee ballot.

PARTIES, CAUCUSES & ELECTIONS

What is a political party?

Minnesota law defines "political party" as an organization presenting candidates in the last preceding general election one or more of whom has been voted for in each county in the state and shall have received not less than five percent of the total vote cast for all candidates in such election.

Who joins a party?

Since Minnesota voters do not register with a declaration of political party, they may choose to affiliate with a party in a variety of ways, including attending its precinct caucus and declaring intent to support that party's candidates in the next election.

What is a precinct caucus?

The legal process of the general election year begins with political party precinct caucuses the fourth Tuesday evening in February.

A precinct is an election area which has one polling place. Each of the 4,020 precincts will elect delegates to represent their residents directly and indirectly at county, district, state, and national conventions.

What is a primary election?

In Minnesota the purpose of a primary election is to nominate political party candidates to the general election ballot and to reduce the number of candidates for a nonpartisan office to no more than twice the number to be elected in the general election.

Partisan candidates, therefore, run among themselves in such an election, and the choice of candidates is within each party. Voters must vote in the primary election of only one political party, and no write-in votes are allowed.

How are other parties' candidates nominated?

Other parties, groups, or individuals may place a candidate on the general election ballot by nominating petitions signed by the required number of voters in the district to be represented by that office.

What is a general election?

All candidates nominated either in the primary election or by petition appear on the ballot at the general election on the first Tuesday after the first Monday in November every even-numbered year. A candidate who did not win nomination in the primary election may not run in the general election. In a general election, voters may write in the names of persons for whom they wish to vote which do not appear on the ballot.

MINNESOTA VOTE FOR PRESIDENT SINCE 1860

Abbreviations of Political Parties

A	— American Party of Minn. (no candidate specified).	L	— Libertarian
AC	— Anderson Coalition	M'76P	— McCarthy '76 Principle
Am	— American	MnPeo	— Minnesota People's
C	— Communist	NGD	— National (Gold) Democratic
CP	— Citizens Party	P&F	— Peace and Freedom
D	— Democratic	Peo	— People's
DFL	— Democratic-Farmer-Labor	PO	— Public Ownership
D-Peo	— Democratic People's	Pro	— Prohibition
DSF	— Democratic (southern faction)	Prog	— Progressive
FL	— Farmer-Labor	R	— Republican
G	— Greenback	S	— Socialist
GL	— Greenback Labor	SD	— Socialist Democrat
I	— Independent	SIn	— Socialist Industrial
IDB	— International Development Bank	SL	— Socialist Labor
		SW	— Socialist Workers
In	— Industrial	U	— Union
InG	— Industrial Government	UL	— Union Labor
InL	— Industrial Labor	WC	— Workers Communist
IR	— Independent-Republican	WW	— Workers World

1860
Abraham Lincoln(R) 22,069
Stephen A. Douglas(D) 11,920
John C. Breckenridge(DSF) 748

1864
Abraham Lincoln(R) 25,055
George B. McClellan(D) 17,367

1868
Ulysses S. Grant(R) 43,722
Horatio Seymour(D) 28,096

1872
Ulysses S. Grant(R) 55,708
Horace Greeley(D) 35,211

1876
Rutherford B. Hayes(R) 72,955
Samuel J. Tilden(D) 48,587
Peter Cooper(G) 2,389
Green Clay Smith(Pro) 144

1880
James A. Garfield(R) 93,902
Winfield S. Hancock(D) 53,315
James B. Weaver(GL) 3,267

Neal Dow(Pro) 286

1884
James G. Blaine(R) 111,685
S. Grover Cleveland(D) 70,065
John P. St. John(Pro) 4,684
Benjamin F. Butler(G) 3,583

1888
Benjamin H. Harrison(R) 142,492
S. Grover Cleveland(D) 104,385
Clinton B. Fisk(Pro) 15,311
Alson J. Streeter(UL) 1,097

1892
Benjamin H. Harrison(R) 122,823
S. Grover Cleveland(D) 100,920
James B. Weaver(Peo) 29,313
John Bidwell(Pro) 14,182
James B. Weaver(Fusion Electors) . 107,077

1896
William McKinley(R) 193,503
William J. Bryan(D-Peo) 130,735
Joshua Levering(Pro) 4,339
John M. Palmer(NGD) 3,222
Charles H. Machett(SL) 954

1900

William McKinley(R)	190,461
William J. Bryan(D-Peo)	112,901
John G. Wooley(Pro)	8,555
Eugene V. Debs(SD)	3,065
Joseph R. Maloney(SL)	1,329

1904

Theodore Roosevelt(R)	216,651
Alton B. Parker(D)	55,187
Thomas E. Watson(Peo)	2,103
Eugene V. Debs(PO)	11,692
Silas C. Swallow(Pro)	6,253
Charles H. Corregan(SL)	974

1908

William H. Taft(R)	195,843
William J. Bryan(D)	109,401
Eugene W. Chafin(Pro)	11,107
Eugene V. Debs(PO)	14,527
Thomas L. Hisgen(I)	426

1912

William H. Taft(R)	64,334
Woodrow Wilson(D)	106,426
Eugene V. Debs(PO)	27,505
Eugene W. Chafin(Pro)	7,886
Elmer Reimer(SL)	2,212
Theodore Roosevelt(Prog)	125,856

1916

Charles E. Hughes(R)	179,544
Woodrow Wilson(D)	179,152
J. Frank Hanly(Pro)	7,793
Allan L. Benson(S)	20,117
Elmer Reimer(InL)	468
Edward J. Meier(Prog)	290

1920

Warren G. Harding(R)	519,421
James M. Cox(D)	142,994
William W. Cox(In)	5,828
Eugene V. Debs(S)	56,106
W.W. Watkins(Pro)	11,489

1924

Calvin Coolidge(R)	420,759
John W. Davis(D)	55,913
Frank F. Johns(SIn)	1,855
Robert M. LaFollette(I)	339,192
William Z. Foster(WC)	4,427

1928

Herbert Hoover(R)	560,977
Alfred E. Smith(D)	396,451
Verne L. Reynolds(In)	1,921
William Z. Foster(WC)	4,853
Norman M. Thomas(S)	6,774

1932

Herbert Hoover(R)	363,959
Franklin D. Roosevelt(D)	600,806
William Z. Foster(C)	6,101
Verne L. Reynolds(In)	770
Norman M. Thomas(S)	25,476
Jacob S. Coxey(FL)	5,731

1936

Alfred M. Landon(R)	350,461
Franklin D. Roosevelt(D)	698,811
John W. Aiken(In)	961
William Lemke(U)	74,296
Earl R. Browder(C)	2,711
Norman M. Thomas(S)	2,872

1940

Wendell L. Willkie(R)	596,274
Franklin D. Roosevelt(D)	644,196
John W. Aiken(In)	2,553
Norman M. Thomas(S)	5,454
Earl R. Browder(C)	2,711

1944

Thomas E. Dewey(R)	527,416
Franklin D. Roosevelt(D)	589,864
Edward A. Teichert(InG)	3,176
Norman M. Thomas(S)	5,073

1948

Thomas E. Dewey(R)	483,617
Harry S. Truman(DFL)	692,966
Edward A. Teichert(InG)	2,525
Farrell Dobbs(SW)	606
Henry A. Wallace(Prog)	27,866
Norman M. Thomas(S)	4,646

1952

Dwight D. Eisenhower(R)	763,211
Adlai E. Stevenson(DFL)	608,458
Eric Hass(InG)	2,383
Vincent Hallinan(Prog)	2,666
Farrell Dobbs(SW)	618
Stuart Hamblen(Pro)	2,147

1956

Adlai E. Stevenson(DFL)	617,525
Dwight D. Eisenhower(R)	719,302
Eric Hass(InG)	2,080
Farrell Dobbs(SW)	1,098

1960

John F. Kennedy(DFL)	779,933
Richard M. Nixon(R)	757,915
Farrell Dobbs(SW)	3,077
Eric Hass(InG)	962

1964

Lyndon B. Johnson(DFL)	991,117
Barry M. Goldwater(R)	559,624
Eric Hass(InG)	2,544
Clifton DeBerry(SW)	1,177

1968

Richard M. Nixon(R)	658,643
Hubert H. Humphrey(DFL)	857,738
George C. Wallace(Am)	68,931
Fred Halstead(SW)	808
Henning A. Blomen(InG)	285
Charlene Michell(C)	415
Leroy Eldridge Cleaver(P&F)	935
Eugene J. McCarthy(write-in votes)	585

1972

Richard M. Nixon(R)	898,269
George S. McGovern(DFL)	802,346
Louis Fisher(InG)	4,261
Linda Jenness(SW)	940
Gus Hall(C)	662
John G. Schmitz(Am)	31,407
Benjamin M. Spock(MnPeo)	2,805

Source: Minnesota Legislative Manual, 1985-86 and Secretary of State's Office.

1976

Gerald R. Ford(IR)	819,395
Jimmy Carter(DFL)	1,070,440
Peter Camejo(SW)	4,149
Roger L. MacBride(L)	3,529
Gus Hall(C)	1,092
Jules Levin(InG)	370
Thomas J. Anderson(Am)	13,592
Eugene J. McCarthy(M'76P)	35,490
Lyndon H. LaRouche(IDB)	543
Frank P. Zeidler(S)	354
Margaret Wright(Peo)	635

1980

No Candidates Specified (Am)	6,139
Jimmy Carter(DFL)	954,174
Ronald Reagan(IR)	873,241
Ed Clark(L)	31,593
Clifton DeBerry(SW)	711
Diedre Griswold(WW)	698
Gus Hall(C)	1,184
John B. Anderson(AC)	174,990
David McReynolds(S)	536
Barry Commoner(Cit)	8,407

1984

Ronald Reagan(IR)	1,032,603
Walter Mondale(DFL)	1,036,364
Mel Mason(SW)	3,180
David Bergland(L)	2,996
Lyndon LaRouche(I)	3,865
Gus Hall(C)	630
Ed Winn(WL)	260
Robert "Bob" Richards(AP)	2,377
Sonia Johnson(Cit)	1,219
Dennis Serrette(NA)	232

MINNESOTA VOTE FOR GOVERNOR SINCE 1857

Abbreviations of Political Parties

A	— Alliance	IProg	— Independent Progressive
AM	— American Party of Minnesota	IR	— Independent-Republican
Am	— American	L	— Libertarian
C	— Communist	M-Pop	— Midroad-Populist
D	— Democratic	N	— National
DFL	— Democratic-Farmer-Labor	Peo	— People's
D-Peo	— Democratic People's	PO	— Public Ownership
FL	— Farmer-Labor	Pro	— Prohibition
G	— Greenback	Prog	— Progressive
HG	— Honest Government 87	R	— Republican
I	— Independent	S	— Socialist
In	— Industrial	SA	— Savings Account
InG	— Industrial Government	SD	— Socialist Democrat
InGSL	— Industrial Government (Socialist Labor)	SIn	— Socialist Industrial
		SL	— Socialist Labor
InL	— Industrial Labor	SW	— Socialist Workers
		WC	— Workers Communist
		WL	—Workers League

1857

Henry H. Sibley(D)	17,790
Alexander Ramsey(R)	17,550
	35,340

1859

Alexander Ramsey(R)	21,335
George L. Becker(D)	17,582
	38,917

1861

Alexander Ramsey(R)	16,274
E.O. Hamblin(D)	10,448
	26,722

1863

Stephen Miller(R)	19,628
Henry T. Welles(D)	12,739
	32,367

1865

William R. Marshall(R)	17,318
Henry M. Rice(D)	13,842
	31,160

1867

William R. Marshall(R)	34,874
Charles E. Flandrau(D)	29,502
	64,376

1869

Horace Austin(R)	27,348
George L. Otis(D)	25,401
Daniel Cobb(Pro)	1,764
	54,513

1871

Horace Austin(R)	46,950
Winthrop Young(D)	30,376
Samuel Mayall(Pro)	846
	78,172

1873

Cushman K. Davis(R)	40,741
Ara Barton(D)	35,245
Samuel Mayall(Pro)	1,036
	77,022

1875

John S. Pillsbury(R)	45,073
D. L. Buell(D)	35,275
R. F. Humiston(Pro)	1,669
	84,017

1877

John S. Pillsbury(R)	57,071
William L. Banning(D)	39,147
William Meigher(G)	2,396
Austin Willey(Pro)	1,421
	100,035

1879

John S. Pillsbury(R)	57,524
Edmund Rice(D)	41,524
W. W. Satterlee(Pro)	2,868
William Meigher(G)	4,264
	106,180

1881

Lucius F. Hubbard(R)	65,025
Richard W. Johnson(D)	37,168
C. H. Roberts(G)	2,676
Isaac C. Stearns(Pro)	708
	105,577

1883

Lucius F. Hubbard(R)	72,462
Adolph Biermann(D)	58,251
Charles E. Holt(Pro)	4,924
	135,637

1886

Andrew R. McGill(R)	107,064
Albert A. Ames(D)	104,464
James E. Childs(Pro)	9,030
	220,558

1888

William R. Merriam(R)	134,355
Eugene M. Wilson(D)	110,251
Hugh Harrison(Pro)	17,026
	261,632

1890

William R. Merriam(R)	88,111
Thomas Wilson(D)	85,844
Sidney M. Owen(A)	58,513
James P. Pinkham(Pro)	8,424
	240,892

1892

Knute Nelson(R)	109,220
Daniel W. Lawler(D)	94,600
Ignatius Donnelly(Peo)	39,862
William J. Dean(Pro)	12,239
	255,921

1894
Knute Nelson(R)	147,943
George L. Becker(D)	53,584
Sidney M. Owen(Peo)	87,890
Hans S. Hilleboe(Pro)	6,832
	296,249

1896
David M. Clough(R)	165,806
John Lind(D-Peo)	162,254
William J. Dean(Pro)	5,154
A. A. Ames(I)	2,890
W. B. Hammond(S)	1,125
	337,229

1898
William H. Eustis(R)	111,796
John Lind(D-Poe)	131,980
George W. Higgins(Pro)	5,299
William B. Hammond(SL)	1,685
Lionel C. Long(M-Pop)	1,802
	252,562

1900
Samuel R. Van Sant(R)	152,905
John Lind(D-Peo)	150,651
Bernt B. Haugan(Pro)	5,430
Sylvester M. Fairchild(M-Pop) . . .	763
Thomas H. Lucas(SD)	3,546
Edward Kriz(SL)	886
	314,181

1902
Samuel R. Van Sant(R)	155,849
Leonard A. Rosing(D)	99,362
Thomas J. Meighen(Peo)	4,821
Charles Scanlon(Pro)	5,765
Jay E. Nash(S)	2,521
Thomas Van Lear(SL)	2,570
	270,888

1904
Robert C. Dunn(R)	140,130
John A. Johnson(D)	149,992
Charles W. Dorsett(Pro)	7,577
Jay E. Nash(PO)	5,810
A. W. M. Anderson(SL)	2,293
	303,802

1906
A. L. Cole(R)	96,162
John A. Johnson(D)	168,480
Charles W. Dorsett(Pro)	7,223
O. E. Loftus(PO)	4,646
	276,511

1908
Jacob F. Jacobson(R)	147,997
John A. Johnson(D)	175,136
George D. Haggard(Pro)	7,024
Beecher Moore(PO)	6,516
William W. Allen(I)	593
	337,266

1910
Adolph O. Eberhart(R)	164,185
James Gray(D)	103,779
J. F. Heiberg(Pro)	8,960
George E. Barrett(PO)	11,173
C. W. Brandborg(SL)	6,510
	295,627

1912
Adolph O. Eberhart(R)	129,688
Peter M. Ringdahl(D)	99,659
David Morgan(PO)	25,769
Engebret E. Lobeck(Pro)	29,876
Paul V. Collins(Prog)	33,455
	318,447

1914
William E. Lee(R)	143,730
Winfield S. Hammond(D)	156,304
Thomas J. Lewis(S)	17,225
Willis G. Calderwood(Pro)	18,582
Hugh T. Halbert(Prog)	3,553
Herbert Johnson(InL)	3,861
	343,255

1916
J. A. A. Burnquist(R)	245,841
Thomas P. Dwyer(D)	93,112
J. O. Bentall(S)	26,306
Thomas J. Anderson(Pro)	19,884
John P. Johnson(InL)	5,476
	390,619

1918
J. A. A. Burnquist(R)	166,515
Fred E. Wheaton(D)	76,793
L. P. Berot(S)	7,794
Olaf O. Stageberg(N)	6,648
David H. Evans(FL)	111,948
	369,698

1920

Jacob A. O. Preus(R)	415,805
Henrik Shipstead(I)	281,402
L. C. Hodgson(D)	81,293
Peter J. Sampson(S)	5,124
	783,624

1922

Jacob A. O. Preus(R)	309,756
Magnus Johnson(FL)	295,479
Edward Indrehus(D)	79,903
	685,138

1924

Theodore Christianson(R)	406,692
Floyd B. Olson(FL)	366,029
Carlos Avery(D)	49,353
Oscar Anderson(Sln)	3,876
Michael Ferch(IProg)	9,052
	835,002

1926

Theodore Christianson(R)	395,779
Magnus Johnson(FL)	266,845
Alfred Jaques(D)	38,008
	700,632

1928

Theodore Christianson(R)	549,857
Ernest Lundeen(FL)	227,193
Andrew Nelson(D)	213,734
Harris A. Brandborg(In)	3,279
J. O. Bentall(WC)	5,760
	999,823

1930

Raymond P. Chase(R)	289,528
Floyd B. Olson(FL)	473,154
Edward Indrehus(D)	29,109
Karl Reeve(C)	5,594
	797,385

1932

Earle Brown(R)	334,081
Floyd B. Olson(FL)	522,438
John E. Regan(D)	169,859
William Schneiderman(C)	4,807
John P. Johnson(In)	1,824
	1,033,009

1934

Floyd B. Olson(FL)	468,812
Martin A. Nelson(R)	396,359
John E. Regan(D)	176,928
Samuel K. Davis(C)	4,334
Arthur C. Townley(I)	4,454
	1,050,887

1936

Elmer A. Benson(FL)	680,342
Martin A. Nelson(R)	431,841
Earl Stewart(In)	7,996
	1,120,179

1938

Elmer A. Benson(FL)	387,263
Harold E. Stassen(R)	678,839
Thomas Gallagher(D)	65,875
John William Castle(In)	899
	1,132,876

1940

Harold E. Stassen(R)	654,686
Hjalmar Petersen(FL)	459,609
Edward Murphy(D)	140,021
John William Castle(In)	3,175
	1,257,491

1942

Harold E. Stassen(R)	409,800
Hjalmer Petersen(FL)	299,917
John D. Sullivan(D)	75,151
Martin Mackie(C)	5,082
Harris A. Brandborg(InG)	4,278
	794,228

1944

Edward J. Thye(R)	701,785
Byron G. Allen(DFL)	430,132
Gerald M. York(InG)	7,151
	1,138,468

1946

Luther W. Youngdahl(R)	519,067
Harold H. Barker(DFL)	349,565
Rudolph Gustafson(InGSL)	11,716
	880,348

1948

Luther W. Youngdahl(R)	643,572
Charles L. Halsted(DFL)	545,766
Rudolph Gustafson(InGSL)	6,598
Orville E. Olson(Prog)	14,950
	1,210,886

1950

Luther W. Youngdahl(R)	635,800
Harry H. Peterson(DFL)	400,637
Vernon G. Campbell(InGSL)	10,195
	1,046,632

1952

C. Elmer Anderson(R)	785,125
Orville L. Freeman(DFL)	624,480
Martin Fredrickson(Prog)	5,227
Eldrid H. Bauers(InGSL)	4,037
	1,418,869

1954

C. Elmer Anderson(R)	538,865
Orville L. Freeman(DFL)	607,099
Ross Schelin(InG)	5,453
	1,151,417

1956

Orville L. Freeman(DFL)	731,180
Ancher Nelsen(R)	685,196
Rudolph Gustafson(InG)	5,785
	1,422,161

1958

Orville L. Freeman(DFL)	658,326
George MacKinnon(R)	490,731
Arne Anderson(InG)	10,858
	1,159,915

1960

Orville L. Freeman(DFL)	760,934
Elmer L. Andersen(R)	783,813
Rudolph Gustafson(InG)	5,518
	1,550,265

1962

Karl F. Rolvaag(DFL)	619,842
Elmer L. Andersen(R)	619,751
William Braatz(InG)	7,234
	1,246,827

1966

Karl F. Rolvaag(DFL)	607,943
Harold LeVander(R)	680,593
Kenneth Sachs(InG)	6,522
	1,295,058

1970

Wendell R. Anderson(DFL)	737,921
Douglas M. Head(R)	621,780
Karl Heck(InG)	4,781
Jack Kirkham(write-in votes)	961
	1,365,443

1974

Wendell R. Anderson(DFL)	786,787
John W. Johnson(R)	367,722
Jane VanDeusen(SW)	9,232
Erwin Marquit(C)	3,570
Harry M. Pool(Am)	20,454
Richard R. Kleinow(L)	2,115
Genevieve Gunderson(InG)	2,720
James G. Miles(I)	60,150
	1,252,750

1978

Al Quie(IR)	830,019
Rudy Perpich(DFL)	718,244
Richard Pedersen(AM)	21,058
Jill Lakowske(SW)	6,287
Tom McDonald(HG)	4,254
Robin E. Miller(L)	3,689
Edwin C. Pommerening(SA)	2,043
	1,585,594

1982

Rudy Perpich(DFL)	1,049,104
Wheelock Whitney(IR)	711,796
Kathy Wheeler(SW)	10,332
Tom McDonald(HG)	7,984
Franklin Haws(L)	6,323
	1,785,539

1986

Rudy Perpich(DFL)	790,138
Cal Ludeman(IR)	606,755
W.Z. "Bill" Brust(WL)	4,208
Tom Jaax(SW)	3,151
Joseph A. Rohner(L)	3,852
	1,408,104

Source: Minnesota Legislative Manual, 1985-86; and Secretary of State's Office.

The Volstead Act

Andrew Volstead, a back-bencher from Goodhue County in Minnesota lent his name to the act passed by Congress which led to the Eighteenth Amendment, prohibiting the manufacture, sale and transportation of alcoholic beverages. In 1919 this ushered in an era of illegal moonshining, bootlegging and the organization of the worst and most powerful criminal elements in the nations history.

The "noble experiment" failed in its aim to stamp out the hated saloons and legislate morality. Though federal agents raided stills and speakeasys, demon rum continued to be made and sold everywhere—Minnesota 13 from Stearns county was sought after as a quality product—and arrests in Minneapolis for drunkenness rose from 2546 in 1902 to 7294 in 1925.

All this came to an end when the Twenty-First Amendment was repealed in 1933.

★ ★ ★

Minnesotan Frank Billings Kellogg was appointed Secretary of State on March 5, 1915 by Calvin Coolidge.

Seth Huntington of Minneapolis designed the reverse side of the special Bicentennial half dollar, winning a prize of $5000 and numismatic immortality.

Another Minnesotan, James Earle Fraser of Winona, designed a famous coin—the Indianhead and buffalo nickel. Issued in 1913, the five-cent piece bore the face of Chief Two Gun Whitecalf, who posed for the portrait.

Taxes

Through the state government, money is taxed and pooled from a wide range of statewide sources and redistributed in response to different statewide needs. For example, the state has equalized educational opportunities in wealthy areas and poor through a system of statewide taxes and aids. And the statewide community shifts funds geographically to equalize the quality of roads and accessibility between major centers and remote areas. Flows of government funds help to build, manage, and maintain the state's cities, towns, transportation systems, and communication networks. Government enterprises not only help to create, operate, and control the settlements, but they also continually respond to changes in the settlement pattern and natural resources.

THE TAX BASE

Individual income is the main component of the state tax base. It is both the direct source of income taxes and the basis for property improvement and consumer purchases. The range of county average incomes per capita in Minnesota is wide. Only seven or eight counties are normally above the state mean, and the lowest county average, in Aitkin, is less than half that of the highest, Hennepin. Higher income counties are generally those with the most productive soils and the largest towns and cities — hence the most prosperous agriculture areas and the main centers of business, the professions, and organized labor.

The pattern is still more uneven if personal income is compared with the number of school children to be educated, mainly because some low-income counties have relatively large school-age populations.

Retail trade povides the basis for the sales tax and numerous excise taxes. Even more than income, the sources of taxes on trade are unevenly distributed on the map of the state. Retail trade is concentrated in a limited number of counties where the main trade centers are located. Among those centers, per capita sales are high not only in the regions of high income but also in the places that serve large numbers of vacationers.

Land and buildings are the base for property taxes. The pattern of assessed value reflects the level of investment in improvements and construction. Intensity of development declines sharply as one moves outward from the most urbanized counties. In rural areas average land value declines northward as the average length and warmth of the growing season decline, and westward as the risk of summer drought increases. Although the patterns are similar if one compares assessed valuation with total population or with school-age population—the major beneficiary from property taxes—the difference between wealthy and poor counties is not quite so large. The property tax base from nonresidential developments is more unevenly distributed than the total property tax base. Taxable utility properties tend to reflect not only the over-all settlement pattern but also the locations of a few very large electric generating stations. Value of commercial land and buildings is heavily concentrated in the major commercial and industrial cities.

State and Local Government Revenue

	State Revenue From Own Sources		State Taxes and Charges			
			Individual income tax	Corporate income tax	General sales tax	Other
Year	Millions of dollars*	As percent of personal income	Millions of dollars*	Millions of dollars*	Millions of dollars*	Millions of dollars*
1942	114	5.7	10	7	0	96
1950	219	5.2	37	16	0	166
1970	1243	8.5	346	80	196	622
1977	2916	10.3	957	258	467	1234

*Not adjusted for inflation.
Sources: U.S. Bureau of the Census, various reports; U.S. Bureau of Economic Analysis.

STATE REVENUES

Income tax collection rates reflect not only the geographic variations in personal income but also the progressive structure of the tax. For example, Hennepin County, with about 2.4 times the per capita income of Aitkin County, generated about three times the per capita income tax in 1976. Sales tax collections are high in the counties with major trade centers and those with greater vacation traffic. Corporate income tax collections, a much smaller part of the state's revenue, come still more heavily from the urban business centers—especially the Twin Cities, the main concentration of corporate headquarters in the Upper Midwest.

Taxes on income and general sales account for nearly three-fourths of the state's tax collections. The remainder comes almost entirely from taxes on gasoline and alcoholic beverage sales, licenses for motor vehicles and operators, and iron ore taxes.

Total state tax collections, excluding iron ore, tend to be relatively high per dollar of personal income in counties where there is greater dependence on the sales tax. In general those are counties with relatively low personal income, counties with a large resort and seasonal home population, counties with large, diversified trade and service centers, or some combination of those characteristics.

States taxes collected in each county come out of the same tax base that supports local taxes, and through state aids, in turn, the state taxes make a significant addition to the local tax effort. Local general governments include counties, towns, and cities. They vary widely in the taxes they collect per dollar of personal income. The reasons for such wide variation are probably known in each individual locality but have not been analyzed statewide. Most striking is the fact that local governments in some low-income counties make high local tax efforts—for example, Cass and Aitkin. Meanwhile, counties with similar per capita incomes and urbanization differ considerably in their tax rates for general local government. Large differences between neighboring communities seem to have gone unquestioned.

School district tax rates show similar patterns of variation. Part of the differences between school districts stems from chance variations in the timing of new building projects and the resulting differences in debt service costs. But again it is especially striking that in some of the poorest counties the local tax effort equalled or surpassed that in some of the wealthiest counties. In general, the wealthier counties, or those unaffected by iron ore taxes, tend to supply a higher percentage of their local government revenue from local taxes. The counties which generate smaller percentages of their revenue from their own sources—mainly in the north—are more dependent upon state aids.

STATE AIDS AND DIRECT EXPENDITURES

State aids serve to narrow or eliminate the gaps between poor and wealthy counties. In general, the more sparsely settled or the lower the average income in a county, the higher the state aids paid to its local governments. Conversely, the higher the personal income and the more compact the settlement pattern, the higher the fraction of general local government expenditures raised through local taxes.

EDUCATION

The same general pattern holds for state aids to local school districts. Higher aids go to more sparsely settled or lower income areas, lower aids to districts with more compact settlements or higher income. The state functions as a community to pool its resources and attempt to buy equal educational opportunities for people in widely different locations and economic circumstances.

Because of the leveling effect of state aids, expenditures per pupil in a very large majority of school districts are within about 10 percent of the state-wide mean. But some districts deviate widely from the typical level. Unusually high expenditures may result from first, a large local tax base from iron mining, urban commercial or industrial property, or prime farm land, in combination with an average or below-average size school-age population; and second, unusually large aid payments —especially federal aids—because of a concentration of minority or low-income households.

ROADS

The County State Aid Highway fund (CSAH) is an important mechanism to transfer money from state to local government. The funds come from a part of the state taxes on gasoline and motor vehicles. In the 1977 fiscal year it amounted to 84.2 million dollars. There were slightly more than 60 thousand lane-miles of County State Aid Highways on which to spend the money. Meanwhile the actual share of highway user taxes generated in each county is not measured; but one can estimate it from the United States Census of Business data on the share of the state's total gasoline service station business done in each county. One can then compare the share of the CSAH allotment fund that comes from each county with the share that goes back to each county.

Most counties receive more from the fund than they generate. A few generate much more than they receive. The parts of the CSAH system that are profitable are those that serve the main urban centers and those that feed most immediately into the main transportation corridors: Twin Cities-Fargo, Twin Cities-Cedar Rapids-Des Moines, and Twin Cities-Chicago.

In effect, everyone is buying access to everyone else: cities to farm suppliers and markets, farmers to city markets and suppliers, and much more. The state collects revenues where users are the most numerous, then spreads expenditures across the entire system.

WELFARE

State income maintenance expenditures, for various welfare and assistance programs, redistribute income to individuals and households. The money transferred in these direct payments is less than the amount transferred through indirect aids to school districts. The geographical pattern reflects the distribution of low income and elderly people on the population maps of the state—areas of least urbanization, marginal farmland, and heavy outmigration.

Federal payments for various social services supplement state income maintenance payments. Social security payments are a major part of the federal outlay.

Local social service and welfare payments also supplement state aids, although they equal a far smaller fraction of personal income than the state welfare payments in each county. The geographic pattern reflects many apparently capricious differences in local effort from one county to another, although there is a general tendency for the highest efforts to be in counties with relatively large elderly or low-income populations.

JOBS

State payrolls also serve to redistribute income among the eighty-seven counties. State payrolls are highest in absolute terms in the Twin Cities area, mainly because of the state capitol and the major university campus. On the other hand, the state payroll accounts for exceptionally large shares of personal income in some counties elsewhere in the state as a result of the locations of state universities and community colleges, hospitals, correctional institutions, district highway headquarters, and regional offices of other major state departments. The state payroll reinforces at least two-thirds of the twenty-six major trade centers outside the Twin Cities area.

Public jobs exceed 20 percent of the total in sixteen counties. Each of these counties has a relatively small urban population and employment base, and a relatively important state institution within its boundaries.

An important component of public employment is the state higher education system. Those campuses concentrate state and federal as well as private expenditures in selected urban areas.

NATIONAL COMPARISONS

In 1975 Minnesota was one of nineteen states whose citizens received less money from federal expenditures than they paid in federal taxes. Relatively low defense spending and low federal government employment were the main reasons for the deficit. While eighteenth in population, Minnesota ranked twenty-eighth in per capita volume of defense contracts, forty-seventh in per capita outlay for defense salaries, and twenty-seventh in federal government employment.

Highest federal aids per capita have been paid mainly to western states. But the trend since 1960 has favored states in the eastern half of the nation, especially those with large metropolitan populations and industrial employment.

STATE AND LOCAL BUDGETS

In 1975 Minnesota had the highest state income tax per dollar of personal income of all fifty states. Minnesota and Pennsylvania were tied for the rank of fourth highest in corporate income tax collections per dollar of personal income. The picture was different outside the income tax field. The state general sales tax rate in 1975 was well below the national median and near or well below neighboring Midwest states. Minnesota property tax collections per dollar of personal income ranked twenty-second among the fifty states and below neighboring Midwest states other than North Dakota.

Nationwide, about one-third of all state and local revenue came from service charges and miscellaneous taxes other than those on income, general retail sales, and property. Examples of miscellaneous taxes and charges include sporting licenses, income from publicly-owned liquor stores and recreational facilities, and special taxes on mineral extraction. Minnesota ranked seventeenth among the fifty states in this category of taxes. If taxes on iron ore were omitted, Minnesota would drop to twenty-second. Local natural resources permit some states to tap into the national income stream by taxing mineral wealth that happens to be concentrated in their domain, and Minnesota has been historically one of those.

When all revenues from state sources were combined, Minnesota taxes and charges per dollar of personal income in 1975 were seventh highest in the nation. Combined state and local taxes were higher than those in all other states except Vermont and New York. Minnesota's state and local public debt were near the national median in 1975. Thus the overall Minnesota picture in 1975 included high combined state and local taxes, with average indebtedness and major reliance on a progressive personal income tax.

STATE AIDS TO LOCAL GOVERNMENTS

Minnesota's high state taxes are the result of high state aid payments. In 1975, if state aids had been reduced to the average rate for the other forty-nine states, and other expenditures had remained unchanged, the Minnesota state and local tax rate per dollar of personal income would have been at the national median rather than very near the top. Of course, schools and other enterprises in poorer localities would have suffered.

State government's ultimate revenue—what state agencies actualy spend on state government and services—was slighlty below the national average. The state actually ranked twenty-sixth in disposable state government revenue from all sources, after paying out state aids. Minnesota state government spent an amount equal to 75 percent of the total revenue it raised through state taxes. (In fact, 56 percent of state tax revenue goes to state aids, and the rest of state expenditures are paid from federal aids which the state retains.)

Only five other states retained and spent as low a share of their revenues. Half the state governments spent more than they raised from taxes and charges, making up the difference from federal aids. Most states apparently have more centralized control of state tax revenue, and in most states local governments depend more upon their own local taxes and charges.

Thus Minnesota local governments are exceptionally dependent on the state. The increased use of state aids to pay local government costs in Minnesota reflects deliberate policies: first an attempt to equalize educational and other opportunities by shifting support from local to statewide sources, second, an attempt to keep management responsibility in the local areas, third, an historic commitment to education as a long-term investment for the community, and fourth, a shift from "almost sole dependence on the property tax to other and more equitable taxes to raise the increased revenue needs of state and local governments in our modern society."[*]

[*]Francis M. Boddy, "Minnesota's Economy: 1900-1977," *Commercial West*, 151:15 (April 10, 1976), P. 138.

Source: Atlas of Minn. Resources and Settlement 1980

Minnesota's varied seasons provide entertainment in sunshine or snow. The hot air balloon race is one of the dozens of activities held during the St. Paul Winter Carnival.

Education

POST-SECONDARY EDUCATION

The University of Minnesota was born in 1851 when a charter was passed and signed by the governor of the territory to authorize an institution of higher learning. But it was 1869 before college classes were finally begun.

A major factor in the university's rebirth was the Morrill Act, signed into law by President Lincoln in 1862. This "land grant act" gave each state a grant of land within its borders, the income from which was to be used in providing education for its people - especially in the areas of agriculture and mechanic art.

In 1867 the preparatory school opened its doors. Following a major reorganization in 1868, the university finally got underway as an institution of higher learning in 1869. The first class that fall numbered 18 students. The faculty totaled nine.

From these faltering origins the university has grown to become one of the largest and strongest universities in the country with an enrollment of 56,443 fulltime students on five state campuses.

Besides campuses in Minneapolis and St. Paul, the university has campuses in Duluth, part of the university system since 1947; in Morris, opened in 1960; a technical college in Crookston, opened in 1966, and a technical college in Waseca, established in 1971.

The University of Minnesota was seventh among public institutions in the U.S. and 17th among all public and private institutions according to a National Academy of Sciences ranking of arts and sciences done in the mid-1980s. (The ranking does not include professional schools or agricultural-related fields.)

Top-ranking programs at the university include diverse areas such as chemical engineering, mechanical engineering, journalism, geography, economics, psychology and architecture.

A 12-member Board of Regents governs the university. The legislature chooses one regent from each of Minnesota's eight congressional districts and four from the state at large. One at-large regent must be a university student or have been graduated from the university within the five years prior to election. Regents serve without pay for six-year terms.

Funding for the university comes from state and federal appropriations; student tuition and fees, department earnings; gifts, grants and contracts; auxiliary services; hospital earnings and endowments and investment income.

Tuition varies, but a typical College of Liberal Arts student on the Twin Cities or Duluth campus taking 14 to 18 credits would pay tuition of $561 per quarter plus the student services fee in 1986-87. (The student services fee was $95.42 in the Twin Cities and $79.75 in Duluth.)

In the late 1970s and early 80s the state's bad economic condition caused large budget cuts at the university, as well as increases in tuition. As the university heads into the late 80s the administration is faced with hard choices about which departments to fund and where to place economic emphasis, especially in the areas of high technology which attract top students to the state.

To help the legislature, regents, and the public, make those choices, university president Kenneth Keller formulated Commitment to Focus, a plan that calls for the university to sharpen its focus and improve quality by emphasizing activities that it can best carry out and phasing out activities that can be carried out more effectively by other public educational institutions.

Despite President Keller's explanations of the plan through much of 1987, the plan remains controversial. Some legislators perceive it as elitist; parents worry that the plan's call for fewer undergraduates will mean their children will not be accepted at the university.

Commitment to Focus is sure to be debated until the end of this decade.

Minnesota's post-secondary educational system also includes 59 public institutions on 64 campuses throughout the state governed by the University of Minnesota Board of Regents, the State University Board, the State Board for Community Colleges and the State Board for Vocational-Technical Education. These public universities, community colleges and area vocational-technical institutes serve more than 170,000 students from freshman through graduate levels. An additional 26,000 students are enrolled in self-supporting extension classes.

Community colleges have been part of education in Minnesota since the early 1900's when they were established by local school districts. As their influence grew, the Minnesota State Legislature, in 1963, created a state-operated Community College System to begin July 1, 1964. Enrollment has grown from less than 4,000 students in 1964 to more than 58,000 served by 18 community colleges during 1983-84.

The Minnesota Community College System offers education that students can afford. Tuition, including fees, for a Minnesota resident during 1985-86 school year is $26.00 per credit. A full-time student carrying 15 credits pays $390.00 per academic quarter. Reciprocal agreements with neighboring states permit residents of those states to pay tuition rates no higher than Minnesota rates. Tuition for all other students is $52 per credit or $780.00 per quarter. A student can expect books and supplies to cost an additional $150 to $250 per year.

Close to half the state's high school graduates enroll in a post-secondary institution the next fall. About 6 to 8 percent of Minnesota high school graduates enter schools outside the state, resulting in an overall participation rate of 55 percent.

Minnesota also boasts 23 private four-year colleges, four private junior colleges, 10 private professional schools and more than 50 private vocational schools.

Of the 37 private colleges and professional schools, 17 were founded by 1900. More than 50,000 students, or about 21 percent of the state's enrollment in post-secondary vocational and higher education, attend a private institution.

Private institutions in Minnesota offer about 36 percent of the academic and vocational programs available in the state.

FACTS ABOUT THE UNIVERSITY OF MINNESOTA

ENROLLMENT (Fall Quarter 1986)

Twin Cities	Men	Women	Total
Agriculture	578	354	932
Biological Sciences	180	152	332
Dental Hygiene		49	49
Dentistry	303	118	421
Education	774	1,579	2,353
Forestry	240	74	314
General College	1,766	1,222	2,988
Graduate School	4,566	3,406	7,972
Home Economics	131	1,189	1,320
Law	451	329	780
Liberal Arts	8,124	8,705	16,829
Management	862	674	1,536
Medical School	1,183	751	1,934
Medical Technology	10	43	53
Mortuary Science	53	11	64
Nursing	36	296	332
Occupational Therapy	4	65	69
Pharmacy	136	185	321
Physical Therapy	13	50	63
Public Health	65	192	257
Technology	4,610	1,058	5,668
University College	52	73	125
Veterinary Medicine	149	145	294
Total Twin Cities	24,286	20,720	45,006
Duluth			
Business and Economics	892	651	1,543
Education	494	782	1,276
Fine Arts	137	170	307
Graduate School	92	90	182
Liberal Arts	2,215	1,663	3,878
Medicine	59	33	92
Social Development	4	19	23
Total Duluth	3,893	3,408	7,301
Crookston	598	615	1,213
Morris	855	919	1,774
Waseca	496	653	1,149
Total Collegiate	30,128	26,315	56,443
Extension Classes			18,605
Grand Total			**75,048**

MINORITY ENROLLMENT

All campuses, 3,353

Asian and Pacific Island, 1,650

Black, 881

Hispanic, 472

American Indian or Alaskan, 350

FINANCIAL INFORMATION

1985-86 Income by Source

State Appropriations	$329,565,000
Federal Appropriations	13,431,000
Student Tuition & Fees	113,970,000
Department Earnings	56,181,000
Gifts, Grants, Contracts	226,543,000
Auxiliary Services Earnings	89,049,000
Hospital Earnings	169,226,000
Endowments & Investment Income	34,310,000
Total	$1,032,275,000

1985-86 Expenditures by Function

Education & General Expense	$697,362,000
Auxiliary & Self-Balancing Funds	256,713,000
Student Aid	36,400,000
Other Transfers	11,249,000
Total	$1,001,724,000

DEGREES GRANTED

Students may earn undergraduate and graduate degrees in more than 250 fields of study. Seventy percent of all graduates stay in Minnesota for their first job.

Total degrees awarded through June 1986—397,390
(Including Ph.D.'s)
Doctor of philosophy degrees awarded through June 1986—16,518

Degrees awarded in 1985-86—10,470 (including Ph.D.'s)
Doctor pf philosophy degrees awarded in 1985-86—549

ADMISSIONS POLICY

Increased preparation requirements for entering baccalaureate programs, including a specified core curriculum, will take effect September 1991. Students will be expected to have completed certain courses in high school; those lacking in the core courses will be able to make them up in several ways. Individual colleges will continue to specify grade and test score requirements for admission.

MINNESOTA COMMUNITY COLLEGES

College	Date Opened
Twin Cities Metropolitan Area	
Anoka-Ramsey Community College	1965
11200 Mississippi Boulevard	
Coon Rapids, MN 55433	
612/427-2600	
Cambridge Center	
West Highway 95	
Cambridge, MN 55008	
612/689-1536	
Inver Hills Community College	1970
8445 College Trail	
Inver Grove Heights, MN 55075	
612/455-9621	
Lakewood Community College	1967
3401 Century Avenue	
White Bear Lake, MN 55110	
612/779-3200	
Minneapolis Community College	1965
1501 Hennepin Avenue	
Minneapolis, MN 55403	
612/341-7000	
Normandale Community College	1968
9700 France Avenue South	
Bloomington, MN 55431	
612/830-9300	
North Hennepin Community College	1966
7411 - 85th Avenue North	
Brooklyn Park, MN 55445	
612/424-0811	

Arrowhead Community College Region

Hibbing Community College
1515 East 25th Street
Hibbing, MN 55746
218/262-6700

1916

Itasca Community College
1851 East Highway 169
Grand Rapids, MN 55744
218/327-1760

1922

Mesabi Community College*
905 West Chestnut Street
Virginia, MN 55792
218/749-7700

1918

Rainy River Community College
Highway 11-71 & 15th Street
International Falls, MN 56649
218/285-7722

1967

Vermilion Community College
1900 East Camp Street
Ely, MN 55731
218/365-3256

1922

Clearwater Community College Region

Brainerd Community College
College Drive at SW 4th Street
Brainerd, MN 56401
218/828-2525

1938

Fergus Falls Community College
1414 College Way
Fergus Falls, MN 56537
218/739-7500

1960

Northland Community College
Highway 1 East
Thief River Falls, MN 56701
218/681-2181

1965

Southern and Western Minnesota

Austin Community College
1600 NW Eighth Avenue
Austin, MN 55912
507/433-0508

1940

Rochester Community College   1915
Highway 14 East
Rochester, MN 55901
507/285-7210

Willmar Community College   1962
County Road 5, P.O. Box 797
Willmar, MN 56201
612/231-5102

Worthington Community College   1936
1450 College Way
Worthington, MN 56187
507/372-2107

*Eveleth and Virginia merged to become Mesabi in 1966

MINNESOTA PRIVATE COLLEGES

Academic Charges for 1987-88

	Tuition and Fees	Room and Board	Total
Augsburg College	$7,385	$2,830	$10,215
Bethel College	$7,100	$2,870	$9,970
Carleton College	$11,015	$2,625	$13,640
College of St. Benedict	$6,730	$2,635	$9,365
College of St. Catherine	$7,026	$2,600	$9,626
College of St. Scholastica	$6,639	$2,634	$9,273
College of St. Teresa	$6,776	$2,540	$9,316
College of St. Thomas	$6,833	$2,735	$9,568
Concordia College-Moorhead	$6,755	$2,145	$8,900
Concordia College-St. Paul	$5,610	$2,295	$7,905
Gustavus Adolphus College	$8,425	$2,375	$10,800
Hamline University	$8,075	$2,915	$10,990
Macalester College	$9,730	$3,050	$12,780
Minneapolis College of Art and Design	$6,940	$2,500	$9,440
St. John's University	$6,730	$2,900	$9,630
St. Mary's College	$6,710	$2,650	$9,360
St. Olaf College	$8,215	$2,535	$10,750

PERCENT OF PUBLIC HIGH SCHOOL GRADUATES ENROLLED IN EDUCATIONAL PROGRAMS ONE YEAR AFTER GRADUATION, 1975 THROUGH 1981

Class of	Four-Year Colleges	Community Colleges	Vocational Schools	Total	Class of	Four-Year Colleges	Community Colleges	Vocational Schools	Total
1975	27.1%	9.5%	12.8%	49.4%	1979	30.7%	8.3%	14.0%	53.0%
1976	31.4%	7.2%	13.3%	51.9%	1980	32.2%	9.2%	14.6%	56.0%
1977	30.9%	7.0%	13.5%	51.4%	1981	32.6%	9.0%	15.3%	56.9%
1978	29.5%	7.3%	14.1%	50.9%					

	Percentage Enrolled In:			

Source: Information on Minn. High School Graduates for 1982-83, Minn. Dept. of Education, Education Statistics Section, Apr., 1984.

Governance—Minnesota State Board for Community Colleges

The Minnesota State Board for Community Colleges is the governing Board for Minnesota Community Colleges and consists of nine members appointed by the Governor with the advice and consent of the Senate. The Chancellor is appointed by the State Board for Community Colleges.

Minnesota State Board for Community Colleges

Congressional District	Board Member
1	Franklin Iossi
2	James B. Collier, Jr.
3	Toyse Kyle
4	Clarence Harris
5	Richard Niemiec
6	Lee Antell
7	Arleen Nycklemoe
8	Pierre Mattei
Student Representative	Rebecca Sawyer
Chancellor	Gerald W. Christenson

Women
in the History
of Minnesota

"History as a subject has been confined chiefly to war, politics and diplomacy. Because women have been excluded from all three, they have been excluded from history."

That's a statement from Gretchen Kreuter, past president of Women Historians of the Midwest. Thanks to organizations such as these, women historians are compiling the story of Minnesota women and their contributions to the state.

That story begins in the 18th century, during the era of fur trading and exploration of the area that would become Minnesota. And it begins with Native American women, the proud women of the Chippewa (Ojibway) and Sioux (Dakota).

"The role of the Indian women has been obscured by generations of prejudice, misunderstanding and false stereotypes," Kreuter wrote in an article published in the 1975-1976 Legislative Manual.

In Native American family life, roles of homemaker and mother were held in dignity and honor. A woman's value, and esteem for her, increased as she got older. And although local customs varied, the women participated in tribal politics.

It was the skilled labor of women, Kreuter says, that processed the skins and hides needed for shelter, clothing and later for the fur trade. The woman's skills helped determine the trading value of many pelts and gave the women of the band an important voice in the business of exchange.

Women also made pottery, wove baskets and mats, gathered fuel, made maple sugar, collected and preserved wild foods, planted gardens and cooperated with the men in fishing, harvesting wild rice and building canoes and houses.

The men were often away for long periods and all the necessary tasks were left to women.

French traders and trappers of the Great Lakes region depended upon Native American women as guides and mediators and there was often inter-marriage.

But as the tribes became Christianized and contact with Europeans increased, the Native American women found their former roles diminished. European men did not understand Indian culture and the important place of women in the tribe.

The first white women in Minnesota territory were wives of missionaries and wives of farmers. These women, who were their husbands' partners, had to adapt to primitive living conditions.

The farmer's wife faced never-ending work that included making soap and candles, washing, churning butter, weaving blankets, mending clothes and sometimes pitching in to help her husband with outdoor jobs as they fought to change forest and prairie to field and farm.

Although they kept busy, these pioneer women had to cope with loneliness and insecurity, especially in difficult times of sickness and childbirth.

For those living during the Sioux wars of the early 1860s, there were fears of Indian attacks.

But there was entertainment in the pioneer women's lives too. As soon as churches were established they became centers of community activities. The American lyceum movement spread to the frontier and women could attend performances.

By 1850 Minnesota was fundamentally agricultural and the Patrons of Husbandry, better known as the Grange, was formed in 1867 as a brotherhood of farmers. Caroline Hall, a relative of the Grange founder, suggested the organization admit women. At Grange meetings the lonely wives of farmers found companionship and a sense of sharing problems. In return, the women made enormous contributions to the educational and social functions of the Grange.

In fact, women made many educational and social contributions to Minnesota. Women historians say they find again and again in their research the importance of "woman as culture bearer" in Minnesota history.

It was women who were to transmit values, whether in education, the arts, social service or healing. That they also fought to influence values in labor and politics -areas where tradition did not put them - says a great deal about Minnesota women and their perseverance.

EDUCATION

Minnesota's first teacher was Harriet Bishop (1817-1883), sent by the New England National Popular Education Society which supplied women teachers to frontier schools. She arrived in 1847 and opened the first permanent school in the region, a one-room log cabin covered with bark.

Bishop and other early teachers were expected, Gretchen Kreuter says, "to be mothers and nurturers, transmitters of white culture and religious missionaries all for very little money."

As education became officially structured around 1858, however, women were ignored and left out of decision-making as men took control of the system.

Toward the end of the 19th century there was much concern in the medical profession and among lay people about whether or not "overeducation" could hurt females, either physically or mentally. Some felt too much education made women contract brain fever or go crazy.

So educators decided to teach women what was "appropriate" - skills they would use in their own sphere of influence, the home. Domestic science courses for girls were introduced. But the women who taught these courses were paid less than the men who taught manual arts classes for boys.

In 1875 women got the right to vote and hold office in school elections in Minnesota and in the years that followed some were elected and re-elected to county superintendencies and school boards.

In 1910 Minneapolis women teachers formed their own organization to serve as a lobbying and pressure group. And in early meetings of the Minnesota Education Association women secured passage of an equal pay resolution.

Among the most distinguished teacher-administrators of the late 19th century was Isabel Lawrence of St. Cloud. A leader in the child-study movement, she became superintendent of the model school in 1878 and influenced its developments.

Despite the controversy about "overeducated" women going crazy, women were a familiar sight on college campuses by the late 1890s, as the first wave of feminism convinced young women they could make contributions to society through higher education.

Three buildings at the University of Minnesota are named for influencial women educators.

Maria L. Sanford (1836-1920) was Minnesota's apostle of culture and patriotism. She was professor of history at Swarthmore college, the first woman to hold that rank in America, then professor of rhetoric at the University of Minnesota.

Ada Comstock (1876-1973) went from teaching and administrative posts at the University of Minnesota to become dean of Smith College and then president of Radcliffe College.

Louise M. Powell (1871-1943) was the first director of the first collegiate school of nursing in the world, established at the University of Minnesota in 1909.

These first women in higher education were determined to make their influence felt and in 1889 St. Paul women established one of the first chapters in the state of American Association of University Women.

In 1905 the Sisters of St. Joseph founded the College of St. Catherine in St. Paul, the nation's first fully accredited Catholic women's college and the first to have a Phi Beta Kappa key.

During the Depression of the 1930s, women who wanted professional employment in education were told they were taking men's jobs. Many school systems established regulations forbidding married women to teach.

Yet women continued to teach in one-room schoolhouses, in city high schools and the state teachers colleges, even though salaries continued to decline.

It wasn't until 1972 that the Minnesota State Department of Education issued guidelines eliminating sex discrimination.

With the coming of the women's movement in the 1970s, there was concern about sexism in textbooks. Groups like the Emma Willard Task Force of Minneapolis helped bring about a State Department of Education order requesting elimination of sex bias in books and teaching material.

A new dimension was added to the state education scene in 1958 when the University of Minnesota started the nation's first Continuing Education for Women program. Started as a reaction to the Russian Sputnik space shot, as a way to get mature women back to school, the program now offers between 400 and 500 classes and 20 to 30 seminars and workshops to 4,500 women students each year.

THE ARTS

For both Native American and pioneer women, crafts were the earliest expression of the arts. Indian women did quill work, beadwork and basketry and their skills were a source or pride. The pioneer women often combined art and craft in practical objects - quilts, for instance.

Women have served as administrators, lobbyists and fund-raisers in musical, theatrical and artistic organizations. Gretchen Kreuter says that as the state became settled, the middle class measured "civilization" by how the arts were flourishing, and this was women's responsibility.

In 1852 the women of the Episcopal Church in St. Paul raised money for the first church organ in the territory.

St. Paul women organized the Ladies' Musicale, later the Schubert Club, in 1882. Minneapolis women founded the Thursday Musicale in 1892 and Duluth's Matinee Musicale was organized in 1900.

Early in the 20th century the Minnesota Federation of Women's Clubs lobbied successfully for the formation of a state art commission and worked to establish libraries in many state cities and towns.

In the Twin Cities today, virtually every arts organization is bolstered by a volunteer group, most of them made up of women. Fund-raising is one of their biggest jobs and they do it by sponsoring balls and other social events. One of the most successful is Women's Association of the Minnesota Orchestra (WAMSO) which raised $218,750 for the orchestra in 1980.

One of the must illustrious Minnesota artists was Wanda Gag (1893-1946), painter, lithographer, author and illustrator of children's books. She became nationally recognized as a maker of fine prints.

Verna Scott of the University of Minnesota established the University Artists Course in 1919. In 1930 she became manager of the Minneapolis Symphony Orchestra.

In June of 1980, 400 people attended a testimonial dinner for Meridel LeSueur, 80, who has been writing about oppressed and helpless women since the 1930s.

Other notable Minnesota women writers include Maud Hart Lovelace, Margaret Culkin Banning, Grace Flandrau and Carol Rye Brink and Judith Guest.

In the dance world Loyce Houlton and Nancy Hauser lead nationally-known and respected companies.

SOCIAL SERVICE AND MEDICINE

Modern government provides services for the elderly, the poor and the sick. But in the 19th century these services were provided by private social agencies and in most cases the staffs and volunteers were women. Helping the less fortunate was one of the acceptable activities women could engage in outside the home. What nobody foresaw was that as the women came in contact with needy people and witnessed exploitation of women and children, they would demand government begin to take responsibility. They became politically active as they pressed for social legislation.

In 1867 a group of St. Paul church women established a home "for the friendless" which eventually became the Protestant Home for senior citizens.

Nuns started some of these charitable institutions, including St. Joseph's Hospital in St. Paul, founded in 1854.

In 1887 Dr. Martha G. Ripley, an ardent feminist, founded Maternity Hospital in Minneapolis for use by the city's unwed mothers. Articles of incorporation said the medical department was to be under the care and control of female physicians. The hospital gave outstanding care until it was closed in 1956.

Catheryne Cooke Gilman was the leading spirit in founding the Women's Cooperative Alliance, an organization which was at its peak in the 1920s, dedicated to protecting young women and children in Minneapolis from the evils of the city, and confronting prejudices of the male-dominated legal system, especially its handling of prostitutes.

Other important women in social services were Gertrude Brown, first director of Phyllis Wheatley House in Minneapolis; I. Myrtle Carden of St. Paul's Hallie Q. Brown House, and Sister Giovanni, who has fought government at several levels on behalf of the Hispanic community on St. Paul's West Side.

THE VOTE TO
CRIMINALS
LUNATICS
IDIOTS AND WOMEN
IS THIS
CHIVALRY

Minnesota women have a long tradition of political involvement.
Photo courtesy Minnesota Historical Society

A nationally-known Minnesotan on the medical scene was Sister Elizabeth Kenny (1880-1951) who dedicated 30 years to the crusade against polio and made Minneapolis the center for her famous treatment.

Nationally known on the social service scene is Women's Advocates, St. Paul. The group opened a shelter for battered women, the first in the country, in 1974.

LABOR AND INDUSTRY

By 1890 nearly 34 per cent of Minnesotans lived in cities and this urbanization was providing jobs in factories, mills, offices and stories to young women who previously could be hired only as maids or teachers. By 1900, more than 12 per cent of Minnesota's working women were employed as garment makers or seamstresses.

But they were not paid a living wage.

One champion of late 19th century working women was Eva McDonald Valesh, a newspaper woman who campaigned for improving conditions, especially those in local mills and clothing factories.

In the mid-1930s, a woman named Nellie Stone Johnson organized a local of the hotel and restaurant employees union. Twin Cities laundry workers were organized in 1934 and St. Paul school teachers formed one of the nation's earliest and strongest American Federation of Teachers locals.

But millwork and piecework gave way, in the 20th century, to paperwork. By 1970, 23 per cent of Minnesota's working women were in sales and clerical jobs. Other service-oriented occupations such as teaching, nursing and the restaurant trades were becoming major employers of women.

On Dec. 16, 1977, eight Minnesota working women made national news when they walked off their jobs at Citizens National Bank in Willmar, beginning the first bank strike in Minnesota history. They appeared on national television shows in the months that followed and actress Lee Grant made a documentary about their experience which received praise at the 1980 San Francisco Film Festival.

POLITICS

One of the first women to involve herself in Minnesota politics was Jane Grey Swisshelm (1815-1884). The St. Cloud woman was a feminist, abolitionist, lecturer and editor of a St. Cloud newspaper. She crusaded for the freeing of Negro slaves and for women's rights in politics, business and public affairs.

In September, 1919, Minnesota became the 15th state to ratify the 19th amendment giving women the right to vote in state and national elections.

Minnesota's first national Democratic committeewoman was Anna Dickie Olesen of Cloquet who became, in 1922, the first female candidate for the U.S. senate ever endorsed by a major party. (She lost.)

Laura E. Naplin was the first woman state senator, elected to two four-year terms in 1926 and 1930.

It wasn't until 1954 that the state sent a female representative to congress. She was Coya G. Knutson of Oklee in the Ninth District, the first woman appointed to the House Agriculture Committee.

Until 1974 the only woman to hold one of the major state executive offices was Virginia Holm, who followed her husband Mike Holm as Secretary of State and served one term.

In 1974, Joan Anderson Growe, a former member of the House of Representatives, became Secretary of State.

The first woman to serve on the Minnesota Supreme court, Justice Rosalie Wahl, was appointed to the court by Gov. Rudy Perpich in June, 1977.

Minnesota's first woman U.S. Senator was Muriel Humphrey, widow of Hubert H. Humphrey, former U.S. Senator and Vice President of the United States. Mrs. Humphrey was appointed to serve out her husband's term of office when he died in January, 1978.

Minnesota women have also been prominent on the national political scene.

Eugenie Anderson was the first American woman ambassador, serving in Denmark from 1949 to 1953 and as Minister to Bulgaria from 1962-1964.

St. Paul native Rozanne Ridgway was Ambassador to Finland and Geri Joseph of Minneapolis was Ambassador to the Netherlands.

Koryne Horbal of Shoreview was U.S. Delegate to the United Nations Commission on the Status of Women and Arvonne Fraser was head of Women in Development for the Agency for International Development. Both women are leaders in the Minnesota women's movement.

Many women who hold elective or appointive office today began as members of the Minnesota League of Women Voters, founded in 1919, which is a training ground for women in research and lobbying techniques.

With the coming of the women's movement, a new form of political alliance was born as women began to insist candidates speak to women's issues.

In July, 1971, the Minnesota Women's Political Caucus was started. It was the first such bipartisan group in the nation. In 1973 feminist caucuses were formed in both the DFL and Republican parties.

Women bank employees in Willmar began the state's first bank strike.
Photo courtesy St. Paul Dispatch/Pioneer Press

The 1981 House of Representatives had 19 women members. The senate had 5 women members.

The women's movement also gave impetus to several groups that are women's advocates in many areas, including politics.

The local National Organization for Women group was founded in September, 1970.

Minnesota sent a well-prepared delegation to the historic International Women's Year meeting in Houston, Texas, in 1977. The state group was the only one to have met several times before the IWY meeting to hammer out a list of resolutions they hoped would pass in Houston.

Out of the larger group came a caucus, Women of Color, established by Black, Native American, Asian and Hispanic women in June of 1976. Caucus members felt they were not heard at the Minnesota Women's meeting in St. Cloud which preceded the national IWY meeting. Women of Color carried a separate agenda to Houston, condemning racism in the women's movement.

A St. Paul woman, Pat Bellander, was one of the founders of Women of All Red Nations, a hemisphere-wide organization established in 1978 in Rapid City to promote survival of Indian people. The women are especially concerned about removal of Indian children from their homes by authorities (Minnesota has passed legislation in this area) and forced sterilization of Native American women.

★ ★ ★

Two Minnesota women, Jeannette R. Piccard and Sister Alla Bozarth-Campbell, were among the first group of women to be ordained to the Episcopal priesthood in 1974. Dr. Piccard is also nationally recognized in the field of aeronautics as the first woman in space in 1934.

MINNESOTA WOMEN TODAY

There are roughly two million women and girls in Minnesota, accounting for 51 percent of the state's population. This percentage has not changed in the last decade.

The legislature has given a mandate to the Commission on the Economic Status of Women to study all matters relating to the ecomonic status of women, including credit, family support, security of the homemaker, educational and employment opportunities, and laws and business practices which constitute barriers to women in the ecomony.

The council's third major publication, "Women in Minnesota," was published in August, 1984, in cooperation with the Hubert H. Humphrey Institute's Women, Public Policy and Development Project. Copies may be obtained from the commission.

Following are highlights of the report.

• In the last ten years the fastest-growing group in the state's female population has been women age 85 and over.

• Women age 65 or over in 1980 could expect to live an additional 19.1 years, to age 84 or older. Their male counterparts could expect to live an additional 14.8 years, to age 80 or older. For those born in 1980, the male-female life expectancy difference is about 7 years.

• Current marital status patterns resemble those in Minnesota at the turn of the century. Overall, 57 percent of women are married, 25 percent are single (never married), 11 percent are widowed, and 7 percent are divorced or separated.

• Median age at marriage has increased by about 2 years for both men and women in the last 10 years, and stands now at 23.3 years for women and 25.1 years for men.

• The overall ratio of divorces to marriages has increased from 1 divorce for every 3.8 marriages in 1970 to 1 divorce for every 2.5 marriages in 1980.

• The number of births to teenagers in Minnesota has dropped from 11.9 percent to 10.4 percent of all births. This is substantially below the national average of 15.6 percent teen births in 1980.

• The proportion of married-couple families has decreased in the last decade, while the proportion of female-headed families has grown. In 1980, 84 percent of families in the state were maintained jointly by a husband and wife, while 13 percent were headed by women and 3 percent were headed by men.

• Married-couple families supported by just one earner represent only about one-fourth of all Minnesota families. Both husband and wife

are in the labor force in 57 percent of all married-couple families.

• Sixty-two percent of female-headed families, compared with 54 percent of married couples and 36 percent of male-headed families, have at least one child at home.

• Eighty-eight percent of children live in married-couple families. However, it is estimated that almost half of children born today will live in a single-parent family at some time in their childhood.

• More than four-fifths of non-family households in the state are occupied by people living alone, and more than three-fifths of people living alone are women.

• Labor force rates for women age 16 to 64 increased from 50 percent in 1970 to 64 percent in 1980. By contrast, the rate for men in the same age group has remained unchanged at 86 percent in this period.

• For all women with children, labor force rates increased from 41 percent to 60 percent. Overall, half of mothers of preschoolers and over two-thirds of mothers with school-age children are now in the labor force.

• Women heading families have very high labor force participation rates: 46 percent of those with children under age 3, 65 percent of those with children age 3 to 5, and 83 percent of those with school-age children.

• Forty-nine percent of all persons in the state labor force in 1980 were in jobs which were either male-dominated (80 percent or more men) or female-dominated (80 percent or more women).

• In 1980, Minnesota women employed full-time year-round earned $10,005 compared with $17,704 for their male counterparts—only 57 cents, on the average, for each dollar earned by men.

• Female college graduates earn about the same as men with an eighth grade education, and women who have attended graduate school earn less than male high school dropouts. Female college graduates earn 62 cents for each dollar earned by men with this much education.

• Median income for male-headed families is 80 percent of the median for married couples, while income for female-headed families is only 50 percent of the married-couple median.

• More than 374,000 Minnesotans were living in proverty in 1980. Of these, 41 percent were women, 33 percent were children, and 26 percent were men.

• Almost one-third of female-headed families with children are poor, and more than half of female-headed families with children under age 6 are living in poverty.

LEGISLATION CONCERNING WOMEN

The Council on the Economic Status of Women endorses legislation involving women's concerns. Here is a summary of council-endorsed legislation passed by the 1984 legislature.

Minimum Wage - Tip Credit: Decreases the tip credit over four years until it is eliminated on January 1, 1988 when tipped employees will receive the minimum wage. Chapter 636.

Pay Equity in Local Government: Requires cities, counties, towns and school districts to conduct job evaluation studies and to establish pay equity. Reports must be made to the Department of Employee Relations by October 1, 1985 regarding implementation. Chapter 651.

Divorce Statistics Reporting: Allows collection of additional data about the economic consequences of dissolution by the Commissioner of Health. Chapter 534.

Child Support Guidelines: Modifies the child support guidelines to allow inclusion of certain debts in determining net income, if the debts will be repaid within 18 months and were incurred for the benefit of the child or to generate income. Chapter 547.

Pension Assignment: Amends pension statutes to eliminate the exemption of pension income from garnishment or attachment when child support is in arrears. Chapter 547.

Child Care Sliding Fee: Maintains the child care sliding fee program and appropriates $1.5 million for one year. Chapter 654.

Child Care - Capitol Area: Authorizes rental of space in the capitol complex for a private day care center for state employees. Chapter 485.

Child Care Tax Credit: Increases the dependent care tax credit to 30% of the cost for families with income below $24,000. Chapter 514.

Human Rights Enforcement: Increases the statute of limitations for filing of charges, prohibits leases which require a waiver of rights by an individual, requires the Commissioner to give certain claims priority, allows an administrative hearing if the department has not acted within 180 days, allows for increased damage awards. Chapter 567.

University of Minnesota Pay Equity: Requests the University of Minnesota regents to conduct a job evaluation study of non-academic employees and hospital workers and report to the legislature by April 1, 1985. Chapter 456.

Other legislation related to the Economic Status of Women.

Apprenticeship: Eliminates the exemption of bona fide apprenticeship programs from the age discrimination provisions of the state Human Rights Act. Chapter 319.

Credit Card: Requires credit card issuers to issue a credit card to a married woman in her current or former surname but allows the issuer of the card to require the opening of a new account if the card is in a former surname. Failure to do so is a violation of the state Human Rights Acts. Chapter 533.

Transitional Housing Demonstration: Appropriates $250,000 to the Department of Economic Security for grants to provide temporary housing and support services to families with children, single persons and persons leaving a shelter for victims of abuse. Chapter 654.

Income Tax Intercept: Makes the law allowing the intercept of income tax refunds of child support debtors permanent and allows the amount intercepted to include attorneys fees and costs of collecting child support. Chapter 514.

Minnesota Emergency Employment Development: Appropriates an additional $30 million for the emergency jobs program. Chapter 654.

PAY EQUITY - THE MINNESOTA EXPERIENCE

Pay equity, also known as comparable worth, was one of the most controversial pieces of legislation passed in the state in recent years. Comparable worth means that jobs should be paid according to their value, regardless of whether the jobs are performed by men or women. This is a women's issue because an estimated 80 percent of employed women work in traditional "women's jobs" which are undervalued and underpaid. The earnings gap between men and women has remained unchanged for 20 years.

Minnesota is one of 22 states which have pay equity legislation. Following is some background on the law and how it is being implemented, published by the Commission on the Economic Status of Women.

Melpomene Institute for Women's Health Research, 1897 Summit Ave., St. Paul, is one of a handful of organizations in the nation dedicated to discovering, through scientific inquiry, the facts inherent in physical activity for women. Named after the first woman marathon runner, Melpomene Institute, founded in 1981, is sponsoring studies on how exercise affects menstruation, pregnancy, body image and osteoporosis. The institute welcomes members, who may attend special seminars.

Marie Ward, known as the developer of the caramel apple, died in August, 1984, in a Minneapolis nursing home at the age of 102. Mrs. Ward introduced caramel apples for the first time at the 1916 Minnesota State Fair and the candy-covered fresh apple soon became popular across the nation. But Mrs. Ward, a native of Austria, never patented the process.

COUNCIL ON THE ECONOMIC STATUS OF WOMEN
400 SW, State Office Building, St. Paul, MN 55155

The following publications are available from the council office and free of charge unless otherwise noted:

MINNESOTA WOMEN: INCOME & POVERTY, with special emphasis on the two groups most vulnerable to poverty—older women and single-parent families. (Feb.78)

MINNESOTA WOMEN & MONEY, insurance, retirement income, credit, and taxes. (Jan. 79)

MINNESOTA WOMEN & EDUCATION, elementary, secondary, vocational, and post-secondary public education. (Nov. 79)

WOMEN IN MINNESOTA, a statistical summary of Minnesota women by age, education, marital and parental status, employment, and income. (July 80)

LEGISLATIVE PROGRAM 79, proposals endorsed by the council with background information on how each proposal would affect the economic status of women. (Feb. 79)

MINNESOTA WOMEN: STATE GOVERNMENT EMPLOYMENT FOLLOW-UP, women in the state's civil service system. (Mar. 79)

MINNESOTA WOMEN: CITY & COUNTY EMPLOYEES, local government employment. (Apr. 80)

WOMEN IN THE TRADES, state apprenticeship programs. (Dec. 79)

Public Information:

A WOMAN'S PLACE, outlining the legal and economic rights of Minnesota women in a question-and-answer format. (Sep. 78 - revised edition July 80)

NEWSLETTER, issued monthly, with summaries of Council research and reports and notice of Council activities.

Special Projects:

FINAL REPORT of the TASK FORCE ON HOUSING, with recommendations related to the cost and availability of housing for single-parent families. (Feb. 79)

VOCATIONAL EDUCATION SUMMARY REPORT, 1978-79, sex equity in secondary and post-secondary public vocational education students and staff. (Sep. 80)

A SURVEY OF FEMALE STUDENTS IN NON-TRADITIONAL AVTI PROGRAMS, the status of women in training for occupations which have been "male" jobs. (Sep. 79)

A SPECIAL REPORT ON FAMILIES, by the Governor's Task Force on Families, reviewing ways public policies and programs affect families. (Feb. 79)

FAMILIES IN CONFLICT, by the Governor's Task Force on Families, a brief report on family violence, including spouse abuse, child abuse, and incest. (June 79)

Women consistently earn less than men, regardless of occupation...

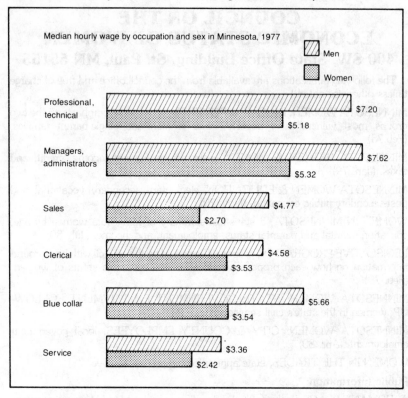

Median hourly wage by occupation and sex in Minnesota, 1977

Men
Women

Professional, technical — $7.20 / $5.18

Managers, administrators — $7.62 / $5.32

Sales — $4.77 / $2.70

Clerical — $4.58 / $3.53

Blue collar — $5.66 / $3.54

Service — $3.36 / $2.42

...or type of employer

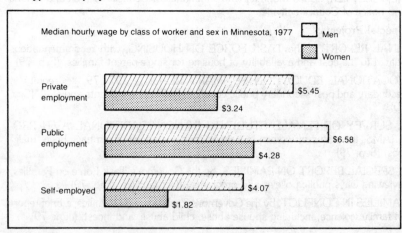

Median hourly wage by class of worker and sex in Minnesota, 1977

Men
Women

Private employment — $5.45 / $3.24

Public employment — $6.58 / $4.28

Self-employed — $4.07 / $1.82

Employment/ Organized Labor

The beginnings of the Minnesota labor movement, 1854-1900, were marked with success and adversity.

The first newspaper report of a Minnesota strike was in October, 1854. The strikers were journeymen tailors of St. Paul and the outcome is not known, but the strikers probably lost.

In 1856 the Typographical Union was formed in St. Paul. Today it is known as Local Union No. 30 of the International Typographical Union and is the oldest existing labor organization in the state.

Post-Civil War—1880s

In the post-Civil War period labor was in the doldrums.

Three laboring groups, however, were organized in 1867. Plasterers of St. Paul first organized that year. The Journeymen Tailors Self-Help Protective Society was incorporated as a result of an earlier strike and German immigrants in Minneapolis established a Workingman's Society to find jobs for all society members.

St. Paul Journeymen Cigar Makers' Union was organized by "tramp" members from other cities in 1868.

At least seven strikes can be traced through newspapers in 1870. Strikers wanted higher wages, a shorter workday, improvements in working conditions, promotion of state intervention on behalf of workers, and promotion of the dignity of labor.

Also in 1870 the Brotherhood of Locomotive Engineers at Austin was formed. It is now the state's oldest labor union with continuous existence.

The Depression of 1873-1879 not only limited union growth, but ruined most unions.

But in 1873 the Custom Tailors Benevolent Union was formed in Minneapolis, and by 1874 the Millers Union was holding regular meetings in Minneapolis.

A local assembly of Knights of Labor was formed in Minneapolis in 1878 and the following year another one arose in St. Paul. That same year Great Lakes sailors organized.

1880 - 1900

Prosperity and growth of industry were boons to the organized labor movement in the 1880s.

The Federal Census of 1880 recorded Minnesota as having 21 unions out of a total of 2,440 in the entire nation. Nine of these were railroad brotherhoods and the remainder manufacturing and craft groups.

During this period tradesmen, particularly in the Twin Cities, became union conscious. Unions grew rapidly, despite the need for utmost secrecy because of workers' fears that their union activities would become known to employers.

During the decade working conditions improved, wages rose and hours fell. The Twin Cities was recognized as two of the best-organized cities in the United States.

In 1882 the St. Paul Trades and Labor Assembly, the first such body in Minnesota, was founded with the assistance of the Knights of Labor Assembly. In 1883 the Minneapolis Trades Assembly was organized. Its name changed several times and finally the name Minneapolis Central Labor Union Council was accepted.

Knights of Labor experienced a rapid growth in Minnesota during the 1880s. Besides the Twin Cities it had local assemblies in Duluth, Stillwater, Albert Lea and Rochester. By 1883 it claimed 85 local asemblies within the state with 6,500 members.

The Knights stimulated workers to make demands for what they considered to be their rightful place in society. But by 1887 the Knights' decline was beginning and skilled workers were finding the new craft-conscious American Federation of Labor more appealing.

In 1886 joint political state conventions were held in St. Paul by Knights of Labor and the Farmers Alliance. (This was one of the first of many efforts which would lead, in the 20th century, to establishment of the Farmer-Labor party.)

By the end of the 1880s, trade unionism had spread over a large part of the state. As membership increased, so did strikes.

In 1885, for instance, only three strikes were recorded. But in 1888 there were 16 and in 1890 there were 20.

The 1890s saw growth of organized labor and the winning of concessions from factory, mill and mine owners.

The Minnesota State Federation of Labor was formed in 1890, proclaiming the following principles: an 8-hour day, contracts for convict labor should be abolished, wages should have first lien on all products, employees should be paid once a week, there should be state inspection of mines and factories, employees should be able under law to recover damages for loss of life or limb at work (a suggestion that was a forerunner of workman's compensation), the state should own and control railroads, telegraph and telephones and textbooks should be supplied free to all school children.

In 1893 the State Board of Labor Statistics was renamed the Bureau of labor, with enlarged powers.

Nationally-known socialist and union organizer Eugene V. Debs in 1894 directed the successful American Railway Union 18-day tie-up of the Great Northern railway after James J. Hill ordered a wage cut.

Union members got their own newspapers in 1896 when both the *Minnesota Union Advocate* in St. Paul and *The Duluth Labor World* were started.

1900 - 1930

In the years between 1900 and 1930 labor experienced both advances and reverses in Minnesota.

By its militant unionism, labor reflected the influence of radical populism in the early 1900s. But organized labor in Minneapolis experienced serious setbacks. Strong anti-union sentiments of flour milling companies proved to be a powerful threat to unionism and gave rise to labor strife.

In 1902 and 1903 there was a general strike against the three largest flour companies in Minneapolis. Workers demanded an 8-hour day to replace the 12-hour one, with no reduction in pay.

In those same years unionism was threatened by the formation of the Citizens Alliance, an organization of employers which fought every major strike in the city for more than 30 years. Its existence made Minneapolis well known nationally among employers as an "open shop" city and among labor as "one of the worst scab cities in the country."

Despite these adversities, the labor movement gained momentum through organization, slowly-won economic gains and a gradual increase in political power.

Between 1900 and 1903 Boot and Shoe workers, Ice Wagon Drivers, St. Paul butchers, Stillwater sawmill workers and St. Paul brewery workers were all organized.

A new, dynamic force on the state labor scene is first mentioned in the early 1900s - the Industrial Workers of the World (IWW). The IWW offered a militant, radical form of industrial unionism that sprang from the socialist-anarchist tradition.

By 1911 the IWW was involved in street fights in Duluth and Minneapolis over the question of the union organizers' right to speak in public.

The two biggest IWW strikes in Minnesota erupted in 1916. The first significant strike in the timber industry involved at one time an estimated 4,000 strikers who demanded an 8-hour day and increased pay. In the mining industry, from 12,000 to 15,000 Iron Range miners struck, also demanding an 8-hour day.

In 1913 Minnesota became only the second state in the nation to pass a Workmen's Compensation law, doing so after a decade of struggle.

But in 1917 labor suffered a severe setback when the legislature voted near dictatorial powers to a seven-man Public Safety Commission. The commission barred strikes, forbade moves to extend unionization and used its powers to cripple the IWW and any other unions they considered "subversive."

1930 - 1940

By 1930 the effects of the worsening Depression were obvious in Minnesota, with 18½ per cent of state union members unemployed. By 1932 the number had risen to 30 per cent unemployed with 17 per cent working part-time.

Labor activity increased dramatically in 1933, largely as a result of the National Industrial Recovery Act, legislation designed to get the nation's economy moving again.

America's first "sit down" strike also took place in 1933 at the Hormel Company in Austin.

The year 1934 was a banner one for labor unions.

The first Bakers Union contract in the Twin Cities covering a machine producer of baked goods was signed. State employees in the Highway Department organized and Twin Cities newsmen organized. Their union became the foundation for the American Newspaper Guild. The first Minnesota contract was won by International Ladies Garment Workers Union and some Twin Cities filling stations were organized.

The 1934 truck drivers' strike in Minneapolis was perhaps the most violent, and yet the most significant, in the state's labor history.

In May a strike for recognition resulted in a pitched battle between pickets and an employers' "army." Gov. Floyd B. Olson intervened and brought about a tentative agreement. But in July a more violent strike erupted when some employers reneged on the May settlement and martial law was invoked.

Four strikers were killed and scores injured until Gov. Olson again intervened and helped the Teamsters win the strike. The Citizens Alliance was finally defeated.

After the strike the Minneapolis labor movement emerged from a period of official hostility and public antagonism to one of acceptance and began to grow to its present strength. (Today Minneapolis is one of the most highly organized cities in the U.S.)

The middle and late 1930s were years of significant labor developments.

Unemployment compensation, long sought by the State Federation, was adopted. The Steel Workers Organizing Committee organized the Mesabi range, the Minnesota State Federation of Teachers was established and state locals participated in the formation of the American Federation of State, County and Municipal Employees.

Long-sought goals were attained in 1937. A Twin Cities-wide contract was won by the Hotel and Restaurant Employees and Bartenders Union, the International Brotherhood of Electrical Workers achieved their first contract with Northern States Power Company, the Twin Cities paperbox and carton industry was organized and the Twin Cities "waterfront" was finally organized.

Greyhound bus line employees organized and the Minnesota State CIO Council representing an estimated 40,000 workers was formed.

In 1939 Gov. Harold Stassen succeeded in having the legislature pass a state labor relations act to apply to intra-state commerce. The bill anticipated many features of the later national Taft-Hartley Act.

1940 - 1980

Labor played a prominent role in the merging of the Democractic and Farmer-Labor parties in 1944.

As the state entered the post-World War II era in 1946 the all-time national record for labor unrest was reflected in Minnesota.

Five thousand members of the National Maritime Union on the Great Lakes struck against the 7-day, 56-hour work week. St. Paul teachers began the first organized teachers' strike in the nation's history.

The issue of communism and how to handle it had risen by 1946. In 1947 a strongly anti-communist executive board was formed by the Minnesota CIO Council, making it easier for the Minnesota Federation of Labor, the DFL party and farm groups to work with the CIO.

In 1951 a strike by Minneapolis schoolteachers during the legislative session provided Conservatives in the legislature an argument to finally enact a law prohibiting strikes by public employees.

But in 1954 a liberal turn in Minnesota politics resulted in favorable labor legislation and other developments. Many measures supported by the AFL State Federation of Labor were passed, including the Fair Employment Practices Act, improvements in workmen's and unemployment benefits and in old age assistance and increased state school aids.

The state's first comprehensive medical care program was negotiated that same year by the Duluth building trades.

In 1956 the AFL and CIO held a state merger convention in Rochester and formed the new Minnesota AFL-CIO Federation of Labor.

A strike in 1959 at Wilson Company meat packing plant in Albert Lea resulted in the worst violence since 1934 when Wilson attempted to reopen the plant with strike breakers. The dispute ended in arbitration.

In 1967 the legislature enacted a "meet and confer" law for teachers, restricting the rights of teachers to genuine negotiations. This law was the chief cause for making 1969 one of the most turbulent years for public education in Minnesota annals.

In 1970 the Minneapolis Federation of Teachers voted to strike, pointing up the deficiencies of the "meet and confer" and "no strike" laws. The "meet and confer" law was repealed in 1971 and new rights were conferred on the state's 230,000 public employees.

The beginning of the 1970s found Minnesota's labor movement numerically strong and financially stronger.

New challenges awaited labor in the 1980s. Among them were automation, the shift from a manufacturing to a service oriented economy, organizing white collar clerical workers and continued recruitment of minorities and women.

1980 - Present

When World War II ended in 1945, the United States emerged as a leading supplier of food, steel, cars and other manufactured basics.

In the last decade, however, this nation has turned from being an industrial nation, whose population centers were in the Eastern manufacturing areas, to a service-oriented economy, where paperwork has replaced the actual creation of goods.

As recently as 1960, this nation held a 52 percent corner on automobile production; by 1984 we manufactured only 25 percent of the world's output. In 1960, we produced 26 percent of the world's steel; now that figure is 11 percent.

This change has been deeply felt in Minnesota, according to the state Department of Jobs and Training.

By 1990, sales, technical, service and clerical occupations are expected to comprise nearly 71 percent of this state's jobs, compared to 68 percent in 1980.

The continuing farm crisis in which family-owned farms are being consolidated by corporations, the closing of mines in northern Minnesota and the restructuring of big corporations like Control Data and Sperry Univac reflect these shifts in world economics.

As the nation moves to a service-oriented economy, many people who had been working in manufacturing, like those in steel, mining and auto making, found themselves without work.

Minnesota Workers and Their Jobs

In 1986, there were 2,213,000 Minnesotans in the state labor force. Of that number, 2,095,000 were employed and 118,000 were not employed.

The unemployment rate in 1986 was between 7 and 8.9 percent, right in the middle of a national unemployment rate that varied from 3 to 4.9 percent in some states to 11-14 percent in the hardest-hit states.

The highest unemployment rate was found across northern Minnesota; the lowest rate was in the Twin Cities and counties immediately to the east, as well as in some southwestern and south-central Minnesota counties.

Unlike the rest of the nation, Minnesota's employment dropped slightly in 1986, due to fewer men working. However, both the number of jobless people and the rate of unemployment fell dramatically from 6 percent in 1985 to 5.3 percent in 1986. Women were responsible for 60 percent of this as their jobless rate decreased from 5.5 percent to 4.6 percent in 1986. (The men's unemployment rate increased from

Minnesota 1986
Employment Distribution by Industry

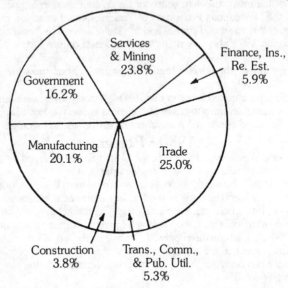

Source: Minnesota Department of Jobs and Training

5.9 percent to 6.4 percent. These figures show the trend for service-oriented businesses, like retailing and foods, to hire females, often on a part-time basis that does not provide benefits such as paid vacations and health insurance.)

In 1986, construction was the only goods-producing employer that added workers. The state lost employees in mining and durable goods faster than the national average.

The metal industry, after losing 13 percent of its workers in 1985, suffered a 25 percent drop in 1986.

Durable goods manufacturing employment also declined by 3.3 percent after barely holding its own during 1985.

Heavy concentrations of computer producing firms - and their shakeups - were the main culprits in dropping both electrical and nonelectrical employment. Although the state's fabricated metals employment rose in 1986, primary metals declined.

Employment Patterns by Region

St. Paul-Minneapolis - Fueled by record-setting demand for new and existing housing in the Twin Cities area, employment in construction and financial service firms grew faster than any major industry category in 1986. The number of jobs in finance, insurance and real estate increased by 6.3 percent in 1986, while construction firms added 5.8 percent more workers. The manufacturing sector lost jobs for the second consecutive year. Most of the loss was among computer producers.

The Job Market
SUPPLY/DEMAND FOR SPECIFIC OCCUPATIONS
February 1987[1]
by Debra Detrick

MINNESOTA
Shortage Occupations: food service workers[2]

Surplus Occupations: clerical workers[2], general laborers[2]

CENTRAL MINNESOTA
Shortage Occupations: experienced non-union construction workers (St. Cloud area)

Surplus Occupations: clerical workers[2], retail sales clerks

MINNEAPOLIS-ST. PAUL
Shortage Occupations: food service workers[2]

Surplus Occupations: assembly workers[2], electronic assemblers[2], general laborers, production workers[2]

NORTHEASTERN MINNESOTA
Shortage Occupations: none

Surplus Occupations: auto mechanics[2], clerical workers[2], construction workers[2], electicians[2], entry level managers[2], laborers[2], machinists[2], maintenance workers, mining crafts[2], painters[2], pipefitters[2], plant workers, sales clerks[2], teachers[2], welders[2]

NORTHWESTERN MINNESOTA
Shortage Occupations: fast food workers[2], specialized mechanics

Surplus Occupations: construction workers[2], general laborers[2], truck drivers

SOUTHERN MINNESOTA
Shortage Occupations: food-service workers[2], part-time sales clerks, printing press operators (Rochester area)

Surplus Occupations: clerical workers[2], construction workers

---

[1] Shortage occupations are those that are difficult to fill or go unfilled due to the lack of qualified applicants. Surplus occupations are those in which the number of qualified applicants greatly exceeds the number of openings.

[2] This occupation has been listed as a shortage or surplus occupation in at least two out of the last three quarters of the *Review*.

Source: Minn. Dept. of Jobs and Training. *Minn. Labor Market Review*, Feb., 1987.

Minnesota 1985 and 1986
Industrial Employment

	Employment 1985	1986	%
Total Nonagricultural			
Wage and Salary	1,864.8	1,891.2	1.4
Manufacturing	3,753	369.0	-1.7
Construction	71.3	74.6	4.6
Transp., Comm.,			
Public Utilities	98.4	97.5	0.9
Trade	465.6	470.4	1.0
F.I.R.E.	110.3	116.3	5.4
Services and Mining	434.4	447.8	3.1
Government	301.2	309.1	2.6

Source: Minnesota Department of Jobs and Training

Overall, nonagricultural wage and salary job growth in 1986 dropped to about half of what it was in 1985. Jobs in the services sector increased by 2.7 percent in 1986, compared to 5.2 percent in 1985. Government employment grew slightly faster in 1986 than in 1985; practically all of this growth took place in public education.

Duluth-Superior - This region lost about five out of every 1,000 nonagricultural jobs from 1985 to 1986. Hardest hit were mining, transportation, communications and public utilities. Unlike the rest of the state, which lost manufacturing jobs, Duluth-Superior generated nearly 200 from 1985 to 1986, a 2.8 percent increase.

Southern Minnesota - The economics of the 34 counties of southern Minnesota are tied to the fortunes of agriculture, supporting service industries and manufacturing. Recent closings and cutbacks among manufacturers in small towns have eroded

LABOR TODAY*

The three major labor oganizations in Minnesota are the AFL-CIO, the Teamsters and the United Auto Workers. The total membership for the three unions is about 330,000.

The AFL-CIO has 575 locals with 280,000 members. There are about 18 Teamster locals with 50,000 members, and the U.A.W. has 13 locals with approximately 8,000 members.

*as of 1 Aug. 1987

Sources: State AFL-CIO, Teamster and U.A.W. locals.

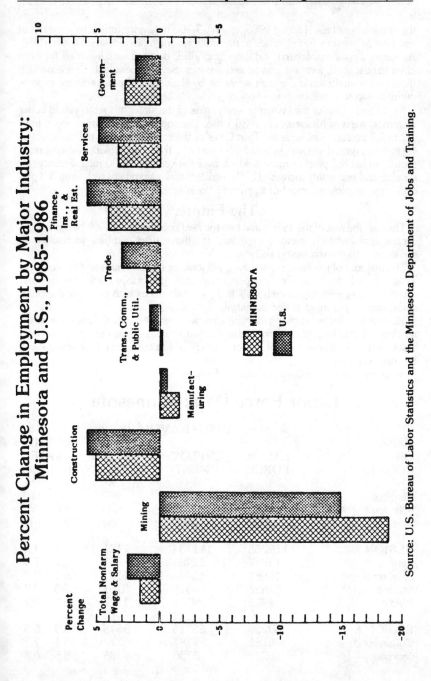

Percent Change in Employment by Major Industry:
Minnesota and U.S., 1985-1986

Source: U.S. Bureau of Labor Statistics and the Minnesota Department of Jobs and Training.

the employment base. During 1986, roughly 7,700 nonagricultural jobs were lost in southern Minnesota. Farming was at the root, bringing other industries down with it. As farms were consolidated and crop land idled, demand was lessened for farm hired hands, seed, fertilizer and related services. Several manufacturers, especially those associated with computers, were hit by shakeups. The department expects outmigration to continue in this region.

St. Cloud - One of the fastest-growing areas of the state, this region fared better than most parts of Minnesota in 1985-1986. The unemployment rate dropped from 7.7 to 5.7 percent. Unlike in the Twin Cities or the state in general, the manufacturing industry gained workers by a hefty 5.1 percent. Trade, particularly the large retail sector, added 8.2 percent more workers over the year, or 1,500 jobs. Finance, insurance and real estate increased by 10 percent, and government picked up 3.3 percent more employees, most of them working in schools.

The Future

Through the rest of the 1980s and into the next decade, growth will be stongest in service and hightech sectors, especially for those who combine technological, managerial and/or marketing skills.

The majority of job seekers, however, will look for clerical, sales and service jobs. They should find excellent opportunities for janitorial, truck driving and waiter/waitress jobs. Others who will find jobs: secretaries with personal computer skills, nurses, paramedics and paralegals.

Minnesota's fastest-growing occupations will be data processing, equipment repairers, dental hygienists, farm managers, health aides (except nursing), teachers aides, waiters/waitresses assistants and sellers of furniture, home furnishings and business services.

State farming occupations will decline fastest.

Labor Force Data: Minnesota

ANNUAL AVERAGE 1986

AREA OR COUNTY	LABOR FORCE	EMPLOY— MENT	UNEMP.	UNEMP. RATE 1986	1985
Kanabec	5716	5219	497	8.7	11.1
Mille Lacs	8413	7743	670	8.0	9.5
Pine	9309	8405	904	9.7	10.4
REGION 7W	**119255**	**112134**	**7121**	**6.0**	**7.3**
Benton	13837	12986	851	6.2	7.4
Sherburne	16583	15446	1137	6.9	7.9
Stearns	57632	54471	3161	5.5	7.2
Wright	31203	29231	1972	6.3	7.1
REGION 8	**60260**	**56715**	**3545**	**5.9**	**6.9**
Cottonwood	6161	5787	374	6.1	7.7
Jackson	6271	5736	535	8.5	6.8

Women in Trades

Although women have been entering the labor market in unprecedented numbers in recent years, they continue to be concentrated in traditionally "female" occupations, which are also traditionally the lowest-paid.

In the last decade, though, some women have been entering the male-dominated trades.

A 1979 survey by the Council on Economic Status of Women found there were 7,521 active apprenticeships in Minnesota. (Apprentice means a person engaged in study and on-the-job training for a skilled trade and enrolled in a program which is registered with the Apprenticeship Division of the Minnesota Department of Labor and Industry.)

Of these active apprenticeships, 91 (or 1.2 per cent) were women.

Minnesota ranks well below the national average in the proportion of its apprentices who are women. In June, 1978, the state ranked 48th of the 54 states and territories in this respect. One reason may be that other states, but not Minnesota, recognize apprenticeship in cosmetology, a trade which accounts for 12 per cent of registered female apprentices nationally.

As of Dec. 31, 1978, Minnesota women in registered apprenticeships represented 31 different trades of the 152 trades statewide. Trades with more than two female apprentices included: carpenter, plant attendant, watchmaker, bookbinder, electrical wirer, painter/decorator, mapper and offset platemaker.

The council's survey of apprentices in the trades found that of the 51 different trades represented, the most frequently reported were carpenter, electrician, painter/decorator, bricklayer and machinist. Both men and women were likely to be carpenters or electricians while women were more likely to be painter/decorators and men were more likely to be bricklayers.

The women apprentices had higher levels of educational attainment - 58 per cent of them had some college education compared to 28 per cent of the men, and 23 per cent of the women had four or more years of college compared to only four per cent of the men.

In addition, the women were more likely to be entering the trades as a second career. Five indicated they had been office workers, one had been a licensed practical nurse, and one a teacher.

There were also substantial differences in marital status between male and female apprentices. The men were much more likely to be married with spouse present than their female counterparts - 61 per cent compared to 27 per cent - and the women were more likely to be divorced.

Job satisfaction was very high for the female apprentices. Only 15 per cent said they were dissatisfied.

The women were most likely to list "good working conditions" or "liking co-workers" as reasons for their satisfaction. Many also indicated they enjoyed the physical challenge of their jobs, working outdoors and having a tangible product.

Both men and women mentioned financial rewards or good benefit plans as a factor in their satisfaction, but this response was more common for women.

Each apprentice was asked whether he or she had experienced barriers when trying to enter their trade. "Yes" answers were given by 44 per cent of the women, but only 26 per cent of the men.

More than half the barriers encountered by women were specifically related to their sex. "Men don't think women belong" and "the guys in the plant don't think women can handle it" were comments which typified many of the women's responses.

The most striking differences in backgrounds of male and female apprentices were in previous related experience and education. Slightly more than half of the men, but only about a third of the women, had worked in related fields before entering their apprenticeship.

In addition, several of the women mentioned the disadvantage of inadequate coursework in high school, including not having drafting or advanced mathematics.

A large majority of both groups - 80 per cent of the women and 89 per cent of the men - belonged to a union. Sixty per cent of the women, but only 21 per cent of the men, were interested in becoming officers of the union or being active in some way.

Equal Opportunity Law

Women who are thinking about entering the trades should know that there is a body of legislation on equal opportunity in employment. Here are the laws and regulations.

TITLE VII of the federal Civil Rights Act of 1964 prohibits discrimination based on sex for employers of 15 or more persons, labor organizations with 15 or more members, and labor-management apprenticeship programs.

EXECUTIVE ORDER 11246 prohibits discrimination based on sex by organizations performing work under a federal construction contract or subcontract exceeding $10,000.

EQUAL EMPLOYMENT OPPORTUNITY IN CONSTRUCTION regulations of the Office of Federal Contract Compliance Programs require certain contractors and subcontractors to take specific affirmative action steps. Goals for the representation of women are set at 3.1 percent as of May 1979, 5.0 percent as of May 1980, and 6.9 percent as of May 1981.

EQUAL EMPLOYMENT OPPORTUNITY IN APPRENTICESHIP regulations of the U.S. Department of Labor require sponsors of apprenticeship programs to set a goal for women of not less than 50 percent of the proportion of women in the sponsor's labor market area. For example, since women account for 51 percent of the labor force in the Minneapolis area, sponsors with more than five apprentices must have a goal of at least 25.5 percent women in new apprenticeship classes. Programs which do not comply may be deregistered by the U.S. Department of Labor and the Minnesota Department of Labor and Industry.

The MINNESOTA HUMAN RIGHTS ACT prohibits discrimination in employment and on the part of a labor organization on the basis of sex. The same law prohibits discrimination on the basis of age, with some exceptions. Exemptions to the age prohibition are provided for apprenticeship programs related to a trade "which predominantly involves heavy physical labor or work on high structures," and which apply the age restriction uniformly to all individuals.

Agriculture

Minnesota has been an agricultural state since the first white settlers came from Scandinavia and Germany in the 19th century to break the virgin prairie soil with hand-made plows.

The state's farmers have fed the nation through a depression and two world wars and our culture is permeated with the values of rural life, including strong family ties, hard work, regular church attendance and Populist-based politics.

Until 1950, most Minnesotans lived in rural areas rather than in cities.

That is why there is so much concern about the "Farm Crisis," the loss of small, family-operated farms that began at the start of the 1980s.

Besides sympathy for the families who have lost their homes and jobs, Minnesotans also seem to sense that the end of family farming as a way of life is a loss for us all.

The story of Minnesota agriculture in the 1980s is a story of loss.

Since the beginning of this decade, Minnesota farms have declined in number from 104,000 to 93,000 - a loss of 11,000 farms. (This compares with farm losses of 11,000 for Wisconsin, 10,000 for Iowa, 19,000 for Illinois, 8,000 for Nebraska and somewhat lesser amounts for the Dakotas.)

From 1984 to 1985 alone, Minnesota recorded a drop of 5,000 farms, the largest year-to-year drop for any state in the nation.

Ironically, the average size of farms in the state has been steadily increasing, from 292 acres in 1981 to 323 acres in 1986. This change reflects the trend from small, family-operated farms to larger tracts run by corporations.

As the number of farms dwindles, Minnesota farm land values continue to fall.

Since the peak year of 1981, land values in the state have dropped 48 percent. Southwestern Minnesota was hardest hit, with land values down 31 percent in 1984-1985.

The drop in farm real estate values in 1986 marked the fifth consecutive annual decline. That year, average land values fell 25 percent to $515 per acre, the largest annual drop in the history of the Land Value Survey that is conducted by the University of Minnesota's Agricultural Extension Service.

Minnesota's farmers have also seen a drop in net farm income.

Despite a 6 percent decline in farm production expenses, the state's total net farm income dropped 14 percent from 1984 to 1985.

Total gross farm income for 1985 dropped 7 percent to $7.31 billion. When production expenses of $6.15 billion were subtracted out, state farmers were left with a net income of $1.16 billion. This averages out to a net of $12,098 per farm, down 9 percent from 1984.

Minnesota's major crops are corn, soybeans, wheat, barley, oats, hay, flax, rye and sugarbeets. Corn is grown mostly in southern Minnesota, especially in the counties bordering Iowa. Wheat is grown primarily in the northwestern corner of the state and soybeans are also grown in the southern third of Minnesota. Oats are grown on a diagonal line running from the northwestern corner of the state to the southeastern corner.

While farms are getting bigger, the number of animals raised on them is declining.

Cattle numbers on state farms as of January 1, 1987, were down 7 percent from a year earlier, the lowest total since 1930. Sheep and lamb numbers increased 11 percent in 1985-1986. Inventory of all hogs on December 1, 1986, was up 4 percent and all chickens on farms increased 1 percent.

The number of farms with cattle fell 4,000 from 1985 to 1986, while milk cows dropped 2000, hogs declined 1500 and sheep operations were down 1200.

The value of the animals that are raised has been dropping.

Combined value of all livestock and poultry on Minnesota farms at the end of 1986 was $1,899 million. All cattle and calves, valued at $1,465 million, were 1 percent more valuable than the previous year. The value of hogs on hand accounted for $396 million, up 42 per cent; all sheep and lambs, $19.8 million, up 23 percent, and all chickens $17.9 million, down 22 percent.

In the mid-1980s, the Minnesota legislature responded to the farm crisis by passing some legislation to help farmers, including stricter rules on bank foreclosures and loan programs.

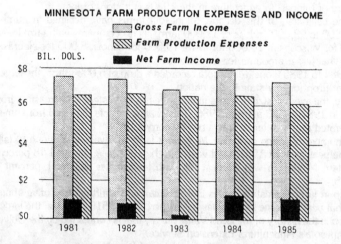

MINNESOTA FARM PRODUCTION EXPENSES AND INCOME

Gross Farm Income
Farm Production Expenses
Net Farm Income

BIL. DOLS.

Sources: (for whole chapter);
   (1) *Census of Ag. 1978,* (U.S. Dept. of Ag., published by U.S. Dept. of Commerce)
   (2) *Minnesota Ag. Statistics 1987,* U.S. Dept. of Ag. and Minn. Dept. of Ag.; July 1987)
   (3) Information from Minnesota Department of Agriculture.

MINNESOTA'S RANK AMONG STATES

ITEM   **RANK**

Number of Farms, June 1, 1987 6

CASH FARM INCOME, 1986:

Total 6
Crops 7
Livestock and Livestock products 6

CROP PRODUCTIONS, 1986

Corn for grain 4
Soybeans 4
Wheat, all 8
Other Spring Wheat 2
Oats 3
Barley 4
Sunflowers, all 3
Hay, all 2
Potatoes, all 9
Sugarbeets 1
Flaxseed 3
Rye 4
Sweet corn for processing 1
Green peas for processing 2
Dry edible beans 7

LIVESTOCK, DAIRY AND POULTRY

Red meat production, 1986 6
Cattle and Calves, Jan. 1, 1987 10
Milk cows, Jan. 1, 1987 4
Cattle and calves on feed, Jan. 1, 1987 9
Cattle and calves marketed, 1986 (head) 9
Hogs, Dec. 1, 1986 3
Pig crop, 1985 3
Hog marketed, 1986 4
Stock sheep and lambs, Jan. 1, 1987 15
Lamb crop, 1986 13
Chickens, Dec. 1, 1986 11
Eggs, produced, December 1985—November 1986 11
Turkeys raised during 1986 2
Milk production, 1986 4

DAIRY PRODUCTS MANUFACTURED DURING 1986

Total Cheese 2
American cheese 2
Butter 3
Nonfat dry milk 2
Ice cream 7
Fertilizer consumption (year ending 6/30/86) 6
Agricultural Exports (fiscal 1986) 7

Source: **Minnesota Agricultural Statistics, July, 1987, published by State of Minnesota Agriculture Department and U.S. Department of Agriculture.**

FARMLAND ACREAGE IN MINNESOTA

Year	Number of Farms (thousands)	Total Acreage (thousands)	Average Size (acres)
1940	198	32,700	165
1950	184	33,300	181
1960	156	32,400	208
1970	121	30,900	255
1975	118	30,600	259
1978	103	30,300	260
1982	103	30,400	295
1983	102	30,400	298
1984	101	30,400	301
1985	96	30,400	317
1986[1]	93	30,000	323

[1] As of June 1, 1987. Farms are defined as places which had annual sales of agricultural products of $1,000 or more.

OVER 15,000 FARMS LOST
IN THESE STATES OVER PAST YEAR

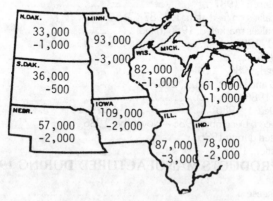

1986 number of Farms and change from last year.

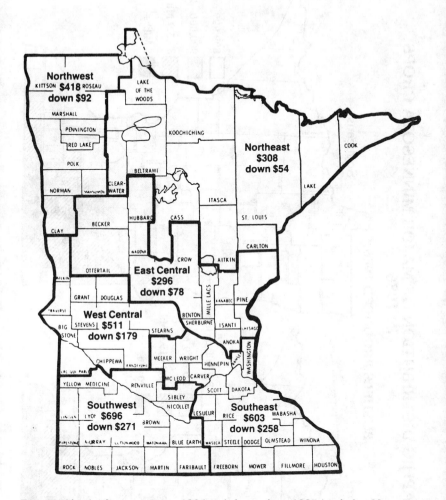

Estimated land values per acre in 1986 and change from 1985 (excluding Hennepin and Ramsey Counties. Based on reported estimates of average value per acre of farmland for the first six months of 1986)*

*Estimated average value per acre of Minnesota Farmland by District.

Minnesota Agricultural Statistics, 1987, published by State of Minnesota Agriculture Department and U.S. Department of Agriculture.

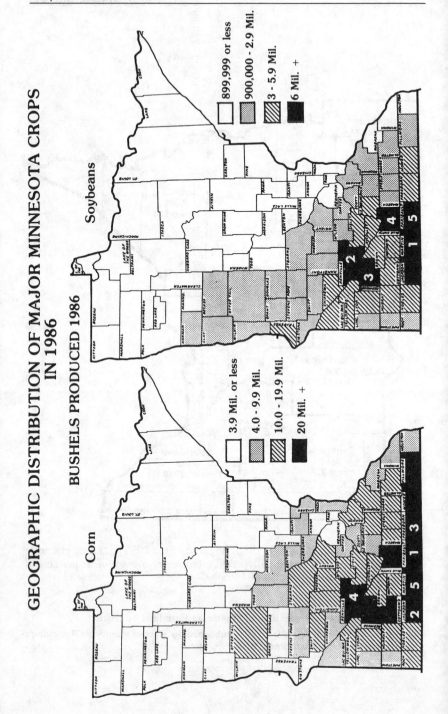

GEOGRAPHIC DISTRIBUTION OF MAJOR MINNESOTA CROPS IN 1986

BUSHELS PRODUCED 1986

Soybeans

899,999 or less
900,000 - 2.9 Mil.
3 - 5.9 Mil.
6 Mil. +

Corn

3.9 Mil. or less
4.0 - 9.9 Mil.
10.0 - 19.9 Mil.
20 Mil. +

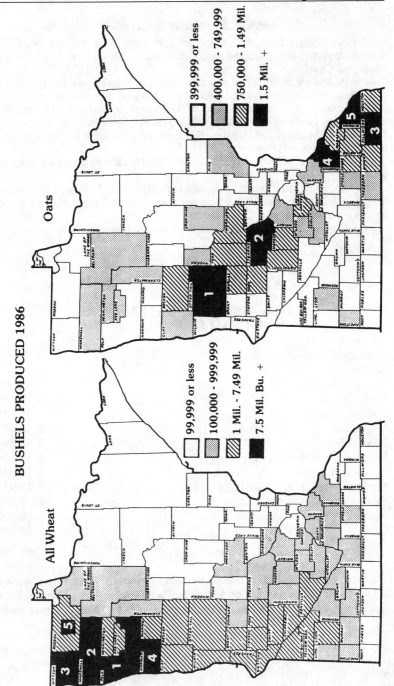

BUSHELS PRODUCED 1986

All Wheat

99,999 or less
100,000 - 999,999
1 Mil. - 7.49 Mil.
7.5 Mil. Bu. +

Oats

399,999 or less
400,000 - 749,999
750,000 - 1.49 Mil.
1.5 Mil. +

1985 Paddy Wild Rice Statistics*

Wild rice, Minnesota's official State Grain, is grown as a field crop on 27,000 acres in northern Minnesota. The leading counties are Aitkin, Clearwater, Beltrami, Itasca and Cass.

Acreage and yields are increasing as production problems are being solved by growers and researchers. Average yield per acre has steadily increased. In 1968 only 900 acres were in production, yielding 36,000 pounds of processed grain. In 1985, 27,000 acres produced over 4,200,000 pounds of processed grain. Average yield per acre at 155 pounds was up from 1984 and represents a 290% gain from the 40 pounds estimated for 1968.

The value of the 1985 crop was $13,650,000 at $3.25 per pound for processed wild rice.

The number of farm operations producing wild rice in 1985 was 68. Average acreage in wild rice production per farm operation increased from 250 acres in 1982 to 398 acres in 1984.

*Information Provided by Minnesota Paddy Wild Rice Research and Promotion Council)

1986 MINNESOTA AG EXPORTS WORTH $1.27 BILLION

Soybeans & Products	$424.9 Mil.
Feedgrains	$389.0 Mil.
Wheat & Products	$152.9 Mil.
Dairy Products	$ 51.1 Mil.
Feeds & Fodders	$ 47.8 Mil.
Vegetables	$ 44.0 Mil.
Hides & Skins	$ 40.7 Mil.
Live Animals & Meat (Excl. Poultry)	$ 39.3 Mil.
Fats, Oils, Greases	$ 14.6 Mil.
Sunflower Seed & Oil	$ 12.9 Mil.
Seeds	$ 9.5 Mil.
Poultry	$ 8.7 Mil.
Other	$ 33.5 Mil.
Total	$1,268.9 Mil.

Shown is the value of these exports by commodity group. These shares are derived from Minnesota's contribution to U.S. production and/or sales. They are not actual exports but reflect Minnesota's important stake in the national export market.

Dairy

Minnesota's milk production totaled 10.8 billion pounds in 1985, 5% more than 1984. The state's share of national production in 1985 was 8%. The 12-month average number of milk cows was 915 versus 887 in 1984.

The average milk per cow was 11,847 in 1985, up 200 pounds from 1984.

The count of plant patrons selling milk or cream in June 1985 totaled 22,168. This compares with the revised totals of 23,247 for June 1984 and 24,776 for June 1983.

GEOGRAPHIC DISTRIBUTION OF MINNESOTA MILK PRODUCTION

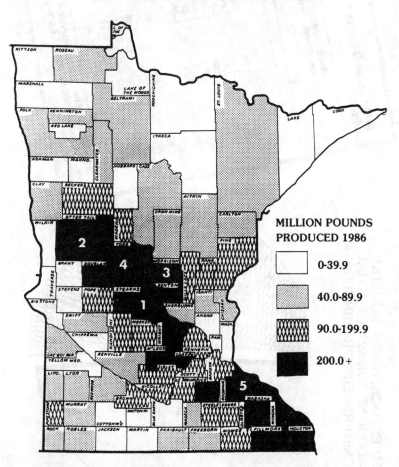

MILLION POUNDS
PRODUCED 1986

0-39.9

40.0-89.9

90.0-199.9

200.0+

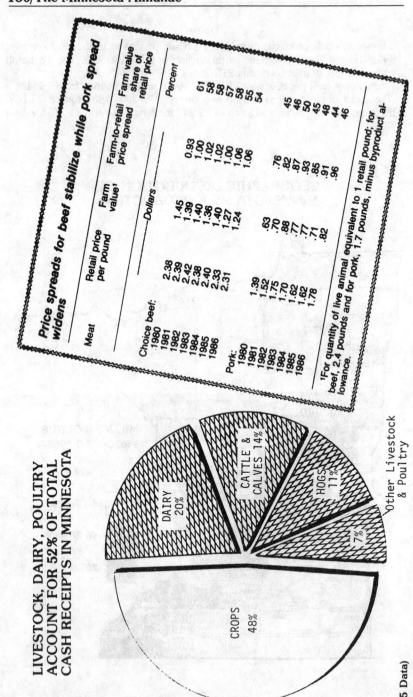

Price spreads for beef stabilize while pork spread widens

Meat	Retail price per pound	Farm value[1]	Farm-to-retail price spread	Farm value share of retail price
		— Dollars —		Percent
Choice beef:				
1980	2.38	1.45	0.93	61
1981	2.39	1.39	1.00	58
1982	2.42	1.40	1.02	58
1983	2.38	1.36	1.02	57
1984	2.40	1.40	1.00	58
1985	2.33	1.27	1.06	55
1986	2.31	1.24	1.06	54
Pork:				
1980	1.39	.63	.76	45
1981	1.52	.70	.82	46
1982	1.75	.88	.87	50
1983	1.70	.77	.93	45
1984	1.62	.77	.85	48
1985	1.62	.71	.91	44
1986	1.78	.82	.96	46

[1]For quantity of live animal equivalent to 1 retail pound; for beef, 2.4 pounds and for pork, 1.7 pounds, minus byproduct allowance.

LIVESTOCK, DAIRY, POULTRY ACCOUNT FOR 52% OF TOTAL CASH RECEIPTS IN MINNESOTA

DAIRY 20%

CATTLE & CALVES 14%

HOGS 11%

7%

Other Livestock & Poultry

CROPS 48%

(1985 Data)

HERE'S WHAT A DOLLAR SPENT ON FOOD PAID FOR IN 1986

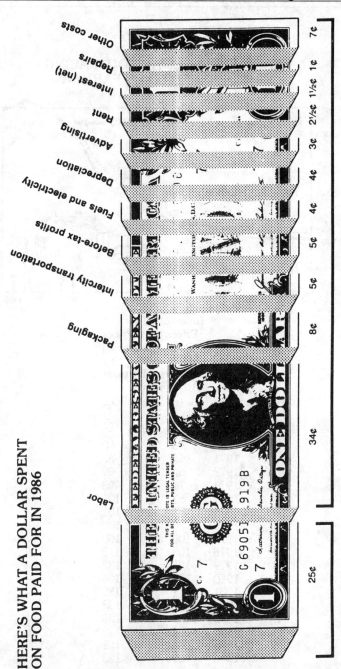

Other costs	7¢
Repairs	1¢
Interest (net)	1½¢
Rent	2½¢
Advertising	3¢
Depreciation	4¢
Fuels and electricity	4¢
Before-tax profits	5¢
Intercity transportation	5¢
Packaging	8¢
Labor	34¢

Marketing Bill

	25¢

Farm Value

Includes food at home and away from home. Other costs include property taxes and insurance, accounting and professional services, promotion, bad debts, and many miscellaneous items.

FARM EXPENSES ARE OUTPACING
PRICES RECEIVED BY FARMERS

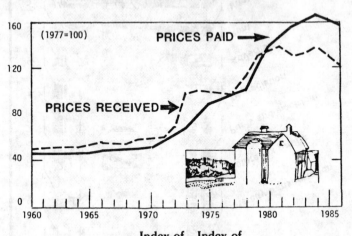

(1977=100)

PRICES PAID →

PRICES RECEIVED →

Year	Index of Prices Paid by Farmers (1977 = 100)	Index of Prices Received by Farmers
1967	49	55
1968	51	56
1969	53	59
1970	55	60
1971	58	62
1972	62	69
1973	71	98
1974	81	105
1975	89	101
1976	95	102
1977	100	100
1978	108	115
1979	123	132
1980	138	134
1981	151	139
1982	157	133
1983	161	135
1984	164	142
1985	163	128
1986	159	123

Poverty and Welfare

Minnesotans have long prided themselves on taking care of those who cannot care for themselves.

The immigrants who settled in this region, particularly the Scandinavians, brought with them a tradition of helphing one another, made more necessary by the harshness of life on the prairie.

In the 19th century, extended families who lived on adjacent farms, or close together in towns, were able to care for the elderly and the sick. Church women's groups provided food and clothing for needy families. "Welfare" help was a private affair.

As the midwest became urbanized in the 20th century, extended families broke apart, servants were not longer affordable, women entered the work force, houses were smaller and the divorce rate rose.

All these factors changed the shape of poverty and forced government to take on the task of caring for those in need through public assistance programs that are known today as welfare.

These days the poverty level for families and individuals is set each year by the U.S. government, based on a definition originated by the Social Security Administration.

For instance, in 1982 a married couple with two children was in poverty if the family income was below $9,783. A single parent with two children was in poverty if the family income was below $7,772. (By contrast, the 1982 Minnesota median family income was $24,027).

Who are Minnesota's financially needy?

In 1979, the last year for which complete figures are available, more than 374,000 Minnesotans were living in poverty. Of these, 41 percent were women, 33 percent were children and 26 percent were men. The majority of poor people, nationally and in Minnesota, were women and children.

Minnesotans most likely to be poor are females, under age 24 or over age 75, not currently married, not in the labor force and living outside the Twin Cities area.

Those least likely to be poor are male, between the ages of 25 and 64, currently married, in the labor force and living in the Twin Cities.

Poverty rates are highest for both men and women among those ages 18 to 21 and among those age 65 and older. The highest rates, 19 percent for women and 13 percent for men, are for persons age 75 and above.

Six percent of women and five percent of men age 40 to 54 are poor, the lowest rate for any age group. (This is explained in part by the fact that most people this age are married and living with their spouses, a life stage that is associated with economic well-being.)

YOUR WELFARE DOLLAR
State and County Dollars

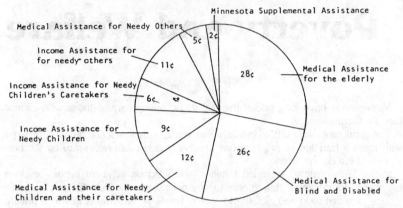

Poverty rates are consistently higher in the balance of the state than in Region 11, which is made up of the seven-county Twin Cities metropolitan area: Anoka, Carver, Dakota, Hennepin, Ramsey, Scott and Washington counties.

The highest poverty rate by region and age is for women age 75 and older living outside the Twin Cities area. Almost a quarter of these women had poverty level incomes in 1979.

Those who live alone are likely to be in poverty.

Median income for female one-person households was $6,483 in 1979, 59 percent of the $11,039 median for male one-person households. Both figures are well below the average of $22,533 for married-couple families in the state.

For both men and women living alone, median income decreases at older ages. For female one-person households, the median ranges from $10,006 for those under age 45 to $4,610 for those age 65 and older. For their male counterparts, the

PERCENT OF WELFARE RECIPIENTS

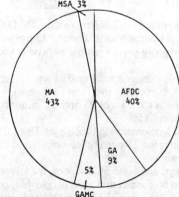

373,511 Recipients.
An unduplicated count is 255,247.

median ranges from $13,311 for those under age 45 to $5,193 for those age 65 and older.

Families, however, can also live in poverty. There were more than 74,000 Minnesota families with income below the poverty level in 1979.

Families maintained by women with no spouse present are most vulnerable to poverty: 23 percent of these families compared with five percent of husband-wife families and eight percent of male-headed families had income below the poverty level in 1979.

More than 122,000 Minnesota children were in poverty that year. Female-headed families with children have a higher poverty rate, 30 percent, than those without children, 6 percent. Those with preschool-age children are more likely than those with only school-age children to be poor, 50 percent compared with 21 percent.

How does the state welfare system help these people?

In 1985, some 255,247 Minnesotans, or about 6 percent of the state's population, received some form of public assistance. For the 1985-87 biennium, total welfare expenditures are 18.4 percent of the state budget.

These monies are distributed through five major welfare programs. They are:

● Aid to Families with Dependent Children (AFDC) — This is a federal/state/county program that provides income maintenance to dependent children and their caretakers who meet eligibility requirements. More than 8 out of 10 caretakers are women.

● Minnesota Supplemental Assistance (MSA) — This is a state program that supplements the federal Supplemental Security Income program and Social Security benefits to needy aged, blind and disabled persons. About 54 percent of MSA recipients are women.

● General Assistance (GA) — This is a state program that provides assistance for basic maintenance needs. It is for needy persons who do not qualify for AFDC, SSI or MSA.

● Medical Assistance (MA) — This is a federal/state program that pays the cost of medical care for eligible persons who cannot afford the cost of necessary medical services.

● General Assistance Medical Care (GAMC) — This is a state/county program that pays medical expenses incurred by general assistance recipients and other needy people not eligible for medical assistance.

These were the percent of welfare recipients in each program in 1985: AFDC, 40 percent; MSA, 3 percent; GA, 9 percent; MA, 43 percent; GAMC, 5 percent.

STANDARD OF NEED FOR FY 86**

Number of Children in Grant	Children Only	Plus One Adult	Plus Two Adults
1	$248	$434	$507
2	342	528	601
3	430	616	689
4	505	691	764
5	581	767	840
6	657	843	916
7	722	908	981
8	786	972	1045

**These grants received a 1 percent increase as of July 1986.

In fiscal 1985, state medical assistance expenditures totalled $994,060,970. Although the majority of persons receiving Medical Assistance are members of AFDC families, their proportion of the dollar amount is much smaller, less than 20 percent. The biggest percent of MA funding goes to the aged (43 percent) and the blind and disabled (39 percent).

Aid to Families with Dependent Children is one of the most controversial of the state's welfare programs.

Minnesota law defines a dependent child as one who is "found to be deprived of parental support or care by reason of death, continued absence from home, or physical or mental incapacity of a parent . . ."

During most of the 50-year history of the program, the predominant deprivation factor has been the continued absence of the father.

To be eligible for the program, a family must also meet income and asset limits.

For fiscal year 1986, the income standard for need for a caretaker with two children was $528 a month.

In fiscal 1985, there were a monthly average of 93,648 children and 55,694 caretakers receiving AFDC benefits.

The AFDC caretaker is most likely to be a mother in her 20s. Prior to 1982,

PERCENT OF SELECTED GROUPS
BELOW POVERTY, 1979

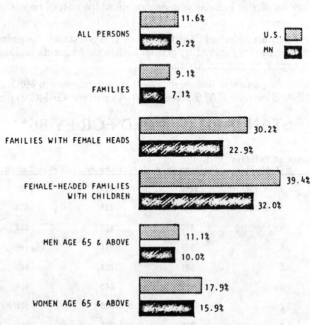

	U.S.	MN
ALL PERSONS	11.6%	9.2%
FAMILIES	9.1%	7.1%
FAMILIES WITH FEMALE HEADS	30.2%	22.9%
FEMALE-HEADED FAMILIES WITH CHILDREN	39.4%	32.0%
MEN AGE 65 & ABOVE	11.1%	10.0%
WOMEN AGE 65 & ABOVE	17.9%	15.9%

PERSONS IN POVERTY BY AGE AND REGION: 1979

Age and Sex	Minnesota		Region 11		Balance of State	
	Total Population	% In Poverty	Total Population	% In Poverty	Total Population	% In Poverty
CHILDREN UNDER AGE 18	**1,174,202**	**10.4%**	**557,087**	**7.8%**	**617,115**	**12.8%**
WOMEN AGE 18 AND OVER	**1,505,769**	**10.2**	**749,686**	**7.5**	**756,083**	**12.9**
Age 18 to 21	164,249	16.0	78,905	13.1	85,344	18.6
Age 22 to 39	578,283	8.7	320,469	6.9	257,814	10.8
Age 40 to 54	294,233	5.9	147,894	3.8	146,339	8.1
Age 55 to 59	97,107	7.2	45,859	4.8	51,248	9.2
Age 60 to 64	89,580	9.1	38,813	6.8	50,767	10.9
Age 65 to 74	150,174	13.0	61,671	9.5	88,503	15.5
Age 75 and Over	132,143	19.2	56,075	13.3	76,068	23.5
MEN AGE 18 AND OVER	**1,395,999**	**7.1**	**679,100**	**4.6**	**716,899**	**9.5**
Age 18 to 21	158,373	10.4	75,425	7.3	82,948	13.2
Age 22 to 39	579,206	6.5	312,597	5.0	266,609	8.2
Age 40 to 54	289,352	5.2	144,230	2.5	145,122	7.8
Age 55 to 59	91,596	5.5	42,969	3.0	48,627	7.8
Age 60 to 64	80,371	6.9	33,557	4.2	46,814	8.8
Age 65 to 74	119,746	8.2	43,618	4.7	76,128	10.2
Age 75 and Over	77,355	12.8	26,704	7.3	50,651	15.7

women turned to AFDC because of divorce, but after 1982, birth out of wedlock became the major reason why fathers were absent. In 1985, "parents not married" continued to be the major cause for the father's absence.

Criteria for eligibility for AFDC was expanded in July, 1970, to include two-parent families where the father met the program's definition of an unemployed father. In 1979, this category was expanded to include unemployed mothers and became the unemployed parent category. In 1985, an unemployed father was the reason for eligibility for 17.3 percent of the children. The "typical" child on AFDC in 1985 was

POVERTY BY REGION

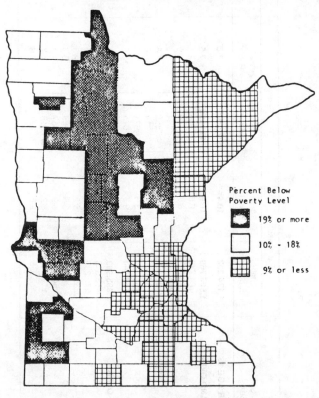

Percent Below
Poverty Level

19% or more

10% - 18%

9% or less

Fifteen percent of Minnesota's poor live in the poorest fourth of Minnesota's counties. Fifty percent of Minnesota's poor live in the most affluent fourth of Minnesota's counties.

1985-87 MINNESOTA STATE BUDGET
Total Spending $10.5 Billion

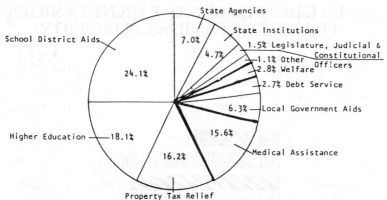

six years old. The largest single age group was three years, accounting for 8 percent of all children in the program. More than one-third of AFDC children are pre-schoolers.

The average length of stay on AFDC in Minnesota is approximately two years. In June, 1985, 59 percent of AFDC families had been on AFDC for less than two years, with more than a third on for less than one year. Almost 85 percent of AFDC families had been on the program for less than five years.

The end of single parenthood seems to account for 40 percent or more of single parent family exits from the program.

Separated and divorced AFDC recipients stay on the program for shorter periods than do mothers who have had their children out of wedlock. (Sixty-eight percent of divorced women and 61 percent of separated women remain on AFDC for less than two years, while only 39 percent of unwed mothers are off of AFDC in less than two years.)

Education seems the key to leaving AFDC. Seventy-five percent of single parents in the program are high school graduates. Ninety-four percent of AFDC recipients who leave the program through work are high school graduates while only 52 percent of the long-term AFDC recipients (84 or more months) have high school diplomas. People who leave AFDC through work also tend to have fewer children.

What's the future of welfare?

With the worsening of the national economy in the late 1970s, and financial short-falls in the early 80s that caused tax increases, "welfare reform" became a major issue in the state.

During the 1986 Minnesota legislative session, legislation was introduced to reduce AFDC grants by 30 percent. It didn't pass, but several study commissions were established to explore welfare reform options.

One of the most controversial of these is "work fare," in which the welfare recipients perform some public service. It is being studied by municipal governments, but advocates for people on welfare argue that the plan is demeaning and unfair.

The debate over welfare is likely to last well in the 1990s.

FEMALE-HEADED SINGLE-PARENT FAMILIES PERCENT OF FAMILIES IN POVERTY
1979

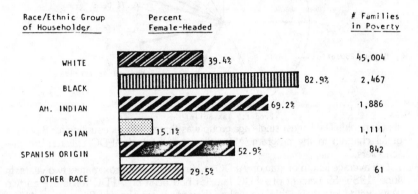

Race/Ethnic Group of Householder	Percent Female-Headed	# Families in Poverty
WHITE	39.4%	45,004
BLACK	82.9%	2,467
AM. INDIAN	69.2%	1,886
ASIAN	15.1%	1,111
SPANISH ORIGIN	52.9%	842
OTHER RACE	29.5%	61

Source: *Minn. Women and Poverty, Commission on the Economic Status of Women,* Jan. 1985.

The nonpartisan Countryside Council interviewed hundreds of residents of 19 southwest Minnesota counties and surveyed 200 social service providers about economic stress in this troubled agricultural area. Among the findings: one-fifth of the individuals had trouble paying for housing or utilities; couldn't afford medical care; worried about career change and felt depressed. One quarter reported their income as below the previous year's. The information was gathered in the summer of 1984.

Arts and Entertainment

Minnesota is tops in the nation in the way state government joins hands with the private sector to support the arts.

This was the message of a formal letter of commendation from President Ronald Reagan presented to Gov. Rudy Perpich in July of 1984.

In his letter the president spoke of "the unique and model partnership that exists in Minnesota between the Minnesota State Arts Board and the private sector corporations and foundation funders who have a commitment to the arts."

That commitment to the arts goes back to the days when Minnesota was still a territory and Indians and voyageurs roamed the land.

PAINTING AND SCULPTURE

Adventuring artists were drawn to Minnesota territory by the beauty of the landscape and interest in the lives of Indians. Soldier-artists stationed at Fort Snelling, whose job was to record important military information, also contributed views of the fort and surrounding scenes.

One of the earliest sketches of what would become Minnesota was done by Jonathan Carver who sketched the Falls of St. Anthony in 1776.

In the early 19th century scenes were recorded by Samuel Seymour who was part of the Stephen Long map-making expedition of 1823 and sketched Maiden Rock on Lake Pepin; Peter Rindisbacher who is believed to have worked along the North Dakota-Minnesota border in the 1820's and was the first to paint the daily lives of Indians and George Catlin of Pennsylvania who visited Fort Snelling and the plains Indians as well as the sacred quarry at Pipestone.

Seth Eastman's name is synonymous with Minnesota. He was assigned to Fort Crawford (near Prairie du Chien) after graduating from West Point and sketched several Indian tribes in the vicinity. Between 1848 and 1854 Eastman illustrated five books on Indian themes written by his wife, Mary Eastman. The first, **Dahcotah: or, Life and Legends of the Sioux Around Fort Snelling** was the inspiration for Henry Longfellow's poem **"Hiawatha."**

Eastman spent five years illustrating Henry W. Schoolcraft's six-volume work on Indian tribes of the United States. Forty-six of the watercolors used as a basis for these illustrations were purchased by railroad tycoon James J. Hill and are owned by the Hill Reference Library of St. Paul.

Other early artists who painted in the Upper Mississippi Valley include James

Otto Leis, the official government representative commissioned to paint portraits at the Treaty of Prairie du Chien; Charles Deas of Philadelphia who painted Fort Snelling; John Casper Wild, whose 1844 "View of Fort Snelling Seen from Mendota" is owned by the Minnesota Historical Society, and John M. Stanley of New York State and Detroit who visited the fort in 1835 and 1853 and made drawings of St. Paul, Minnehaha Falls and White Bear Lake.

By the time Minnesota became a state in 1858 fewer itinerant artists were visiting the area. But settlers in the more cosmopolitan cities of St. Paul, Stillwater, Winona and Red Wing were beginning to appreciate art - although "art" could mean anything from ladies' collars to drawings and paintings.

By the 1870s some citizens were considered patrons of the arts, including Henry M. Rice, E. S. Goodrich, J. C. Burbank and James J. Hill, whose collection became to extensive he had to add a gallery onto his house.

Among St. Paul's resident painters in the 1880s were J. D. Larpenteur, Mrs. G. B. Grant, W. H. Frisbie, Vincent de Gornon, and Nicholas R. Brewer and Charles Noel Flagg.

In the 1890s a group of women started classes that evolved into the St. Paul School of Fine Arts. The school became the St. Paul Gallery and School of Art.

In Minneapolis at about this time a Dane named Peter Clausen executed frescoes in the Church of the Redeemer (Universalist), the first work in fresco done in Minneapolis.

The Minneapolis Society of Fine Arts was formed in January of 1883, a group which started with no endowment and no quarters of its own. Today the society supports and governs the Minneapolis Institute of Arts and the Minneapolis College of Art and Design.

The society's first president was William Watts Folwell, then president of the University of Minnesota. The other important man on the Minneapolis arts scene at the time was Thomas Barlow Walker, a civic-minded businessman and collector who established the Walker Foundation and deeded his 6,000 art objects to it, as well as property on which to build a museum. Walker Gallery opened in 1927 and has become an important midwest repository for modern art as the Walker Art Center.

Among turn-of-the-century artists was Stephen A. Douglas Volk, first director of the Minneapolis School of Art; Alexis Fournier, identified with the French Barbizon school and Robert Koehler, a German whose prize-winning painting, "The Strike", was presented to the city of Minneapolis by the Society of Fine Arts.

Koehler, director of the Minneapolis School of Art until 1914, saw a number of students enrolled at the school who made their mark on the national art scene, including Adolf Dehn who specialized in watercolors; Arnold Blanch, born in Mantorville; Elizabeth Olds of Minneapolis; Wanda Gag, New Ulm children's book author and illustrator; Dewey Albinson who used northern Minnesota scenes or subjects and Cameron Booth, the man who brought Minnesota a national reputation. In the early 1920s Booth painted farmlands, the Iron Range and streets of Minnesota but after World War II he worked in the abstract vein. Booth was director from 1929 to 1942 of the St. Paul School of Art, now the Minnesota Museum of Art.

The museum was founded in 1924 by a group of art students known as the Art Students League of St. Paul. The League operated the St. Paul Gallery and School of Art in an old Summit Avenue mansion until 1964 when the institution moved into the new St. Paul Arts and Science Center; in 1969 the name was changed to Minnesota Museum of Art. In 1972 the museum purchased the old Women's City Club in downtown St. Paul and now operates two facilities.

With a budget of just $1 million the museum mounts 15 to 18 exhibitions a year and runs an extensive education program as well as a museum school.

Other Minnesotans with wide reputations are Josephine Lutz Rollins, Jerome Kamrowski, Eddy May and LeRoy Neiman.

The gallery scene today in the Twin Cities is active; a survey by the Arts Resource and Information Center showed 160 non-profit and for-profit galleries in the Twin Cities in the summer of 1984. Young artists have been especially active in St. Paul's Lowertown area and there are women's art collectives in both St. Paul and Minneapolis.

Jakob H. F. Fjelde was the first trained sculptor known to have been a resident of the state. Born in Norway, he came to the U. S. in 1887 and lived in Minneapolis until his death in 1896. Fjelde was responsible for the bust of dramatist Ibsen in Como Park and the statue of "Hiawatha and Minnehaha" in Minnehaha Park.

Sculptors who had Minnesota connections and gained national renown are Paul Manship, John B. Flannagan, John Rood and Alonzo Hauser.

Manship was born in St. Paul in 1885 and studied at the St. Paul School of Fine Arts before leaving the state for further schooling. His best-known work is the "Prometheus" sculpture in New York's Rockefeller Center. His "Europa and the Bull" is owned by Walker Art Center.

Rood worked in wood, stone and welded metals and his commissions are at St. Mark's Cathedral in Minneapolis and Hamline University in St. Paul.

Hauser was head of the Macalester College art department until 1949. One of his most visible works is a bronze figure of a young girl seated amidst petals of a large flower. The piece is on the Capital Approach in St. Paul.

Women sculptors include Evelyn Raymond of Duluth and Katherine Nash.

MUSIC

The earliest known music in what was to become Minnesota was created by the Sioux and Chippewa Indians who used chants as part of their religious ceremonies.

The late Frances Densmore of Red Wing is responsible for collecting some 3,600 Indian songs, using wax cylinders available in the early part of the century.

The first white men's music was brought into the territory by voyageurs, French-Canadian canoemen and guides. They sang of love and sunny climates, home and adventure, often using a rhythm set by paddle strokes.

By mid-19th century immigrants were arriving, bringing with them music from all parts of Europe, especially Scandinavia and Germany.

As settlements grew into villages instruments began arriving in St. Paul - pianos, harpsichords and melodeons. Violins, coronets and flutes began to be heard and churches began putting together choirs.

By 1863 St. Paul had a Musical Society, a small orchestra which lasted a quarter of a century, often playing in the newly-created city of Minneapolis.

In Minneapolis one of the first instrumental groups was the Quintette Club of the 1850s. In the '60s the Germans formed the Harmonia Society and, in 1868, the Musical Union, both choral groups.

Two men responsible for bringing music to the Twin Cities were George Seibert, who directed the St. Paul Musical Society, and his brother-in-law, a Fort Snelling bandleader named Frank Danz. Seibert organized the Great Western Band and Orchestra in St. Paul and Danz organized a similar group in Minneapolis.

By the last two decades of the 19th century some 30 opera companies were traveling through Minnesota. The Boston Symphony Orchestra visited in 1890 and the Metropolitan Orchestra in 1893.

The most important organization of the 1890s was the Philharmonic Club, a mixed choral group which sprang out of a Minneapolis organization called the Filharmonix.

By 1902 the Philharmonic Club had become so successful it was organized into the Minneapolis Symphony - now the Minnesota Orchestra.

The orchestra eventually became the first major civic orchestra associated with a university, giving regular concerts in Northrop Auditorium. In 1968 the orchestra became the Minnesota Orchestra, and in 1974 it moved into the new Orchestra Hall in Minneapolis, a building praised for its acoustic perfection and a fitting home for an orchestra that had built a world-wide reputation.

Musicians of exceptional skills have led the Minnesota Orchestra, including Eugene Ormandy, Dimitri Mitropolous, Antal Dorati, Stanislaw Skrowaczewski and Neville Merriner.

The orchestra's programming today, based on a budget of about $13 million, includes three orchestral series, a Great Performers and Masters of the Keyboard series, holiday specials including the "Nutcracker Fantasy," jazz concerts, radio and television broadcasts, orchestral, tours and education programs.

Although there was a fully professional St. Paul Symphony Orchestra between 1906 and 1914, it was the atmosphere of the 1930s and '40s that led to establishment of St. Paul's current most renown group - The St. Paul Chamber Orchestra.

In the '30s and '40s John J. Becker, a pioneer in the 12-tone technique, conducted a professional group of free-lance musicians in programs featuring American contemporary composers. When Becker moved to California in 1959, Leopold Sipe became director of the St. Paul Philharmonic Society. Becoming a professional group in 1968, the Society became the Chamber Orchestra.

Sipe was replaced by Dennis Russel Davies in 1972 and the orchestra developed a reputation for its 20th century repertoire. Today the orchestra's artistic director is Pinchas Zukerman and the repertoire spans four centuries.

The Duluth-Superior Symphony Orchestra dates from 1932; the Fargo-Moorhead Symphony celebrated its 50th anniversary in 1981 and the Rochester Symphony began in the 1920s.

CHORAL MUSIC

Many people maintain that Minnesota is one of the leading states in choral singing.

Much credit for that attitude must go to the Apollo Club, a male chorus started in Minneapolis in the 1890s.

In the early 20th century F. Melius Christiansen, a 32-year-old Norwegian violinist and teacher, turned the St. Olaf Choir of St. Olaf College, Northfield, into a world class choral group.

The high St. Olaf standards have permeated the state. At Concordia College in Moorhead Paul J. Christiansen, Melius' son, proved that a cappella singing could be nurtured in a small town. Augsburg College, Hamline University and the University of Minnesota Chorus have also been important in the choral music field.

The Bach Society originated in the early 1930s with a group of University of Minnesota music students who loved and wanted to sing Bach's choral music. They were under the leadership of Donald Ferguson from 1933 to 1950. The group ceased functioning, then was reorganized in 1959 by Dr. David Le Berge. The Society has from 80 to 90 members and has been under the musical dictatorship of Henry Chas. Smith since 1980. They perform concerts throughout the year, including an annual Bach Festival and Christmas concert.

Today the Dale Warland Singers are bringing praise to Minnesota. The group began in 1970 as the Opera Chorale and the name was changed to the Dale Warland Singers in 1972. The chorus offers an extensive repertoire of a cappella choral music as well as 20th century works. The ensemble is featured on 10 record albums and consistently sells out concerts in the Twin Cities.

One of the most important organizations fostering musical excellence is the Schubert Club of St. Paul, started in the 1880s by Marion Ramsey Furness, Gov. Alexander Ramsey's daughter. Through the years the club has sponsored programs by some of the world's greatest musicians, including Isaac Stern, Beverly Sills and the Juilliard String Quartet. The Schubert Club will be one of the tenants of the new Ordway Music Center, scheduled to open in January of 1985 in St. Paul.

Verna (Mrs. Carlyle) Scott organized the University Artists Course in 1919 and thereafter brought to town scores of the world's finest and most popular artists.

From 1939 to 1971 the St. Paul Women's Institute sponsored big-name entertainers ranging from Victor Borge to Yehudi Menuhin. In those pre-television days the institute, sponsored by the St. Paul Dispatch and Pioneer Press, would draw as many as 5,000 women to the old St. Paul Auditorium.

OPERA

Minnesotans' taste for opera was satisfied by touring companies from the 1870s to the 1890s. From the early 1880s on stars and casts of New York's Metropolitan Opera House traveled under various company names. They continued to appear during the first part of the 20th century, then did not return until 1944 when a statewide sponsors' group was set up to arrange a yearly season at Northrop Auditorium. The Met's spring season now runs for a week and, although touring has become increasingly expensive, patrons and sponsors of the Metropolitan Opera of the Upper Midwest have given enough money to allow the company to continue its appearances here.

The Minnesota Opera Company was started in 1963 as a performing wing of the Walker Art Center called Center Opera. The company has established a national reputation for excellence of its productions and dedication to new American music. In 1979 Minnesota Opera received a national award for service to American opera from the National Opera Institute.

Opera St. Paul, formerly St. Paul Opera, is dedicated to providing practical operatic experience for performers and stage personnel from the Midwest.

When the Arts Resource Information Center did a survey of Minnesota arts in 1979 they found 122 music organizations. There's no doubt - Minnesotans love to make music.

THEATER

The first theater performances in Minnesota territory may have been put on by bored soldiers stationed at Fort Snelling.

The earliest troupes came to St. Paul in the 1850s, usually in summer when the steamboats were operating. By 1885, when railroads made outlying towns accessible, there were 47 towns housing plays and variety shows.

In the 1860s St. Paul built an Opera House and a wide variety of shows played the Twin Cities, including Shakesperean productions, horse operas and minstrel shows.

In the late 19th century the Twin Cities hosted some of the nation's finest performing artists and the pick of plays from New York.

It was 1878 when John Murray founded a stock company in Minneapolis, the Murray-Carland Company, which lasted until 1883. People's Stock Company of St. Paul lasted about the same length of time.

Through the 1890s there were numerous theaters in the Twin Cities, several owned by L. N. Scott.

The first part of the 20th century is dominated by "Buzz" Bainbridge, Minnesota's most enterprising manager-producer of time. He founded the longest-lived stock company in the history of the state, the Bainbridge Players, which lasted from 1912 to 1933.

By the 1920s the heyday of great touring companies was over as movies became popular; old theaters became movie houses or were razed.

The Duluth Playhouse, founded in 1914, is the oldest amateur community theater in the United States. The state's oldest "straw hat" theater is the Old Log in Excelsior, an Equity house (which pays actors full professional wages).

Another Equity phenomenon is the Chanhassen Dinner Theater, a four-stage complex that offers a wide variety of plays.

One of the most applauded volunteer theaters is Theater in the Round of Minneapolis. In 1973 TRP represented the U. S. at the international theater festival in Monaco and in 1983 the troupe took first place in biannual competition for the state of Minnesota.

Credit for current interest in theater and the wide variety of vibrant, small groups must go to the Guthrie Theater, giant of the Midwest entertainment scene.

Founded in 1963 by the late Sir Tyrone Guthrie, the theater opened with support from arts patrons and the business community. The Guthrie began as a repertory company but through the years it has changed to a format of bringing in stars and, occasionally, entire productions. Under the leadership of Rumanian director Liviu Ciulei the theater has tended toward what many feel is "director's theater," offering the world's avant-garde directors, such as Andre Serban, a chance to show their 20th century vision.

Another theater with a national reputation is the Children's Theater of Minneapolis. The theater began in the 1960s as the Moppet Players committed to the idea that theater for young people should and could be artistically excellent. In 1965 artistic director John Clarke Donahue took the newly-named Children's Theater Company to the Minneapolis Institute of Arts and in 1974 the company and its school moved to a new building adjoining the institute.

DANCE

Roy Close, dance writer and critic for the St. Paul Pioneer Press and Dispatch, said in the summer of 1984 that dance is the fastest growing art form in the Twin Cities.

A 1983 survey of arts in the metropolitan area by the St. Paul-Ramsey United Arts Council shows 19 dance companies in the cities, ranging from small, specialized groups through jazz and folk groups.

Among the most prominent is **Loyce Houlton's Minnesota Dance Theater and School**. The theater, which has been praised for innovations, has had its ups and downs through financial difficulties but has entertained thousands with its yearly performances of the "Nutcracker Fantasy" presented in cooperation with the Minnesota Orchestra.

ARTS SERVICE ORGANIZATIONS

Arts Service organizations, which encourage and support arts producers, have been an important force in the growth and success of artist and arts organizations in the metro area and the state.

The granddaddy of all the arts service organizations is the Arts Resource and Information Center (ARIC), funded by the Minneapolis Institute of Arts and located in the institute building at 2400 Third Ave. S., Minneapolis.

Director Robert Booker says the ARIC is the oldest and largest such organization in the nation. For 10 years, with the help of volunteers, the ARIC has answered 300 calls a day about the literacy, visual and performing arts. ARIC publishes an annual-director of art fairs and will publish sometime in 1984 a list of Twin Cities art galleries. Arts Reach, which offers guides to educational materials, is also an ARIC function. The telephone number is (612)870-3131.

Minnesota Citizens for the Arts, Landmark Center, 75 W. Fifth St., St. Paul, is a group of about 800 individuals and 100 organizations. MCA calls itself "a statewide political action organization" working to establish a common ground for arts supporters and to promote unity within the arts community. MCA publishes a quarterly newsletter with information on arts issues, current projects and legislation affecting the arts. Since it was formed in 1975 MCA has been devoted to ensuring opportunities for all people to experience and participate in the arts. The telephone number is (612)227-5963.

Affiliated State Arts Agencies of the Upper Midwest, 528 Hennepin Ave., Suite 302, Minneapolis, is one of eight regional arts organizations in the U. S. and works with the state arts agencies in Iowa, Minnesota, North Dakota, South Dakota and Wisconsin to foster and promote the arts resources of the region and develop and expand arts activities and audiences. The affiliation provides programs and services which, without multi-state cooperation, would not be feasible or available to people of the Upper Midwest. Principal activity recently has been assisting presenters of select touring programs in the performing and visual arts with partial financial assistance.

Recently a number of new service organizations have emerged to serve individual artists in particular disciplines.

The Playwrights' Center, 2301 Franklin Ave. E., Minneapolis, was founded in 1971. In 1975 the center began to devote all of its time, energy and money to script development. In 12 years the center has grown from serving four playwrights with a budget of $2,000 to serving more than 60 playwrights with a budget exceeding a quarter of a million dollars annually.

Minnesota Independent Choreographers Alliance, 528 Hennepin Ave. S., Minneapolis, began in 1979 when 11 choreographers got together to identify common needs. Membership has grown to more than 100 choreographers who meet monthly.

Minnesota Composers' Forum, Markethouse, Fifth and Broadway, Minneapolis, was founded in 1973 by two composers. In 11 years the forum has grown to a membership of more than 200 composers drawn largely from Minnesota but including many from throughout the United States.

The Loft, which moved into new quarters on the lower level of the Playwright's Center in the summer of 1984, is a support center for aspiring writers offering classes, sponsoring readings and maintaining a small press library.

FESTIVALS

Minnesotans love festivals. A story in the April 29, 1984 St. Paul Pioneer Press listed more than 300 festivals in the state just between May and August.

In 1984 the Minnesota State Fair, the largest festival of all, celebrated its 100th birthday at the State Fairgrounds in Falcon Heights. And Minnesota citizens gave the fair a great birthday present - they attended in record numbers of 1,446,450.

MINNESOTA STATE FAIR
YEARLY ATTENDANCE TOTALS
(Vehicles Excluded)
PERIOD OF FAIR - 12 DAYS

1978	1,386,457
1979	1,405,669
1980	1,325,360
1981	1,414,809
1982	1,321,785
1983	1,347,884
1984	1,446,450
1985	1,496,014
1986	1,565,349
1987	1,612,170

Prior to 1885 the State Agricultural Society, governing body of the fair, held expositions at a variety of locations. But public sentiment called for a permanent fair site; the Twin Cities was logical, since the area was a major population and railway center. St. Paul and Minneapolis vied for the fair and, after some intense maneuvering, the Ramsey County Board of Commissioners donated the 210-acre poor farm northwest of St. Paul for a fair site.

The first fair was held there in 1885. Only twice since then have fairs been cancelled - in 1945 because of World War II and in 1946 because of a polio epidemic. The fair was 10 days long until 1972 when it went to 11 days and in 1975 it went to 12 days.

One of the highlights of fair-going for many people is seeing Grandstand shows by some of the biggest names in the entertainment world. Sammy Davis, Jr., Englebert, Johnny Cash, Buster Keaton, Linda Ronstadt, Andy Williams, the Smothers Brothers and Chuck Mangione have all appeared in the Grandstand. The 1984 lineup included Spanish singer Julio Iglesias in his first Minnesota appearance, country stars Willie Nelson and Alabama and rock star Rod Stewart.

While the State Fair is unwinding the Renaissance Festival is offering and alternative in a field four miles southwest of Shakopee.

Some 300,000 people attend the Renaissance Festival which runs for seven weekends. The 1984 event was the 14th.

Jugglers, minstrels, acrobats, magicians, royalty, food and games all evoke a renaissance village festival. There are arts and crafts for sale and performances by more than 500 performers.

Minnesota's largest indoor festival may be the Festival of Nations, held each April at the St. Paul Civic Center. Some 60,000 people attend the festival to sample ethnic foods, see folk dancing and folk art demonstrations as well as costume shows.

The festival began in 1932 when there was tension between "Americans and foreign born" and feelings against immigrants were running high. Alice Sickels proposed a festival that would dispel discrimination and prejudice, promote understanding among people of different ethnic backgrounds and preserve the traditions of ethnic groups.

Working with the International Institute and scores of volunteers Sickels staged the first three-day festival.

By 1934 groups representing 30 nationalities were participating in the festival. Over the years displays and groups have been added as new immigrants arrive; in recent years Southeast Asians have made their debuts. In some families several generations have participated in the festival.

Arts and crafts festivals are popular in Minnesota. Some are at shopping malls and are open to everyone; others, like the Minnesota Craft Council show at the College of St. Catherine, are juried.

One of the largest art fairs is the Uptown art fair which celebrated its 21st birthday in 1984. The three-day event stretches out along streets and alleys in the Hennepin-Lake area of south Minneapolis, drawing some 200,000 visitors to look at more than 100,000 pieces of artwork shown by 660 exhibitors from 28 states.

A new festival may become a tradition in Detroit Lakes, 45 miles east of Fargo-Moorhead. The "More in '84" country-western music festival staged in August, 1984, the second such festival, drew between 60,000 and 75,000 people to hear Merle Haggard, Ronnie Milsap and Johnny Cash.

Two St. Paul-based festivals are becoming among the biggest in the state.

Taste of Minnesota has been sponsored for five years by the St. Paul Downtown Council. It is held on the grounds of the State Capitol where participants can buy food from Twin Cities restaurants and caterers and hear music, including a Fourth of July concert by the Minnesota Orchestra. The 1987 festival drew a record 220,000 people.

Right after Taste of Minnesota, in mid-July, RiverFest takes up residence for 10 days on the banks of the Mississippi River across from downtown St. Paul. About 250,000 people attended the 1987 celebration, which included entertainment by some nationally-known singers. Whitney Houston drew crowds of 50,000 during each of her two nights of performances.

FILM

Although Minnesota is not the Hollywood of the North, there is much interest in films, as shown by the rapid expansion of film in the cities of St. Paul and Minnesota Film Center/University Film Society located in Minneapolis.

Film in the Cities started in 1970 as a program of the St. Paul-Ramsey Arts and Science Council in response to the need of the public schools for an alternative communications program. It has expanded in scope and increased its programs until FITC is now a comprehensive media arts center offering education and service programs. In 1980 FITC was awarded a $300,000 grant from the National Endowment for the Arts in recognition of its achievements.

University Film Society, founded in 1962, was a student group at the University of Minnesota through most of the 1960s, sponsoring showings of foreign and domestic films overlooked by commercial theaters. Incorporated in 1980 as the Minnesota Film Center it is now the fourth largest non-profit film exhibitor in the U. S. The society has sponsored visits by more than 300 prominent guest filmmakers and critics.

"Personals" was filmed in Minneapolis in the early 1980s. The comedy-drama was written, directed and filmed by Peter Markle and original music was written by Will Sumner, leader of the St. Paul fusion jazz group Tropic Zone.

John Hanson, St. Paul-born independent filmmaker used Eveleth as a setting for "Wildrose," a film about life on the Iron Range which opened in the summer of 1984 to good reviews. Many critics praised Hanson for his sensitivity and his ability to fuse professional actors and townspeople.

In August of 1984 filming began in St. Paul's Capitol Hill area on "That Was Then, This Is Now," based on a novel by S. E. Hinton and produced by Media Ventures of Minneapolis, a company which produced "Touch", a film on sexual abuse.

In the summer of 1984, the summer of Michael Jackson's fabulously successful Victory Tour, national critics bestowed the coveted "star" title on a slight, dark 26-year-old rock singer from Minneapolis named Prince after his movie, "Purple Rain" began packing movie houses around the country. "Purple Rain" was filmed in late 1983 at First Avenue, a Minneapolis club.

JAZZ

When Jazz impressario George Wein visited the Twin Cities in 1982, he was amazed that there were 1,500 dues-paying members of the Twin Cities Jazz Society.

Jazz is a growing scene in the Twin Cities with more activity by local musicians and more concerts by national groups than there have ever been, according to Bob Protzman, jazz and entertainment writer for the St. Paul newspapers. Jazz acts are being booked by Cricket Theater, Walker Art Center, the University of Minnesota, Orchestra Hall and the new Ordway Music Center in St. Paul. There's even jazz at the State Fair.

There is a jazz degree program at the University of Minnesota, summer jazz concerts in some parks and jazz film showings.

In 1982 there were some 30 clubs in the Twin Cities where some jazz was played several nights a week. The Artists Quarter in Minneapolis is devoted exclusively to jazz and the Emporium of Jazz in Mendota is dedicated to Dixieland and swing.

Most amazing to those from other cities is the fact that all kinds of jazz can be heard here.

Among the big name artists who have appeared in the Twin Cities are avant-garde or free-jazz people booked by the Walker, including Cecil Taylor and Ornette Coleman; Orchestra Hall's pop-jazzers like Jeff Lorber and mainstreamers like Stephanie Grappelli and Oscar Peterson; Northrop's commercially attractive performers such as Betty Carter, Joe Williams and Alberta Hunter. And the Emporium of Jazz has hosted the greats - Pee Wee Erwin, Jay McShann, Ruby Braff, Bud Freeman and Urbie Green.

Well known jazz musicians with Minnesota roots include drummer Kenny Horst, trumpeter Red Wolfe and bass player Oscar Pettiford. Known locally are Butch Thompson, the Hall Brothers, Percy Hughes, McCoy Tyner, Milo Fine, Manfredo Fest, Roberta Davis, Eddie Berger, Morris Wilson, Sue Drude and Debra Joyce and Shirley Witherspoon.

THE ARTS TODAY - FOCUS ON FUNDING

If Minnesota arts and arts patrons came of age at any specific time, it would have been in the early 1970s. In 1974 the state made national news when a Ford Foundation-sponsored study showed that the Twin Cities metropolitan area was second only to New York in individual exposure to the performing arts and movies.

But the report was also prophetic. It predicted that by 1981 the national performing arts deficit could be increased sixfold.

By the late 70s inflation and increased costs left Twin Cities arts organizations looking for new methods of financing, slimming their operating expenses and rethinking their missions.

Ripples of worry spread from the arts community to the community at large, for by the end of the 1970s art had become big business in Minnesota.

A Twin Cities Arts Alliance study reported that the 10 largest Twin Cities arts organizations accounted for more than $21.7 million in wages paid to 3,000 people in 1978. The researchers estimated that the amount of money spent in the community by the institutions and their patrons totaled more than $57 million. Local government received another $2.13 million in taxes.

Over all, the researchers concluded that the economic impact of the 10 organizations on the local economy in 1978 was $85 million.

Major support for the arts in Minnesota today comes from three sources:
* public and private foundations
* businesses
* government agencies, chiefly the Minnesota State Arts Board

Major foundations which funnel arts support through the Minnesota State Arts Board are:
* The McKnight Foundation which funds a program to support Minnesota arts organizations for day-to-day operations.
* The Dayton-Hudson Foundation, which provides grants to enable Minnesota artists to work on interdisciplinary or collaborative projects.
* The Jerome Foundation, which grants studio residency fellowships in New York City to emerging Minnesota artists.
* The Northwest Area Foundation, which underwrites tours by performing artists from Minnesota.

A 1977 report by the Minnesota Council on Foundations said total foundation support for the arts was $15,626,620, or about 20 percent of all charitable giving by foundations. A 1979-1980 study by the Council on Foundations of giving by the state's 30 largest foundations showed 23.5 percent of giving was directed to the arts, compared to 15.3 percent given to the arts in 1981 by foundations nationwide.

Minnesota is a national leader in corporate support of the arts as well. Federal law allows businesses to contribute up to 5 percent of pre-tax earnings to charitable causes and Minnesota was one of the first states to institutionalize the practice in 1975. By 1980 almost 50 companies belonged to the "Five Percent Club" and their total contributions were about five times the national average, according to the Council on Foundations.

Federal and state money is the third major source of arts income. These monies are funneled through the Minnesota State Arts Board.

The legislative appropriation from the arts board grew steadily from 1966, when the state allocated only $5,000, to the arts until 1980. For the 1976-77 biennium the total was $1 million and in 1980 it was over $2 million.

In 1980 Minnesota was ninth among the 50 states in its public support of the arts. The state also ranked third, behind New York and Massachusetts, in the amount of public money available to individual artists in the form of fellowships and project grants.

In 1980 the state arts appropriation was $2,078,993. But in 1981, 1982 and 1983 the appropriation dropped each year.

In 1981 too, President Reagan proposed an $85-million budget cut in the National Endowment for the Arts and arts organizations again began the scramble for money.

The good news in 1981 was that the McKnight Foundation would put $1.6 million into the arts each year for the next six years.

By 1983 the Minnesota State Arts Board budget had been sliced 22.7 percent. Small arts group were especially hard hit.

Some of the lost money was made up by giving from private citizens and corporations. An example is what happened to the United Arts Fund which provides the greatest single source of support for six affiliated St. Paul arts groups - Chimera Theater, COMPAS, Minnesota Landmarks, the Minnesota Museum of Art, the St. Paul Chamber Orchestra and the Schubert Club.

Since 1981, the arts appeal has grown more successful each year. In 1983 contributions rose to $1.61 million from $1.37 million two years earlier. The 1984 goal was $1.65 million.

By early 1984, although arts organizations' managers were not entirely optimistic, it looked as though the worst was over.

Said one arts administrator, "the recession made us smarter."

MINNESOTA STATE ARTS BOARD

The Minnesota State Arts Board, an agency of state government, is a reorganization of the Minnesota State Arts Council, which was created by the Minnesota legislature in 1966. The agency was created initially for educational purposes and in response to the availability of federal funds from the National Endowment for the Arts for establishment of state arts agencies.

Primary purpose of the board today is to provide grants and related services to arts organizations, individual artists and schools.

In fiscal 1986, the board was governed by 11 private citizens appointed by the governor to serve non-salaried terms of four years. Eight of the members are selected to represent each of the state's congressional districts; the other three serve at-large.

Primary funding sources for the board are:

- appropriations from the State of Minnesota
- grants from the National Endowment for the Arts (a federal agency)
- partnership with the private sector including foundations and business.

The agency (a total budget for fiscal 1986 was $3,760,461. Federal monies included a block grant of $379,900, an Arts in Education grant of $117,800, a $2,650 initiative to fund a professional artist-in-residence in a state prison and a Folk Arts grant of $30,000.

Private funding was:

- McKnight Foundation - $575,000
- Dayton-Hudson Foundation - $12,800
- Northwest Area Foundation - $50,000
- American Express Travel Related Services Company - $137,000

The board is also a partner with regional arts councils and during fiscal 1986, distributed $797,300 to the various councils throughout the state. Here is the breakdown:

REGIONAL ARTS COUNCIL STAFF

REGION 1
Mary Jo Crystal
NW Regional Development Comm.
425 Woodland
Crookston, MN 56716
(218) 281-1396

REGION 2
Eileen Stankavich
Region Two Arts & Humanities Cncl.
Bemidji Community Arts Center
426 Bemidji Avenue
Bemidji, MN 56601
(218) 751-5447

REGION 3
Eleanor Hovda
Arrowhead Regional Arts Council
217 Old Main Building
2215 East 5th Street
Duluth, MN 55812
(218) 724-3610

REGION 4
Sonja Peterson
West Central Regional Arts Cncl.
PO Box 661, City Hall
112 W. Washington Avenue
Fergus Falls, MN 56537
(218) 739-4617

REGION 5
Virginia MacArthur
Region Five Regional Dev. Comm.
611 Iowa Avenue
Staples, MN 56479
(218) 894-3233

REGIONS 6E, 6W, 8
Jerry Schaefer
SW MN Arts & Humanities Cncl. (SMAHC)
PO Box 1193
Marshall, MN 56258
(507) 537-1471
Toll-Free 800-622-5284

REGION 7E
Phil Schroeder
East Central Regional Dev. Comm.
119 South Lake Street
Mora, MN 55051
(612) 679-4065

REGION 7W
Greg Reigstad
Central Minnesota Arts Council
PO Box 1442
St. Cloud, MN 56301
(612) 253-9517

REGION 9
Marliss Johnston
Region Nine Regional Dev. Comm.
410 South 5th St., Box 3367
Mankato, MN 56001
(507) 387-5643
Toll-Free 800-722-9389

REGION 10
Pat Beaver
Southeastern MN Arts Council
1312 1/2 7th St. NW
Suite 207
Rochester, MN 55901
(507) 281-4848

REGION 11
Marion Angelica or Linda Hennessey
Metropolitan Arts Council
300 Metro Square Building
7th & Robert St.
St. Paul, MN 55101
(612) 291-6571

Sources:
Arts Resource and Information Center, **Nonprofit Arts Organizations in Minnesota,** (Mpls., Minn., 2nd edit., 1979)

John K. Sherman, **Music and Theater in Minnesota History,** (Mpls., Minn., Univ. of Minn. Pr., 1958)

Donald R. Torbert, **A Century of Art and Architecture in Minnesota,** (Mpls., Minn., Univ. of Minn. Pr., 1958)

Minnesota State Fair Communications Office, Jerry Hammer

Minnesota State Arts Board, Margie Casey

Saint Paul-Ramsey United Arts Council, **Metropolitan Arts Survey,** (Saint Paul, Minn., Nov., 1983)

Minnesota Renaissance Fair, Information Office, Marilyn Ruedy

LITERATURE

The first written description of what would become Minnesota appeared in Paris in 1683. **Description of Louisiana,** written by Father Louis Hennepin, told of a journey to the Upper Mississippi in 1680.

Other works by early writers about Minnesota territory include Pierre Esprit Radisson's **Voyages of Peter Esprit Radisson,** written in 1688-69; Pierre Margray's six-volume work about travels in Minnesota country between 1650 and 1763 and Englishman Capt. Jonathan Carver's **Travels through the Interior Parts of North American in the Years 1766, 1767 and 1768** which was an instant success in London in 1778.

Lt. Zebulon Montgomery Pike wrote one of the first important American accounts of travel through Minnesota country. He journeyed to Leech Lake in 1806 and his personal diary was published in 1807.

The Mississippi began to attract adventurers from America and Europe in the early 1800s, many with names familiar to today's Minnesotans. Lewis Cass, Stephen H. Long, Giacomo Beltrami, Henry R. Schoolcraft and Joseph N. Nicollet all left travel narratives.

By the 1830s missionaries had begun to record their observations for eastern and European magazines. Some of them put the Chippewa and Sioux languages in writing.

At the same time Mary Henderson Eastman, wife of artist Seth Eastman, published her work on the legends of the Sioux around Fort Snelling. Henry Hastings Sibley, fur trader and future governor of the state, wrote sports stories for sports journals and sketches for the St. Paul Pioneer newspaper.

Joseph Snelling, son of Col. Josiah Snelling, first commandant of Fort Snelling, roamed the countryside as a youth and wrote **Tales of the Northwest,** published in 1830, describing the colorful traders, voyageurs and Indians he knew. He also published many magazine articles and juvenile books.

In 1846 and 1848 a French scientist, Auguste Lamare-Picquot visited Minnesota territory and wrote about his adventures and scientific investigations. The plant "picquotinae" is named for him.

William Whipple Warren, part-Chippewa son of a fur trader, wrote a history of his tribe and its culture in the 1840s which was published in 1853 by the Minnesota Historical Society.

In St. Cloud Jane Grey Swisshelm was protesting slavery and advocating women's rights in her newspaper, *Visitor,* and in Sauk Rapids newspaper editor and author Julia Sargent Wood was turning out novels, articles, poems and short stories.

One of Minnesota's first novelists was Edward Eggleston, whose *The Mystery of Metropolisville* depicts the land speculation craze of the 1850s. By 1894 he was a well known short story writer.

In the history of Minnesota journalism a name that blazes is James Madison Goodhue, owner and editor of Minnesota's first newspaper, the *Minnesota Pioneer,* now the St. Paul Pioneer Press and Dispatch. He wrote fierce editorials and was known beyond the boundaries of the state during his career in the 1850s.

That era also brought national attention to writer Ignatius Donnelly. Orator and advocate of third-party movements, he was also the author of a wide variety of books, including *Atlantis, the Antediluvian World; Ragnarok, The Age of Fire and Gravel* and *The Great Cryptogram, Francis Bacon's Cipher in the So-Called Shakespeare Plays.*

Presbyterian minister Edward Duffield Neill, founder and first president of Macalester College in St. Paul, was a respected historian and published his *History of Minnesota* in 1858.

Norwegian Thorstein Veblen spent much of his boyhood in Minnesota and graduated in 1880 from Carleton College, Northfield. In 1899 he published his most famous book, *The Theory of the Leisure Class.* Although Veblen was an economist, he is thought of today as a sociologist and his theory of "conspicuous consumption" is still discussed.

Hamlin Garland became the voice of disenchanted midwest farmers at the turn of the century. He lived much of the time on the Minnesota-Wisconsin border and his best-known work, *A Son of the Middle Border,* was published in 1914.

In 1927 Ole E. Rolvaag's famous *Giants in the Earth* was published, having been translated from its original Norwegian. Rolvaag, born in Norway in 1876, taught in the Norwegian department at St. Olaf College, Northfield. *Peder Victorius,* published in 1929, and *Their Father's Gods,* completed the trilogy about a Norwegian immigrant family.

The 1920s brought forward two more of Minnesota's greatest writers.

Sinclair Lewis' sixth novel, *Main Street,* published in 1920 and based on Sauk Centre, was a portrait of what he saw as the smug, complacent views of small-town America. His novel *Babbitt* (1922) brought a new word to the language in a story about a man who had no standards. He also wrote *Elmer Gantry* and other novels. Lewis declined the Pulitzer Prize in 1926 but accepted the Nobel Prize for Literature in 1930.

F. Scott Fitzgerald still fascinates biographers and in the past five years there have been at least three new works about the tortured author who documented life among St. Paul's society people in the 1920s. Fitzgerald's legacy includes *The Great Gatsby,* about wealth and youth; *Tender is the Night,* which he wrote while living on St. Paul's Summit Avenue, and *The Last Tycoon.*

In the 1940s Frederick Manfred achieved recognition. His novels, mostly set in the midwest, include the still popular *Lord Grizzly,* published in 1954.

Allen Tate and Robert Penn Warren, both of whom have been on the University of Minnesota faculty, are well known contemporary poets. Tate has written literacy criticism as well as poetry. Warren is critic, novelist, short story writer and poet. Among his most famous works is *All the King's Men,* which won a Pulitzer Prize in 1947.

Another poet of distinction, John Berryman, inspired students at the University of Minnesota until he committed suicide in 1972.

Several nationally-known journalists began their careers in Minnesota, including Harrison Salisbury, who covered Russia for *The New York Times;* Eric Sevareid, author and radio and television commentator who was a Minneapolis newspaperman, and television's Harry Reasoner.

Twentieth century fiction writers include Margaret Culkin Banning, Herbert Krause, Max Shulman, Kay Boyle and Meridel LeSueur, who is also a short story writer and poet.

Writers for juveniles include Carol Brink, Wanda Gag, Laura Ingalls Wilder and Maud Hart Lovelace.

Writers who are creating national names today are Garrison Keillor, Jon Hassler, Carol Bly and Robert Bly, Susan Allen Toth, Patricia Hampl, Judith Guest and Tim O'Brien.

In 1983 two St. Paul writers, Evelina Chao and Dr. Tim Rumsey, sold first novels to major publishers for record sums.

Source: Grace Lee Nute, A History of Minnesota Books and Authors, (Mpls., Minn., Univ. of Minn. Pr., 1958.)

SMALL PRESSES AND JOURNALS

Since the mid-1980s, Minnesota has been developing a national reputation as a home for non-profit small presses devoted to publishing prose and poetry with an emphasis on quality, rather than marketability.

New Rivers Press of St. Paul, founded in 1968 by C.W. Truesdale, now principal officer and chief editor, is the oldest continuously-publishing small press in the nation.

Two other nationally-known small presses — Coffee House and Greywolf — have relocated in the Twin Cities.

Literary journals are not as prevalent in the state now as they were in the past decade, a trend that is obvious in other parts of the country too.

Milkweed Journal, which for seven years published the work of unknown authors, has become Milkweed Editions, a small publisher that produced "Spillville," a collaboration between writer Patricia Hampl and artist Steve Sorman that sold for $1,500 in a fine art edition.

Other journals include the Lake Street Review of Minneapolis, edited by Kevin FitzPatrick; Sing, Heavenly Muse!, a feminist journal; and Great River Review, published from Winona State University in Winona.

The Great Midwestern Book Show, held for two days each year at various Twin Cities locations, is the largest in the nation. It draws more than 5,000 people who browse through offerings of small presses from around the country.

MINNESOTA PUBLIC RADIO

If the arts are appreciated in Minnesota, some of the credit should go to Minnesota Public Radio, considered a model for public radio nationally.

Designed to offer programming that is a complement and alternative to what is available on commercial stations, MPR began in 1967 at St. John's University, Collegeville, Minn. as KSJR, a non-commercial fine arts station for central Minnesota. In 1969 KSJN was established in St. Paul under the sponsorship of the St. Paul-Ramsey Arts and Science Council. At the same time a new community corporation Minnesota Public Radio, was formed to extend broadcast coverage to the rest of the state. In 1971 a news and information component was added and by 1975 a network of six stations reaching 95 percent of the population of Minnesota had been built.

In 1980 MPR finished a $7.2 million capital project to construct a network headquarters and production center in St. Paul, to acquire a second station in the Twin Cities and to connect to the new national satellite transmission system. The MPR network now consists of 10 stations reaching 98 percent of the state's population.

METRO ARTS SURVEY

In 1983 the St. Paul-Ramsey United Arts Council did a wide-ranging metropolitan arts survey, the most comprehensive survey of the '80s.

Preliminary computer analysis of 74 non-profit organizations and 12 which are not tax exempt gives some interesting information about arts in the Twin Cities metro area.

The 92 organizations surveyed cover the full range of arts disciplines:

theater	22 percent
music	20 percent
visual arts	17 percent
multi-disciplinary	12 percent
dance	10 percent
film/video/broadcast	9 percent
literature	3 percent
service organizations	3 percent
other	2 percent

The study shows that new groups continue to be formed regardless of recent cuts in government funding from the arts. Only half the 92 groups are more than seven years old; 18 percent have been incorporated within the last three years.

Twin Cities arts organizations do not tend to restrict their activities to a limited geographic region, the study shows. Thirty-four percent of the groups serve the Twin Cities metro area; 21 percent serve the state and 18 percent serve a multi-state area while 10 percent serve nationwide. Only 12 percent serve a specific city or neighborhood.

The computer analysis also considered budgets. While 10 percent had budgets of more than $2 million, the largest group of respondents (19 percent) had budgets between $50,000 and $100,000.

Of these budgets almost half the organizations spent the great majority (between 71 percent and 90 percent) on artistic expenses. Another 37 percent spent between 41 percent and 70 percent on artistic costs.

Audience served annually varied greatly:

less than 1,000 patrons .... 13 percent
1,001-5000 patrons .... 19 percent
5,001-10,000 patrons .... 16 percent
10,001-25,000 patrons .... 19 percent
25,001-50,000 patrons .... 6 percent
50,001-100,000 .... 13 percent
100,001-500,000 .... 11 percent
500,000-99,999 .... 3 percent

Thirty-eight of the 92 organizations analyzed had membership programs. Of these, 34 percent had between 250 and 1,000 members; 21 percent had between 101 and 250 members and 18 percent had between 50 and 100 members.

The survey shows how the arts are distributed in the Twin Cities:

theater .... 57 organizations
music .... 53 organizations
dance .... 19 organizations
multi discipline................................... 18 organizations
visual arts .... 15 organizations
service .... 14 organizations
literature .... 8 organizations
film/video/broadcast .... 7 organizations

MINNESOTA STATE ARTS BOARD APPROPRIATIONS

	State Legislative Monies	State/ Federal (N.E.A.)	Other Federal Grants*	Private (Foundations)
1987	$2,767,647	$523,100		$803,770
1986	2,495,313	528,671		736,477
1985	2,265,107	447,985		738,821
1984	1,788,400	127,900	100,000	570,000
1983	1,313,100	223,500	102,241	590,000
1982	1,735,200	282,900	122,746	550,000
1981	1,958,410	216,580		0
1980	2,078,993	269,600	110,641	0

Source: *Minn. State Arts Board, Margie Casey.*

*Since 1985 Other Federal Grants are grouped under State/Federal (N.E.A.).

Business/Industry

The people of Minnesota, through their farms, mines, industries, and trade and service organizations, produce approximately 1.9 percent of the American gross national product. Minnesota's share of national production has a distinctive composition because of the state's unique location on the maps of America's natural resources and settlement. One finds great economic variety within the state boundaries. But the dominant theme has been vigorous adaptation to a continuing barrage of technologic, social, and economic changes that have repeatedly altered both the meaning of the natural resource base and the relative location of state production within the world's markets.

In the northeast the world's largest iron mining district shifted from small, underground mines in pioneer days to the vast, open pits that fed American industrial growth during the automotive age and that ultimately exhausted the easily recovered, high-grade ores. Since the 1950s the same region has been converted again, this time to the world's foremost producer of taconite pellets.

In the southern and western two-thirds of the state, farmers have performed in a remarkable drama. They created a large part of the agricultural Midwest in the pioneer period. They created the nation's first major hard spring wheat region and from that crop earned the first surge of agricultural income to start the upward spiral of farm mechanization and improvement. They created a major part of the nation's commercial dairying region during the heyday of butter and milk consumption in American society and thus laid the foundation for a continuously evolving system of dairy farms, milk processing plants, farm-to-market roads, and financial institutions.

In the twentieth century in the southern half of the state, farmers have thrust the traditional corn-hog system farther north than it has ever been before. Through changes in farm organization and development of specialized sub-regions, farmers have subsequently adapted the Minnesota corn belt to hybrid seeds, shifts in the national diet, introduction of new crops, fluctuations in world-wide demands, and revolutionary changes in machinery, fertilizer, pest-control, tillage, labor costs, lifestyle, and environmental awareness.

In the northwest the bonanza farms of the Red River valley have been converted to family-operated enterprises with the flexibility to shift enormous acreages dramatically within a wide range of cash crop options in quick response to changes in world-wide needs.

Now the whole productive system stands at the brink of a new era, as the age of cheap fossil fuel draws to a close. Significant changes appear inevitable in the technology and the organization of transportation, building construction, and basic energy supply. New energy supplies may be either more centralized or more dispersed, and conflicting trends will run for a long time. In the face of perhaps one or two generations of experimentation, trial and error, the historic adaptive abilities that have characterized the Minnesota productive system will be needed more than ever. To meet that need, the vital resources of diversified, technologically advanced industries and capital are large and in place.

MINNESOTA 100 TOP RANKED COMPANIES

RANK	Company	City	Revenues ($millions¹)	Description of business
1	Dayton Hudson Corp.	Minneapolis	9,259.1	Retail department and specialty stores
2	Super Valu Stores Inc.	Eden Prairie	9,065.8	Wholesale foods; supermarket operations; general merchandise department stores
3	3M Company	St. Paul	8,602.0	Diversified industrial and consumer products
4	Pillsbury Co.	Minneapolis	6,127.8	Consumer food products; agricultural products; restaurants
5	Honeywell Inc.	Minneapolis	5,378.2	Aerospace & defense systems; environmental control & industrial automation
6	General Mills Inc.	Minneapolis	5,189.3	Consumer foods; restaurants; specialty retailing
7	NWA Inc.	St. Paul	3,589.2	Commercial passenger & freight airline; related travel services
8	Control Data Corp.	Bloomington	3,346.7	Computer systems, services; educational and business services
9	St. Paul Companies Inc.	St. Paul	3,181.6	Insurance management; property/liability underwriting, reinsurance, risk mgmt.
10	First Bank System Inc.	Minneapolis	2,930.2	Bank holding company; diversified financial services
11	Norwest Corp.	Minneapolis	2,419.8	Consumer and mortgage banking; trust services; venture capital; leasing
12	Hormel & Co., Geo. A.	Austin	1,960.2	Livestock processing; meat and meat products
13	Northern States Power Co.	Minneapolis	1,781.6	Gas and electric utilities; non-regulated energy services

14	Northwestern National Life Insurance Co.	Minneapolis	1,725.2	Life and health insurance services
15	Nash Finch Co.	St. Louis Park	1,573.7	Wholesale and retail foods; general merchandise distribution
16	International Multifoods Corp.	Minneapolis	1,403.0	Diversified food products for foodservice, commercial & agricultural markets
17	Gelco Corp.	Eden Prairie	1,016.4	Transportation management; leasing; corporate management services
18	Minstar Inc.	Minneapolis	989.5	Energy services; boats and sporting equipment
19	Deluxe Check Printers Inc.	St. Paul	886.8	Bank checks; financial and business forms; financial services and software
20	Bemis Co. Inc.	Minneapolis	864.7	Flexible packaging materials; specialty coated graphics products
21	Diversified Energies Inc.	Minneapolis	780.4	Natural gas distribution; heating and cooling equipment; mobile communications
22	Ecolab Inc.	St. Paul	762.8	Chemical products and systems for cleaning, sanitation, and lawn care
23	Soo Line Corporation	Minneapolis	631.8	Holding company: railroads, trucking, real estate
24	Pentair Inc.	St. Paul	623.9	Paper; portable electric tools; woodworking machinery
25	TCF Banking and Savings, F.A.	Minneapolis	616.0	Savings and loan association
26	Cray Research Inc.	Minneapolis	596.7	Large-scale, high-performance scientific computers
27	Jostens Inc.	Bloomington	587.3	Products for education, business, and athletics
28	Fuller Co., H.B.,	St. Paul	528.5	Adhesives, sealants, paints, waxes and specialty chemical products
29	Medtronic Inc.	Minneapolis	502.0	Pacemakers; heart valves; catheters; grafts; patient monitors

	Company	Location		Description
30	Musicland Group Inc.	Minneapolis	412.0	Records; audio and video cassettes; compact disks; music supplies
31	Toro Co.	Bloomington	406.7	Institutional turf care equipment; consumer lawn care and snow removal products
32	Minnesota Power	Duluth	395.5	Electric utilities and rural independent telephone services
33	American Hoist & Derrick Co. (Amhoist)	St. Paul	358.4	Cranes; metal recycling equipment; vacuum coating; wholesale hardware
34	Valspar Corp.	Minneapolis	345.2	Paint, coatings, stains, varnishes, and specialty products
35	Genmar Industries Inc.	Minneapolis	340.4	Recreational powerboats; marine sales and service
36	Lieberman Enterprises Inc.	Minneapolis	322.0	Pre-recorded music; software; merchandising services
37	Tonka Corp.	Minnetonka	293.4	Toys for retail, mass merchandising and wholesale markets
38	Inter-Regional Financial Group Inc.	Minneapolis	284.0	Securities brokerage; investment banking services
39	Apogee Enterprises Inc.	Bloomington	279.0	Glass fabrication; auto glass replacement; non-residential aluminum windows
40	Donaldson Co. Inc.	Minneapolis	271.7	Air cleaners, filters, mufflers, and specialized separation technologies
41	National Computer Systems Inc.	Eden Prairie	262.1	Optical mark readers; specialized information management products & services
42	Best Buy Company Inc.	Bloomington	239.5	Consumer electronics, major appliances & factory warranty services
43	Graco Inc.	Minneapolis	225.0	Fluid handling and bulk materials equipment
44	United Healthcare Corp.	Minnetonka	216.2	Managed health care delivery systems, HMOs
45	MEI Diversified Inc.	Minneapolis	216.1	Packaged and bulk snack, health food products

46	North Star Universal Inc.	Minneapolis	190.9	Holding company: food processing, graphics manufacturing
47	Krelitz Industries Inc.	Minneapolis	184.8	Wholesale drugs; medical, surgical, lab supplies; computerized pharmacy systems
48	International Dairy Queen Inc.	Minneapolis	183.9	Food and soft-serve dairy product retail franchises
49	Data Card Corp.	Minneapolis	176.1	Plastic transaction cards; embossing and encoding equipment
50	Green Tree Acceptance Inc.	St. Paul	172.6	Purchase, pooling of sales contracts on manufactured housing, RVs
51	Otter Tail Power Co.	Fergus Falls	172.2	Electric utility
52	Regis Corp.	Minneapolis	171.9	Hairstyling salons; hair care products
53	Piper Jaffray Inc.	Minneapolis	165.2	Securities and commodities broker-dealer; investment banking
54	Minnetonka Inc.	Chaska	163.2	Fragrances; hair care and gift products
55	Michael Foods Inc.	Minneapolis	153.3	Retail and wholesale foods; food ingredients
56	Tennant Co.	Minneapolis	151.5	Industrial, institutional, and commercial floor maintenance equipment
57	CVN Companies Inc.	Minneapolis	150.1	Cable television and retail sales of consumer products; liquidations
58	Munsingwear Inc.	Minneapolis	147.9	Apparel for men, women, and children
59	ADC Telecommunications Inc.	Bloomington	143.7	Electro-mechanical and electronic products for telecommunications industry
60	Robel Beef Packers Inc.	St. Cloud	137.7	Beef processing and packaging
61	Lamaur Inc.	Minneapolis	126.8	Hair care and personal grooming products for salon and consumer use

	Company	City		Description
62	BMC Industries Inc.	St. Paul	123.4	Precision etched and optical products
63	Lee Data Corp.	Eden Prairie	114.5	Multifunction interactive terminal systems
64	MTS Systems Corp.	Minneapolis	109.8	Computer-based systems for product development, simulation, and analysis
65	Network Systems Corp.	Minneapolis	108.8	Data communications products
66	Shelter Corp. of America Inc.	Minneapolis	101.7	Real estate construction and development
67	CPT Corp.	Minneapolis	101.3	Office workstations; networking; peripherals
68	Norstan Inc.	Plymouth	96.2	Private telecommunications systems; lease financing
69	G & K Services Inc.	Minneapolis	80.8	Commercial, institutional, industrial garment supply and service
70	Consul Restaurant Corp.	Minneapolis	73.5	Family-style Mexican restaurants
71	Sunstar Foods Inc.	Minneapolis	72.2	Consumer food products; wholesale food ingredients
72	Colwell Industries Inc.	Minneapolis	70.0	Holding company for graphic arts, printing, home furnishing samples
73	Poly-Tech Inc.	Minneapolis	62.7	Consumer trash bags; plastic sheeting products
74	Sheldahl Inc.	Northfield	62.0	Electronic circuits; interconnect devices; graphic display systems
75	St. Jude Medical Inc.	St. Paul	60.5	Heart valves; implantable cardiovascular products and devices
76	Analysts International Corp.	Edina	56.7	Consulting; project management; systems analysis; software services
77	Advance Circuits Inc.	Minnetonka	55.4	Printed circuit boards for military, aerospace, and commercial use

78	National City Bancorporation	Minneapolis	54.2	Bank holding company
79	Twin City Barge Inc.	South St. Paul	52.0	Marine transportation services; shipyard and terminal operations
80	Knutson Mortgage Corp.	Bloomington	51.4	Residential mortgage loan services
81	Merrill Corporation	St. Paul	49.4	Financial forms and documents; printing; typesetting services
82	Golden Valley Microwave Foods Inc.	Edina	47.9	Microwave popcorn and breakfast products
83	Hutchinson Technology Incorporated	Hutchinson	47.2	Components for computer peripherals and military guidance systems
84	Kahler Corp.	Rochester	47.2	Hotels, resorts, conference centers; formal wear; laundry services
85	Ag-Chem Equipment Co. Inc.	Edina	41.0	Agricultural chemical and industrial spraying equipment
86	Security American Financial Enterprises	Minneapolis	38.5	Individual or group life and health insurance; annuities
87	Dahlberg Inc.	Minneapolis	38.0	Hearing aids, accessory products, and replacement parts
88	Crown Auto Inc.	Eden Prairie	36.8	Automotive parts, accessories, and services for retail after-market
89	Communications Systems Inc.	Hector	35.9	Telecommunications equipment; independent phone companies
90	Advertising Unlimited, Inc.	Sleepy Eye	31.1	Specialty advertising products and worship bulletins
91	Washington Scientific Industries Inc.	Long Lake	31.0	Precision-machined components; power transmissions
92	Hawkins Chemical Inc.	Minneapolis	30.7	Industrial and laboratory chemicals
93	Sterner Lighting Systems Inc.	Winsted	30.5	Outdoor and indoor lighting systems

94	K-tel International Inc.	Minnetonka	29.4	Entertainment products, records and tapes
95	Hickory Tech Corp.	Mankato	27.0	Local phone services; cable TV
96	Reuter Inc.	Hopkins	25.1	Refuse systems; plastics machining
97	Zycad Corp.	St. Paul	24.0	Electronic processors for computer-aided engineering
98	TSI Inc.	St. Paul	23.8	Flow instrumentation
99	Norwesco Inc.	Minneapolis	23.7	Plastic resin products
100	Mesaba Aviation Inc.	Minneapolis	21.8	Regional airline service

*For fiscal years ending 7-31-86 through 6-30-87
Source: Corporate Report Minnesota magazine.

Communications

Minnesota's first newspaper was James M. Goodhue's Minnesota Pioneer, founded in St. Paul in 1849. In the early years of the 20th century there were approximately 700 newspapers in Minnesota with an impressive number of them giving European news to the early immigrants in their native languages.

Today the Minnesota Newspaper Association lists 325 weekly, semi-weekly and suburban papers in the state, and 28 dailies.

The state's communication network also includes some 18 television stations, 182 radio stations and a growing number of cable television channels.

MINNESOTA WEEKLY, SEMI-WEEKLY
AND SUBURBAN NEWSPAPERS

CODE
p — publisher
cp — co-publisher
gm — general manager

me — managing editor
e — editor
m — manager
c — county seat

Press room of "Tomahawk" weekly newspaper at White Earth, founded in 1902.
Photo Courtesy Minnesota Historical Society

MINNESOTA DAILY NEWSPAPERS

Town and Zip Code	Newspaper and Year Estab. and County Seat (c)	Publisher	Circ.	Publ. Day
Albert Lea 56007	Albert Lea Tribune (1897) c	Don Jones	10364	Su-F
Austin 55912	Austin Daily Herald (1891) c	Ed E. Smith	9994	Su-F
Bemidji 56601	The Pioneer (1896) c	Elaine Reeves	7385	Su-F
Brainerd 56401	Brainerd Daily Dispatch (1881) c	William J. McCollough	14420	Su-F
Breckenridge (MN) Address:				
Wahpeton, ND 58075	Wahpeton/Breckenridge Dly. News	Newell C. Grant	6350	M-F
Crookston 56716	Crookston Daily Times (1885) c	Wes Plummer	5018	M-F
Duluth 55082	Duluth News-Tribune & Herald	John McMillion	62124	Su-Sa
Fairmont 56031	Fairmont Sentinel (1874) c	Richard Norman	11633	M-Sa
Faribault 55021	Faribault Daily News (1914) c	Thomas B. Gagnon	9000	M-Sa
Fergus Falls 56537	Fergus Falls Daily Journal (1873) c	Charles Underwood	13416	M-Sa
Hibbing 55746	Hibbing Daily Tribune (1893)	Bernard J. Krauth gm	12151	Su-F
International Falls 56649	Int'l Falls Daily Journal (1911) c	Arlin Albrecht	5323	M-F
Mankato 56001	Mankato Free Press (1857)	H.A. Thompson	27636	M-Sa
Marshall 56258	Marshall Independent (1873)	Roger M. Smed	8819	M-Sa
Minneapolis 55415	Finance and Commerce (1887)	Warren E. Maul	3827	Tu-Sa
Minneapolis 55488	Minneapolis Star & Tribune	Roger P. Parkinson	372179	M-Sa
Minneapolis 55488	Minneapolis Sunday Star & Tribune	Roger P. Parkinson	586876	Su
New Ulm 56073	New Ulm Journal (1898) c	Bruce Fenske	10954	Tu-Su
Owatonna 55060	Owatonna People's Press (1874) c	S.L. (Sam) Morocco	7779	Tu-Su
Red Wing 55066	Red Wing Republican Eagle (1857) c	Arlin Albrecht	9167	M-Sa
Rochester 55901	Rochester Post-Bulletin (1912)	William C. Boyne	39065	M-Sa
St. Cloud 56301	St. Cloud Daily Times (1861) c	Steven A. Studt	28478	M-Sa
St. Paul 55101	Dispatch and Pioneer Press	Tom Carlin (See SRDS)	246565	Su
	Sunday Pioneer Press		246565	Su
	Pioneer Press		104335	M-F

Location	Newspaper	Editor/Publisher	Circulation	Day
	Dispatch		100635	M-F
	Saturday Dispatch and Pioneer Press		171872	am
St. Paul 55101	St. Paul Legal Ledger	Samuel E. Leweis Jr.	587	Tu-Sa
Stillwater 55082	Stillwater Gazette (1870) c	John Easton	5112	M-F
Virginia 55792	Mesabi Daily News (1893)	Larry Asbach, gm	15143	Su-F
Willmar 56201	West Central Tribune (1895) c	Paul E. London	16383	M-Sa
Winona 55987	Winona Daily News (1855) c	R.J. Semple	16737	Su-F
Worthington 56187	Worthington Daily Globe (1872) c	J.L. Vance	16880	M-Sa

MINNESOTA WEEKLY, SEMI-WEEKLY AND SUBURBAN NEWSPAPERS

Location	Newspaper	Editor/Publisher	Circulation	Day
Ada 56510	Norman County Index (1880) c	John R. Pfund	2962	W
Adams Address:				
Stacyville, IA 50476	Adams Monitor Review (1897)	James/Gail Morris	1454	Th
Adrian 56110	Nobles County Review (1890)	Douglas Haugom	1554	Th
Aitkin 56431	Aitkin Independent Age (1883) c	Evonne Agnello	5726	W
Albany 56307	Steams-Morrison Enterprise (1910)	Don Larson	3068	Tu
Alden 56009	Alden Advance (1891)	Wayne/Shirley Wright	994	Th
Alexandria 56308	Lake Region Echo (1970) c	Jon Haaven	9705	W
Alexandria 56308	Lake Region Press (1946) c	Jon Haaven	9742	F
Amboy 56010	Country Times (1890)	Kathie S. Davis	1688	Tu
Annandale 55302	Annandale Advocate (1887)	John Fisher/Ann Jennen	2875	W
Anoka 55433	Anoka County Union (1865) c	Arch Pease	5253	Th
Apple Valley 55435	Apple Val./Rsmt. Countryside (1977)	Mary Ziegenhagen	16950	M
Appleton 56208	Appleton Press (1880)	Curtis Johnson	2745	W
Arlington 55307	Arlington Enterprise (1884)	Val Kill	1850	W
Askov 55704	Askov American (1914)	Joel Mortenson	1789	Th

MINNESOTA WEEKLY, SEMI-WEEKLY AND SUBURBAN NEWSPAPERS

Town and Zip Code	Newspaper and Year Estab. and County Seat (c)	Publisher	Circ.	Publ. Day
Atwater 56209	Atwater Herald (1878)	Dennis G. Baker	1244	W
Aurora 55708	Aurora-Hoyt Lakes Range Facts (1933)	Gary Albertson	1603	Th
Babbitt 55706	Babbitt Weekly News (1961)	A.B. Austreng	1454	W
Badger 56714	Badger Enterprise (1951)	Marie E. Lockhart	966	Th
Bagley 56621	Farmers Independent (1898) c	Eugene Beltz Jr.	2952	Th
Balaton 56115	Balaton-Russell Press (1903)	Lou Gellerman	1041	Th
Barnesville 56514	Barnesville Record-Review (1900)	Eugene A. Prim	2130	Th
Battle Lake 56515	Battle Lake Review (1883)	Jon A. Tamke	2650	W
Baudette 56623	Baudette Region (1903) c	John C. Oren	2535	W
Belgrade 56312	The Observer (1899)	James Lemmer	1120	W
Belle Plaine 56011	Belle Plaine Herald (1882)	C. Edward Townsend	3417	W
Benson 56215	Swift County Monitor/News (1876) c	Ronald Anfinson	3246	F
Bertha 56437	Bertha Herald (1895)	Ernest J. Silbernagel	1081	W
Big Lake 55309	West Sherburne Tribune	Gary Meyer	7350	Tu
Bird Island 55310	Bird Island Union (1879)	Arthur J. Noecker	1110	W
Biwabik 55708	Biwabik Times (1907)	Gary Albertson	1292	Th
Blackduck 56630	Blackduck American (1901)	Bernard/Kathy Elhard	2079	Tu
Blaine 55433	Blaine-Spring Lake Park Life (1958)	Arch Pease	1680	F
Blooming Prairie 55917	Blooming Prairie Times (1893)	John Iacovino	2116	W
Bloomington 55435	Bloomington Sun Current (E & W)	Mary Ziegenhagen	29000	Th
Bloomington 55437	Let's Play Hockey	Bob/Donna Utecht	15000	F
Blue Earth 56013	Blue Earth Post-Ambassador (1869) c	Robert W. Tuff	3790	W
Blue Earth 56013	Town Crier Publications	Bob Bromeland mgr	9200	M
Bovey 55709	Scenic Range News (1923)	Douglas D. Deal	1738	Th
Braham 55006	Braham Journal (1899)	Frank Przybilla	1290	W

City/ZIP	Newspaper (Year)	Editor/Publisher	Circ.	Day
Brooklyn Center 55428	Brooklyn Center Post (1955)	See New Hope	4779	Th
Brooklyn Park 55428	Brooklyn Park Post (1950)	See New Hope	5595	Th
Brooten 56316	Bonanza Valley Voice (1969)	Howard & Kayla Johnson	1125	Th
Browerville 56438	Browerville Blade (1906)	Theresa Quirt/Tom Allen	1963	Th
Browns Valley 56219	The Valley News (1926)	William N. Kremer	1232	Th
Brownton 55312	Brownton Bulletin (1892)	Chuck Warner	956	W
Buffalo 55313	Wright County Journal-Press (1887) c	James P. McDonnell, Jr.	5952	Th
Burnsville 55337	Dakota County Tribune	Daniel/Joseph Clay	8621	Th
Burnsville 55435	Burnsville/Savage Current	Mary Ziegenhagen	16600	M
Byron 55920	Byron Review (1967)	Larry Miller	963	W
Caledonia 55921	Caledonia Argus (1862) c	Thomas Murphy	2830	Th
Cambridge 55008	Cambridge Star (1905) c	Frank Przybilla	2910	Th
Canby 56220	Canby News (1878)	Gerald R. Bohn	3380	W
Cannon Falls 55009	Cannon Falls Beacon (1876)	George E. Dalton	4128	W
Cass Lake 56633	Cass Lake Times (1899)	John P. Utley	1582	Th
Champlin 55369	Champlin-Dayton Press (1974)	Don/Carole Larson	1435	Th
Chaska 55318	Carver County Herald (1861) c	Stan Rolstud	3566	W
Chatfield 55923	Chatfield News (1856)	Neil L. Snider	1865	W
Chisholm 55719	Chisholm Free Press (1947)	Veda Ponikvar	3500	Th
Chisholm 55719	Chisholm Tribune Press (1957)	Veda Ponikvar	3500	Tu
Chokio 56221	Chokio Review (1898)	Owen/Michele Heiberg	998	Th
Circle Pines 55014	Circulating Pines (1950)	Andrew/Grace Gibas	1382	Th
Clara City 56222	Clara City Herald (1895)	Kermit Swanson	1706	W
Claremont 55924	Claremont News (1909)	John Iacovina	831	Th
Clarissa 56440	Clarissa Independent (1900)	Eugene Watts	955	Th
Clarkfield 56223	Clarkfield Advocate (1892)	Byron/Dorie Higgins	1373	Th
Clinton/Graceville 56225	The Northern Star (1883)	J.D. Kaercher	2195	Th
Cloquet 55720	Pine Knot-Billboard (1884)	Charles R. Johnson	9786	M&Th
Cokato 55321	Cokato Enterprise (1884)	Ivan Barnaal	2190	Th
Cold Spring 56320	Cold Spring Record (1899)	Terry O'Keefe	2880	W

MINNESOTA WEEKLY, SEMI-WEEKLY AND SUBURBAN NEWSPAPERS

Town and Zip Code	Newspaper and Year Estab. and County Seat (c)	Publisher	Circ.	Publ. Day
Columbia Heights 55435	Col. Hgts/St. Anthony Focus	Mary Ziegenhagen	7800	Th
Comfrey 56019	Comfrey Times (1900)	Gary Richter	1030	Th
Cook 55723	Cook News-Herald (1906)	Gary Albertson	3245	F
Coon Rapids 55433	Coon Rapids Herald (1866)	Arche Pease	3173	W
Cosmos 56228	Cosmos Sun (1955)	Dennis G. Baker	722	W
Cottage Grove 55016	Washington County Bulletin (1958)	Wm. J. Krueger	4884	Th
Cottonwood 56229	Cottonwood Ind./Current (1893)	Robert Lancaster	2175	W
Crosby 56441	Crosby-Ironton Courier (1912)	Thomas M. Swensen	4140	W
Dassel 55325	Dassel Dispatch (1918)	Carolyn H. Holje	1715	W
Dawson 56232	Dawson Sentinel (1884)	Norman Bacon	2425	Th
Deer River 56636	Western Itasca Review (1896)	Tom Klein ed.	1387	W
Delano 55328	Delano Eagle (1872)	Don/Carole Larson	1750	M
Detroit Lakes 56501	Becker County Record (1871) c	John Meyer	7662	M
Detroit Lakes 56501	Detroit Lakes Tribune (1907) c	John Meyer	7652	Th
Dodge Center 55927	Dodge Center Star Record (1873)	Larry Miller	1526	W
Duluth 55807	Duluth Budgeteer	Richard F. Palmer	45950	Su
Duluth 55802	The Coalition Voice	Senior Citizen Coalition	2400	M&Th
Eagan 55435	Eagan Chronicle	Mary Ziegenhagen	9500	M
Eagle Bend 56437	Eagle Bend News (1892)	(See Bertha)	1880	Th
East Grand Forks 56721	The Exponent (1886)	Warren H. Strandell	2095	Th
Eden Prairie 55344	Eden Prairie News (1974)	Mark Weber	9200	W
Eden Prairie 55435	Eden Prairie Sailor	Mary Ziegenhagen	8299	
Eden Valley 55329	Eden Valley Journal (1892)	H.W. (Bill) Cutten	1369	W
Edgerton 56128	Edgerton Enterprise (1883)	Rick A. Fey	2185	W
Edina 55435	Minnesota Suburban Newspapers	All Zones	286398	

Location	Newspaper	Editor/Publisher	Circulation	Day
Edina 55435	Edina Sun-Current	Mary Ziegenhagen	18390	W
Elbow Lake 56531	Grant County Herald (1874) c	Dave Simpkins	2564	*Bi/Mo
Elbow Lake 56531	Sodbuster (zoned)	Dave Simpkins	12500	
Elk River 55330	Elk River Star News (1875) c	Elmer Anderson	13000	Th
Ellendale 56026	Ellendale Eagle (1901)	John Iacovino	1286	W
Ely 55731	Ely Echo (1972)	Anne Wognum	3632	M
Ely 55731	Ely Miner (1875)	A.B. Austreng	2092	M
Elysian 56028	Elysian Enterprise (1893)	Jack Webster	710	W
Erskine 56535	Erskine Echo (1899)	Robert M. Hole	975	Th
Evansville 56531	West Douglas County Record	Dave Simpkins	1535	W
Eveleth 55734	Eveleth Range Scene (1976)	James/Kathie Krause	1248	W
Excelsior 55435	Excelsior/Shorewood Sailor	Mary Ziegenhagen	9064	
Fairfax 55332	Fairfax Standard (1897)	Charles Warner	1600	W
Fertile 56540	Fertile Journal (1882)	David Evans	1745	W
Floodwood 55736	Floodwood Forum (1936)	Henry/Nancy Raihala	1450	Th
Foley 56329	Benton County News (1900) c	Ronald Youso	2754	Tu
Forest Lake 55025	Forest Lake Times (1903)	Duane A. Rasmussen	4068	Th
Fosston 56542	The Thirteen Towns (1884)	Franklin Vikan	3179	Th
Frazee 56544	Frazee Forum (1960)	Jerold J. Brenk	1559	Th
Fridley 55435	Fridley/Spring Lk. Pk. Focus	Mary Ziegenhagen	11754	
Fulda 56131	Fulda Free Press (1882)	Gerald/Louise Johnson	1483	Th
Gaylord 55334	Gaylord Hub (1886) c	James Deis	2137	Th
Gibbon 55335	Gibbon Gazette & Tribune (1894)	Alan/Jeri Morland	1125	Th
Gilbert 55741	Gilbert Herald (1908)	James/Kathie Krause	1236	W
Glencoe 55336	Glencoe Enterprise (1873) c	Annamarie Tudhope	4339	Th
Glencoe 55336	McLeod County Chronicle	Bill Ramige	2053	W
Glenville/Emmons 56036	Glenville/Emmons Leader-Press (1975)	Stuart Madson	763	Th
Glenwood 56334	Pope County Tribune (1920) c	John/Mary Stone	4015	Th
Gonvick 56644	Gonvick Leader Record (1901)	Richard D. Richards	2196	Tu
Goodhue 55027	Goodhue County Tribune (1895)	Earl Campbell	603	W

MINNESOTA WEEKLY, SEMI-WEEKLY AND SUBURBAN NEWSPAPERS

Town and Zip Code	Newspaper and Year Estab. and County Seat (c)	Publisher	Circ.	Publ. Day
Grand Marais 55604	Cook Co. News Herald (1891) c	Ken Kettunen	3235	Th
Grand Rapids 55744	Grand Rapids Herald Review (1894) c	George A. Rossman	8070	Su&W
Granite Falls 56241	Granite Falls Tribune (1883) c	Dave Putnam	3548	Th
Greenbush 56726	Greenbush Tribune (1908)	Rex Clay Jr.	1480	Th
Grygla 56727	Grygla Eagle (1973)	Richard D. Richards	695	W
Hallock 56728	Kittson Co. Enterprise (1881) c	Keith Axvig	2020	Tu
Halstad 56548	Halstad Valley Journal (1907)	Harold/Doris Nelson	3220	W
Hancock 56244	Hancock Record (1899)	Viki L. Beuckens	874	W
Hanska 56041	Hanska Herald (1901)	Norman L. Becken	890	Th
Harmony 55939	Harmony News (1896)	Larry Salge/Bill Carlson	1135	M
Hastings 55033	Hastings Star Gazette (1857) c	Mike O'Connor	5270	Th
Hawley 55549	Hawley Herald (1890)	Robert A. Brekken	2335	Th
Hayfield 55940	Hayfield Herald (1895)	Dale Sargent	1755	Tu
Hector/Buffalo Lake 55342	Hector News-Mirror (1887)	John/Ken Hubin	2325	W
Henderson 56044	Henderson Independent (1872)	Leonard J. Blaschko	1186	Th
Hendricks 56136	Hendricks Pioneer (1900)	Marlin/Janice Thompson	1468	Th
Henning 56551	Henning Advocate (1891)	Curtis A. Anderson	1859	Th
Herman 56248	Herman Review (1900)	Owen/Michele Heiberg	1370	Th
Hermantown 55811	Hermantown Star (1977)	Ray H. Pearson	1400	Th
Heron Lake 56138	The Tri-County News (1886)	James/Leora Golda	1120	Tu
Hills 56138	Hills Crescent (1893)	John Minette	616	Th
Hinckley 55037	Hinckley News (1890)	John C. Lyon	1739	Th
Hoffman 56339	Hoffman Tribune (1922)	H.V./A.A. Bueckens	1291	Th
Hopkins 55435	Hopkins Sailor	Mary Ziegenhagen	10331	
Houston 55943	Houston Gazette & Cntry. Jml. (1976)	Betty W. Kellstrom	1584	Th

Howard Lake 55349	Howard Lake Herald (1878)	Floyd/Jo Ann Sneer	1941	W
Hutchinson 55350	Hutchinson Leader (1880)	Wayne Kasich	5859	Tu&Th
Isanti 55040	Isanti County News (1900)	Elmer Andersen	3155	Th
Isanti 55040	North Anoka American	Elmer Andersen	1446	Th
Isle 56342	Mille Lacs Messenger (1913)	Richard Norlander	4150	W
Ivanhoe 56142	Ivanhoe Times (1900) c	Vincent/Bev Turner	1080	Th
Jackson 56143	Jackson County Pilot (1889) c	Dan DeBettingnies	2813	Th
Janesville 56048	Janesville Argus (1875)	Tom West	1651	W
Jasper 56164	Jasper Journal (1888)	Chuck Draper	1073	M
Jordan 55352	Jordan Independent (1884)	John F. Neely	1457	Th
Karlstad 56732	North Star News (1900)	Dane H. Nordine	3268	Th
Kasson 55944	Dodge Co. Independent (1866)	Folmer Carlsen	2223	W
Kenyon 55946	Kenyon Leader (1885)	Robert D. Noah	2069	Th
Kerkhoven 56252	Kerkhoven Banner (1896)	T.J. Almen	1439	Th
Kiester 56051	Courier-Sentinel (1900)	Elton/Lois Matson	2349	Th
Kimball 55353	Tri-County News (1947)	Phyllis Greely Hoeft	1390	Th
La Crescent 55947	Houston County News/Signal (1882)	Myron/Darlene Schober	2147	Th
Lafayette 56054	Lafayette-Nicollet Ledger (1904)	Douglas W. Hanson	1659	Th
Lake Benton 56149	Lincoln Co. Valley Journal (1880)	Marlin D. Thompson	1462	W
Lake City 55041	Lake City Graphic (1861)	Dennis Schumacher	2941	Th
Lake Crystal 56055	Lake Crystal Tribune (1882)	Don R. Marben	1927	Th
Lakefield 56150	Lakefield Standard (1884)	R.H. Douglass	2090	Th
Lake Lillian 56253	Lake Lillian Crier (1948)	Dennis G. Baker	840	W
Lake Park 56554	Lake Park Journal (1896)	Gerald Schlueter	970	Th
Lakeville 55044	Lakeville Life & Times	Richard M. Sherman	8274	M
Lamberton 56152	Lamberton News (1922)	Joseph G. Dietl	1772	Th
Lanesboro 55949	Lanesboro Leader (1898)	Larry Salge/Bill Carlson	940	M
Le Center 56057	Le Center Leader (1895) c	Raymond G. Plut	2570	W
Le Roy 55951	Le Roy Independent (1875)	Carl B. Cassidy	1206	Th
Le Sueur 56058	Le Sueur News-Herald (1880)	Patrick J. Eastwood	2275	Th

MINNESOTA WEEKLY, SEMI-WEEKLY AND SUBURBAN NEWSPAPERS

Town and Zip Code	Newspaper and Year Estab. and County Seat (c)	Publisher	Circ.	Publ. Day
Lester Prairie 55354	Lester Prairie Journal (1896)	Floyd/Jo Ann Sneer	773	Th
Lewiston 55952	Lewiston Journal (1926)	Timothy Mack	1306	Tu
Lindstrom 55045	Chisago County Press (1898)	John A. Silver	3569	Th
Litchfield 55355	Litchfield Independent Review (1876) c	V. Madson/S. Roeser	4842	Th
Little Falls 56345	Morrison Co. Record c	Carolyn Hoheisel	14594	M
Littlefork 56653	Littlefork Times (1903)	Rick/Barb Painter	1051	Th
Long Prairie 56347	Long Prairie Leader (1883) c	Gary/Sharon Brown	3794	W
Luverne 56156	The Star-Herald (1873) c	Roger S. Tolletson	2756	M
Mabel 55954	Mabel Record (1906)	I.A. Scheel	1333	W
Madelia 56062	Madelia Times-Messenger (1870)	Michael Whalen ed	2143	W
Madison 56256	The Western Guard (1890) c	Alvin Henningsgaard	4016	W
Madison Lake 56063	Lake Region Times (1914)	Patricia J. Will	678	Th
Mahnomen 56557	Mahnomen Pioneer (1905) c	Patrick Kelly	2800	Th
Maple Lake 55358	Maple Lake Messenger (1898)	Harold Brutlag	1721	W
Mapleton 56065	Mapleton Enterprise-Herald (1888)	Kenneth Warner	1103	W
Maplewood 55109	Maplewood Review (1962)	(see No. St. Paul)	1910	W
Maplewood 55435	Maplewood/Little Canada Focus	Mary Ziegenhagen	14073	
Maynard 56260	Maynard News (1914)	Beverly Schaller	1000	
Mazeppa 55956	Mazeppa Journal (1877)	Earl Campbell	782	W
Mc Intosh 56556	Mc Intosh Times (1888)	Richard D. Richards	1283	W
Melrose 56352	Melrose Beacon (1889)	Don/Carole Larson	2640	W
Middle River 56737	The New River Record (1903)	Richard D. Richards	985	W
Milaca 56353	Mille Lacs County Times (1892) c	Elmer L. Andersen	3341	W
Milan 56262	Milan Standard Journal (1896)	Loren Johnson	935	Th
Minneapolis 55416	American Jewish World	Stacey Bush	6500	F

Location	Publication	Contact	Circulation	Day
Minneapolis 55412	Camden Community News	Tom Lamb	14000	M&Th
Minneapolis 55403	City Pages	Tom Bartel	110000	W
Minneapolis 55440	Cooperative World	Terry Nagle	300000	M&Th
Minneapolis 55404	Freeway News (see Skyway News)	Clint Andrus	33600	W
Minneapolis 55403	Loring Community Crier	Burt Berlowe	4000	M&Th
Minneapolis 55454	Many Corners	Barry Casselman	20000	M&Th
Minneapolis 55409	Minneapolis Spokesman (1934)	(See St. Paul Recorder)	15700	Th
Minneapolis 55402	Register Mirror	Philip G. Bradley	290	Sa
Minneapolis 55404	Skyway News (comb)	Clint Andrus	95000	Tu&Th
Minneapolis 55418	The Northeaster (2 zones)	Margo/Kerry Ashmore	3000	*eoW
Minneapolis 55414	The Southeast	J. Theodore Tucker	10000	M&Th
Minneapolis 55408	The Southside Journal	Ira Hauptman	65000	M&Th
Minneapolis 55404	The Surveyor	Dave Scheie	15000	M&Th
Minneapolis 55403	The Town Pump	Roy Ebertson	3000	M&Th
Minneapolis 55440	TV Forum	Rashad Hasan	45000	F
Minneapolis 55455	U of M Club Gazette	A.M. Shapiro	125000	M&Th
Minneapolis 55405	The Whittier Globe	Marilyn Kaye Moore	10000	M&Th
Minneapolis 55402	Twin Cities Courier (1966)	Mary J. Kyle	16051	Th
Minneota 56264	Minneota Mascot (1891)	Jon Guttormsson	1376	Th
Minnesota Lake 56068	Minnesota Lake Tribune (1894)	Marlys/Kenneth Hiscock	885	Th
Minnetonka 55435	Minnetonka Sailor	Mary Ziegenhagen	10950	
Minnetonka 55435	Westonka Sailor	Mary Ziegenhagen	7500	
Montevideo 56265	Montevideo American-News (1876) c	John Skaalen me	4925	Th
Montgomery 56069	Montgomery Messenger (1888)	Helen C. Keohen	2394	W
Monticello 55362	Monticello Times (1857)	Donald Q. Smith	2892	Th
Moose Lake 55767	Arrowhead Leader	Ruth Hanson	2080	Tu
Moose Lake 55767	Star-Gazette (1885)	Jerry DeRungs	6350	M&Th
Mora 55051	Kanabec County Times (1883) c	Wade Weber	3000	W
Morgan 56266	Morgan Messenger (1890)	Walter/Arlene Olson	1145	W
Morris 55267	Morris Sun (1883) c	Jim Morrison	4162	Tu

MINNESOTA WEEKLY, SEMI-WEEKLY AND SUBURBAN NEWSPAPERS

Town and Zip Code	Newspaper and Year Estab. and County Seat (c)	Publisher	Circ.	Publ. Day
Morris 55267	Morris Tribune (1876) c	Jim Morrison	4082	Th
Morristown 55052	Morristown Life (1890)	Jack Webster	505	W
Mound 55364	The Laker (1974)	Bill Holm	8640	M
Mountain Lake 56159	Mt. Lake Observer/ Advocate (1893)	C. Bill Paulson	2479	W
Nashwauk 55769	Eastern Itascan (1909)	Keith O. Axvig	1540	Th
Nevis 56467	Hubbard County Independent (1962)	Victor W. Olson	1298	Th
New Brighton 55109	New Brighton Bulletin (1910)	N. Theodore Lillie	4957M	Th
New Brighton 55435	New Brighton/Moundsview Focus	Mary Ziegenhagen	11032	
New Hope 55428	New Hope-Golden Valley Post (1962)	Gary L'Herault	5318	Th
New London 56273	New London-Spicer Times (1886)	Peter/Lynn Jacobson	3130	W
New Prague 56071	New Prague Times (1889)	E. Charles Wann	4408	Th
New Richland 56072	New Richland Star (1886)	Margaret A. Engesser	2099	W
New York Mills 56567	New York Mills Herald (1915)	Mike Parta	2375	Th
North Branch 55056	East Central MN Post-Review (1875)	Howard D. Lestrud	2559	Th
North St. Paul 55109	Ramsey County Review (1887)	T.R. Lillie	2272	W
Northfield 55057	Northfield News (1876)	Robert L. Bradford	5325	Th
Northome 56661	Northome Record (1903)	B./K. Elhard	1074	Tu
Norwood/Young America 55368	Norwood Times (1890)	James Berreth	2450	Th
Oakdale 55109	Washington County Review	(see North St. Paul)	913	W
Oklee 56742	Oklee Herald (1914)	Richard D. Richards	1171	W
Olivia 56277	Olivia Times-Journal (1872) c	P. Schmidt/C. Warner	2618	W
Ortonville 56278	Ortonville Independent (1920) c	James Kaercher	3865	W
Osakis 56360	Osakis Review (1890)	John J./Pamela Thein	1754	W
Osseo 55369	Osseo-Maple Grove Press (1921)	Don Larson	4074	W
Park Rapids 56470	Park Rapids Enterprise (1882) c	Doug Hirsch	6109	W&Sa

City	Publication (founded)	Editor	Circ.	Day
Parkers Prairie 56361	Parkers Prairie Independent (1902)	Thomas/Sheryl Myers	1853	W
Paynesville 56362	Paynesville Press (1887)	Peter J. Jacobson	3103	W
Pelican Rapids 56572	Pelican Rapids Press (1897)	G.E./R.E. Peterson	3599	Th
Pequot Lakes 56472	Country Echo (1972)	Keith H. Anderson	2220	Th
Perham 56573	Perham Enterprise-Bulletin (1882)	Mike Parta	2823	Th
Pine City 55063	Pine City Pioneer (1885) c	Dennis Winskowski	2726	Th
Pine Island 55963	Pine Island Record (1935)	Earl Campbell	996	W
Pine River 56474	Pine River Journal	Amanda Amy	2350	W
Pipestone 56164	Pipestone County Star (1879) c	Chuck Draper	4089	Th
Plainview 55964	Plainview News (1894)	Timothy Mack	2941	Tu
Plymouth 55428	Plymouth Post	(See New Hope)	3229	
Preston 55965	Preston Republican (1860) c	Wayne Haugerud	2570	Th
Princeton 55371	Princeton Union-Eagle (1876)	Elmer L. Andersen	3774	Th
Prior Lake 55372	Prior Lake American (1960)	Stan Rolfsrud	2855	W
Prior Lake 55435	Prior Lk/Spring Lk Clipper	Mary Ziegenhagen	4445	M
Proctor 55810	Proctor Journal (1906)	Jake Benson	1745	Th
Raymond 56282	Raymond News (1900)	William Paterson	780	Th
Red Lake Falls 56750	Red Lake Falls Gazette (1883) c	Keith O. Axvig	1770	Tu
Redwood Falls 56283	Redwood Gazette (1896) c	John Schneider	5615	Tu&Th
Renville 56284	Renville Star-Farmer (1889)	Daniel A. Licklider	1902	Tu
Richfield 55435	Richfield Sun-Current	Mary Ziegenhagen	15005	Th
Robbinsdale-Crystal 55428	North Hennepin Post (1912)	(See New Hope)	6351	Th
Rockford 55369	Rockford Crow River News (1913)	Don Larson	3489	W
Rockford 55373	Rockford Newsleader	Larry/Kathy Windom	5400	M
Roseau 56751	Roseau Times-Region (1891) c	Tom/Jan Dutcher	4748	Tu
Rosemount 55435	Apple Vly-Rosemnt Countryside	Mary Ziegenhagen	16583	
Roseville-Arden Hills 55435	Rsvlle-Falcon Hgts. Focus	Mary Ziegenhagen	19097	
Rushford 55971	Tri-County Record (1915)	Myron/Darlene Schober	1775	Th
Ruthton 56170	Buffalo Ridge Gazette	Duane D. DeBettingnies	603	W
Sacred Heart 56285	Sacred Heart News (1920)	Daniel A. Licklider	1015	Th

MINNESOTA WEEKLY, SEMI-WEEKLY AND SUBURBAN NEWSPAPERS

Town and Zip Code	Newspaper and Year Estab. and County Seat (c)	Publisher	Circ.	Publ. Day
St. Charles 55972	St. Charles Press (1879)	Timothy Mack	1980	Tu
St. James 56081	St. James Plaindealer (1891) c	Kris/Robin Offerdahl	3260	Th
St. Louis Park 55435	St. Louis Park Sailor	Mary Ziegenhagen	16675	
St. Paul 55102	Catholic Bulletin (1911) c	Dennis W. Heaney gm	58691	Th
St. Paul 55119	District I News	Julie A. Lehr	10400	M&Th
St. Paul 55106	The Farmers Voice	Dan Hogstad	33000	eoTu
St. Paul 55104	Frogtown Forum	John Fuerst	10000	M&Th
St. Paul 55105	Grand Gazette	Maurice Mischke	20000	M&Th
St. Paul 55116	Highland Villager	Maurice Mischke	39375	eoW
St. Paul 55104	Midway/Como Monitor	Denis Woulfe ed	19000	M&Th
St. Paul 55117	North End News	Dave Petersen	12000	M&Th
St. Paul 55108	Park Bugle	Kevin Richard	11000	M&Th
St. Paul 55101	St. Paul Recorder	Launa/Oscar Newman	10100	Th
St. Paul 55101	St. Paul Skyway News	(see Mpls. Skyway News)	20000	W
St. Paul 55119	Sunrise	Mark Truso	11000	M&Th
St. Paul 55107	West Side/West St. Paul Voice	Susan Carlson	19500	eoF
St. Peter 56082	St. Peter Herald (1860) c	H. Evanhoff	2678	Th
Sanborn 56083	Sanborn Sentinel (1896)	Walter M. Olson	795	W
Sandstone 55072	Pine County Courier (1894)	Dennis Winskowski	1861	Th
Sauk Centre 56378	Sauk Centre Herald (1867)	D.W. Griswold	3495	W
Sauk Rapids 56379	Sauk Rapids Herald (1854)	Roland Doroff	1247	W
Sebeka/Menahga 56477	Sebeka/Menahga Review Msgr. (1898)	John F. Bloomquist	3500	Th
Shakopee 55379	Shakopee Valley News (1861) c	John F. Neely	3393	W
Shoreview 55435	Shoreview/Arden Hills Focus	Mary Ziegenhagen	7865	
Silver Lake 55381	Silver Lake Leader (1901)	K.B./W.W. Merrill	1658	Th

City/ZIP	Newspaper	Editor	Circ.	Day
Slayton 56172	Murray County Herald (1892) c	Seth Schmidt	2378	Th
Sleepy Eye 56085	Sleepy Eye Herald-Dispatch (1880)	Mark W. Beito	3867	Tu
South St. Paul 55435	Inver Grove Hgt. Sun-Current	Mary Ziegenhagen	12450	
Springfield 56087	Springfield Advance-Press (1887)	P.C./D.J. Hedstrom	2700	W
Spring Grove 55974	Spring Grove Herald (1891)	B.A. Onsgsard	1534	Th
Spring Valley 55975	Spring Valley Tribune (1879)	Fred E. Phillips	2585	Th
Staples 56479	Staples World (1890)	Paul Caquelin	3074	Th
Starbuck 56381	Starbuck Times (1898)	Ron Lindquist	2216	W
Stephen 56757	Stephen Messenger Banner (1883)	Earl L. Anderson	2003	Th
Stewartville 55976	Stewartville Star (1890)	Sandy/Pam Forstner	2135	W
Storden/Jeffers 56174	Storden/Jeffers Times/Review (1915)	Steven T. Jessop	1110	Th
Thief River Falls 56701	Thief River Falls Times (1910) c	C.W. Mattson	6557	M&W
Tower 55790	Tower News (1900)	Paula Bloczynski	1950	M
Tracy 56175	Tracy Headlight Herald (1879)	Victor/James Keul	2878	Th
Trimont 56176	West Martin Weekly News	Robert Francis	2500	W
Truman 56088	Truman Tribune (1899)	P.C./D.J. Hedstrom	1803	W
Twin Valley 56584	Twin Val. Times/Gary Graphic (1896)	Keith O. Axvig	1998	W
Two Harbors 55616	Lake County News-Chronicle (1912) c	Hugh Bishop	3283	W
Tyler 56178	Tyler Tribute (1912)	William Clark	1598	Th
Ulen 56585	Ulen Union (1896)	David G. Evans	1377	W
Verndale 56481	Verndale Sun (1966)	Mary A. Tangemen	976	Th
Victoria 55386	Victoria Gazette	Sue Orsen	2900	M&Th
Wabasha 55981	Wabasha County Herald (1857) c	Gary D. Stumpf	2877	W
Wabasso 56293	Wabasso Standard (1900)	John/Betty Moe	1137	Th
Waconia 55387	Waconia Patriot (1897)	James D. Berreth	3225	Th
Wadena 56482	Wadena Pioneer Journal (1877) c	Mike Parta	4671	Tu&Th
Walker 56484	Walker Pilot-Independent (1920) c	James D. Smith	3240	Th
Wanamingo 55983	Wanamingo Progress (1908)	Earl Campbell	860	W
Warren 56762	Warren Sheaf (1880) c	E. Neil Mattson	3624	W
Warroad 56763	Warroad Pioneer (1897)	Charles Pryor	1901	W

MINNESOTA WEEKLY, SEMI-WEEKLY AND SUBURBAN NEWSPAPERS

Town and Zip Code	Newspaper and Year Estab.	Publisher	Circ.	Publ. Day
Waseca 56093	Waseca County News	Michael Johnson	9667	Tu
Waseca 56093	Waseca County News		3100	Th
Watertown 55388	Carver County News (1887)	James D. Berreth	2400	Th
Waterville 56096	Lake Region Life	Jack Webster	1620	W
Watkins 55389	Watkins Patriot (1972)	Terry O'Keefe	605	W
Wayzata 55435	Wayzata/Plymouth Sailor	Mary Ziegenhagen	14408	
Wells 56079	Wells Mirror (1870)	Michael Johnson	1951	Th
West Concord 55985	West Concord Enterprise (1892)	Richard W. Stafford	1000	W
West St. Paul 55435	Mendota Heights Sun-Current	Mary Ziegenhagen	9450	
Westbrook 56183	Westbrook Sentinel and Tribune	R./G./T. Merchant	2286	Th
Wheaton 56296	Wheaton Gazette (1885) c	William N. Kremer	2895	Th
White Bear Lake 55110	White Bear Press (1882)	Eugene Johnson	1095	W
Williams 56686	Williams Northern Light (1916)	La Rae A. Prosser	942	W
Windom 56101	Cottonwood County Citizen (1882) c	Kenneth M. Anderson	4270	W
Winona 55987	The Courier (Catholic)	Ivan Kubista		eoF
Winona 55987	Winona Post & Shopper	John/Frances Edstrom	23456	W
Winsted 55395	Winsted Journal (1922)	Floyd/Jo Ann Sneer	1608	Tu
Winthrop 55396	Winthrop News (1887)	Dana Melius	1435	W
Wood Lake 56297	Wood Lake News (1897)	Curtis B. Warnke	715	W
Zimmerman 55330	Zimmerman Frontier	Elmer Andersen	3500	W
Zumbrota 55992	Zumbrota News (1873)	David A. Grimsrud	2010	W

Source: Courtesy of Minn. Newspaper Assoc.

MINNESOTA TELEVISION STATIONS

City	Call letters	Channel
Alexandria	KCMT	7
Austin	KAAL	6
Duluth	KBJR-TV	6
Duluth	KDAL-TV	3
Duluth	WDIO-TV	10
Hibbing	WIRT	13
Mankato	KEYC-TV	12
Mpls.-St. Paul	KMSP-TV	9
Mpls.-St. Paul	KSTP-TV	5
Mpls.-St. Paul	WCCO-TV	4
Mpls.-St. Paul	WTCN-TV	11
Rochester	KTTC-TV	10
Walker	KNMT	12

MINNESOTA RADIO STATIONS

City	Call letters	Frequency
Aitkin	KKIN	930 khz
Aitkin	KEZZ-FM	94.3 mhz
Albany	KASM	1150 khz
Albert Lea	KATE	1450 khz
Albert Lea	KCPI-FM	95.3 mhz
Alexandria	KCMT-FM	100.7 mhz
Alexandria	KXRA	1490 khz
Alexandria	KXRA-FM	92.7 mhz
Anoka	KANO	1470 khz
Anoka	KTWN-FM	107.9 mhz
Austin	KAUS	1480 khz
Austin	KAUS-FM	99.9 mhz
Austin	KEDQ-FM*	90.7 mhz
Austin	KQAQ	970 khz
Bemidji	KBHP-FM	101.1 mhz
Bemidji	KBUN	1450 khz
Bemidji	KBSB-FM*	87.9 mhz
Bemidji	KKBJ	1360 khz
Benson	KBMO	1290 khz
Benson	KBMO-FM	93.5 mhz
Blue Earth	KBEW	1560 khz
Brainerd	KLIZ	1380 khz
Brainerd	KLIZ-FM	95.7 mhz
Brainerd	KVBR	1340 khz
Breckenridge	KBMW	1450 khz
Breckenridge	KKWB-FM	104.9 mhz
Buffalo	KRWC	1360 khz
Cambridge	KABG-FM	105.5 mhz
Cloquet	WKLK	1230 khz
Cloquet	WKLK-FM	100.9 mhz
Collegeville	KSJR-FM*	90.1 mhz
Crookston	KROX	1260 khz
Crookston	KCUM-FM*	91.7 mhz
Detroit Lakes	KDLM	1340 khz
Detroit Lakes	KVLR-FM	95.3 mhz
Duluth	KAOH	1390 khz
Duluth	KAOH-FM	94.9 mhz
Duluth	KDAL	610 khz
Duluth	KUMD-FM*	89.1 mhz
Duluth	WAKX-FM	98.9 mhz
Duluth	WDTH-FM*	103.3 mhz
Duluth	WEBC	560 khz
Duluth	WGGR-FM	105.1 mhz
Duluth	WWJC	850 khz
Duluth	WSCD-FM*	92.9 mhz
East Grand Forks	KRAD	1590 khz
East Grand Forks	KRAD-FM	103.9 mhz
Ely	WELY	1450 khz
Eveleth	WEVE	1340 khz
Fairmont	KSUM	1370 khz
Faribault	KDHL	920 khz
Faribault	KDHL-FM	95.9 mhz
Fergus Falls	KBRF	1250 khz
Fergus Falls	KBRF-FM	103.3 mhz
Fosston	KEHG	1480 khz
Fosston	KEHG-FM	107.1 mhz
Golden Valley	KQRS	1440 khz
Golden Valley	KQRS-FM	92.5 mhz
Golden Valley	KUXL	1570 khz
Grand Rapids	KOZY	1320 khz
Grand Rapids	KAXE-FM*	91.7 mhz
Grand Rapids	KXGR-FM	96.7 mhz
Hastings	KDWA	1460 khz
Hibbing	WKKQ	1060 khz
Hibbing	WMFG	1240 khz
Hibbing	WWFG-FM	106.3 mhz
Hutchinson	KDUZ	1260 khz
Hutchinson	KDUZ-FM	107.1 mhz
International Falls	KGHS	1230 khz
International Falls	KICC-FM*	91.5 mhz
Litchfield	KLFD	1410 khz
Litchfield	KLFD-FM	95.3 mhz
Little Falls	KLTF	960 khz
Long Prairie	KEYL	1400 khz
Luverne	KQAD	800 khz
Luverne	KQAD-FM	100.9 mhz
Mankato	KEEZ-FM	99.1 mhz
Mankato	KTOE	1420 khz
Mankato	KMSU-FM*	90.5 mhz
Mankato	KYSM	1230 khz

City	Call letters	Frequency
Mankato	KYSM-FM	103.5 mhz
Maplewood	WMIN	1010 khz
Marshall	KMHL	1400 khz
Marshall	KMHL-FM	100.1 mhz
Minneapolis	KBEM-FM*	88.5 mhz
Minneapolis	KTCR	690 khz
Minneapolis	KTCR-FM	97.1 mhz
Minneapolis	KUOM*	770 khz
Minneapolis	WCCO	830 khz
Minneapolis	WCCO-FM	102.9 mhz
Minneapolis	WDGY	1130 khz
Minneapolis	WLOL	1330 khz
Minneapolis	WLOL-FM	99.5 mhz
Minneapolis	WCTS-FM*	100.3 mhz
Minneapolis	WWTC	1280 khz
Montevideo	KDMA	1460 khz
Moorhead	KCCM-FM*	91.1 mhz
Moorhead	KVOX	1280 khz
Moorhead	KVOX-FM	99.9 mhz
Morris	KMRS	1230 khz
Morris	KMRS-FM	95.7 mhz
Morris	KUMM-FM*	89.7 mhz
Newport	KDAN	1370 khz
New Prague	KCHK	1350 khz
New Ulm	KNUJ	860 khz
New Ulm	KNUJ-FM	93.1 mhz
Northfield	KRLX-FM*	90.3 mhz
Northfield	KYMN	1080 khz
Northfield	WCAL*	770 khz
Northfield	WCAL-FM*	89.3 mhz
Ortonville	KDIO	1350 khz
Owatonna	KRFO	1390 khz
Owatonna	KRFO-FM	104.9 mhz
Park Rapids	KPRM	1240 khz
Park Rapids	KPRM-FM	97.5 mhz
Pine City	WCMP	1350 khz
Pine City	WCMP-FM	92.1 mhz
Pipestone	KLOH	1050 khz
Pipestone	KLOH-FM	98.7 mhz
Pipestone	KRSW-FM*	91.7 mhz
Preston	KFIL	1060 khz
Preston	KFIL-FM	103.1 mhz
Princeton	WQPM	1300 khz
Princeton	WQPM-FM	106.3 mhz
Red Wing	KCUE	1250 khz
Red Wing	KCUE-FM	105.5 mhz
Redwood Falls	KLGR	1490 khz
Redwood Falls	KLGR-FM	97.7 mhz
Richfield	KDWB-FM	101.3 mhz
Richfield	WAYL	980 khz
Richfield	WAYL-FM	93.7 mhz
Rochester	KRCH-FM	101.7 mhz
Rochester	KRPR-FM*	89.9 mhz
Rochester	KKEE	1520 khz
Rochester	KWEB	1270 khz
Rochester	KNXR-FM	97.5 mhz
Rochester	KWWK-FM	96.7 mhz
Rochester	KROC	1340 khz
Rochester	KROC-FM	106.9 mhz
Roseau	KRWB	1410 khz
Roseville	KTIS*	900 khz
Roseville	KTIS-FM*	98.5 mhz
Rushford	KLSE-FM*	91.7 mhz
St. Cloud	KCLD	1450 khz
St. Cloud	KCLD-FM	104.7 mhz
St. Cloud	KVSC-FM*	88.5 mhz
St. Cloud	WJON	1240 khz
St. Cloud	WWJO-FM	98.1 mhz
St. Louis Park	KRSI	950 khz
St. Louis Park	KFMX-FM	104.1 mhz
St. Paul	KDWB	630 khz
St. Paul	KEEY	1400 khz
St. Paul	KEEY-FM	102.1 mhz
St. Paul	KNOF-FM	95.3 mhz
St. Paul	KSJN-FM*	91.1 mhz
St. Paul	KSTP	1500 khz
St. Paul	KSTP-FM	94.5 mhz
St. Peter	KRBI	1310 khz
St. Peter	KRBI-FM	105.5 mhz
Sauk Centre	KMSR-FM	94.3 mhz
Sauk Rapids	WHMH-FM	101.7 mhz
Sauk Rapids	WVAL	800 khz
Shakopee	KSMM	1530 khz
Stillwater	WAVN	1220 khz
Thief River Falls	KAVS-FM*	89.5 mhz
Thief River Falls	KTRF	1230 khz
Thief River Falls	KOSN-FM	99.3 mhz
Virginia	WHLB	1400 khz
Virginia	WIRN-FM	107.1 mhz
Wabasha	KWMB	1190 khz
Wadena	KWAD	920 khz
Wadena	KKWS-FM	105.9 mhz
Walker	KLLR	1600 khz
Waseca	KOWO	1170 khz
Waseca	KQDE-FM	92.1 mhz
Willmar	KWLM	1340 khz
Willmar	KQIC-FM	102.5 mhz
Windom	KDOM	1580 khz
Windom	KDOM-FM	94.3 mhz
Winona	KAGE	1380 khz
Winona	KAGE-FM	95.3 mhz
Winona	KQAL-FM*	89.5 mhz
Winona	KWNO	1230 khz
Worthington	KWOA	730 khz
Worthington	KWOA-FM	95.1 mhz

*Denotes non-commercial stations

★ ★ ★

In 1928, WAMD and KFOY merged to form KSTP, and President Calvin Coolidge pressed a key in the White House to activate the transmitter.

CABLE TELEVISION

Cable television initially developed to serve isolated markets beyond the range of broadcast reception. From the state's first operational cable system in Peterson in 1954, the number of systems has grown to 128 serving 223 municipalities by Jan. 1, 1980, with an additional five systems under construction. These range in size from five systems with fewer than 100 subscribers each to one system with more than 18,000 subscribers in Rochester.

Most cable systems in Minnesota have a capacity of 12 channels, but some can receive as many as 35 channels. Two systems - Fosston and St. Peter - have operational two-way capability, which allows listener participation; an additional 61 systems have the technical capability to activate two-way operations.

On a stationwide average, 13 per cent of Minnesota's households were served by cable television in mid-1979, ranging from 36 per cent in region 9 (south-central Minnesota) to 1 per cent in the Twin Cities area, according to the Minnesota Cable Communications Board. Past growth of cable television has been concentrated outside the Twin Cities metropolitan area. Only three cities of 10,000 population or more outside the Twin Cities area remain uncabled - Northfield, Owatonna and Worthington.

In the Twin Cities, cable television companies are in hot competition and cable has become a political football, embroiling the city councils of both Minneapolis and St. Paul in controversy over who should win the lucrative contract.

In January, 1981, five southwest Minneapolis suburbs voted unanimously to award a joint cable television franchise to Minnesota Cablesystems, a subsidiary of Canadian Cablesystems Ltd.

The company has plans to lay about 690 miles of cable in Eden Prairie, Edina, Hopkins, Minnetonka and Richfield.

Information for much of this chapter came from 1980 Atlas of Minnesota

Resources & Settlement by John R. Borchert and Neil C. Gustafson, published by the Center for Urban and Regional Affairs, University of Minnesota, and the Minnesota State Planning Agency.

EDUCATIONAL TELEVISION

CITY OR TOWN	CALL LTRS.	CHANNEL	EST.
Appleton	KWCM	10	1966
Austin	KAVT	15	1972
Duluth (Minn.)			
Superior (Wis.)	WDSE	8	1964
Minneapolis-St. Paul	KTCA	2	1957
	KTCI	17	

Minnesota's first commercial radio station was started by Dr. George W. Young, an eye doctor, in 1923 at 909 West Broadway, Minneapolis; hence the call letters WDGY.

In 1923, the first radio broadcast of a symphony concert in the state, and possibly the nation, was aired by WLAG, the precursor of WCCO, with Walter Damrosch of Boston as the guest conductor. A prominent Minneapolis businessman, E.L. Carpenter, offered a $25 prize for the best critique of the performance. It was won by a 12-year-old boy, Stephen B. Humphrey, later a prominent teacher of English at the University of Minnesota and St. John's University.

★ ★ ★

In 1973, WCCO was the first commercial station in the U.S. to receive the Peabody Award.

★ ★ ★

Before becoming mayor of Minneapolis, Hubert Horatio Humphrey did a stint as a newscaster on station WTCN.

★ ★ ★

The first broadcast from an airplane to the ground for dissemination to public listeners was done by KSTP radio.

★ ★ ★

First live coverage of a baseball game, the Minneapolis Millers baseball team from Old Nicollet Park. This was in fact KSTP's first TV broadcast, a remote on April 27th, 1948.

★ ★ ★

In May, 1950 unemployed Dave Moore stopped in to use the mens' room at 50 S. 9th St., Minneapolis, while his wife went to see a movie at Radio City next door. Minutes later, he was drafted to read a news broadcast (regular staffers had gone to the Korean police action) and was hired on the spot. Hastening to the theater to give his frau the news, he was shocked to hear Shirley say, "I know, I heard it on the loudspeaker." (The broadcasts were piped into the film house as an added feature) Thus began an illustrious career on WCCO - TV.

★ ★ ★

KSTP purchased one of the first RCA commercial cameras manufactured and remote equipment for the purpose of experimenting with closed circuit, and to assist in training personnel for TV work. 1938.

Science/Health

THAT part of the earth known as Minnesota contained a foundation for science thousands of years before people from western Europe reached this area and countless ages before the Indians gave the place a name, calling it "Land of the Sky Blue Waters."

Appropriately enough, the scientific foundation was, and to a great extent still is, based on what nature had provided here. Skies are clear, water is plentiful, the soil is rich with the elements of life and minerals underneath. Utilizing the obvious bountifulness, plus many more elements and conditions that are not so easily noticed, Minnesotans have, during the tiny speck of time called modern history, made scientific contributions ranging from A to Z. From the ATOM to the ZIPPER and encompassing discoverings in technology, medicine, agriculture, theoretical pioneering and humanistic research.

Before attempting to put a statistical finger on man-made contributions, however, it should be informative to introduce a concise inventory of those Minnesota resources that have been particularly significant to science.
These must include:

  *Extensive and excellent farm land.
  *Clear skies that diffuse more than enough sunlight to compensate for a short growing season, influencing numerous activities of scientific nature.
  *Water in abundance, nourishing all growing things and providing power. The power potential of Minnesota's running water is exceptional because large rivers flow from and through the state in all directions; north, south, east, and west.
  *Minerals, not only in abundance but also in variety. Iron has been the most plentiful, the most accessible, and the most exploited in the past. More recent years have seen substitution of taconite, an iron-bearing rock from which Minnesota scientists have learned to extract and concentrate ferrous material, replacing the higher grade ore that is no longer easily available.
  *Timber, for direct utilization and also as a replenishable source of supply for manufacturing and chemical industries.
  *Glacial residues destined to become increasingly valuable as present-day earth materials are used toward the point of practical extinction.
  *Climate that is invigorating and healthful for human and animal life.

The way or ways in which those resources have been utilized and the people who have played a role in the process constitute the history and the future potential of science in Minnesota. The input of human effort is naturally most vital, spreading the impact of this area's science far beyond the borders of the state or limits that may exist for physical exploitation of natural resources. It has touched technological, educational, medical, social, and economic facets of life around the world and is reaching out in space.

Because science is essentially a function of the present and the future, this almanac tends to emphasize the contemporary in the discussion which follows.

The great contribution to atomic science from Minnesota was a demonstration for a practical method of isolating and separating two isotopes of uranium, known as U-235 and U-238. This was accomplished in 1940 with development and successful use of a mass spectrograph by Dr. Alfred O. C. Nier, a native of the state and a professor of physics at the University of Minnesota.

Nier's work made it possible for scientists, many of whom also were concentrating on atomic investigations, to establish the fissionable or atom-splitting capabilities of U-235, the power-containing isotope. From that knowledge it then became possible to develop the apparatus and control systems that made utilization of atomic energy practical. Initial application of the power of the atom was in bombs at the climax of World War II. Subsequent developments saw utilization of nuclear power for generating electricity for medical uses and for massive earth movement.

The original mass spectrometer that Nier constructed at the University of Minnesota for his U-235 investigation is in the Smithsonian Institution in Washington D.C. It is one of two Minnesota-made items in the permanent exhibition there.

Nier, who was born in St. Paul in 1911, received bachelor, masters and doctoral degrees from Minnesota and also studied at Harvard. His mass spectrography research has been directed to other scientific investigations, including studies important to geology, chemistry, and medicine as well as nuclear physics.

While Nier's original mass spectrograph was a two-ton mechanical monster, he has since been a principal developer of smaller instruments that are being utilizied in industry as well as in academic research. One such compact model, weighing about eight pounds, was included in the instrument package carried to Mars on the historic *Viking Project Flight* in 1975-1976. Nier himself had been active for several years on the scientific cadre in the Mars program and was assigned to head a five-man group known as the *Science Entry Team.* The group's responsibility covered research equipment to probe the atmosphere surrounding the famed red planet and its surface material; and a mass spectrometer incorporating some of Nier's principles was linked to function in conjunction with the soil testing apparatus of the Viking.

Scientific equipment aboard the Viking also included an instrument developed under the direction of Professor William Hanson of the University of Texas, who is a graduate of the University of Minnesota and a native of this state.

Following the mass spectrograph from Minnesota to the Smithsonian was a small flying machine called the "tailless airplane." This had its origins at the University of Minnesota in the mid-thirties and was accepted for permanent display in the National Air and Space Museum in 1970.

Identified with the official numbers XI4880 (one of less than 5,000 recognized "experimental" aircraft) the little machine had been conceived by Prof. John D. Akerman, then director of the university's fledgling program in aeronautical engineering. Final design and construction were the work of students supported by the WPA (*Works Progress Administration*) during the depression years.

The scientific significance of the tailless airplane was in its unique aerodynamic characteristics. The same principles were later to contribute to the delta wing design high speed military jet planes and supersonic aircraft.

The mid-thirties spawned another contribution to the science of high altitude flight and eventual space exploration from the University of Minnesota campus.

At 6:58 a.m. on June 24, 1936, the first of a series of so-called "stratosphere balloons" was sent aloft from the University's Memorial Stadium by Prof. Jean Piccard and a small army of students. Made of very thin plastic strips, that balloon carried simple instruments, later recovered, which indicated that it had risen somewhere between 13 and 16 miles above the land. It was an altitude that few in that time dreamed it possible to attain.

Refinement of the plastic balloon technology, in which General Mills played a part as it began to diversify from flour milling and grain processing, led to construction of successively larger plastic stratosphere balloons in accordance with Piccard's research findings. Those giant balloons when inflated with helium were as tall as a 20-story building, and they carried research instruments to altitudes calculated to be above 99 percent of the earth's oxygen envelope.

Launched from numerous land stations and from the decks of aircraft carriers, the balloons and their instruments gathered information of weather and navigational importance in war or peace.

Prof. Piccard's balloon research, in which he was assisted by his scientist wife, Jeannette, contributed to scientific know-how that was later applied in development of windows for high-altitude jets and other pressurized structures.

The record of high altitude research with a Minnesota angle cannot be complete without mention of Dr. William Randolph Lovelace, formerly a surgeon at the Mayo Clinic and an air force lieutenant colonel. Investigating human physiology and the efficiency of oxygen equipment as well as the performance of parachutes in the rarified upper air, Dr. Lovelace made his first parachute jump from an altitude of 40,200 feet, the highest officially recognized leap. The surgeon-soldier-scientist suffered no serious trouble, but one of his hands was frozen when his glove was jerked off as the parachute opened at an altitude where the temperature was 50 degrees below zero, fahrenheit.

The transistor, tiny source of gigantic power for the electronic industry, owes its birth to three physicists, two of them with research backgrounds at the University of Minnesota. John Bardeen and Walter Brattain, who had studied and taught at the university, and William Shockley shared the 1956 Nobel Prize in physics for their invention of the transistor. Bardeen also shared the 1972 Nobel Prize in physics for other work, mainly at the University of Illinois.

The "Iron Century"

It is awesome to realize how short the recorded history of Minnesota's science has been when compared with the age of rocks in this state, estimated to be among the oldest material of Earth. Iron ore, the state's greatest resource for technology, can be used to dramatize the time scale. The age of rocks in northeastern Minnesota, where the iron concentrations exist, has been estimated into the billions of years. The *"Iron Age"* as a period in the reckoning of human history began little more than three thousand years ago; the iron history of Minnesota has not yet completed a full century.

In the 1860's Newton Horace Winchell came from the East to be Minnesota's first state geologist and professor in the new Geology department at the university.

Traversing the state afoot and by canoe, Winchell developed the first Minnesota geological map. This pinpointed the areas that later became the world's most productive iron mines and also forecast the agricultural potential of the prairies to the West.

It was not until 1890, however, that Leonidas Merritt and his six brothers — the fabulous *"Seven Iron Men"* of history — were granted their first mining leases on the Mesabi range. Mined mostly by the economical open pit method, the Minnesota ore was so rich in iron content that one pit alone became known as *"the mine that won two world wars,"* supplying the hungry steel mills during the booms of World Wars I and II.

Within little more than half a century, however, Minnesota researchers began to realize that the rich Mesabi ore would run out within foreseeable time. Many of the mines were shut down, some abandoned permanently, because they could no longer be worked profitably and efficiently.

Fortunately for Minnesota, scientists and economists were sufficiently aware of the declining supply of rich iron ore and had begun to do something about it. The most effective "something" was accomplished by E. W. Davis, a professor at the University of Minnesota. Knowing that billions of tons of iron-bearing rock, called taconite, existed around the bodies of rich iron, Davis and his associate devised methods and built equipment to mine that rock and extract the iron from it.

A flame-spewing mechanical monster known as the jet piercing drill was developed to begin cutting the taconite rock. The world's biggest trucks and special railroad cars were designed to transport the rock to huge crushing plants where the material was ground down to the fineness of talcum powder. Then the iron was extracted by magnets and processed into balls or pellets for shipping to the steel mills. When it was learned that some of the crushed iron ore was non-magnetic, the Minnesota scientists found ways to remagnetize it so it could be recovered for further processing.

Taconite revolutionized America's steel industry as mills were converted to handle the uniformly rich and sized pellets instead of crude ore of varying quality. Taconite also brought great changes to the shipping industry on the Great Lakes, making it possible to move a relatively greater amount of usable ore in fewer ships. They did not have to carry the waste rock; and because the pellets are of standard size, loading and unloading was speeded up with new machinery.

Despite its technical and economic advantages, however, taconite also brought new problems. The non-ferrous (iron) waste material which used to go to the steel plants for disposal there had been deposited in its powder-fine condition in the Minnesota environment. As much as 67,000 tons of this material has been dumped daily into Lake Superior from one taconite plant at Silver Bay; and elsewhere onetime lakes and river beds are being filled with this waste material. Some of the powdery material is discharged into the air, too, and this may be creating a health hazard because it contains asbestos fibers. Dumping of taconite tailings was stopped after years of legal action.

The end of the state's iron century is now less than five years away, counting from the initial mining on the Vermillion range in 1884. But the scientific discoveries and developments that made taconite usable assure a supply of iron into more centuries and probably will stimulate further scientific probing for new and improved utilization of iron as a raw material.

Nature and Science Merge in Timber

Timber and wood product industries, being both providers and consumers of scientific material and methods, are future-oriented in Minnesota and becoming more so every year. Lumbering used to be characterized in this state by the Paul Bunyan legends, tall stories of a giant lumberjack who could clear a quarter section or so of pine trees with one sweep of his axe. The more modern picture is of scientists and woodsmen working together in laboratories as well as in the field to save and restore woodlands and learn new ways to use the forests and their products. It is a technological shifting of gears from thinking only of ways to cut down the most trees with the least cost in the shortest time to looking at practices that should insure a perpetual supply of timber for construction, for fuel, and for processing through chemistry and mechanical means.

In its earlier days in Minnesota, roughly the last two decades of the 1800's and something less than three decades of this century, lumbering was strictly an extractive industry. Its employment, though large, was seasonal and thus of restricted economic value. The railroad employment offices, which probably maintained the best job records of those times, reported moving as many as 200,000 loggers each season through the Twin Cities. That number was greater than the regular population of either Minneapolis or St. Paul.

Papermaking, which has been a leader in bringing chemistry and other sciences together with lumbering, was itself a transient industry as long as paper mills could move easily from one place to another as timber lands were cleared of their source of pulp. During the same years that Yankee entrepreneurs were following the timber supply from New England through Pennsylvania, New York, Michigan and Wisconsin into Minnesota, machinery for making paper or finishing lumber was becoming too costly and two complicated to be moved easily. At the same time, the paper companies were getting the know-how from scientists for growing trees as a constant crop and learning how to get chemical by-products from the trees.

Alcohol, though it can be an important scientific chemical extracted from trees, is reported to have been a factor in early-day lumbering, but from an entirely different aspect. According to many accounts, some more or less scientific, alcohol was the medium of exchange by which lumber barons acquired forest land and again the key to separating the lumberjacks from their money when they came out of the woods at the end of each logging season.

In today's context, alcohol has to be considered just one of the valuable chemical materials available from wood. Sugar is another; and there are other saps or fibers proving their economic worth in the *"new lumbering."*

The paper industry depends heavily on chemistry to create papers with special qualities and also needs chemists to solve the problems of pollution of rivers where the big mills discharge wastes. But nowadays the woods are literally full of other scientists—botanists, biologists, physicists, and ecologists studying the complex schemes by which nature grows trees and replenishes the earth. The human sciences also are involved in the lumber and paper industries, being concerned with recreational or social values of this state's abundant forests. And not least of these efforts is the fact that trees are among the growing things through which solar energy can be transmitted to Earth.

Farm and Food Science

Minnesota scientists, responding to the world's need for food, have made distinguished contributions to both better crops and better equipment to process and preserve the products coming off the land. Additionally, economists from this state have played leadership roles in directing the marketing and distribution of food worldwide.

The major discoveries have come from agricultural research at the University of Minnesota, and the rust-resistant strains of wheat and improved crops of many kinds developed by men like Profs. Alvin Stakman, Clyde Bailey and J. J. Christensen have to be rated high on the food chain of all mankind. Wendelin Grim is credited with having developed hard and hardy alfalfa, a boon to livestock raisers; and Peter Gideon developed the Wealthy apple for successful production in northern climates.

On the mechanical side of agriculture, Edmon LaCroix, a Frenchman who worked in mills at Faribault and Minneapolis, designed and built the first *"middlings purifier,"* and with that device revolutionized flour milling.

While those contributions have worldwide impact, the most notable recognition of Minnesota agricultural achievement came in 1970 when Norman Borlaug received the Nobel Peace Prize for his contributions to food production. Borlaug's research had its roots at the University of Minnesota and was continued with global significance after he joined the Rockefeller Institute.

Minnesota Nobel Laureates

Borlaug was one of seven scientists, two in medical fields, who have had University of Minnesota backgrounds and were honored with Nobel Prizes. Three of those award winners were physicists: Ernest O. Lawrence, who was at the state university in 1939 and then followed through with development of the cyclotron, an atom-smasher device of research significance, in California; Walter H. Brattain and John Bardeen (a double Nobel winner) who shared the 1956 Nobel Prize in Physics as inventors of the modern transistor. Melvin Calvin, a Minnesota graduate, received the Nobel in Chemistry in 1961; and Drs. Philip S. Hench and Edward C. Kendall were Nobel Laureates in Physiology and Medicine in 1950. They were cited for research on chemicals known as ACTH and the discovery of cortisone, one of the miracle drugs of the mid-century period.

This state's first Nobel Laureate native was Sinclair Lewis of St. Cloud, who received the coveted prize in 1930 and was the first American so honored, but he was not a product of the University of Minnesota.

Firsts and Foremosts from Minnesota Medicine

Although Hench and Kendall became famous as Nobel winners, other Minnesotans also have made contributions of top impact in the medical world. An outstanding example revolves around the work and influence of Dr. C. Walton Lillehei, who pioneered surgery on the open heart at University Hospitals in 1954. Surrounding Lillehei under the bright lights in the surgical theater or observing from above through the glass dome of the operating room were perhaps a dozen other doctors who later were to make medical history as follow-ons of Minnesota-inspired training.

Included among those trainees, participants, students and colleagues were Christiaan Barnard, who later performed the first successful heart transplant, Norman Shumway, probably the most prolific of the transplanters, Richard Varco, who remained as lead surgeon of the Minnesota teams, Dr. Robert Good, Morley Cohen and practically all the other surgeons who were to perform successful heart transplants during the ensuing years or lead in development of the pumps and blood-purifying devices that are essential adjuncts of heart and organ transplants.

Many of those same doctors had been students or associates of Dr. Owen H. Wangensteen, who was not only an outstanding surgery educator but also an inventor, having created, among other devices, the suction unit that bears his name and is a basic tool of gastric surgery.

For generations, surgical talent and improvisation were central elements of medical practice not only at the university but also at the Mayo Clinic and hospitals in Rochester, Minn., which is self-identified in a clinic publication as "an adventure in medicine." Drs. Will J. and Charles H. Mayo, sons of Dr. William Worrall Mayo who established the institution in 1863 on what was then a medical frontier, both exemplified the surgeon tradition. But they also led the Mayo organization through numerous expansions, diversification, and life-serving discoveries in research, diagnosis and non-surgical phases of medicine.

No recounting of this state's medical-scientific accomplishments can be considered complete without mention of Sister Elizabeth Kenny. Not particularly welcome to the medical establishment of either the Mayo Clinic or the University, she defiantly pressed ahead with a unique hotpack and mobility treatment of poliomyelitis in Minneapolis. Self-trained as an Australian bush nurse, Sister Kenny has nevertheless left her mark on the healing profession and made Minneapolis a key center during the polio epidemics of the 1940's and 1950's.

Minnesotans and Minnesota resources have made their full share of notable and long-lasting scientific contributions. But science is future-oriented, never standing still while human needs and desires are changing constantly. Other life-saving or life-prolonging discoveries, future Nobel prizes, and further improvements in the production of food and fiber are sure to come from this state. It should be equally certain, too, that those future advances are most likely to be built on the same strong foundation provided here by nature. The air, water, soil, and minerals will remain, but scientists will be challenged increasingly to preserve as well as to invent and produce.

Sunshine and flowing water will be utilized more effectively than now to supply power. Fewer acres of the land will produce more of the source materials for food, shelter, clothing, and chemical uses. The rocks and depths of the earth will give up more treasure, though at greater effort and cost.

But of all Minnesota's resources, the human element will continue to be the greatest contributor to science, for that is the true propellant of progress.

At the "Z" end of the alphabet among scientific and technical developments with a Minnesota angle, the modern zipper is credited at least in part to Gideon Sundback, a rural Minnesotan who received a patent in 1913 for a meshed-tooth fastener, one of several items based on a similar idea that gave practical and commercial impetus to widespread use of zippers.

Minnesota Mentions in the Guinness Book of World Records

Before his death Jean Paul Getty who was born in Minneapolis was listed as one of four proclaimed U.S. billionaires. At his death his personal assets and trust funds exceeded $1,750,000,000·

★ ★ ★

Ralph S. Samuelson of Lake Pepin is credited with having pioneered the present-day sport of water skiing in 1922 on curved boards and also of having made the first recorded jump on water skis from a greased ramp in Miami Beach in 1928.

★ ★ ★

The St. Lawrence Seaway is the world's longest artificial seaway. It enables ocean going vessels to sail the 2,342 miles from the North Atlantic to Duluth, Minnesota, 602 feet above sea level.

★ ★ ★

The greatest horsepower developed by a locomotive engine was by the Northern Pacific (now the Burlington Northern) 2-8-8-4 built in 1929. It generated 45,500 h.p., but a tractive effort of 140,000 lbs.

★ ★ ★

Mrs. Cecilia Grimsmo of Pine River, Minnesota had a duck named Susie which laid a 17 oz. egg in 1972; it's thought to be the biggest.

★ ★ ★

The first solo transatlantic flight was achieved by Minnesotan Charles A. Lindbergh in a 220 h.p. Ryan Monoplane "Spirit of St. Louis" on May 20th and 21st 1927. The 3610 mile flight lasted 33 hours 29½ minutes. Lindbergh was born in Minnesota in 1902, the son of a prominent politician. He died in 1974.

Weather

MINNESOTA'S climate is strongly shaped by its location near the center of the North American continent. Because the state is remote from the oceans, it is warm in the summer, cool in the winter, and basically dry as compared with most places, especially those which are populated to any great extent. The climate will likely prevent Minnesota from ever being heavily populated. The climate produces a people who must be prepared to cope with certain vigors and who must cooperate to some degree from time to time to survive. The remoteness from the sea means that drought must occasionally be expected so that individuals and the people of the state as a group must sometimes expect economic adversity. Various physical and mental tasks are thrust upon Minnesotans that most persons need never face. The climate does have its rewards, however, in providing a favorable outdoor recreational environment eleven months of the year.

Most people are not aware that four atmospheric pressure systems have their "boundaries" in Minnesota. To the northwest and southeast are general high pressure regions. The high pressure system to the southeast, over the Atlantic and the low pressure region to the northeast, near Greenland, are year-round strong features, while high pressure to the northwest is especially well developed in winter and the low pressure to the southwest is especially well developed in the summer.

Good development of the low pressure to the southwest, which is strongest from around June 1 to July 10 and again from August 20 to September 15, results in an inflow of air during those 66 days from the Gulf of Mexico which gives the state about one-third of the total amount of precipitation that falls every year. In winter, development of the high pressure to the northwest results in the spilling of cold air over the state providing a nearly permanent snow cover from around December 6 to about March 19.

Dominance of the low pressure system to the northeast brings in generally ideal outdoor weather from about July 10 to August 20, while the presence of the high pressure system over the Atlantic acts year-round to encourage the intermittent northward flow of moisture-bearing winds. The low pressure system to the northeast during the cold half of the year helps provide a steering current for migrating storms bearing snow.

Quirks in the pressure systems act to create mini-seasons within the four main seasons. The first favorable mini-season of the year occurs during the last half of February, which is marked by a very great amount of sunshine and a general lack of stormy weather.

This is followed by a general stormy period from about March 1 to April 5, marked by large storms up to March 19, the snowiest time of the year. This period is generally unfit for any recreational activity, except to offer a challenging opportunity for the sport of orienteering (navigating with a map and compass). The only other type of sport that is possible and still pleasurable at this time needs to be weather independent, such as cross-country soccer. Cross-country soccer consists of each player kicking a ball to a series of predetermined targets (such as trees, large rocks etc.) each about 1/8 of a mile apart, with the player hitting the targets with the fewest kicks being the winner.

The period from April 5 to May 28 is marked by warmer weather and afternoon showers. The first week of May usually brings widespread storms, however. The last days of May are characterized by fine, warm weather, but from June 1 to about July 10, the establishment of the low pressure to the southwest results in large, widespread evening thunderstorms and sometimes tornadoes or other severe weather.

From July 10 to August 20 is a time of sunny skies, warm temperatures and general lack of rain except for occasional thunderstorms heavily prone to occurring during the night. Southwesterly winds prevail at this time. An exception occurs during the first week of August, when northeasterlies generally blow for a day or two, and when rain becomes more likely.

From August 20 to mid-September, the second rainy season occurs. Severe weather and tornadoes becomes more likely, with storms likely to develop around sunrise. After Labor Day, thunderstorms actually are most common during the hours soon after dawn.

The last week of September usually brings the first really cool weather. During the first week of October warm stormy weather often arises, while the period between the 5th and the 20th is usually marked by clear cool nights and mild, hazy and sunny days with lots of southwesterly winds.

Around October 20, northwesterly winds begin to prevail along with sharply colder temperatures and the beginning of large scale storms. Mid-November brings really cool air and storms, or occasionally blizzards, which are interspersed with cloudy days and light winds.

The arrival of December brings an end to blizzards, with storms until about Christmas nearly always being accompanied by low or moderate winds. Nearly always, a gentle snowstorm occurs within a few days of December 6. When there are no storms, skies are usually overcast with low stratus clouds at this time.

Between Christmas and mid-February, the weather is characterized by alternations between cold continental polar air and warmer air from the Pacific ocean. The battles between these air masses bring snows, with an occasional blizzard. Continental air often means sunny, cold days while the Pacific air brings warm, hazy days. A warm winter is one dominated by Pacific air; a cold one is under the control of continental air.

Climatic Regions in the State

The general weather prevailing in Minnesota has two major modifiers that cause variations from place to place: one is latitude, and the other is earth surface peculiarity.

Latitude has the well-known effect of making the north colder than the south, especially in the winter. In January, temperatures in southwestern Minnesota are 15 degrees warmer than in the northwest, while in July the difference is only five degrees.

However, an even greater modifier of the weather is the nature of the earth's sur-

KITTSON ROSEAU LAKE OF THE WOODS

KOOCHICHING

MARSHALL

ST. LOUIS

POLK PENNINGTON BELTRAMI

RED LAKE CLEAR WATER

COOK

LAKE

NORMAN MANN OMEN HUBBARD CASS ITASCA

NORTHERN AND CENTRAL
HIGHLANDS
CLIMATIC REGION

LAKE CLIMATIC REGION

CLAY BECKER

OTTERTAIL WADENA CROW WING AITKIN CARLTON

WILKIN

PINE

PRAIRIE CLIMATIC REGION

TODD MORRISON MILLE LACS KANA-BEC

ANT DOUGLAS

TRAVERSE BIG STONE EVENS POPE STEARNS BENTON ISANTI

SWIFT KANDI-YOHI SHER-BURNE ANOKA CHISAGO

LAC QUI PARLE CHIPPEWA MEEKER WRIGHT HENN EPIN RAM SEY WASHINGTON

RENVILLE MCLEOD CARVER

YELLOW MEDICINE

LIN-COLN LYON REDWOOD SIBLEY SCOTT DAKOTA

NICOLLET LE SUEUR RICE GOODHUE

BROWN

SOUTHEASTERN HILLS

PIPE-STONE MURRAY COTTON-WOOD WATO-WAN BLUE EARTH WAS-ECA STEELE DODGE OLMSTED WINONA

CLIMATIC REGION

ROCK NOBLES JACKSON MARTIN FARI-BAULT FREE-BORN MOWER FILLMORE HOUS-TON

Climatic Regions of Minnesota

face itself. Minnesota has four basic climatic provinces: the prairie, the southeastern hill region, the north-and-central highlands and the Lake Superior region. These regions cause the state both storms and fair weather systems to behave differently as they cross.

The southeastern hill region is a place of generally reliable rainfall, with topography and vegetation offering protection against winds. Of all the regions of the state, it has the most evenly distributed rainfall during the summer months, but with definite peaks in mid-June and early September. Partly because this area has a less harsh climate than the prairie and northern highlands, it is the most heavily populated. The climate is reflected in the natural vegetation in the form of general hardwood forest or hardwood trees and savannah.

The prairie region is marked by occasional serious drought and high winds. Over this area, there is great variation in temperature from north to south in the winter, but in summer, isotherms (these tend to run north-south) indicate similar temperatures. Thus, western Kittson County on the Canadian border is only five degrees cooler than Rock County on the Iowa line. The prairie is also a region of high winds. The countryside is flat so the wind can blow unhindered. Southerly winds generally prevail in this area and are enhanced by a dynamic low pressure trough that forms over the eastern Dakotas in the lee of the mountains to the west. This region of western Minnesota and the eastern Dakotas is the "wind alley" of the United States. In winter the prairie winds often cause problems in the form of drifting and blowing snow. The hot winds of summer undoubtedly helped to create the ancient prairie by drying the vegetation and spreading fires when they occurred.

The central-and-north highland region is generally an area of rolling or long hills covered with trees and interspersed with many lakes, swamps, meadows and bogs. The summer is much cooler and wetter than on the prairie and the region is much less prone to drought. The rough topography breaks the sweep of the wind so that winter winds produce a pleasant aspect—blizzards, even though they occur, are not as wild as they are on the prairie. Relative humidity is generally high year-round and evaporation is considerably lower than to the south and west. In certain low spots frost occurs even in July and August and temperatures as low as minus 50 degrees are not uncommon in winter.

The shore region along Lake Superior is the most temperate part of the state, owing to the cool waters which are near 40 degrees out in the lake year-round. This shore area rarely experiences extremes of heat or cold, with average daily temperatures ranging from around 62 degrees in August to about 13 degrees in winter. Precipitation is generous, with rain often occurring along the shore in winter while snow falls inland. Snows can be heavy, however, when they do occur. The heaviest snow region in the state lies along the high ground about a dozen miles inland from Lake Superior, where upslope motion combines with moisture-laden east winds to produce 100 inches or more in some areas in a season.

Technically, the portion of the state with the least temperature variation is near the point where Minnesota, Wisconsin and Michigan meet in Lake Superior. Here the average monthly temperature runs from 20 degrees in January to about 60 degrees in August. Minnesota waters of Lake Superior provide fogs and storms at times, but tranquil beauty at others.

Micro-Climates

Lurking within each of Minnesota's climatic regions are local micro-climates. These small scale climates, wrought by differences in topography and vegetation, often cause strong weather differences within distances on the order of hundreds of feet and sometimes just a few feet.

Wind is very strongly influenced by differences in topography and vegetation. Trees have a strong braking effect on the wind for distances many times their height. In a deep forest there is nearly a calm while the wind around and above blows with gusto. Hills offer considerable protection from the full force of wind on the other side. Manmade structures may give good protection, but poor design often results in negative wind effects.

Topography often causes spectacular differences in nighttime temperature in short distances. This happens because the earth's surface cools by radiation to the night sky. Air moving over the surface is cooled by the ground. The chilled air is denser and seeks a lower elevation under the influence of gravity. Pools of cool air build up in low places during the night with ever-colder air flowing near the surface.

Temperature differences of 20 degrees in an area of several square miles are not uncommon in many parts of the state on clear nights. Even on nights with appreciable cloudiness and winds of 10 miles per hour, differences of 10 degrees appear. Those who live in dells and other low places should not be surprised if their heating bills seem to be higher than their neighbors. In some shadowy low places, the air may chill from a few hours before sunset to well after sunrise.

City dwellers, even in places of 500 inhabitants, generally have lower heating bills than rural people because of heat released by homes and other activities. The "heat island" of Minneapolis-St. Paul warms winter-time temperatures by an average of about 4 degrees, and has even raised the average airport winter temperature by about 2 degrees over the natural.

In rural northern Minnesota there are many places where frost occurs the year round. Weather stations are normally located in areas other than these "frost pockets", so that the cold areas are not highly visible.

Cold areas are places of less atmospheric water vapor; by the same token they are areas where dew concentrates. When the air is chilled by the surface vegetation a considerable amount of atmospheric water vapor is deposited on the surfaces of plants.

The micro-climate features are best developed in the central and northern highland climatic region and most poorly on the flat prairie region. The presence of micro-climatic features make some enormous differences in selecting proper building sites for dwellings and other structures. Those who ignore the micro-climate in planning in Minnesota do so at the peril of their comfort and their pocketbooks.

Sunshine is also much affected by topography and vegetation. Locations on north slopes can be quite miserable, being often in winter's shadows while at the same time suffering from exposure to the cold winds from the arctic regions.

Here are some rules for selecting and developing a dwelling site in Minnesota:
1. Pick a spot on a south-facing slope; one which has higher ground immediately to the west is ideal.
2. If there is no high ground to the west or north, plant evergreen trees to break the wind and shield against the hot setting sun of the summer.
3. Plant broadleaf trees to the south and east of the structure. They will provide shade in the summer and interfere little with the sunshine in the cold winter. It is best to plant these trees some distance from the house so you can take advantage of solar energy. Every south facing window can become a solar collector if you remove any screens and open drapes when the sun is shining. Fuel savings can be substantial.

4. Choose a neighborhood that is not too densely populated. Concentration of dwellings leads to an insufferable summertime micro-climate. Non-vegetated surfaces store up heat during the day and release it at night, causing miserable conditions for sleeping.

5. Avoid dells, low spots, hilltops and north slopes.

6. A lake to the southwest is very desirable. During the period from mid-July through about Labor Day, lots of hot southwesterly winds blow. The passage of air over the water has the effect of cooling the air and allowing the wind to pick up speed for cooling the body. Strong southwesterly winds are rare in winter, so no problem from them arises.

There are two good places in Minnesota to observe for ideas on site selection. One, Glenwood, is located on south slope along the northeast end of Lake Minnewaska. It is ideally situated from the standpoint of the micro-climate principle. Another is the Windsor Green Townhouses in New Brighton—they are on a south slope to the northeast of Silver Lake.

Storms

Blizzards, tornadoes and severe thunderstorms rake Minnesota every year, wreaking property damage and often death.

A blizzard generally affects the entire state, a severe thunderstorm several counties and a ttornado one or two counties. Over the years, the severe thunderstorms kill more people than blizzards and tornadoes combined, though the latter two get most of the publicity since they often take more lives in one blow.

Without question, the greatest blizzard, in terms of intensity, was that of January, 1975, the "Blizzard of the Century". The greatest tornado of all, in terms of deaths, was the St. Cloud-Sauk Rapids storm of April 14, 1886. It is impossible to identify clearly the most severe thunderstorm of all time, since the criteria have become difficult to establish. Candidates for such storms where tornado activity was not a significant feature would include that of Aug. 29, 1948, which killed 37 persons and featured some very rare cloud forms, the Black Thursday storm of June 20, 1974, and the Great Hailstorm of July 20, 1903, which laid waste entire townships in Lincoln, Pipstone, Rock and Nobles counties. The August storm was clearly foremost in deaths, the June storm in terms of wind damage, and the July storm because of hail damage.

Blizzards

The blizzard is a blinding stew of heavy snow, blowing snow, blowing dust, rain, freezing rain, high winds (sometimes of hurricane velocity), sleet, low barometer and stark temperature contrast—to the 60's and even 70's to the front and sub-zero to the rear.

A great blizzard begins with a pickup of northerly winds across the Great Plains and a rush of warm air northward across the Mississippi Valley. The blizzard must take place between November 3 and April 10. Only during that time are the needed ingredients present.

The worst blizzard, that of January 1975, took place between the 9th and 12th of the month. The center of the storm passed over the Twin Cities area around 10 p.m. with a measured low pressure of 28.62 inches. The storm center reached the Grand Portage area at dawn on the 11th, with gales and, in some places, hurricane force winds causing zero and near zero visibility from blowing snow and dust on the afternoon of the 11th over most of Minnesota. Gale driven snow was already blowing in western Minnesota. On the morning of the 10th and still on the 12th, high winds were occurring in most parts of the state.

The storm included lightning and thunder near the storm center and there were great temperature variations. While sub-zero readings were being observed in the Dakotas, Wisconsin was reading values in the 50's. Minnesota, in the path of the center had temperatures in the 40's in the southeast while below-zero values were present in the western portion of the state.

Prior to the 1975 blizzard, the worst in the history of Minnesota was brobably that of Feb. 13, 1866. The eight most intense blizzards in the state's history were:
1. The Blizzard of the Centuries, January 9 - 12, 1975
2. The Great Blizzard, Feb. 13 - 15, 1866
3. Blizzard of Jan. 7 - 10, 1873
4. The Armistice Day Storm, Nov. 11 - 12, 1940
5. The Blizzard of Jan. 13 - 15, 1888
6. The Blizzard of Feb. 23 - 26, 1835
7. The Ides of March Blizzard, March 15 - 16, 1941
8. The Blizzard of Jan. 14 - 15, 1827

Severe Thunderstorms

A ferocious thunderstorm squall line roared through eastern Minnesota and western Wisconsin on the morning of August 29, 1948. The clouds of this system represented the classic profile of a squall line development. The advance edge of the storm cloud was an immense smooth wall approximately 100 miles long that extended from near the ground to about 50,000 ft. in the sky. Ahead of the mass was a rotor cloud roughly 200 feet in diameter and scores of miles in length. It rotated at about 35 revoulations per minute as very cold air from its bowels slashed along the ground, sending the old warm August morning air aloft.

As the violence struck Winona County, an unfortunate airliner was caught in the storm's path. Aircraft in those days could not fly above the path of foul weather, and the plane was chewed up in the vicious jaws of the wall cloud. All 37 people aboard were killed.

Similar in appearance was the great squall line of July 20, 1903. The wall cloud roared over four southwestern counties of Minnesota. Wind destruction was tempered somewhat by the fact that mostly open prairie was under the storm, but hail damage was the big story. It fell nearly everywhere in the counties, with total damage involving whole townships. Many stones weighed several pounds, and huge holes were torn in the roofs of buildings. The stones in some instances smashed down nearly entire roofs.

Noteworthy for its high winds was the storm of Black Thursday on June 20, 1974. It moved into Minnesota from North Dakota between Fargo and Grand Forks. A pilot described the area under the storm as being "as black as night."

As the disturbance moved over many counties from Fargo to the Iowa line in southeastern Minnesota, it became enlarged and knocked down thousands of trees. Its passage caused farm yard lights activated by automatic switches sensitive to failing light, to glare as the eerie darkness enveloped the land. Short intense hail and rain pelted the region. Winds were clocked at speeds over 100 miles per hour as the storm ground through the state.

On July 23, 1987 the heaviest rain ever fell at the National Weather Service Office in Minneapolis. A total of 10.00 inches was recorded within eight hours from the evening of the 23rd to the early part of the 24th.

A rain of this magnitude can be expected at a given point about once every 10,000 years. However, it should be noted that a rain such as this occurs somewhere in Minnesota every few years. What is unusual is that this storm picked the official airport rain gauge as one of its principal targets.

Tornadoes

Tornadoes make news not according to their size and number in a family, but also according to where they hit. A dozen severe tornadoes slashing through remote forest areas may be little noted, while a single small tornado striking a mobile home park will make headlines because of death and injury.

Very damaging and newsworthy was a family of six or more tornadoes which struck the Twin Cities on May 6, 1965. The western and northern suburbs were hardest hit. A total of 16 persons were killed and 512 injured, with 325 homes and 278 mobile homes destroyed. In addition, 1197 dwellings and 82 mobile homes were damaged and 241 farms and 65 businesses were demolished.

The eight worst tornadoes in state history, in terms of fatalities were:

		Deaths
1. St. Cloud-Sauk Rapids	April 14, 1886	74
2. Fegus Falls	June 21, 1919	57
3. Tyler	August 21, 1918	36
4. Rochester	August 21, 1883	26
5. Twin Cities	May 6, 1965	16
6. Northern Minnesota	August 6, 1969	15
7. Twin Cities	August 20, 1904	15
8. Albert Lea-Wells Waseca-Owatonna	April 30, 1967	12
9. Mankato-Wells	August 17, 1946	11

One of the most unusual tornadoes was that of May 27, 1930. While traveling through Norman County, the famous old train, the Empire Builder, collided with a twister. The crack train was picked off the tracks and overturned, killing one person.

Other Storms

Climatic disturbances of another nature and less intensity visit Minnesota. Notable in violence but rare in occurrence are "land hurricanes". These are spring and fall phenomena that bring winds of hurricane force (73 miles per hour or over) to the area. They usually originate in the vicinity of New Mexico and move across Minnesota to Canada. Three of these monumental climatic movements occurred on Sept. 16, 1856, Oct. 10, 1949 and May 5, 1950. On at least one such occasion, a well-developed "eye" was observed.

The common "all-day rainstorm" usually appears a few days after a cold front passage when the front stalls to the south. A low pressure zone coming from the west will "pick up" the front, causing it to move northward toward Minnesota as a warm front. The low pressure center moves eastward along the front, with the front to the rear of the storm again moving south as a cold front. When it passes as far as Iowa, Minnesota can receive a lot of heavy rain.

Minnesota Sky and Weather Phenomena

Ice fogs, composed of ice crystals, often present pretty sights on cold winter mornings. They sparkle in the air like millions of diamonds, a delight to natives and a source of amazement to visitors from southern climates. They are caused by freezing of air-borne water and begin to appear most often at temperatures below minus 20 Fahrenheit. Heavy auto traffic may cause considerable loss of visibility since combustion processes release copious amounts of water into the air.

The aurora borealis, or northern lights, are caused by reactions to the bombardment of the upper atmosphere by solar particles. These fireworks make the air glow, resulting in brilliant displays. They are so common in the state because it is close to the north magnetic pole, just northwest of Hudson Bay. The aurora borealis appears more frequently farther north.

Climatic Averages, Extremes

Temperature, degrees fahrenheit	Duluth	Intl. Falls	Moor.-Fargo	Roch.	St. Cld.	Twin Cities
Yearly Normal	38.6	36.5	40.8	43.6	41.7	44.1
January Normal	8.5	1.9	5.9	12.9	8.9	11.8
April Normal	38.6	38.2	42.3	44.5	42.9	44.6
July Normal	65.6	65.8	70.7	70.1	70.2	71.2
October Normal	45.3	43.5	46.9	49.6	47.6	49.2
Record High	106	98	114	108	107	108
Record Low	-41	-46	-48	-42	-42	-41
Hottest July	70.8	76.4	80.2	77.6	78.9	78.7
Coldest January	-7.2	-10.4	-6.2	-3.8	-5.7	-6.0
Normal Degree Days	9756	10,547	9271	8227	8868	8159
Precipitation, Inches						
Yearly Normal	30.18	25.65	19.62	27.47	26.84	25.94
Wettest Year	40.08	32.20	31.48	43.69	39.32	40.15
Driest Year	18.11	15.12	8.87	11.65	14.64	11.59
January Normal	1.16	.85	.50	.65	.76	.73
April Normal	2.55	1.67	2.08	2.36	2.30	2.04
July Normal	3.73	3.98	3.19	3.74	3.23	3.69
October Normal	2.30	1.69	1.10	1.82	1.69	1.78
Wettest Month	11.52	11.26	9.58	11.95	12.81	11.87
Driest Month	.07	.10	T	T	0	T
Days .01 or More	135	133	104	107	109	110
Snowfall						
Average Season	77.6	58.2	33.9	42.4	42.1	45.0
Snowiest Season	131.6	93.7	82.2	77.5	87.9	88.9
Most in One Month	48.2	31.5	30.4	35.1	51.7	40.0
Most in One Day	25.4	17.0	19.2	12.9	14.5	16.2
Days 1" or More	22	18	11	13	13	15
Other						
Fastest Wind, MPH	75	52	115	52	53	110
Average Sky Cover	6.7	6.7	6.0	6.3	6.1	6.0
Average No. of Clear Days	75	82	103	92	111	103
Average No. of Pt.-Cldy Days	104	103	115	115	100	110
Average No. of Cloudy Days	186	180	150	158	154	152
Average Thunderstorm Days	35	30	32	41	35	38

See inside back cover.

Minnesota Weather Extremes
Miscellaneous Minnesota Weather Facts

On a weighted basis, an average of 25.153 inches of rain fell per year in the state between 1901 and 1960. This is 33.37 cubic miles of water per year, enough water to fill a tank 3.2 miles long, 3.2 miles wide and 3.2 miles high. However, it would take 88 years at this rate to equal a volume the size of Lake Superior.

The record highest and lowest temperature are not generally listed correctly. The true high was 114.5 degrees Fahrenheit at Beardsley. Moorhead once had 113.6. Both round off at 114, but the Beardsley reading was actually 0.9 degrees higher. The coldest temperature was minus 59 recorded at Leech Lake at Pokegema. However, examinations of the records shows the Leech Lake value to be reliable, and the Pokegema figure invalid.

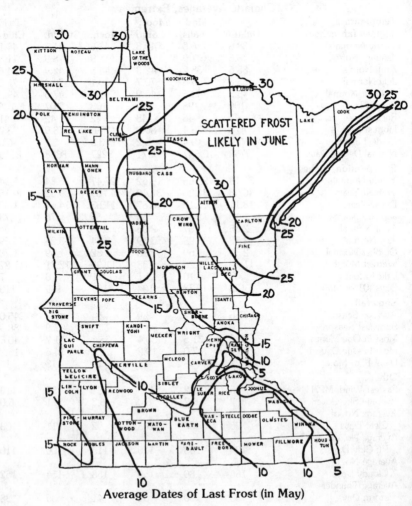

Average Dates of Last Frost (in May)

Minnesota Weather Safety

It is no secret that thousands of Minnesotans have died from weather related causes. However, for the most part, the deaths have been needless and proper precautions could have averted most of the fatalities. Here are some weather safety hints:

A blizzard can stop your car in its tracks or force it to become stuck in a snowbank. You may face danger from the car being buried in the snow, causing suffocation, by becoming too cold in the metal prison causing frostbite or worse, or making a decision to leave the vehicle and dying by getting lost and freezing.

Generally, it is best you stay in the car and not venture out. Blowing snow can limit visibility to a few feet, and one becomes disoriented. In winter, no trip should

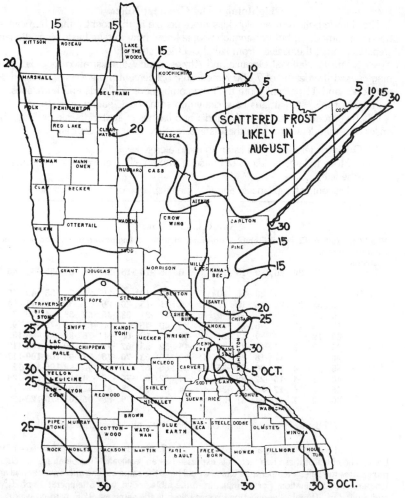

Average Dates of First Frost (in September)

begin without blankets, food and drink for a few days and a 3-pound coffee can for body wastes. A portable radio with fresh batteries is an imperative for receiving information about weather and road conditions.

Anyone driving extensively in winter should have a CB radio and an updated road map. Don't forget a flashlight and first aid kit.

When it is raining very hard in warmer weather, pull over, preferably into the driveway of a restaurant or service station. Heavy rain seldom lasts long. Avoid low stream areas where flooding may occur.

Always keep an eye out for squall line clouds, especially if you are in a boat. Learn to recognize them. They bring not only rain, but high winds.

Lightning - The Greatest Killer

The thunderbolt from on high kills more people in the country than hurricanes, floods or tornadoes; but not enough people know how to take basic precautionary steps to protect themselves from lethal electrical strikes.

According to National Oceanic and Atmospheric Administration records, lightning caused the deaths of 7,000 Americans, 55 percent more than were killed by tornadoes and 41 percent more than the combination of floods and hurricanes.

In light of this, statisticians have drawn up some basic safety rules, to wit:

When approaching rumbles of thunder and flashes of light in the sky indicate the onset of a thunderstorm, take these steps for they may save your life:

DO Watch television and listen to radio alerts

DO Move to large buildings or house or into an all - metal vehicle (car, truck or or the like)

DO Disconnect appliances, and use the telephone only for emergencies

Wind Chill Table

Wind Chill Index: (Equivalent temperature) Equivalent in cooling power on exposed flesh under calm conditions.

Degrees (F.)		35	30	25	20	15	10	5	0	-5	-10	-15	-20	-25	-30	-35	-40	-45
MPH	0	35	30	25	20	15	10	5	0	-5	-10	-15	-20	-25	-30	-35	-40	-45
	5	33	27	21	16	12	7	1	-6	-11	-15	-20	-26	-31	-35	-41	-47	-54
	10	21	16	9	2	-2	-9	-15	-22	-27	-31	-38	-45	-52	-58	-64	-70	-77
	15	16	11	1	-6	-11	-18	-25	-33	-40	-45	-51	-60	-65	-70	-78	-85	-90
	20	12	3	-4	-9	-17	-24	-32	-40	-46	-52	-60	-68	-76	-81	-88	-96	-103
	25	7	0	-7	-15	-22	-29	-37	-45	-52	-58	-67	-75	-83	-89	-96	-104	-112
	30	5	-2	-11	-18	-26	-33	-41	-49	-56	-63	-70	-78	-87	-94	-101	-109	-117
	35	3	-4	-13	-20	-27	-35	-43	-52	-60	-67	-72	-83	-90	-98	-105	-113	-123
	40	1	-4	-15	-22	-29	-36	-45	-54	-62	-69	-76	-87	-94	-101	-107	-116	-128
	45	1	-6	-17	-24	-31	-38	-46	-54	-63	-70	-78	-87	-94	-101	-109	-118	-128
	50	0	-7	-17	-24	-31	-38	-47	-56	-63	-70	-79	-88	-96	-103	-110	-120	-128

(Wind speeds greater than 40 mph have little additional chilling effect)

How Cold is cold? Temperature and wind both affect the heat loss from the surface of the body. The effect of these two factors is expressed as an "equivalent temperature," which approximates the still-air temperature which would have the same cooling affect as the wind and temperature combination. For example, from the table above, with a temperature of 20° F. and a wind of 20 mph, the effect on exposed flesh is the same as -9° F. with no wind.

Minnesota Weather Extremes

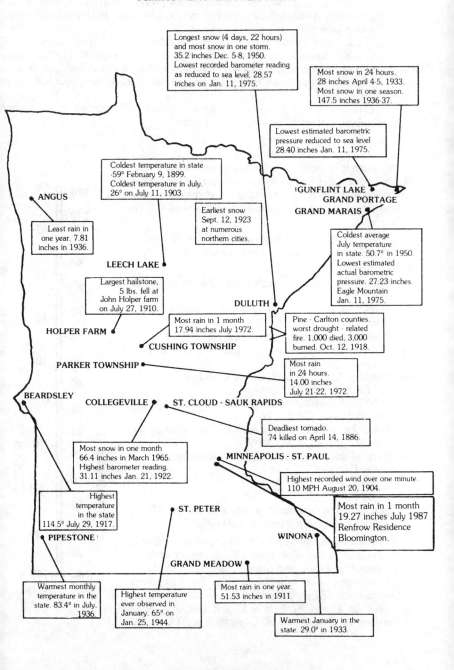

Longest snow (4 days, 22 hours) and most snow in one storm. 35.2 inches Dec. 5-8, 1950. Lowest recorded barometer reading as reduced to sea level. 28.57 inches on Jan. 11, 1975.

Most snow in 24 hours. 28 inches April 4-5, 1933. Most snow in one season. 147.5 inches 1936-37.

Lowest estimated barometric pressure reduced to sea level 28.40 inches Jan. 11, 1975.

Coldest temperature in state -59° February 9, 1899. Coldest temperature in July. 26° on July 11, 1903.

Earliest snow Sept. 12, 1923 at numerous northern cities.

GUNFLINT LAKE
GRAND PORTAGE
GRAND MARAIS

Coldest average July temperature in state. 50.7° in 1950. Lowest estimated actual barometric pressure. 27.23 inches. Eagle Mountain Jan. 11, 1975.

ANGUS

Least rain in one year. 7.81 inches in 1936.

LEECH LAKE

Largest hailstone, 5 lbs. fell at John Holper farm on July 27, 1910.

DULUTH

Most rain in 1 month 17.94 inches July 1972.

Pine - Carlton counties. worst drought - related fire. 1,000 died, 3,000 burned. Oct. 12, 1918.

HOLPER FARM

CUSHING TOWNSHIP

PARKER TOWNSHIP

Most rain in 24 hours. 14.00 inches July 21-22, 1972.

BEARDSLEY

COLLEGEVILLE

ST. CLOUD - SAUK RAPIDS

Deadliest tornado. 74 killed on April 14, 1886.

Most snow in one month 66.4 inches in March 1965. Highest barometer reading. 31.11 inches Jan. 21, 1922.

MINNEAPOLIS - ST. PAUL

Highest recorded wind over one minute. 110 MPH August 20, 1904.

Highest temperature in the state 114.5° July 29, 1917.

ST. PETER

Most rain in 1 month 19.27 inches July 1987 Renfrow Residence Bloomington.

PIPESTONE

WINONA

GRAND MEADOW

Warmest monthly temperature in the state. 83.4° in July, 1936.

Highest temperature ever observed in January. 65° on Jan. 25, 1944.

Most rain in one year. 51.53 inches in 1911.

Warmest January in the state. 29.0° in 1933.

If Outside:

> DO NOT stay anywhere near metal farm equipment, golf scooters, motorcyles, metal fences, pipes, rails or any other metal objects that could conduct electricity to or near you.
>
> DO NOT seek shelter in small sheds or isolated buildings in open areas.
>
> DO seek a haven in low ground, preferably under a thick growth of small trees.
>
> DO drop to your knees and bend forward, putting your hands on your knees — this reduces the chances of a bolt striking near you and using your body as a conductor.
>
> DO warn members of a group to spread out, not huddle together, to reduce the numbers that might be affected by a strike.

Celsius Scale

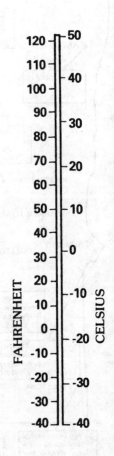

Although it has thus far failed to gain acceptance in the United States, the Celsius temperature scale is becoming increasingly familiar to Americans. It is the measuring system used by virtually the entire world beyond U.S.A. boundaries.

There are some clever techniques that can be used to relate Celsius to Fahrenheit. Here are some benchmarks that are easy to remember.

1. Both Celsius and Fahrenheit are equal at 40 below zero.

2. At -23° Fahrenheit, turn the numbers around to get approximate degrees Celsius; -32°.

3. Twelve degrees Fahrenheit is minus eleven Celsius, and eleven degrees Fahrenheit is minus twelve degrees Celsius.

4. Freezing, 32° Fahrenheit, is zero Celsius.

5. 39° Fahrenheit is 3.9° Celsius.

6. At 61° Fahrenheit, turn the numbers around to get approximate degrees Celsius, 16.

7. At 82° Fahrenheit, turn the numbers around to get approximate degrees Celsius, 28°.

8. Some of the easier relationships to remember are:

> 95 F is 35 C
> 68 F is 20 C
> 50 F is 10 C

9. Like 32 Fahrenheit occurs at a memorable O Celsius, 32 Celsius occurs at a memorable 90 Fahrenheit.

If you remember these benchmarks, you can estimate temperatures in the other system by recalling that there are almost 2 Fahrenheit degrees (actually 1.8) for 1 Celsius degree. For example, if it is 86 Fahrenheit, remember that 82 Fahrenheit is 28 Celsius. The difference between 86 F and 82 F is 4 F, and half of 4 is 2. Therefore, 28 C + 2 C is 30 C, so 86 F is 30 C.

CALENDARS

The Twin Cities Weather Calendar has been part of the local Metropolitan scene since 1969. Except for minor alterations, the format is the same now as it was back then.

The long Twin cities weather record, dating continuously back to 1819, is the third longest in the United States, and is the best in the United States, and perhaps the world, for so long a time. After such a long time, many climatic fluctuations have occurred. It is likely that the weekly averages on these calendars will remain stable for at least the next several thousand years to a high degree of similarity. Considerable efforts are being made in computer modeling to preclude the possibility that mankind will engage in activities that will alter world climate to a significant extent. These studies, though basic in research, are of great potential applied value, for they could enable America as a nation to change activities or to warn other nations to change their activities so as to not endanger the food supply of the world by ruining the present climate, to which crops are adapted. Argument is strong for the general climate of the past 160 years to prevail for a long time to come. Thus this Weather Calendar should stay valid for many millenia.

The Gregorian Calendar

This calendar, now the world calendar, is known as the Gregorian Calendar. It was proclaimed by Pope Gregory XIII in Rome in 1582 to be in effect as the calendar of the Roman Catholic Church as of October 15th (old October 4th) of that year. The calendar came about after long concern over the fact that the calendar of the Roman Empire as revised by Julius Caeser was losing days by not dropping an extra day every 100 years in 3 centuries out of 4. Caeser had revised and fixed an ever-changing calendar, traditionally originated by Romulus, the founder of Rome.

Gregory's calendar became the official calendar in the American Colonies on September 14, 1752 (Gregorian) under our ruler at the time, His Brittanic Majesty, King George II. Despite the fact that an Englishman, the Venerable Bede of Jarrow, pointed out the need for the correction as early as the year 730, England and her subject lands were among the last to adopt the Gregorian calendar.

It is important for many reasons, such as the study of weather and climate, that the calendar stay in synchronization with the seasons. For this purpose, our calendar is fixed on a point in the sky, called the First Point of Aries. This point is related to the moment that spring begins—the moment at which the earth is at the point in its orbit about the sun such that the most vertical "ray" of the sun strikes the earth's equator exactly as the sun appears to proceed northward in the sky as seen from Earth. Our calendar is determined such that this occurs from March 19 to March 21.

The Gregorian calendar makes every year evenly divisible by four a leap year, except for years evenly divisible by 100 but not by 400. Thus, 1800, 1900, 2100, 2200, and 2300 are not leap years, but 2000 and 2400 will be. These adjustments will keep the calendar within 1 day of accuracy until about 5000 if no significant changes occur in the various motions involved in the calculation of time. Around 4800 or 5200, we should need to drop a day—that decision has not yet been made according to sources I contacted. Another day may have to be dropped around the years 10,000, 15,000 and 20,000 etc.

The Gregorian calendar recycles to the same dates and days of the week every 400 years, so that the calendars for 1600,2000, 2400, and each of the next 399 years thereafter are in synchronization.

One unfortunate change was made in the calendar between the time of Julius Caeser and Pope Gregory. Augustus Caeser took a day out of February and put it into August, the month which he named after himself. One simple calendar reform might be to take a day from January and March and give them to February, so that all those months will have 30 days, a more even distribution. Leap day then could be February 31.

Other Calendars

We use the calendar that evolved from Rome since the dominant cultural heritage of today's world came from or through Rome as a result of the spread of civilization by that city's vast empire and the subsequent world-wide expansion of its former domains such as England, Spain and France. The calendar of Rome became the calendar of the colonies and dominions of these lands and remains such though the colonies and dominions are now free.

Both other calendars were in use at one time by other cultures, with some being superior to the Roman calendar.

Locally, the Ojibwe calendar was reckoned by moons and by days of each moon. The Ojibwe moons were highly related to weather or weather-associated events. They bear such names as the Freezing Moon and Deep Snow Moon. One way to reckon Ojibwe Moons is by the following method: Let the first full moon after the vernal equinox be the Snowshoe Breaking Moon (the moon when snowshoes are no longer needed because the snow melts away during the moon). Let the next 12 months follow in order by the names listed below except when it becomes necessary to drop one moon due to the year. To do this, let the last full moon before the vernal equinox always be the Crust of Snow Moon, with the Sucker Moon dropping out if there is no full moon between February 8th and 18th. The names are according to Duane Chatfield.

TABLE OF OJIBWE MOONS

FULL MOON DATES		MOON NAMES	NEW MOON DATES	
Earliest	Latest		Earliest	Latest
Mar 20	Apr 18	Snowshoe Breaking	March 6	Apr 13
Apr 19	May 17	Maple Sugar	April 14	May 2
May 18	Jun 16	Budding Plants	May 3	June 1
Jun 17	July 16	Strawberry	June 2	June 30
July 16	Aug 14	Midsummer	July 1	July 29
Aug 15	Sep 12	Harvest	July 30	Aug 28
Sep 13	Oct 12	Wild Rice Harvest	Aug 29	Sep 26
Oct 13	Nov 10	Falling Leaves	Sep 27	Oct 26
Nov 11	Dec 10	Freezing	Oct 27	Nov 25
Dec 11	Jan 8	Descending Cold	Nov 26	Dec 25
Jan 9	Feb 7	Deep Snow	Dec 26	Jan 24
Feb 8	Feb 18	Sucker	Jan 25	Feb 4
Feb 19	Mar 20	Crust of Snow	Feb 5	Mar 6

ASTRONOMICAL EVENTS FOR 1988

OJIBWE MOON NAME	NEW MOON	FIRST QUARTER	FULL MOON	LAST QUARTER
Descending Cold			Jan 3 7:40 PM	Jan 12 1:04 AM
Deep Snow	Jan 18 11:26 PM	Jan 25 3:53 PM	Feb 2 2:51 PM	Feb 10 5:01 PM
Crust of Snow	Feb 17 9:54 AM	Feb 24 6:15 AM	Mar 3 10:01 AM	Mar 11 4:56 AM
Snowshoe Breaking	Mar 17 8:02 PM	Mar 24 10:41 PM	Apr 2 3:21 AM	Apr 9 2:21 PM
Maple Sugar	Apr 16 7:00 AM	Apr 23 5:32 PM	May 1 6:41 PM	May 8 8:23 PM
Budding Plants	May 15 5:11 PM	May 23 11:49 AM	May 31 5:53 AM	Jun 7 1:21 AM
Strawberry	Jun 14 4:14 AM	Jun 22 5:23 AM	Jun 29 2:46 PM	Jul 6 6:36 AM
Midsummer	Jul 13 4:53 PM	Jul 21 9:14 PM	Jul 28 10:25 PM	Aug 4 1:22 PM
Harvest	Aug 12 7:31 AM	Aug 20 4:51 AM	Aug 27 5:56 AM	Sep 2 10:50 PM
Wild Rice Harvest	Sep 10 11:49 PM	Sep 18 10:18 PM	Sep 25 2:07 PM	Oct 2 11:58 AM
Falling Leaves	Oct 10 4:49 PM	Oct 18 8:01 AM	Oct 24 11:35 PM	Nov 1 4:11 AM
Freezing	Nov 9 8:20 AM	Nov 16 3:35 PM	Nov 23 9:53 AM	Dec 1 12:49 AM
Descending Cold	Dec 8 11:36 PM	Dec 15 11:40 PM	Dec 22 11:29 PM	Dec 30 10:57 PM

Astronomical Events for 1989

OJIBWE MOON NAME	NEW MOON	FIRST QUARTER	FULL MOON	LAST QUARTER
Deep Snow	Jan 7 1:22 PM	Jan 14 7:58 AM	Jan 21 3:33 PM	Jan 29 8:02 PM
Crust of Snow	Feb 6 1:37 AM	Feb 12 5:15 PM	Feb 20 9:32 AM	Feb 28 4:08 PM
Snowshoe Breaking	Mar 7 12:19 PM	Mar 14 4:11 AM	Mar 22 3:58 AM	Mar 30 4:21 AM
Maple Sugar	Apr 5 10:33 PM	Apr 12 6:13 PM	Apr 20 10:13 PM	Apr 28 3:46 PM
Budding Plants	May 5 6:46 AM	May 12 9:19 AM	May 20 1:16 PM	May 27 11:01 PM
Strawberry	Jun 3 2:53 PM	Jun 11 1:59 AM	June 19 1:57 AM	June 26 4:09 AM
Midsummer	Jul 2 11:59 PM	Jul 10 7:19 PM	Jul 18 12:42 PM	Jul 25 8:31 AM
Harvest	Aug 1 11:06 AM	Aug 9 12:28 PM	Aug 16 10:07 PM	Aug 23 1:40 PM
Wild Rice Harvest	Aug 31 12:44 AM	Sep 8 4:49 AM	Sep 15 6:51 AM	Sep 21 9:10 PM
Falling Leaves	Sep 29 4:47 PM	Oct 7 7:52 PM	Oct 14 3:32 PM	Oct 21 8:19 AM
Freezing	Oct 29 9:27 AM	Nov 6 8:11 AM	Nov 12 11:51 PM	Nov 19 10:44 PM
Descending Cold	Nov 28 3:41 AM	Dec 5 7:26 PM	Dec 12 10:30 AM	Dec 19 6:54 PM
Deep Snow	Dec 27 9:20 PM			

Major Events 1988

January

The earth is at perihelion on January 3 at 6 PM.

* Brilliant Venus and the crescent moon will be close in the western sky at dusk on Thursday the 21st.

February

* Saturn, Mars, and the waning crescent moon are seen close together in the sky before dawn on Saturday the 13th.

* Brilliant Venus, Bright Jupiter, and the moon are seen close together in the west at dusk on Saturday the 20th.

March

* Saturn, Mars, and the last quarter moon are seen close together in the wee hours on Saturday the 12th.

* Spring begins on Sunday, March 20 at 3:39 AM. On that evening, Venus, Jupiter, and the crescent moon will be seen close together in the west.

April

* Venus and the moon are seen close together in the northwest at dusk on Tuesday the 19th.

May

* Venus is seen close to the crescent moon at dusk on Tuesday the 17th.

June

* Summer begins on the 20th at 10:57 PM.

July
*The earth is at aphelion on Tuesday the 5th at 6 PM.
* Jupiter and Mars are seen close to the crescent moon before dawn on Sunday the 20th.

August
*The moon is close to Mars on the 2nd, to Jupiter on the 6th, and to Venus on the 8th. All three of these planets are bright in the morning sky this month.
*There will be a partial eclipse of the moon before sunrise on Saturday the 27th. It will be darkened most around 6:05 AM.

September
*The moon is close to Jupiter on the 2nd, to Venus on the 7th, to Saturn on the 18th, and to Mars on the 25th.

*Fall begins at 2:29 PM on Thursday the 22nd.

October
*The moon is close to Venus on the 7th, to Saturn on the 16th, to Mars on the 22nd, and to Jupiter on the 27th.

November
*The moon is near Venus before dawn on Sunday the 6th. It is near Mars on the 19th and near Jupiter on the 23rd, when the moon is full.

December
*Venus is near the crescent moon before dawn on Tuesday the 6th.
The moon is near Mars on the 17th, and Jupiter on the 20th.
*Winter begins on Wednesday the 21st at 9:28 AM.

Major Events 1989

January
*The earth is at perihelion at 4 PM on January 1.
*Jupiter is seen near the moon on the evening of the 16th.

February
*Mars is seen near the moon on the evening of the 11th.
*Jupiter is seen near the moon on the evening of the 12th.
*An eclipse of the moon will begin at 6:30 AM on the 20th. However, Minnesotans cannot see the total phase of the eclipse since the moon will set too soon.

March
*A partial eclipse of the sun can be seen from Minnesota from around noon to 1:15 PM on the 7th.
*Mars and Jupiter are seen near the moon on the evening of the 12th.
*Spring begins at 9:28 AM on the 20th.

April
*Jupiter and Mars are seen near the moon on the evening of the 9th.

*Saturn is seen near the moon on the night of the 26th-27th.

May
*Mars is seen near the moon on the evening of the 8th.
Saturn is seen near the moon on the 30th before dawn.

June
*Venus is seen near the crescent moon at dusk on the 4th. Mars, dimmer, is not far away.
*Summer begins at 4:53 AM on the 21st.

July
*Brilliant Venus and dimmer Mars are seen close to the crescent moon at dusk on July 4th.
*The earth is at aphelion on July 4th.
*The moon is near Saturn on the evenings of the 16th and 17th, and near Jupiter before dawn on the 29th and 30th.

August
*The moon is seen near Venus on the evening of the 4th, near Saturn on the night of the 13th-14th, and near Jupiter before dawn on the 26th.

*There will be a total eclipse of the moon visible from all of Minnesota on the evening of the 16th from 9:19 PM to 10:56 PM, Central Daylight Time.

September
*The moon is seen near Venus on the evening of the 3rd, near Saturn on the evening of the 9th, and near Jupiter during the wee hours on the 22nd.

*Fall begins on the 22nd at 8:20 PM.

October
*The moon is seen near Venus at dusk on the 3rd, near Saturn on the evening of the 6th, and near Jupiter on the night of the 19th-20th.

*The Harvest Moon is full on the 14th.

November
*The moon is seen near Venus on the evening of the 2nd, near Saturn on the evening of the 3rd, and Jupiter on the night of the 16th-17th.

December
*Venus is seen very near the moon on the evening of the 1st, and near Jupiter on the night of the 13th-14th.

*Winter begins on the 21st at 3.22 PM.

MONTHLY STATISTICS

TEMPERATURE, F	JAN	FEB	MAR	APR	MAY	JUN	JUL	AUG	SEP	OCT	NOV	DEC
Mean	11.2	15.0	28.1	44.3	57.5	66.2	71.0	68.5	59.3	47.5	31.2	17.0
Mean Maximum	20.7	24.8	37.5	54.9	69.0	77.3	82.6	80.0	70.6	58.3	40.0	26.2
Mean Minimum	1.6	5.2	18.6	33.8	45.9	55.1	59.5	57.0	48.0	36.7	22.3	7.8
Hottest	59	61	83	95	106	104	108	103	104	91	77	63
Coldest	-41	-40	-32	1	18	34	41	34	26	7	-23	-39

PRECIPITATION, In.	JAN	FEB	MAR	APR	MAY	JUN	JUL	AUG	SEP	OCT	NOV	DEC
Mean	.87	.83	1.42	2.17	3.34	4.07	3.42	3.29	3.06	1.90	1.38	.94
Wettest	4.34	3.25	4.75	5.88	10.33	11.67	17.90	9.31	10.61	6.42	5.75	4.27
Driest	0	T	.02	.13	.21	.02	.11	.20	.27	0	.02	T
Mean Snowfall	9.0	7.7	9.6	3.1	0.2	0	0	0	T	0.5	5.1	7.3
Most Snowfall	46.4	26.5	40.0	21.8	3.0	0	0	0	1.7	14.0	30.4	33.2
Absolute Humidity	2.0	2.1	3.2	5.0	7.6	10.6	13.4	12.4	9.2	6.1	3.9	2.5
Relative Humidity	73	72	71	62	61	64	68	69	70	68	74	76
Dew Point	5.7	9.9	20.3	31.8	43.1	54.7	60.4	59.3	49.8	39.3	25.1	12.6
Thunder Days	x	.1	.8	2.2	5.4	7.8	7.5	6.6	4.5	2.1	.5	.1
Wind Speed MPH	10.2	10.3	10.0	12.1	11.2	9.7	8.9	8.8	9.1	10.0	10.4	9.9
Possible Sunshine	50	56	57	58	59	63	72	68	60	55	41	40
Barometer	30.12	30.11	30.04	29.98	29.94	29.91	29.95	29.97	29.99	30.01	30.05	30.08
Degree Days	1668	1330	1110	570	230	41	12	16	160	488	954	1420

**Spring: March 20 9:28 AM - Summer: June 21 4:53 AM
Fall: September 22 8:20 PM - Winter: December 21 3:22 PM**

Total Eclipse of Moon: August 17

ORDER BLANK

☐ Set of perpetual Twin City Weather Calendars (14 in all) $5.00
☐ Calendar for the year of my birth, year_____. .50¢
☐ Calendar for the following years, at 50¢ each:_____
_____

☐ Calendar for the Year 1, Gregorian. 50¢
☐ Windchill chart—1 degree & 1 mph increments 96¢
☐ Comfort temperature chart $1.00
☐ Average monthly temperature charts, Twin Cities 1819-1987 96¢
☐ Total monthly precipitation charts, Twin Cities 1836-1987 96¢
☐ Watson Weather Card on Temperature 25¢
☐ Watson Weather Card on Precipitation 25¢
☐ Weather on My Birthday Picture Chart—custom-made. Specify date of
birth, year, and hour $12.00_____
(Twin Cities weather—chart may be ordered for any day of interest such
as wedding day, etc.).

Name_____

Street _____ Apt_____

City _____ State_____Zip_____

Minnesota residents add 6% sales tax. Due to restriction, not for sale to
residents of Minneapolis.

Total amount enclosed $_____

Bruce F. Watson Consulting Meteorologist
2514 Brenner Street Roseville, Minnesota 55113

Fun Considerations

In the year 2000, only 13 years away, we will have a February 29th in a year
divisible by 100 for the first time since His Majesty, King George II, declared the
Gregorian calendar to be that of his realms. We thus get an extra day that our
forefathers in this country never had.

In the year 2001, the calendar will be the same as it would have been for the year 1
if the Gregorian calendar had been in use. Christmas day, December 25, in those
years is on a Tuesday.

Every year, except leap years, begins and ends on the same day of the week.

Calendars and Other Materials You Can Buy

Calendars for all possibilities. They are all in the Twin City Weather Calendar format with weekly averages of temperature, mean daily high for the week, mean daily
low for the week, average sunshine for the week, and average weekly precipitation.
They can be ordered in various ways.

Recreation

The Minnesota Department of Natural Resources Division of Parks and Recreation oversees 65 state park and recreation areas for nearly seven million visitors each year.

Income from park permits, campground fees, refreshments, and souvenirs exceeds $2 million.

The National Park Service administers three park areas in Minnesota. These include Voyageurs National Park with about 219,000 acres of land and water on the Canadian Border, Pipestone National Monument near the southwest corner of the state and the National Wild and Scenic Riverway on the St. Croix.

CAMPSITES

There are more than 6,000 state and federal campsites in Minnesota, not including county, municipal and private campsites. More than 3,700 campsites are provided in 64 of the state's parks. State forests provide nearly 700 campsites in the two national forests and an additional 1,700 water-access sites in the Boundary Waters Canoe Area. The Corps of Engineers maintains 300 campsites on lands near Upper Mississippi River Water Control Areas.

TRAILS

Hiking, bicycling, snowmobiling and cross-country skiing trails provide year-round outdoor recreational opportunities. More that 9,992 miles of marked and maintained snowmobile trails are offered in Minnesota, more than any other state.

Cross-country skiing trails are maintained in many state parks and some state forests. Both national forests have skiing trails, and facilities are available at several national wildlife refuges. One of the most interesting cross-country trails is at the Minnesota Zoo in Apple Valley where skiers share the winter beauty with the animals.

RECREATION TRAILS

ARROWHEAD (THREE SEGMENTS):
- **Ely to Grand Marais.** 95-mile, multiple-use trail. *Undeveloped.*
- **Ely to International Falls.** 100-mile, multiple-use trail. *Undeveloped.*
- **Duluth to Grand Portage (North Shore Trail).** 190-mile, multiple-use trail paralleling Lake Superior. 55 miles of wooded trail developed for hiking and snowmobiling.

CASEY JONES: 37-mile, multiple-use trail from Lake Shetek State Park to Slayton to Pipestone. The western 10 miles of this prairie trail, which follows an abandoned railroad right-of-way, has been developed for hiking and horse back riding.

COUNTRYVIEW BICYCLE: 22-mile bicycle trail on public roads from Lake Phalen on St. Paul's East Side to Stillwater.

DOUGLAS: 12-mile, multiple-use trail from Rochester to Pine Island. Eleven miles are developed for hiking, horseback riding, snowmobiling and bicycling.

GLACIAL LAKES: 100-mile, multiple-use trail through lake country from Lake Carlos State Park to Glacial Lakes State Park to Sibley State Park to Green Lake. *Undeveloped.*

HEARTLAND: 48-mile, multiple-use trail from Park Rapids to Walker to Cass Lake, which follows an abandoned railroad right-of-way. A 27 mile segment is developed from Park Rapids to Walker for hiking, horseback riding and snowmobiling.

LUCE LINE: 104-mile, multiple-use trail from Plymouth to Hutchinson to Gluek. Follows an abandoned railroad right-of-way. Eastern 24 miles have been developed for hiking; 6 miles are available for horseback riders, 18 miles for snowmobilers, and 24 miles for bicyclists.

MINNESOTA-WISCONSIN BOUNDARY: 220-mile, multiple-use trail from New Brighton to Taylors Falls to St. Croix State Park to Jay Cooke State Park. 60 miles of trail between St. Croix State Park and Nemadji State Forest has been developed for hiking and snowmobiling, 30 miles for horseback riding.

MINNESOTA VALLEY: 72-mile, multiple-use trail from Fort Snelling State Park to LeSueur. 24 miles have been developed for hiking, 10 miles for horseback riding, 20 miles for snowmobiling and 12 miles for cross-country skiing.

- **Carver Rapids Wayside.** Near Jordan. Hiking, horseback riding, cross-country skiing, and snowmobiling.
- **Lawrence Wayside:** U.S. Hwy. 169, between Jordan and Belle Plaine. Picnicking, fishing, primitive camping, cross-country skiing, hiking, horseback riding and snowmobiling.
- **Rice Lake Wayside:** Near Shakopee. Picnicking and boat access.
- **Rush River Wayside:** State Hwy. 19, 2 miles west of Henderson. Picnicking.
- **State Highway 41 (Chaska Access):** Fishing, horseback riding, and snowmobiling.

ROOT RIVER: This proposed trail would wind through hilly southeastern Minnesota countryside from Ramsey to LaCrescent. *Undeveloped.*

SAKATAH SINGING HILLS: 48-mile, multiple-use trail which follows an abandoned railroad right-of-way from Faribault to Mankato. 24 miles have been developed for hiking and snowmobiling and 8 miles for bicycling.

TACONITE: 165-mile, multiple-use trail in northern Minnesota from Grand Rapids to Ely. 50 miles have been developed for hiking and snowmobiling.

RECREATIONAL WATERS

Nearly a thousand water access sites are administered by the Minnesota Department of Natural Resources. An additional 500 water access sites are administered by other state and local governmental agencies, and the federal government has developed approximately 200 water access sites.

The state and federal governments have passed legislation called the Wild and Scenic Rivers Program to protect the character of three types of rivers - Wild rivers, Scenic rivers, and Recreational rivers. The legislation, designed to preserve the scenic and recreational features of a river, regulates residential and commercial development and authorizes purchase of land easements from willing sellers.

Wild river segments are:

* **Kettle** — 52 miles in Pine County
* **Mississippi** — 52 miles between St. Cloud and Anoka
* **Crow** — 41 miles of the North Fork in Meeker County
* **Minnesota** — 96 miles from Lac qui Parle to Franklin
* **Rum** — 147 miles between Ogeechie Lake and Anoka

The U.S. Congress designated the St. Croix River north of Taylors Falls as a national wild riverway in 1968 and added—as a scenic or recreational riverway—the lower St. Croix south to its junction with the Mississippi in 1972.

CANOE AND BOATING ROUTES

All rivers have accesses and a number of campsites and picnic sites depending upon their length and usage.

Rivers designated **Family** are generally mild, slow moving rivers giving a person or group with the basic knowledge of canoeing skills a pleasant experience.

Rivers designated **Experienced** require more advanced knowledge of canoeing and rapid water behavior. Will require some navigation of rapids and swift current. Quick decisions necessary.

Rivers designated **Whitewater** are for the experienced whitewater paddler only. Dangerous water conditions arise rapidly and require split second decisions and maneuvering.

BIG FORK: *From Dora Lake to the Rainy River — 165 miles.*
Experienced, some stretches of Whitewater. Few towns, mostly primitive.

CANNON: *From Highway 13 bridge west of Sakatah Lake to the Mississippi River — 80 miles.*
A family river. Good fishing. Very scenic.

CLOQUET: *From Indian Lake to the St. Louis River — 75 miles.*
Experienced upper section to Island Lake Reservior. **Family** in southern section. Very scenic, primitive.

CROW (NORTH FORK): *From Lake Koronis to the Mississippi River — 130 miles.*
A family river. Few towns. Good fishing.

CROW WING: *From Tenth Crow Wing Lake to the Mississippi River — 110 miles.*
A family river. Scenic. Good fishing.

DES MOINES: *From Talcot Lake to Iowa — 70 miles.*
A family river. Scenic from Windom to Jackson.

KETTLE: *From Minnesota 27 to St. Croix River — 55 miles.*
Experienced river to Banning State Park. Whitewater from Banning to Croix River. Very scenic, primitive.

LITTLE FORK: *From Cook to the Rainy River — 140 miles.*
Experienced to Whitewater, most of river. Primitive, almost no towns.

MINNESOTA: *From Big Stone to the Mississippi River — 330 miles.*
Family river. Wide, good current in places. Large barges near Twin Cities.

MISSISSIPPI: *From Lake Itasca to Anoka — 480 miles.*
Family river. From Wilderness at Headwaters to wide, large, busy at Anoka. Good fishing in some locations.

RED LAKE: *From East Grand Forks to Lower Red Lake — 196 miles.*
Family river. Few towns. Good fishing.

ROOT: *From Highway 75 to the Mississippi River — 95 miles.*
A family river. Scenic bluffs, good fishing.

RUM: *From Mille Lacs Lake to the Mississippi River — 140 miles.*
Experienced from Lake Onamia to Princeton. Excellent fishing. Few towns. Family river from Princeton to Anoka.

ST. CROIX: *From Danbury to the Mississippi River — 140 miles.*
Family river. Very busy on weekends. Good fishing.

ST. LOUIS: *From U.S. 53 to Cloquet — 90 miles.*
Family to experienced. Mostly primitive.

SNAKE: *From County Road 26 to St. Croix River — 85 miles.*
Experienced to Whitewater. Mostly primitive. Good fishing.

STRAIGHT: *From U.S. 14 to Faribault — 30 miles.*
Family river. Best from mid-March to mid-June.

ZUMBRO: *From Rochester to the Mississippi River — 125 miles.*
Family river. Scenic, excellent fishing.

MOTOR VEHICLE PERMITS	
Annual	$15
Minnesota Senior	$7.50
(owner 65 or older, MN license plates)	
Minnesota Handicapped	$7.50
(MN handicapped license plates)	
Daily	$3
Minnesota Senior	$1.50
(owner 65 or older, MN license plates)	
Minnesota Handicapped	$1.50
(MN handicapped plates or certificate)	

CAMPING FEES	
Semi-modern site (showers)	$6
Rustic site (no showers, pit toilets)	$5
Hike-in or canoe-in site (hand pump, pit toilet)	
Family	$4
Group (6 or less)	$4
Group (over 6)	$4
plus 50¢/person over 6	
Minnesota residents 65 and older or handi-	
capped — half-price camping Sunday through	
Thursday.	
Electricity (where available)	$1.50/night

MINNESOTA STATE PARK CAMPGROUNDS

Afton, 2 mi. S. of Afton, 24 backpacking sites, picnic grounds, fishing, swimming, 14 mi. hiking, 14 mi. ski touring. Visitor center.

Banning, 2 mi. N. of Sandstone, 31 rustic sites, picnic ground, fishing, 13 mi. hiking, 10 mi. ski touring and 4 mi. snowmobile trails. Primitive group camp, canoeing.

Bear Head Lake, 16 mi. E. of Tower, 24 semi-modern campsites, 50 rustic campsites, picnic ground, swimming, fishing, boats. 17 mi. hiking, 14 mi. ski touring and 6 mi. snowmobile trails, 5 backpacking sites. Primitive group camp. Naturalist.

Big Stone Lake, 3 areas - 7½ and 18 mi. N.W. of Ortonville, 42 rustic campsites, picnic ground, swimming, fishing, boat rental and access. 2 mi. hiking and 3 mi. snowmobile trail, primitive group camp, dump station.

Blue Mounds, 7 mi. N. of Luverne, 73 semi-modern campsites, and 58 rustic campsites, picnic ground, swimming, fishing canoe rental. 10 mi. hiking. 7 mi. snowmobile and 3 mi. ski touring trails, primitive group camp, dump station. Naturalist.

Buffalo River, 13 mi. E. of Moorhead. 44 semi-modern campsites, picnic ground, swimming, fishing, 12 mi. hiking and 12 mi. ski touring trails. Primitive group camp, dump station.

Camden, 7 mi. S.W. of Marshall, 37 semi-modern campsites, picnic ground, swimming, fishing, 9 mi. hiking. 10 mi. snowmobile and 4 mi. horse trails. Primitive group camp. Naturalist. Visitor center.

Carley, 4 mi. S. of Plainview. 20 rustic campsites, picnic ground, fishing, 3 mi. hiking and 3 mi. ski touring trails, primitive group camp.

Cascade River, 10 mi. S.W. of Grand Marais. 38 semi-modern campsites, picnic ground, 15 mi. hiking, 2 mi. snowmobile and 30 mi. ski touring trails, fishing.

Charles A. Lindbergh, 2 mi. S. of Little Falls, 38 semi-modern campsites, picnic ground, 6 mi. foot trail, primitive group camp, dump station. Museum.

Crow Wing, 9 mi. S.W. of Brainerd. 65 semi-modern campsites, picnic ground, fishing, 14 mi. hiking, 9 mi. snowmobile and 6½ mi. ski touring trails, dump station, Naturalist, boat access.

Father Hennepin, 1 mi. N.W. of Isle, 103 semi-modern campsites, picnic ground, swimming, fishing, 4 mi. hiking, 2 mi. snowmobile and 7 mi. ski touring trails, boat access, dump station. Naturalist. Historic site.

Flandrau, E. side of New Ulm. 57 semi-modern and 33 rustic campsites, picnic ground, fishing, group camp, 7 mi. hiking, 1 mi. snowmobile, 7½ mi. ski touring and 3 mi. horse trails, dump station, primitive group camp. Naturalist.

Forestville, 7 mi. S.E. of Wykoff. 60 semi-modern campsites, picnic ground, fishing, 15 mi. hiking, 7 mi. snowmobile, 8 mi. ski touring and 15 mi. horse trails, primitive group camp, dump station. Naturalist.

Fort Ridgely, 7 mi. S. of Fairfax. 35 rustic modern campsites, picnic ground, 12 mi. hiking, 3 mi. ski touring, 4 mi. snowmobile and 4 mi. horse trails, primitive group camp, golf course and outdoor summer theater.

Franz Jevne, 3 mi. N.E. of Birchdale, 10 rustic campsites, picnic ground, fishing, 1 mi. hiking trail.

Frontenac, 5 mi. N.W. of Lake City. 58 semi-modern campsites, picnic ground, fishing, 6 mi. hiking, 10 mi. snowmobile and 2 mi. ski touring trails, dump station.

George H. Crosby Manitou, 8 mi. N.E. of Finland. 22 backpacking campsites, picnic ground, and 6 mi. ski touring trails, rental canoes. 10 mi. snowmobile trails.

Glacial Lakes, 5 mi. S. of Starbuck. 21 semi-modern and 18 rustic campsites, picnic ground, swimming, fishing, boat rental and access, 11 mi. hiking and 9 mi. snowmobile trails, primitive group camp, backpacking. 9 mi. horse trails.

Gooseberry Falls, 14 mi. N.E. of Two Harbors, 70 semi-modern campsites, primitive group camp, picnic ground. 18 mi. hiking, 2 mi. snowmobile and 15 mi. ski touring trails, year-round showers and toilets. Naturalist. Interpretive center. Reservations accepted. Fishing. Dump station.

Hayes Lake, 15 mi. S.E. of Roseau, 35 semi-modern campsites, picnic ground, fishing, swimming. 12 mi. hiking and 6 mi. snowmobile trails. 3 mi. horse trails. 6 mi. ski trail, boat access. Naturalist.

Helmer Myre, 3 mi. E. of Albert Lea. 100 semi-modern campsites, picnic ground, fishing, 18 mi. hiking, 17 mi. snowmobile and 8 mi. ski touring trails, primitive group camp, boat access, dump station. Naturalist.

Interstate, 1 mi. S. of Taylors Falls. 47 semi-modern campsites, picnic ground, fishing, canoe rental and boat access. 3 mi. hiking trail, primitive group camp, dump station. Naturalist. Visitor center.

Itasca, 21 mi. N. of Park Rapids. 220 semi-modern and 30 rustic campsites, picnic ground, fishing, swimming, boats and access, tourist cabins, 33 mi. hiking, 31 mi. snowmobile and 27 mi. ski touring trails, primitive group camp. Naturalist.

Jay Cooke, 2 mi. W. of Duluth. 80 semi-modern campsites, picnic ground, fishing, 50 mi. hiking, 12 mi. snowmobile, 36 mi. ski touring trails, 4 backpacking sites, dump station, group camp. Naturalist. Interpretive center. 10 mi. horse trail. Reservations accepted.

Judge C. R. Magney, 14 mi. N.E. of Grand Marais. 39 rustic campsites, picnic ground, fishing, 3 mi. hiking trail.

Kilen Woods, 9 mi. N.W. of Jackson. 20 semi-modern campsites. Picnic ground, fishing, 5 mi. hiking, 4 mi. snowmobile and 2 mi. ski touring trails, primitive group camp. Naturalist.

Lac Qui Parle, 12 mi. N.W. of Montevideo. 56 semi-modern campsites, picnic ground, fishing, swimming, boat access. 7 mi. hiking, 7 mi. ski touring and 7 mi. horse trails, primitive group camp. Historical museum.

Lake Bemidji, 5 mi. N.E. of Bemidji. 103 semi-modern campsites, picnic ground, swimming, fishing, boats and access, dump station, 7 mi. hiking and 3 mi. ski touring trails, primitive group camp. Naturalist.

Lake Bronson, 2 mi. E. of Lake Bronson. 190 semi-modern campsites, picnic ground, swimming, fishing, boats and access, dump station, 14 mi. hiking, 10 mi. snowmobile and 3 mi. ski touring trails. Naturalist.

Lake Carlos, 8 mi. N. of Alexandria. 138 semi-modern campsites, picnic ground, swimming, fishing, boats and access, modern group camp, dump station. 12 mi. hiking, 9 mi. snowmobile. 5 mi. ski touring and 6 mi. horse trails, horse group camp. Naturalist. Reservations accepted.

Lake Louise, 1 mi. N. of LeRoy. 22 semi-modern campsites, picnic ground, swimming, fishing, 11 mi. hiking, 7 mi. snowmobile, 4 mi. ski touring and 7 mi. horse trails, primitive group camp. Museum.

Lake Maria, 8 mi. W. of Monticello. 11 backpacking campsites, picnic ground, canoe rental and boat access, 13 mi. hiking, 13 mi. ski touring and 6 mi. horse trails. Primitive group camp. Naturalist. Visitor center. Fishing.

Lake Shetek, 14 mi. N.W. of Slayton. 78 semi-modern and 20 rustic campsites, picnic ground, swimming, fishing boats and access, modern group camp, dump station, 5 mi. hiking, 4 mi. snowmobile trails and 10 backpacking sites, primitive group camp. Naturalist. 2 mi. ski trail.

Little Elbow Lake, 16 mi. E. of Waubun. 22 rustic campsites, picnic ground, fishing, boat access, 10 mi. hiking and 10 mi. snowmobile trails.

McCarthy Beach, 20 mi. N.W. of Hibbing. 45 semi-modern and 14 rustic campsites, picnic ground, swimming, fishing, boats and access, dump station, 17 mi. hiking, 12 mi. snowmobile and 8 mi. ski touring trails. Naturalist.

Maplewood, 7 mi. S.E. of Pelican Rapids. 61 semi-modern campsites, picnic ground, swimming, fishing, boat access, 25 mi. hiking, 15 mi. snowmobile, 17 mi. ski touring and 20 mi. horse trails, primitive group camp.

Mille Lacs Kathio, 5 mi. N.W. of Onamia. 71 semi-modern campsites, picnic ground, swimming, fishing, boats and access, 35 mi. hiking, 20 mi. snowmobile and 27 mi. horse trails, primitive group camp. Naturalist. 18 mi. ski touring.

Minneopa, 6 mi. W. of Mankato. 65 semi-modern campsites, picnic ground, fishing, historic site. 4 mi. hiking and 4 mi. ski touring trails, primitive group camp. Naturalist.

Monson Lake, 4 mi. S.W. of Sunburg. 20 rustic campsites, picnic ground, fishing, boat access, 1 mi. hiking trail.

Moose Lake, 18 rustic campsites, picnic grounds, fishing, swimming, boat rental, 3 mi. ski touring, 10 mi. snowmobile trails.

Nerstrand Woods, 16 mi. S.E. of Northfield. 61 semi-modern and 17 rustic campsites, picnic ground. 14 mi. hiking, 6 mi. snowmobile and 8 mi. ski touring trails, primitive group camp, dump station.

O. L. Kipp, 15 mi. N.W. of La Crescent. 31 rustic campsites, picnic ground, 6 mi. hiking and 9 mi. ski touring trails, primitive group camp.

Old Mill, 17 mi. N.E. of Warren. 24 semi-modern campsites, picnic ground, swimming, 7 mi. hiking, 3 mi. snowmobile and 3 mi. ski touring trails, primitive group camp. Historic site.

Rice Lake, 7 mi. E. of Owatonna. 42 rustic campsites, picnic ground. 3 mi. hiking, 2 mi. snowmobile and 4 mi. ski touring trails, primitive group camp. Dump station.

St. Croix, 16 mi. E. of Hinckley. 217 semi-modern campsites, 2 backpacking campsites, 8 canoe campsites, picnic ground, swimming, fishing, modern group camps, canoe rental and boat access, 127 mi. hiking, 21 mi. ski touring, 75 mi. snowmobile and 75 mi. horse trails, dump station, primitive group camp. Naturalist. Interpretive center. Reservations accepted. Horse camp.

St. Croix Wild River, 14 mi. E. of North Branch. 73 semi-modern, 20 canoe and 20 backpacking campsites, picnic ground, fishing and boat access. 45 mi. hiking, 1 mi. snowmobile, 45 mi. ski touring and 30 mi. horse trails, dump station, primitive group camp, year-round showers and toilets. Naturalist. Interpretive center. Reservations accepted. Horse camp.

Sakatah Lake, 2 mi. E. of Waterville. 60 semi-modern campsites, picnic ground, swimming, fishing, boat access. 5 mi. hiking, 2 mi. snowmobile and 2 mi. ski touring trails, dump station, primitive group camp. Naturalist. Access to Sakatah Singing Hills State Trail. Visitor Center.

Savanna Portage, 16 mi. N.E. of McGregor. 62 semi-modern and 5 backpacking campsites, picnic ground, swimming, fishing, rental boats and boat access, 22 mi. hiking and 60 mi. snowmobile trails, 17 mi. ski touring trails, dump station, primitive group camp.

Scenic, 7 mi. E. of Big Ford, 110 semi-modern campsites, picnic ground, swimming, 20 rustic sites, 6 backpacking sites, 6 canoe sites, fishing, rental boats and boat access. 14 mi. hiking, 10 mi. snowmobile and 12 mi. ski touring trails, primitive group camp. Dump station. Naturalist. Visitor Center.

Schoolcraft, 8 mi. S. of Deer River. 38 rustic campsites, picnic ground, fishing, 2 mi. hiking trail, boat access, 12 canoe sites.

Sibley, 7 mi. W. of New London. 138 semi-modern campsites, picnic ground, swimming, fishing, boats and access, modern group camp, dump station. 18 mi. hiking, 6 mi. snowmobile, 10 mi. ski touring and 5 mi. horse trails, primitive group camp. Naturalist. Interpretive center. Reservations accepted.

Split Rock Creek, 1 mi. S. of Ihlen. 28 rustic campsites, picnic ground, swimming, fishing, boat access. 2 mi. hiking and 2 mi. ski touring trails, primitive group camp. Trail center.

Split Rock Lighthouse, 19 mi. N.E. of Two Harbors. Picnicking, fishing. 6 mi. hiking, 6 mi. ski, 20 cart-in campsites, year-round toilets, visitor center, historic site.

Temperance River, 23 mi. S.W. of Grand Marais. 51 semi-modern campsites, fishing, picnic ground, 6 mi. hiking and 8 mi. ski touring trails.

Tettegouche, 4 mi. N. of Silver Bay on North Shore of Lake Superior. Class #1 rest area, public recreation information station, picnic area, fishing opportunities, 35 semi-modern campsites, 13 miles ski touring, 18 miles hiking, 4 miles snowmobile connects to North Shore Trail.

Whitewater, 9 mi. N. of St. Charles. 106 semi-modern campsites, picnic ground, swimming, fishing, modern year round group camp. 10 mi. hiking and 1 mi. ski touring trails, primitive group camp. Naturalist. Interpretive center. Reservations accepted.

William O'Brien, 16 mi. N. of Stillwater. 125 semi-modern campsites, 35 canoe campsites, picnic ground, fishing, swimming, boats. 10 mi. hiking and 9 mi. ski touring trails, primitive group camp, naturalist. Trail center. Reservations accepted.

Zippel Bay, 9 mi. N.E. of Williams. 60 rustic campsites, picnic ground, fishing, boat access, 6 mi. hiking, 15 mi. snowmobile and 2 mi. ski touring trails, primitive group camp, swimming.

MINNESOTA STATE FOREST CAMPGROUNDS

State Forest campgrounds are of the primitive type designed to furnish only the basic needs of individuals who camp for the enjoyment of the outdoors. Each campsite consists of a cleared area, fireplace and table. In addition, pit toilets, garbage cans and drinking water from a hand pump may be provided. A $5.00 fee per night per campsite is charged. The honor system is used. The maximum recreational vehicle length which can be accommodated is 20 feet. For more information concerning other state forest campgrounds and recreation facilities contact the Department of Natural Resources, Forestry, Box 44, DNR Building, 500 Lafayette, St. Paul, Minnesota 55146.

BIRCH LAKE STATE FOREST

Birch Lake Campgrounds, from Melrose take County Road 13 north 5½ miles to County Road 17; turn right (east) 1½ miles; turn left (north) 2 miles; turn right (east) on Forest Road. (612) 689-2832. 27 campsites, 8 picnic sites, swimming, concrete boat ramp, fishing, 2 mile hiking trail, group camping by reser. Area Forester, 915 South Highway 65, Cambridge, Minnesota 55008.

CHENGWATANA STATE FOREST

Snake River Campground, from Pine City take County Road 8 and 118 East 9 miles and North ½ mile. (218) 485-4474. 26 campsites, on canoe route, fishing, hiking and horse trails. Forester, Route 2, 701 South Kenwood, Moose Lake, Minnesota 55767.

CROW WING STATE FOREST

Greer Lake Campground, from Crosby take State Highway 6 North 12 miles to County Road 36; turn left (West) 3 miles to County Road 14; turn left (South) 1½ miles; turn right (West) and follow signs 2 miles. (218) 828-2565. 34 campsites, 2 picnic sites, swimming, boat ramp, fishing, 1 mile hiking trail. Area Forester, 203 West Washington Street; Brainerd, Minnesota 56401.

DORER MEMORIAL HARDWOOD STATE FOREST

Kruger Recreation Area, from Wabasha take County Road 60 West 5 miles then County Road 81 South ½ mile (on Zumbro River). (612) 345-3216. 18 campsites, 13 picnic sites, fishing, on canoe route, 5 mile hiking and 4 mile horse trails. Area Forester, Box 278, Lewiston, Minnesota 55952.

FINLAND STATE FOREST

Eckbeck Campground, from Finland take State Highway 1 South 3 miles (on Baptism River). (218) 723-4669. 35 campsites, fishing. Forester, 6163 Rice Lake Road, Duluth, Minnesota 55803.

Finland Campground, from Finland take County Road 6 East ¼ mile (on Baptism River). (218) 723-4669. 19 campsites, 10 picnic sites, fishing. Forester, 6163 Rice Lake Road, Duluth, Minnesota 55803.

GENERAL C.C. ANDREWS STATE FOREST

Willow River Campground, in Village of Willow River take North Street East to service road of Interstate Highway 35 turn left (North) ½ mile (on Willow River Flowage). (218) 485-4474. 32 campsites, 1 picnic site, boat ramp, fishing, Forester, group camping by reser. Route 2, 701 South Kenwood, Moose Lake, Minnesota 55767.

GEORGE WASHINGTON STATE FOREST

Bear Lake Campground, from Nashwauk take State Highway 65 North 23 miles to County Road 52 (Venning Road); turn left (West) 2 miles; turn left (South) 2½ miles. (218) 262-6760. 28 campsites, swimming, boat ramp, fishing, 2 hiking trails. Forester, 1208 East Howard, Hibbing, Minnesota 55746.

Beatrice Lake Campground, from Hibbing take Highway 169 North 5 miles County Road 5 North 17 miles West 3½ miles. (218) 262-6760. 25 campsites, boat access, fishing. Park Manager, Star Route 2, Hibbing, Minnesota 55746.

Larson Lake Campground, from Effie take State Highway 1 East 11 miles to Bass Lake Road; turn right (South) about 1½ miles to junction (1½ miles South of Bass Lake); turn right (West) 1 mile. (218) 246-8343. 6 campsites, 2 picnic sites, concrete boat ramp, fishing. Forester, Deer River, Minnesota 56636.

Lost Lake Campground, from Bigfork take Scenic Highway (County Road 7) Southeast 10 miles to County Road 340; turn left (East) about 7 miles to ranger station; turn left (North) across from ranger station and follow signs 3½ miles. (218) 246-8343. 20 campsites, swimming, concrete boat ramp, fishing. Forester, Box 157, Deer River, Minnesota 56636.

Owen Lake Campground, from Bigfork take Scenic Highway (County Road 7) Southeast 10 miles to County Road 340; turn left (East) 7 miles to ranger station; turn left (North) across from ranger station and follow signs 3½ miles. (218) 246-8343. 26 campsites, 2 hiking trails, swimming, boat ramp, fishing. Forester, Box 157, Deer River, Minnesota 56636.

Thistledew Lake Campground, from Togo take Hwy. 1 West 4½ miles to ranger station turn left (South) 2 miles. (218) 262-6760. 20 campsites, 9 picnic sites, swimming, concrete boat ramp, fishing. Forester, 1208 East Howard, Hibbing, Minnesota 55746.

HUNTERSVILLE STATE FOREST

Shell City Landing Campground, from Menahga take County Road 17 East 4 miles to County Road 23; turn left (North) 1 mile to County Road 18 turn right (East) 6 miles to County Road 25; turn left (North) 2 miles (on Crow Wing River on Crow Wing Saddle Trail). (218) 947-3232. 18 campsites, boat access by portage, fishing, canoe route. Forester, Box 34, Backus, Minnesota 56435.

Huntersville Forest Landing Campground, from Menahga take County Road 148 East 4 miles; continue East 3 miles on County Road 150; continue East 1½ miles on Forest Road (on Crow Wing River on Crow Wing Saddle Trail). (218) 947-3232. 13 campsites, boat access by portage, fishing, canoe trail. Forester, Box 34, Backus, Minnesota 56435.

KABETOGAMA STATE FOREST

Ash River Campground, from Orr take U.S. Highway 53N 26 miles to Ash River Road (County Road 126); turn right (East) 9 miles. (218) 757-3274. 9 campsites, 2 picnic sites, concrete boat ramp, fishing, Forester, Orr, Minnesota 55771.

Wakemup Bay Campground, from Cook take County Road 24 North 2½ miles to County Road 78; turn right (East) 3 miles, left (North) 1 mile (on Lake Vermillion). (218) 757-3274. 21 campsites, 2 picnic sites, fishing, swimming, change houses, boat ramp. Forester, Orr, Minnesota 55771.

Woodenfrog Campground, from Orr take U.S. Highway 53 North 30 miles to County Road 122 (Gamma Road); turn right (North) and follow signs about 6 miles (on Kabetogama Lake. (218) 757-3274. 59 campsites, 5 picnic sites, swimming, concrete boat ramp. Forester, Orr, Minnesota 55771.

LAND O'LAKES STATE FOREST

Clint Converse Memorial Campground, from Outing take State Highway 6 North 2 miles to County Road 48; turn left (West) 2 miles. (218) 947-3232. 30 campsites, 7 picnic sites, swimming, fishing, boat ramp, 20 miles hiking trails. Forester, Box 34, Backus, Minnesota 56435.

NEMADJI STATE FOREST

Gavert Campground, from Nickerson take State Highway 23 Northeast ½ mile; turn right (South) across railroad tracks ½ mile; turn left (East) 1½ mile to Nett Lake Forest Road; turn right (South) 1½ miles; turn left (East) about ½ mile (on Pickeral Lake). (218) 485-4474. 9 campsites, 1 picnic site, fishing, boat ramp. Forester, Route 2, 701 South Kenwood, Moose Lake, Minnesota 55767.

PAUL BUNYAN STATE FOREST

Mantrap Lake Campground, from Park Rapids take County Road 4 North 12 miles to Emmaville (County Road 24); turn right (East) 1½ miles to County Road 104 turn left (North) and follow signs ¾ miles. (218) 732-3309. 38 campsites, 5 picnic sites, swimming, boat ramp. Forester, 607 West 1st Street, Highway 34, Park Rapids, Minnesota 56470.

PILLSBURY STATE FOREST

Rock Lake Campground, from Pillager take State Highway 210 West ½ mile to County Road 1; turn right (North) 6 miles turn left (West) and follow road along lake. (218) 828-2565. 18 campsites, 4 picnic sites, swimming, boat ramp, fishing. Forester, 203 West Washington Street, Brainerd, Minnesota 56401.

ST. CROIX STATE FOREST

Boulder Campground, from Sandstone take County Road 30 East 17 miles to County Road 24; (Duxbury); turn right (South) 2 miles to County Road 25; turn left (East) 4 miles to County Road 173; turn right (South) ¾ mile to Tamarack Forest Road; turn left (East) about 5 miles; (on Rock Lake on hiking and riding trail). (218) 485-4474. 19 campsites, 6 picnic sites, boat ramp, 21 miles of hiking and riding trails. Forester, Route 2, 701 South Kenwood, Moose Lake, Minnesota 55767.

SAND DUNES STATE FOREST

Ann Lake Campground, from Elk River take State Highway 169 North 9 miles to County Road 4 (Zimmerman); turn left (West) 6 miles; turn left (South) and follow signs 1½ miles. (612) 689-2832. 36 campsites, 7 picnic sites, swimming, fishing, 18 miles hiking and horse trails. Group camping by reservation. Forester, 915 South Highway 65, Cambridge, Minnesota 55008.

SAVANNA STATE FOREST

Hay Lake Campground, from Jacobson take State Highway 65 South 2½ miles turn left (East) 3 miles; turn right (South) 1 mile. (218) 697-2476. 20 campsites, 10 picnic sites, swimming, boat ramp, fishing, 1 mile hiking trail. Forester, P.O. Box 9, Hill City, Minnesota 55748.

TWO INLETS STATE FOREST

Hungry Man Lake Campground, from Park Rapids take State Highway 71 North 10 miles to County Road 41; turn left (West) 1½ mile; turn right (North) 1 mile. (218) 732-3309. 14 campsites, 4 picnic sites, swimming, concrete boat ramp, fishing. Forester, 607 West 1st Street, Park Rapids, Minnesota 56470.

FORESTRY ADMINISTERED FACILITIES

Moose Lake Campground, from Deer River take State Highway 6 North 4 miles to County Road 19; turn right (East) 5½ miles turn left (North) 1 mile. (218) 246-8343. 12 campsites, 1 picnic site, swimming, concrete boat ramp. Forester, Box 157, Deer River, MN 56636.

Waskish Campground, Hwy. 72 at Waskish just South of bridge (on Tamarack River). (218) 835-6684. 33 campsites, 4 picnic sites, boat ramp, fishing. Forester, Blackduck, Minnesota 56630.

One of the most successful advertising campaigns in history—the Burma-Shave signs—was born in Minnesota. Burma-Vita, producer of a shaving cream called Burma-Shave, was headquartered in Minneapolis. The first signs were erected by Lloyd and Allen Odell, sons of the founder, in the autumn of 1925. One set of signs went up on Highway 65 between Minneapolis and Albert Lea, and the other was placed on the road from the Twin Cities to Red Wing.

The signs were set some distance apart, so people driving by had to keep their heads turned toward the side of the road if they wanted to read the whole message.

Among the best of the signs were:

Don't stick/Your elbow/Out so far/It might go home/in another car.

The signs have been gone since 1963, but in their time those red and white placards were not only wildly successful sales producers, they were beloved by the public.

MINNESOTA TOURISM REGIONS

(1) ARROWHEAD, Mr. Charles Bloczynski, Minnesota Arrowhead Assoc.; 734 E. Superior St., Lower Level; Duluth, MN 55802. Phone: (218) 722-0874.

(2) HEARTLAND, INC., Mr. Joe Egge, Exec. Dir., Minnesota Heartland, Inc.; P.O. Box 443, 411 Laurel St.; Brainerd, MN 56401. Phone: (218) 829-1615.

(3) SOUTHERN MINNESOTA TOURISM ASSOC., Mr. Bob Kennebeck, Executive Director, Southern Minnesota Tourist Association; P.O. Box 999, Mankato, MN 56001. Phone: (507) 345-4517.

Courtesy of The Boundary Waters Journal

PHOTO BY ROBERT BEYMER

NATIONAL FOREST CAMPGROUNDS

Overnight camping fees will be charged at designated campgrounds in the Chippewa and Superior National Forests. The amount charged at designated campgrounds ranges from $2 to $4 per night depending on the facilities available at the campground. Each area is signed at the entrance with the amount charged per night indicated. The Golden Age Passport is issued free to persons 62 years of age or older upon proof of age, which allows for a 50 percent reduction in the camping fee. Golden Age Passports are available at the Forest Supervisors' Offices in Duluth and Cass Lake and at the Forest Service District Rangers' Offices in Aurora, Grand Marais, Isabella, Ely, Cook, Tofte, Virginia, Blackduck, Cass Lake, Deer River, Marcell and Walker. Golden Age Passports cannot be obtained by mail. Dogs are allowed in National Forests but must be on a leash at all times, and reservations are not accepted at any of the National Forest campgrounds.

The information in this guide was collected in February, 1980. You may want to call in advance to confirm dates and facilities.

NUMERICAL CODES

1—Tent Camping
2—Camper sites
3—Trailer sites
4—Mobile home sites
5—Cabins/Cottages
6—Hot showers
7—Electrical connections
8—Water connections
9—Sewage hookup
10—Sanitary disposal
11—Laundry facilities
12—Drinking water
13—Picnic tables
14—Fireplaces
15—Swimming beach
16—Pool
17—Playground
18—Recreation Hall
19—Winter activities
20—Restaurant
21—Groceries
22—Ice
23—Firewood
24—Fishing & location
25—Bait
26—Fishing tackle
27—Boats for rent
28—Outboard motors for rent
29—Gas and oil
30—Canoes
31—Pontoon boats
32—Boat launching ramp
33—Inside flush toilets
34—Outdoor latrine
35—TV
36—Fish freezing
37—Fishing licenses

CHIPPEWA NATIONAL FOREST, CASS LAKE, MN 56633

Caribou Lake, from Marcell, 4 mi. S.E. on Hwy. 38, 3 campsites. On-site 1, 12, 13, 14, 24, 32, 34; Nearby 20, 21. No trailers. May 15-Sept. 10. No fee.

Clubhouse Lake, from Marcell, ½ mi. N. on Hwy. 38, 5 mi. E. on Co. Hwy. 45, 1½ mi. N. on Forest Rd. 2181, 1½ mi. E. on Forest Rd. 3758. 51 campsites. On-site 1, 2, 3, 12, 13, 14, 15, 23, 24, 32, 34. Nearby: 27. Berry picking. May 15-Sept. 10. Camp fee.

Deer Lake, from Deer River, 1 mi. N.W. on Hwy. 2, 19 mi. N.W. on Hwy. 46, 3 mi. S.W. on Co. Hwy. 33. 48 campsites. On-site 1, 2, 3, 12, 13, 14, 15, 24, 32, 34. Nearby: 21, 22, 27, 29. Berry picking. May 15-Sept. 15. Camp fee.

East Seeleye Bay, from Deer River, 1 mi. N.W. on Hwy. 2, 19 mi. N.W. on Hwy. 46, 2½ mi. S.W. on Co. Hwy. 33. 13 campsites. On-site: 1, 2, 3, 12, 13, 14, 15, 24, 32, 34. Nearby: 21, 22, 27, 29 and nature trails. Berry picking. May 15-Nov. 15. Camp fee.

Knutson Dam, from Cass Lake, 6 mi. E. on Hwy. 2, 5½ mi. N. on Co. Hwy. 10, 1 mi. W. on Forest Rd. 2176. 14 campsites. On-site: 1, 2, 3, 12, 13, 14, 23, 24, 32, 34. Nearby: 20, 21, 22, 27, 29. Berry picking. May 1-Oct. 15. Camp fee.

Mabel Lake, from Remer, 7½ mi. W. on Hwy. 200, ½ mi. N. on Forest Rd. 2104. 21 campsites, On-site: 1, 2, 3, 12, 13, 14, 15, 24, 32, 34. Camp fee.

Middle Pigeon, from Squaw Lake, 4 mi. S. on Hwy. 46, 3 mi. W. on Forest Rd. 2196. 3 campsites. On-site: 1, 2, 3, 12, 13, 14, 24, 32, 34. Nearby: 27. Berry picking. May 15-Sept. 15. No fee.

Mosomo Point, from Deer River, 1 mi. N.W. on Hwy. 2, 18 mi. N.W. on Hwy. 46, ½ mi. S.W. on Forest Rd. 2190. 24 campsites. On-site: 1, 2, 3, 12, 13, 14, 24, 32, 34. Nearby: 15, 21, 27, 29 and nature trails. Berry picking. May 15-Sept. 15. Camp fee.

Noma Lake, from Wirt. 2 mi. N.W. on Co. Hwy. 31. 14 campsites. On-site: 1, 2, 3, 12, 13, 14, 23, 34. Nearby: 21, 22, 24, 27, 32. Berry picking. May 15-Sept. 15. Camp fee.

North Star, from Marcell, 3½ mi. S.E. on Hwy. 38. 42 campsites. On-site: 1, 2, 3, 10, 12, 13, 14, 15, 23, 24, 33. Nearby: 11, 20, 21, 22, 27, 29, 32. Berry picking. May 1-Sept. 10. Camp fee.

Norway Beach, from Cass Lake, 4½ mi. E. on Hwy. 2, ½ mi. N. on Forest Rd. 2171, ½ mi. N. on Forest Rd. 2007. 74 campsites. On-site: 1, 2, 3, 6, 10, 12, 13, 14, 23, 32, 33, 34 and native trails. Nearby: 11, 15, 20, 21, 22, 27, 29. Berry picking. May 15-Sept. 15. Camp fee.

Norway Beach-Wanaki, from Cass Lake, 4½ mi. E. on Hwy. 2, 2 mi. N.E. on Forest Rd. 2171. 43 campsites. On-site: 1, 2, 3, 6, 12, 13, 14, 15, 23, 33, 34. Nearby: 10, 20, 21, 22, 24, 27, 29, 32 and nature trails. May 15-Sept. 15. Camp fee.

Ojibway, from Cass Lake, 3½ mi. E. on Hwy. 2, ½ mi. S. on Forest Rd. 2137. 40 campsites. On-site: 1, 2, 3, 12, 13, 14, 15, 23, 24, 32, 33 and nature trails. Nearby: 6, 10, 11, 20, 21, 22, 27, 29. May 15-Sept. 15. Camp fee.

O-Ne-Gum-E, from Deer River, 1 mi. N.W. on Hwy. 2, 18 mi. N.W. on Hwy. 46, 1/10th mi. E. on Forest Rd. 2507. 50 campsites. On-site: 1, 2, 3, 12, 13, 14, 24, 34. Nearby: 10, 15, 21, 27, 29, 32 and nature trails. Berry picking. May 15-Nov. 15. Camp fee.

Plug Hat Point, from Deer River 1 mi. N.W. on Hwy. 2, 11½ mi. N.W. on Hwy. 46, 1½ mi. W. on Co. Hwy. 9, ½ mi. N.W. on Forest Rd. 2160. 13 campsites. On-site: 1, 2, 3, 12, 13, 14, 15, 24, 32, 34. Nearby: 20, 21, 22, 27, 29. Berry picking. May 15-Sept. 15. Camp fee.

Richard's Townsite, from Bena, 2¾ mi. W. on Hwy. 2, ½ mi. N.W. on Forest Rd. 2167, 2 mi. N.E. on Forest Rd. 2074. 6 campsites. On-site: 1, 2, 3, 12, 13, 14, 23, 24, 32, 34. Nearby: 20, 21, 22, 29. Berry picking. May 15-Sept. 15. No fee.

Shingobee Group Camp, from Walker, 5 mi. S.W. on Hwy. 34, ½ mi. N.E. on Forest Rd. 2110. 1 campsite limited to 75 campers, maximum. On-site: 12, 13, 34. Nearby: 11, 15, 20, 21, 22, 24, 27, 29, 32 and nature trails. Jan. 1-Dec. 31. No fee.

Six Mile Lake, from Bena, 1½ mi. E. on Hwy. 2, 4 mi. S.E. on Forest Rd. 2127. 11 campsites. On-site: 1, 2, 3, 12, 13, 14, 24, 34. Nearby: 21, 22, 27, 29. Berry picking. May 15-Sept. 15. Camp fee.

South Pike Bay, from Cass Lake, 3 mi. E. on Hwy. 371, 1 mi. E. on Co. Hwy. 146, 1½ mi. E. on Forest Rd. 2137 and ½ mi. N. on Forest Rd. 2137A. 21 campsites. On-site: 1, 2, 3, 12, 13, 14, 15, 23, 24, 32, 34. Nearby: 11, 20, 21, 22, 27, 29 and nature trails. Berry picking. May 15-Sept. 15. Camp fee.

Star Island, Boat from Cass Lake or Norway Beach. 3 campsites. On-site: 1, 12, 13, 14, 23, 34. Nearby: 6, 11, 15, 20, 21, 22, 24, 27, 29, 32 and nature trails. Berry picking. May 15-Sept. 15. No fee.

Stony Point, from Walker, 4 mi. S.E. on Hwy. 371, 2 mi. E. on Hwy. 200, 4½ mi. N. on Co. Hwy. 13, 4 mi. N.E. on Forest Rd. 3797. 45 campsites. On-site: 1, 2, 3, 10, 12, 13, 14, 15, 24, 32, 33, 34 and nature trails. Nearby: 20, 21, 22, 27, 29. May 13-Oct. 1. Camp fee.

Tamarack Point, from Bena, 1½ mi. E. on Hwy. 2, 6 mi. N.E. on Co. Hwy. 9, 3½ mi. N.W. on Forest Rd. 2163. 35 campsites. On-site: 1, 2, 3, 12, 13, 14, 15, 27, 32, 34 and nature trails. Nearby: 24. Berry picking. May 15-Nov. 15. Camp fee.

Webster Lake, from Blackduck, ½ mi. S.W. on Hwy. 71, 10 mi. S. on Co. Rd. 39, 1½ mi. E. on Forest Rd. 2206, 1½ mi. N. on Forest Rd. 2208. 24 campsites. On-site: 1, 2, 3, 12, 13, 14, 23, 34. Nearby: 21, 22, 24, 27, 29, 32. Berry picking. May 15-Sept. 15. Camp fee.

West Seeleye Bay, from Deer River, 1 mi. N.W. on Hwy. 2, 20 mi. N.W. on Hwy. 46, 3 mi. S.W. on Co. Hwy. 33, ¼ mi. S. on Forest Rd. 3153. 22 campsites. On-site: 1, 2, 3, 12, 13, 14, 24, 34. Nearby: 15, 21, 22, 27, 34 and nature trails. Berry picking. May 15-Nov. 15. Camp fee.

West Seeleye Overflow, from Deer River, 1 mi. N.W. on Hwy. 2, 19 mi. N.W. on Hwy. 46, 3 mi. S.W. on Co. Hwy. 33, 60 campsites. On-site: 12. Nearby: 10, 13, 15, 21, 22, 24, 27, 29, 32 and nature trails. May 15-Sept. 15. No fee. Campground only used for fishing opener and holidays when other campgrounds are full.

Williams Narrows, from Deer River, 1 mi. N.W. on Hwy. 2, 15 mi. on Hwy. 46, 2 mi. N.W. on Co. Hwy. 148. 17 campsites. On-site: 1, 2, 3, 12, 13, 14, 15, 24, 32, 34. Nearby: 21, 22, 27, 29 and nature trails. Berry picking. May 15-Nov. 15. Camp fee.

Winnie, from Cass Lake, 6 mi. E. on Hwy. 2, 2½ mi. N. on Co. Hwy. 10, 7 mi. N.E. on Forest Rd. 2171, 3½ mi. S.E. on Forest Rd. 2168. 42 campsites. On-site: 1, 2, 3, 12, 13, 14, 23, 24, 32, 34. Nearby: 21, 22, 27, 29. Berry picking. May 15-Oct. 15. Camp fee.

SUPERIOR NATIONAL FOREST, DULUTH, MN 55801

Baker Lake, from Tofte, ½ mi. N.E. on Hwy. 61, 17 mi. N. on Hwy. 2, 5 mi. N.E. on Forest Rd. 165, ½ mi. W. on Forest Rd. 1272. 5 campsites. On-site: 1, 2, 3, 12, 13, 14, 24, 32, 34. Nearby: 27. Berry picking. May 10-Oct. 31. Camp fee.

Birch Lake, from Ely, 9 mi. S. on Hwy. 1, 4½ mi. S. on Forest Rd. 429, 32 campsites. On-site: 1, 2, 3, 12, 13, 14, 23, 24, 32, 34. May 15-Oct. 30. Camp fee.

Boundary Waters Canoe Area Wilderness, 84 access points near Cook, Ely, Isabella, Tofte, and Grand Marais. 2400 managed campsites. Free permit to camp required from May 1-Nov. 15, available from U.S. Forest Service offices or participating cooperators. Wilderness area with canoeing, boating, x-country skiing, snowmobiling, fishing, swimming, and hiking. Year-round.

Cadotte Lake, from Brimson, 8 mi. N. on Co. Hwy. 44, 1½ mi. W. on Co. Hwy. 16, ½ mi. N. on Forest Rd. 425, 1 mi. S.W. on Forest Rd. 778. 27 campsites. On-site: 1, 2, 3, 12, 13, 14, 15, 23, 24, 32, 34. Nearby: 20, 21, 22, 27, 29. May 15-Sept. 15. Camp fee.

Cascade River, from Grand Marais, ½ mi. N. on Co. Hwy. 12, 4 mi. W. on Co. Hwy. 7, 9 mi. N.W. on Forest Rd. 158. 3 campsites. On-site: 1, 2, 3, 12, 13, 14, 23, 24, 34. Nearby: 20, 21, 27, 29, 32. May 15-Oct. 15. No fee.

Clara Lake, from Lutsen, 1 mi. N.E. or Hwy. 61, 8 mi. N. on Co. Hwy. 4, 4 mi. N.W. on Forest Rd. 339. 2 campsites. On-site: 1, 2, 3, 13, 14, 24, 34. Berry picking. May 10-Oct. 31. No fee.

Crescent Lake, from Tofte, ½ mi. N.E. on Hwy. 61, 17 mi. N. on Hwy. 2, 7 mi. N.E. on Forest Rd. 165. 35 campsites. On-site: 1, 2, 3, 12, 13, 14, 24, 32, 34. Nearby: 27. Berry picking. May 10-Oct. 31. Camp fee.

Devil's Track Lake, from Grand Marais, 4 mi. N. on Co. Hwy. 12, 1 mi. W. on Co. Hwy. 6, 8 mi. N.W. on Co. Hwy. 8. 19 campsites. On-site: 1, 2, 3, 12, 13, 14, 23, 24, 34. Nearby: 20, 21, 27, 29, 32. May 15-Oct. 15. Camp fee.

Divide Lake, from Isabella, 1 mi. N.W. on Hwy. 1, 5 mi. E. on Forest Rd. 172. 2 campsites. On-site: 1, 13, 14, 24, 34. Nearby: 20, 21, 22, 29, 32. May 1-Sept. 10. No fee.

East Bearskin Lake, from Grand Marais, 26 mi. N.W. on Co. Hwy. 12, 1½ mi. N.E. on Forest Rd. 146. 43 campsites. On-site: 1, 2, 3, 12, 13, 14, 23, 24, 32, 34, and nature trails. Nearby: 20, 21, 27, 29. May 15-Oct. 15. Camp fee.

Echo Lake, from Buyck, 4 mi. N. on Co. Hwy. 3, 1 mi. E. on Co. Hwy. 116, 1 mi. N. on Forest Rd. 841. 24 campsites. On-site: 1, 2, 3, 12, 13, 14, 15, 23, 24, 32, 34 and nature trails. Nearby: 20, 21, 22, 29. May 15-Oct. 5. Camp fee.

Fall Lake, from Ely, 5½ mi. E. on Hwy. 169, 5 mi. E. on Co. Hwy. 18, 2 mi. N.E. on Forest Rd. 551. 69 campsites. On-site: 1, 2, 3, 12, 13, 14, 15, 23, 24, 32, 33, 34. Berry picking. May 15-Nov. 15. Camp fee.

Fenske Lake, from Ely, 2 mi. E. on Hwy. 169, 2½ mi. N. on Co. Hwy. 88, 8½ mi. N. on Co. Hwy. 116. 16 campsites. On-site: 1, 2, 3, 12, 13, 14, 15, 23, 24, 32, 34 and nature trails. Nearby: 20, 27. Berry picking. May 15-Nov. 15. Camp fee.

Flour Lake, from Grand Marais, 27 mi. N.W. on Co. Hwy. 12, 2½ mi. N.E. on Forest Rd. 147. 44 campsites. On-site: 1, 2, 3, 12, 13, 14, 23, 24, 32, 34 and nature trails. Nearby: 20, 21, 27, 29. May 15-Oct. 15. Camp fee.

Iron Lake, from Grand Marais, 38 mi. N.W. on Co. Hwy. 12. 7 campsites. On-site: 1, 2, 3, 12, 13, 14, 23, 24, 34. May 15-Oct. 15. Camp fee.

Isabella River, from Isabella, 4 mi. W. on Hwy. 1. 11 campsites. On-site: 1, 2, 3, 12, 13, 14, 23, 24, 34. Berry picking. Nearby: 11, 15, 20, 21, 22, 29, 32. May 1-Sept. 10. Camp fee.

Kawishiwi Lake, from Tofte, ½ mi. N.E. on Hwy. 61, 17½ mi. N. on Hwy. 2, 10 mi. W. on Co. Hwy. 3, 4 mi. N.W. on Forest Rd. 354. 5 campsites. On-site: 1, 2, 3, 12, 13, 14, 15, 24, 32, 34. Berry picking. May 10-Oct. 31. No fee.

Kimball Lake, from Grand Marais, 11 mi. N.E. on Co. Hwy. 12, 2 mi. E. on Forest Rd. 140. 9 campsites. On-site: 1, 2, 3, 12, 13, 14, 23, 24, 32, 34. Nearby: 15, 27. May 15-Oct. 15. Camp fee.

Lake Jeanette, from Buyck, 4 mi. N. on Co. Hwy. 24, 12 mi. E. on Co. Hwy. 116. 9 campsites. On-site: 1, 2, 3, 12, 13, 14, 23, 24, 32, 34 and nature trails. Berry picking. May 15-Oct. 5. No fee.

McDougal Lake, from Isabella, 12 mi. W. on Hwy. 1, 1 mi. S.E. on Forest Rd. 106. 21 campsites. On-site: 1, 2, 3, 12, 13, 14, 15, 23, 24, 32, 34. May 1-Sept. 10. Camp fee.

Nine Mile Lake, from Schroeder, ½ mi. S.W. on Hwy. 61, 10 mi. W. on Co. Hwy. 1, 4 mi. N. on Co. Hwy. 7. 24 campsites. On-site: 1, 2, 3, 12, 13, 14, 24, 32, 34. Nearby: 20, 21, 22, 27, 29. May 10-Oct. 31. Camp fee.

Pfeiffer Lake, from Virginia, 22 mi. N.E. on Hwy. 169, 5 mi. W. on Hwy. 1, 2 mi. S. on Forest Rd. 256. 21 campsites. On-site: 1, 2, 3, 12, 13, 14, 23, 34. Nearby: 15, 24, 32. Berry picking. May 1-Sept. 30. Camp fee.

Poplar River, from Tofte, ½ mi. N.E. on Hwy. 61, 11 mi. N. on Hwy. 2, 6 mi. E. on Forest Rd. 164. 4 campsites. On-site: 1, 13, 14, 24, 34. May 10-Oct. 31. No fee.

Sawbill Lake, from Tofte, ½ mi. N.E. on Hwy. 61, 24 mi. N. on Hwy. 3. 50 campsites. On-site: 1, 2, 3, 6, 11, 12, 13, 14, 21, 22, 29, 32, 34. Nearby: 27. May 10-Oct. 31. Camp fee.

South Kawishiwi River, from Ely, 12 mi. S. on Hwy. 1. 31 campsites. On-site: 1, 2, 3, 12, 13, 14, 15, 23, 24, 32, 34 and nature trails. May 15-Nov. 15. Camp fee.

Temperance River, from Tofte, ½ mi. N.E. on Hwy. 61, 11 mi. N. on Hwy. 2. 9 campsites. On-site: 1, 2, 3, 12, 13, 14, 23, 24, 34. May 10-Oct. 31. Camp fee.

Trails End, from Grand Marais, 58 mi. N.W. on Co. Hwy. 12. 36 campsites. On-site: 1, 2, 3, 12, 13, 14, 21, 22, 23, 24, 29, 32, 34 and nature trails. Nearby: 20, 27. May 15-Oct. 15. Camp fee.

Two Island Lake, from Grand Marais, 4 mi. N. on Co. Hwy. 12, 1 mi. W. on Co. Hwy. 6, 5 mi. N.W. on Co. Hwy. 8, 5 mi. N.W. on Co. Hwy. 27. 38 campsites. On-site: 1, 2, 3, 12, 13, 14, 23, 24, 32, 34 and nature trails. Nearby: 27. May 15-Oct. 15. Camp fee.

Whiteface Reservoir, from Aurora, 5½ mi. S. on Co. Hwy. 100, 6½ mi. S. on Co. Hwy. 99, 5 mi. E. on Co. Hwy. 16, 3 mi. S. on Forest Rd. 417. 58 campsites. On-site 1, 2, 3, 12, 13, 14, 23, 24, 34 and nature trails. Nearby: 15, 32. May 15-Sept. 30. Camp fee.

VOYAGEURS NATIONAL PARK

King Williams Narrows, Boat in from Crane Lake. 5 campsites. Pets on leash. 1, 13, 14, 34. No fee.

Mukooda Lake, Boat in from Crane Lake. 5 campsites. Pets on leash. 1, 13, 14, 34. No fee.

Voyageurs National Park, Boat in from Crane Lake, Ash River, Kabetogama or Island View. 100 dispersed campsites. 1, 13, 14, 34. Pets on leash. No fee.

MISSISSIPPI RIVER HEADWATER AREAS

Department of the Army, Corps of Engineers, 1135 U.S.P.O. & Custom House, St. Paul, MN 55101

Cross Lake Area on Cross Lake at Pine River Dam, Corps of Engineers, Crow Wing County. Off Co. Rd. 3 at Village of Cross Lake, 22 mi. N. of Brainerd, over Hwy. 25 and connecting county roads. 97 spaced camping pads for either tents or trailers, with parking spurs and 15 overflow camping pads. 1, 2, 3, 6, 10, 12, 13, 14, 15, 17, 23, 24, 32, 33, 34. $4.00 per night; 14 day limit; dogs on leash only; day use facilities available; water skiing. Nearby: 20, 21, 22, 25, 26, 28. Information station/Ranger station and interpretive area.

Leech Lake Area on Leech Lake at Corps of Engineers damsite, in Cass County. 8 mi. S. on Hwy. 2 off Co. Rd. 8 about 2 mi. N.W. of village of Federal Dam. 56 spaced camping pads for either tents or trailers, and 10 overflow with parking spurs. 1, 2, 3, 6, 10, 12, 13, 14, 17, 22, 23, 24, 25, 26, 27, 28, 32, 33, 34. $4.00 per night; 14 day limit; dogs on leash only; day use facilities available; water skiing.

Sandy Lake Area on Sandy Lake at Corps of Engineers damsite in Aitkin County. 12 mi. N. of McGregor and ½ mi. off Hwy. 65 at Libby. 35 spaced camping pads for either tents or trailers, with parking spurs and 11 spaced tent pads with footpath access only from adjacent parking area. 1, 2, 3, 6, 10, 12, 13, 14, 17, 23, 24, 33, 34. French Voyageur and Indian Museum. $4.00 per night; 14 day limit; dogs on leash only; day use facilities available; water skiing.

Pokegama Lake Area on Pokegama Lake at Corps of Engineers damsite in Itasca County. Just off Hwy. 2 about 2 mi. W. of Grand Rapids. 15 spaced camping pads for either tents or trailers, with parking spurs. 1, 2, 3, 10, 12, 13, 14, 17, 23, 24, 32, 34. Nature trail; water skiing. Nearby: 20, 21, 22, 25, 26, 28. Free use; 5 day limit; dogs on leash only; day use facilities available; water skiing.

MINNESOTA RECREATION AT A GLANCE

State Parks

State parks	64 (171,000 acres)
State recreation areas	6 (4,552 acres)
State waysides	11 (3,285 acres)
State park attendance	6,889,125
State parks with naturalists	30
Private nature centers	20
Historical sites — national register	258
National historical landmark sites	19
National natural landmark sites	4
Snowmobile trails — state parks	495 miles
Snowmobile trails — state forests	1,494 miles
Snowmobile trails — grants-in-aid	4,200 miles
Snowmobile trails — corridor trails	433 miles
Snowmobile permits — annual	110,000
Cross country ski trails	651 miles
Hiking trails	1153 miles
Horseback riding trails	713 miles
Boating water (lakes 50 acres or more)	More than 2.6 million acres
Watercraft registered	526,323
Canoeing water, river and lake routes	3,550 miles
Canoeing rivers (designated Canoeing & Boating Rivers)	18 rivers (2,208 miles)
Public accesses	1,717

STATE PARKS AND RECREATION AREAS

NAME	POST OFFICE - HWY / TELEPHONE NO.	ACRES	CAMPSITES: RUSTIC	SEMI-MODERN	BACKPACKING	CANOE	CAMPING: ELECTRICITY	DUMPING STATION	SHOWERS	FLUSH TOILETS	PIT TOILETS	LODGE & CABINS	GROUP CAMP	PICNICKING	SWIMMING	FISHING	BOAT RAMP	BOAT RENTALS	TRAILS (in miles): FOOT	X-SKI	HORSE	SNOWMOBILE	BICYCLE	SNACK BAR	PARK NATURALIST	SPECIAL FEATURES
AFTON	Afton — CTY 21, 612/436-5391	1,152			3									●					9	9	4					Lower St. Croix park. Varying terrain. One of Minnesota's excellent birding areas. Adjacent to historic Afton.
BANNING	Sandstone — MN 23, 612/245-2668	4,398		31										●		●			4	5				●		Kettle River flowing through scenic rock gorges. Historic "Sandstone" quarry and townsite.
BAPTISM RIVER	— US 61	706								●				●					4							Outstanding scenic beauty. Highest waterfall in the state with several smaller falls.
BEAR HEAD LAKE	Ely — CTY 128, 218/365-4253	4,264	24	50			●	●	●	●			●	●	●	●	●	●	14	14	9			●		Scenic Bear Head Lake in a wilderness setting. Located on Taconite State Trail.
BEAVER CRK. VALLEY	Caledonia — CTY 128, 507/724-2107	671	28	20			●							●		●			6	3						Beautiful steep bluff valley. Trout stream rises from an artesian spring and threads its way through the valley.
BIG STONE LAKE	Ortonville — MN 7, 612/839-3663	1,099		42			●	●	●	●				●	●	●	●	●	2		5					Two areas along big Stone Lake. Important for scenic values and prehistoric record of man in America.
BLUE MOUNDS	Luverne — CTY 20, 507/283-4892	1,357	73			●	●	●	●	●				●	●	●	●		7	3	7					Historic prairie hunting grounds of the Sioux. Unusual geologic Sioux quartzite. Buffalo herd.
BUFFALO RIVER	Glyndon — CTY 44, 218/498-2124	990	44											●	●				4	4						Prairie oasis and prehistoric Campbell Beach of Lake Agassiz.
CAMDEN	Lynd — MN 23, 507/865-4530	1,468	37	10			●	●	●	●				●	●	●			9	10	10			●		Natural wilderness valley in prairie farming area.
CARLEY	Plainview — CTY 4, 507/534-3400	211		20										●					3	3						Rugged, steep wooded valley of north branch of Whitewater River.
CASCADE RIVER	Lutsen — US 61, 218/387-2543	2,813	38							●				●		●			15	30	2					Rugged, Rocky terrain along Lake Superior. River flows through a twisting, rocky gorge.
CHARLES A. LINDBERGH	Little Falls — CTY 52, 612/632-9050	294	38				●	●	●	●				●		●			2							Boyhood home of famous flying Colonel. Along wooded bank of Mississippi River.
CROW WING	Brainerd — CTY 27, 218/829-8022	1,739	65				●	●	●	●				●		●	●		12	4	9			●		Location of historic Crow Wing Indian village. Important in fur trade and Red River ox cart days. Located at confluence of two rivers.
FATHER HENNEPIN	Isle — MN 27, 612/676-8763	274	62				●	●	●	●				●	●	●	●		7		5			●		Deciduous forest with extensive shoreline on Mille Lacs Lake.
FLANDRAU	New Ulm — Cty, 507/354-3519	801	57				●	●	●	●				●	●	●	●		7	1	4			●		Cottonwood River valley with high wooded bluffs.
FORESTVILLE	Preston — CTY 12, 507/352-5111	2,260	68				●	●	●	●				●		●			15	8	7			●		Scenic segment of the Root River valley and abandoned townsite of Civil War era.
FORT RIDGELY	Fairfax — CTY 29, 507/426-7840	504		35			●	●	●	●				●	●	●			12	3	4		●			Site of fierce battles of 1862 Sioux Uprising. Golf course. Outdoor summer theatre.

STATE PARKS AND RECREATION AREAS

NAME	POST OFFICE - HWY NO. / TELEPHONE	ACRES	Semi-Modern	Rustic	Backpacking	Canoe	Electricity	Dumping Station	Showers	Flush Toilets	Pit Toilets	Lodge & Cabins	Group Camp	Picnicking	Swimming	Fishing	Boat Ramp	Boat Rentals	Foot	X-Ski	Horse	Snowmobile	Bicycle	Snack Bar	Park Naturalist	SPECIAL FEATURES
FORT SNELLING	St Paul — I-494 612/727-1961	2,407												■					15	18		1		■	■	Oldest building in state. Instrumental in opening territory to settlement. High bluffs overlooking broad Minnesota River Valley
FRANZ JEVNE	— CTY 85	117		10															1							Fishing area and rapids on Rainy River
FRONTENAC	Lake City — US 61 612/345-3401	1,291	58				■	■	■	■			■	■		■			6	2	10					Rolling woodlands along the northwest shore of Lake Pepin. Site of fur trading post (1727) and Indian town (1860)
GEO. H.C. MANITOU	Finland — CTY 7	2,960		22										■	■	■	■		23	11						Mountainous rock and forest area with 4 miles of Manitou River, including two waterfalls
GLACIAL LAKES	Starbuck — CTY 41 612/239-2860	1,279	21	18		2	■	■	■	■				■	■	■	■	11	11		9					Several spring fed lakes surrounded by virgin prairie on one side and a virgin oak forest on the other
GOOSEBERRY FALLS	Two Harbors — US 61 218/834-3855	1,520		4					■	■				■	■	■	■	6	6	10	2					Located on beautiful rocky Lake Superior. Stream has series of falls and rapids
HAYES LAKE	Roseau — CTY 4 218/425-7504	2,760	35				■	■	■	■				■	■	■	■	6	6		6					Wooded area on edge of prairie
HELMER MYRE	Albert Lea — CTY 38 507/373-5084	1,535	142	6			■	■	■	■			■	■	■	■	■	18	18	2	12					Remnants of natural prairie and a heavily wooded island in Albert Lea Lake
INTERSTATE	Taylors Falls — US 8 612/465-5711	173	47			■	■	■	■	■	■			■	■	■	■	3	3				■	■		Glacial Gardens of outstanding geologic formations. In narrow Dalles of St. Croix River. Excursion Boat
ITASCA	Lake Itasca — US 71 218/266-3656	30,220	220	30		4	■	■	■	■	■	■	■	■	■	■	■	33	33	27	31	2	■	■	■	Large area of lakes and virgin forests. Source of Mississippi River. Famous Douglas Lodge. Ideal objective for a vacation trip
JAY COOKE	Carlton — MN 210 218/384-4610	9,461	94				■	■	■	■			■	■		■		40	40	30		12	■	■	■	Spectacular terrain with St. Louis River running through picturesque gorge
JUDGE C.R. MAGNEY	Grand Marais — US 61 218/387-2929	4,094	42											■		■		3	3							Waterfalls and boiling rapids of Brule River. Exceptional geologic and scenic values
KILEN WOODS	Lakefield — CTY 24 507/662-6258	201	20				■	■	■	■				■	■	■	■	5	5	2	4			■		In Des Moines River Valley. Scenic hills and woods amidst rolling farm land
LAC QUI PARLE	Montevideo — CTY 33 612/752-4736	529	56				■	■	■	■			■	■	■	■	■	7	7	7	7	5				Dense timber along historic Lac Qui Parle and Minnesota Rivers
LAKE BEMIDJI	Bemidji — CTY 20 218/751-1472	302	103				■	■	■	■			■	■	■	■	■	3	3	3		1		■	■	Virgin pine forest on sandy shore of Lake Bemidji
LAKE BRONSON	Lake Bronson — CTY 28 218/754-3200	1,654	150				■	■	■	■				■	■	■	■	10	10	3	6			■	■	Artificial lake with irregular shoreline in middle of open farm country
LAKE CARLOS	Carlos — MN 29 612/852-7200	1,198	146				■	■	■	■				■	■	■	■	12	12	3	10			■	■	Rolling topography with variety of deciduous trees along sandy shoreline

STATE PARKS AND RECREATION AREAS

NAME	POST OFFICE – HWY / TELEPHONE NO.	ACRES	Semi-Modern	Rustic	Backpacking	Canoe	Electricity	Dumping Station	Showers	Flush Toilets	Pit Toilets	Lodge & Cabins	Group Camp	Picnicking	Swimming	Fishing	Boat Ramp	Boat Rentals	Foot	X-Ski	Horse	Snowmobile	Bicycle	Snack Bar	Park Naturalist	SPECIAL FEATURES
LAKE LOUISE	Leroy — CTY 14 / 507/324-5249	816	23							■				■	■	■	■	4	4	7	7		■	■	A wooded area at junction of two streams forming a lake impoundment in upper Iowa River
LAKE MARIA	Monticello — CTY 11 / 612/878-2325	1,318		25						■				■		■		13	13	6				■	Heavy rolling land with deciduous tree cover which surrounds two small lakes
LAKE SHETEK	Currie — CTY 37 / 507/763-3256	1,016	88	20		■	■	■	■	■		■	■	■	■	■	■	3			5		■		Wooded shoreline on one of the few larger lakes in this section of Minnesota. Site of massacre in 1862 Sioux Uprising
LITTLE ELBOW LAKE	Waubun — MN 113 / 218/734-2230	3,048	22								■			■	■	■	■	10			10				Heavily rolling land with deciduous tree cover; three lakes.
MC CARTHY BEACH	Hibbing — CTY 5 / 218/254-2411	1,367	45	14			■		■	■				■	■	■	■	17	5	12			■		Heavy virgin pine timber on rolling hills between two lakes; exceptional sand beaches
MAPLEWOOD	Pelican Rapids — MN 108 / 218/863-8383	7,263	53	10							■			■	■	■		25	17	15	15				Spectacularly beautiful portion of Minnesota, including about 20 lakes
MILLE LACS KATHIO	Onamia — CTY 26 / 612/532-3523	8,063	71				■	■	■	■				■	■	■	■	20	9	9	20		■	■	Large park of hills, meadows and forests. Site of the major battle between Sioux and Chippewa 1745. Capitol Dakota Indian Nation.
MINNEOPA	Mankato — CTY 69 / 507/625-4388	917	65								■			■				4	4					■	Waterfalls in a deep wooded gorge; historic mill site and village
MONSON LAKE	Sunburg — CTY 95 / 612/366-3797	187	20								■			■	■	■	■	1							Site of 1862 Sioux Uprising Massacre
MOOSE LAKE	Moose Lake — I-35 / 218/485-4059	1,016	18								■			■	■	■	■		3		10				State recreation area bordered by two beautiful lakes
NERSTRAND WOODS	Nerstrand — CTY 88 / 507/334-8848	1,073	62				■	■	■	■			■	■		■		11	5		5			■	Remnant of big woods in central Minnesota with picturesque prairie creek
OLD MILL	Argyle — CTY 39 / 218/437-8174	287	24				■	■	■	■			■	■	■	■		4	1	3	3				Typical prairie terrain except for rolling valley with winding river
O.L. KIPP	Winona — CTY 3 / 507/643-6849	1,982	31								■			■				6	9	9				■	Inspiring view of Mississippi River Valley. High hills offer picturesque panoramas
RICE LAKE	Owatonna — CTY 19 / 507/451-7406	757	42				■				■			■		■	■	3	4		2				Virgin deciduous forest surrounding undeveloped lake
ST. CROIX	Hinckley — MN 48 / 612/384-6591	23,608	217	4	2	5	■	■	■	■		■	■	■	■	■	■	127	21	75	75	6	■	■	A large park with pine, spruce, hardwoods and wildlife. The St. Croix river and several small rivers flow through this area
ST. CROIX ISLAND		34		4	4																				Islands in St. Croix River scenic valley area
ST. CROIX WILD RIVER	Center City — CTY 12 / 612/583-2125	5,998	73	4	4		■	■	■	■			■	■	■	■		30	30		1		■	■	At the scenic confluence of the St. Croix and Sunrise Rivers

STATE PARKS AND RECREATION AREAS

NAME	POST OFFICE - HWY NO. / TELEPHONE	ACRES	CAMPSITES				CAMPING					LODGE & CABINS	GROUP CAMP	PICNICKING	SWIMMING	FISHING	BOAT RAMP	BOAT RENTALS	TRAILS (in miles)					SMACK BAR	PARK NATURALIST	SPECIAL FEATURES
			SEMI-MODERN	RUSTIC	BACKPACKING	CANOE	ELECTRICITY	DUMPING STATION	SHOWERS	FLUSH TOILETS	PIT TOILETS								FOOT	X-SKI	HORSE	SNOWMOBILE	BICYCLE			
SAKATAH LAKE	Waterville — MN 60 / 507/362-4438	762	60				■	■	■	■	■		■	■	■	■	■		4						■	Heavily wooded primarily virgin hardwood forest.
SAVANNA PORTAGE	McGregor — CTY 36 / 218/426-3271	14,934	63	8			■	■	■	■	■		■	■	■	■	■		22	16		61				The major link in the route Mississippi to St. Louis River; primitive wilderness character.
SCENIC	Big Fork — CTY 7 / 218/743-3362	1,632	120			■		■	■	■	■		■	■	■	■	■		7	10		10			■	One of Minnesota's primitive parks, virgin norway pine stands beside unspoiled lakes.
SCHOOLCRAFT	Ball Club — CTY 138 / 218/566-2383	217		38						■				■		■			2							Historic Indian wild ricing site; embraces a section of the Mississippi River.
SIBLEY	New London — CTY 48 / 612/354-2443	1,954	83			■	■	■	■	■			■	■	■	■	■	■	15	10	5	6			■	Virgin hardwoods cover moraine hills along a sand shore of Lake Andrews.
SPLIT ROCK CREEK	Jasper — CTY 54 / 507/348-7908	228	25								■			■	■	■	■									Recreational area along artificial lake.
SPLIT ROCK LIGHTHOUSE	Two Harbors — US 61 / 218/226-3065	660									■			■		■			1	1		1				Beautiful view of Lake Superior.
TEMPERANCE RIVER	Schroeder — US 61 / 218/663-7476	133	51					■		■	■			■	■	■			6	8		14				Spectacular rocky river gorge with large potholes; on Lake Superior.
TOWER SOUDAN	Soudan — US 169 / 218/753-2245	1,000												■		■	■									Minnesota's deepest and oldest underground iron mine at Lake Vermilion. Mine Tours.
TRAVERSE DES SIOUX	— US 169	1,147												■		■						7				Site of historic village of Traverse des Sioux, and location of 1850 treaty signing with the Sioux which opened vast areas to settlement.
UPPER SIOUX AGENCY	Granite Falls — MN 67 / 612/564-4777	1,066	67								■	■	■	■	■	■	■		8	2		9		■	■	On the banks of picturesque Yellow Medicine River. Historic location of a government outpost called the Yellow Medicine or Upper Sioux Agency.
WHITEWATER	Altura — MN 74 / 507/932-3007	1,699	68	25						■	■	■	■	■	■	■			10	6					■	Southern Minnesota's most popular park formed by a deep ravine with limestone formations and hardwood forests.
WILLIAM O'BRIEN	Marine on St.Croix — MN 95 / 612/433-2421	1,270	125		4	■	■	■	■	■	■		■	■	■	■	■	■	12	12			■	■	■	Beautifully wooded rolling countryside with frontage on the St. Croix River.
ZIPPEL BAY	Williams — CTY 34 / 218/783-6252	2,826	60							■	■		■	■	■	■	■		6	2		15			■	Gently sloping lands bordering an exceptional beach area on Lake of the Woods.

DEFINITIONS OF CAMPSITES:
Semi-Modern = Back-up spur, usually flush toilets, hot showers.
Rustic = Back-up spur, usually pit toilets, no showers.
Backpacking = Accessible only by hiking.
Canoe = Usually only accessible by canoe.

Ralph S. Samuelson pioneered the sport of water skiing in 1922.

Fishing, Hunting & Wildlife

Minnesota Fishing

"Where-to-go and how-to-get'em" is important. But "when" may be even more so for Minnesota anglers.

The "when" is anytime—24 hours daily, 365 days yearly.

While the general fishing season for the big ones—muskies, northern pike and walleyes—opens on the weekend nearest May 15, crappie, sunfish, silver bass, catfish and bullhead fishing never closes.

State fisheries officials believe many more persons fish for crappies and sunfish than for any other species. Even with generous limits—15 crappies and 30 sunfish or silver bass—the supply remains constant. In fact, some lakes may actually be underfished, leading to catches of smaller sized fish.

The "where" is just as easy.

Fishing starts right in the Twin Cities. Catches of northern pike are common in the great river. Crappies and silver bass strike in both the Mississippi and the Minnesota River in the Fort Snelling State Park area.

Minneapolis city lakes, Calhoun, Harriet and Cedar in particular, are deep and have been benefited by plantings of large game fish seined by state crews from lakes threatened by winter kills. All of the city lakes also furnish hours of pleasant sport for shore casters seeking sunfish and crappies.

West of the Twin Cities, 14,000-acre Lake Minnetonka has been labeled by a state fisheries official as the best natural crappie lake in the state. It also has had stockings of muskies and holds almost any game fish found in the state except trout.

The St. Croix River, east of the Twin Cities, adds scenery including pine shores, to excellent angling for northern pike, walleyes and smallmouth bass. It has given up sensational catches of silver bass.

The seven-county metropolitan area of Hennepin, Ramsey, Anoka, Carver, Dakota, Scott and Washington holds a total of 197 known game-fish lakes. In addition to Minnetonka, some of the best are White Bear, Waconia, Bald Eagle, Coon, Medicine, Forest, Big Marine and Prior.

Spreading out from the Twin Cities, Mille Lacs, 100 miles north, draws more walleye anglers than any other state water. Walleyes usually are found in the larger lakes. Mille Lacs, at 132,000 acres usually is a high producer, particularly for early season anglers.

Other big waters are Red Lake, at 288,800 acres the largest entirely within Minnesota; Leech, 111,500 acres; Winnibigoshish 69,821; Vermilion 37,915; Pepin (a wide spot on the Mississippi) 25,000 and Kabetogama 19,000.

Trout enthusiasts head principally for streams that run into Lake Superior. Lower portions of most of those north shore streams are open to angling all year. Southeastern Minnesota's hill country also has some excellent brown trout streams. Lake trout fishing is confined principally to waters in the northeastern corner of the state.

Lake Superior, or the portion that washes the Minnesota shore, has made a comeback in rainbow trout fishing. The "steelhead" run up streams along that shore is heaviest during late April and early May. Another phenomenon there is the annual run of smelts, a small, silvery fish, taken by netters. That run usually occurs in late April.

The "how" is up to the individual. Minnesota has 2 million anglers, each with his or her own idea how to catch them.

The minnow, once a standard bait for walleyes, has been replaced to some extent in recent years by the use of nightcrawlers and leeches.

Artificials are the favorite for muskies, northern pike and bass. Spinner or spoon type lures appear to be irresistable for northerns. Bucktails or heavy plugs are used for muskies. Bass fishermen usually try surface lures in the shallows during the early season and then switch to deep diving types later in the summer.

Fishing is always good—whether the catch is or not.

LICENSE REQUIREMENTS

Fishing regulations for 1988 will be available about March 1, 1988 when they become effective. License fees have not been determined at the time of publication.

Residents:

• All residents who have attained the age of 16 and are under the age of 65 must have on their person an appropriate license while angling.

• Resident licenses may be issued only to U.S. citizens who have maintained a legal residence in Minnesota for a period of 60 days immediately preceding the date of application for a license.

• Residents under the age of 16 years are not required to have an angling, spearing, or dip netting license.

• A license to take fish shall be issued without charge to any citizen of Minnesota who is a recipient of supplemental security income for the aged, blind, and disabled.

• Residents serving in the U.S. military or naval forces, or the reserve components thereof, who are stationed outside the state may fish without a license when in Minnesota on regularly granted leave or furlough.

• Residents who have attained the age of 65 years may take fish by angling or spearing without a license. However, they must have on their persons evidence of their age and proof of Minnesota residency.

GENERAL RESTRICTIONS
IT IS UNLAWFUL:

• To be on board watercraft without a readily accessible personal flotation device of the type approved by the U.S. Coast Guard.

• To deposit any refuse, poisonous substances, or chemicals injurious to fish life in any waters of the state.

• To buy or sell game fish, except fish taken under a commercial or private hatchery license.

• To operate any unregistered boat (except duck boats during the duck hunting season and rice boats during the harvest season).

• To stock fish in any waters or transfer fish from one body of water to another with out written permit from the Director or his authorized agents.

• To drive a motor boat through a posted spawning bed or fish preserve.

• To deposit garbage, rubbish, offal, in public waters or on the ice, or on public lands.

• To take fish by angling with a set or unattended line.

DID YOU KNOW....?

• That there are about 2.6 million acres of fishing waters in Minnesota.

• That there are about 2,000 miles of trout streams and about 15,000 miles of fishable warm water streams.

• That fish intended for release should not be held by the eye sockets while extracting the hook. Blindness and death are a frequent consequence.

• That the objective is to provide a maximum, sustained yield of fish from the waters of the state and the maximum number of satisfactory sport fishing hours.

• That fish management activities include habitat improvement; acquisition, development, and management of natural spawing areas; operation of fish hatcheries and rearing ponds for the propagation and distribution of fish; rescue of fish from lakes where they are subject to winterkill; rough fish control; lake rehabilitation through the use of fish toxicants; administration of licensed commercial fishing; and formulation of regulations governing the harvest of fish.

Source: Minnesota D.N.R. Div. of Fish and Wild Life.

Daily Limits and/or Possession Since 1922

Species	1922	1930	1939	1947	1948	1951	1953	1956	1962	1975	1981	1987
Lake Trout	25	15	15	5	5	5	5	5	3	3	3	5*
Trout	25	15	15	15	15	15	10	10	10	5	5	10*
Black Bass	15	6	6	6	6	6	6	6	6	6	6	6
Muskellunge	5	2	2	2	2	2	2	1	1	1	1	1+
Northern Pike	no limit	10	8	6	3	3	3	3	3	3	3	3
Walleye	15	8	8	8	8	8	8	6	6	6	6	6
Sunfish	25	15	15	15	15	30	30	30	30	30	30	30
Crappie	20	15	15	15	15	15	15	15	15	15	15	15

* Trout stamp required. Size limit: not more than 3 over 16".
+ Minimum size: 36".

Minnesota Department of Natural Resources

RECORD FISH

If you catch a fish by hook and line which you think could be a record for Minnesota waters, follow these steps:

1. Weigh it on state certified scale, witnessed by an observer.
2. Take the fish to a Section of Fisheries office for positive identification.
3. Obtain a "State Record Fish Application" from the same office, complete it and submit it with a clear, full length photo of the fish to the address indicated.

If the fish is approved as a state record, you will receive a certificate from the Department of Natural Resources verifying your catch.

MINNESOTA RECORD OF LARGEST FISH

Source: Minnesota Department of Natural Resources Division of Fish and Wildlife Section of Fisheries as of Jan. 6, 1987.

Species	Weight Lbs.	ozs.	Method	Where taken	Date	Taken by:
Walleye	17	8	Angling	Seagull R. at Saganaga Lake, Cook Co.	5-13-79	LeRoy Chiovitte, Hermantown, MN
Walleye-Sauger Hybrid	7	2	Angling	Mississippi R.	1975	Timothy C. Violet St. Paul, MN
Sauger	6	2½	Angling	Mississippi River below Alma Dam (L&D No.4)	1964	Mrs. Wylis Larson, Winona, MN
Yellow Perch	3	4	Angling	Lake Plantaganette Hubbard Co.	1945	Merle Johnson, Bemidji, MN
Muskellunge	54		Angling	Lake Winnibigoshish, Itasca County	1957	Art Lyons, Bena, MN
Tiger Muskellunge	30	4	Angling	Deer Lake, Itasca County	8-6-79	Stephen Friberg, Northbrook, IL
Northern pike	45	12	Angling	Basswood Lake	5-16-29	J.V. Schanken, MN
Northern pike (Silver Phase)	18	14	Angling	Disappointment Lake, Lake Co.	6-28-78	Robert Quigley, Mattson, IL
Largemouth Bass	8	9½	Angling	Fountain Lake Freeborn Co.	9-6-86	Timothy Kirsch Albert Lea, MN
Smallmouth Bass	8		Angling	W. Battle Lake, Otter Tail County	1948	John A. Creighton, Minneapolis, MN

Species	lbs.	oz.	Location	Method	Date	Angler
White Bass	4		St. Croix in channel from NSP Plant	Angling	2-12-72	Dan Dickhausen, Lake Elmo, MN
tie	4		Genoa fishing barge	Angling	5-14-74	Richard Zehrt, Racine, WI
Black Crappie (This tied the world's record)	5		Vermillion River, Dakota County	Angling	1940	Tom Christenson, Red Wing, MN
Channel Catfish	38		Mississippi River, No. Mpls.	Angling	1975	Terrence Fussy, Minneapolis, MN
Brown Bullhead	7	1	Shallow Lake, Itasca County	Angling	5-21-74	William Meyer, Holland, IA
Dogfish	10		Priest's Bay, Lake Minnetonka	Angling	1941	Roger Lehman Bemidji, MN
Freshwater Drum (Sheepshead)	35	2	Mississippi River, near Genoa	Angling	6-18-83	Michael C. Foreman, Viroqua, WI
Carp	55	5	Clearwater Lake, Wright County	Angling	7-10-52	Frank J. Ledwein, Annandale, MN
Mooneye	1	15	Minnesota River, Redwood County	Angling	6-18-80	Scott M. Neudecker Redwood Falls
Goldeye	2		Minnesota River, near Carver	Angling	7-6-82	Richard Nesgoda, Hopkins, MN
Tullibee	4	3	Big Sandy Lake, Aitkin County	Angling	1974	Robert Graff, McGregor, MN

Species	lbs	oz	Location	Method	Date	Angler
Longnose Gar	16	12	St. Croix River, Prescot	Angling	5-4-82	Doug Fullerton, Maplewood, MN
American Eel	5	15	Mississippi River, Red Wing	Angling	6-23-82	Ed Krawiecki, Red Wing, MN
White Sucker	9	1	Big Fish Lake, Stearns Co.	Angling	5-1-83	Thomas Waibel, St. Cloud, MN
Big Mouth Buffalo	36	5	North Long Lake, Ottertail Co.	Angling	6-12-80	Carolyn A. Wilkinson, Bullhead City, AZ
Shorthead Redhorse	7	15	Rum River, near Ramsey Anoka Co.	Angling	8-5-83	Robert G. Litke, Anoka, MN
Burbot	17	8	Trout Lake, St. Louis County	Angling	1-22-83	Allen Lindgren, Virginia, MN
Silver Redhorse	7	9⅓	Rainy River, near Loman Koochiching Co.	Angling	4-30-83	Joel M. Anderson, Little Canada, MN
Green Sunfish	1	2.7	Scheuble Lake, Carver County	Angling	1-9-84	Richard R. Kunze, Waconia, MN
Bluegill	2	13	Alice Lake, Hubbard County	Angling	1948	Bob Parker, Bemidji, MN
Rock Bass	1	15	Lake Mille Lacs, Mille Lacs County	Angling	8-19-81	Jason Junghans, Plymouth, MN
Brown Trout	16	8	Grindstone Lake, Pine County	Angling	1961	Carl Lovgren, St. Paul, MN

Species	lbs.	oz.	Location	Method	Date	Angler
Rainbow Trout	17	6	Knife River	Angling	1-19-74	Ottway R. Stuberud, Knife River, MN
Brook Trout	6	2	Pine Mountain, Cook County	Angling	5-20-67	Wes Smith, Grand Marais, MN
Lake Trout	43	8	Lake Superior, near Hovland	Angling	5-30-55	G.H. Nelson
Splake	10	4⅓	Birch Lake, Cook County	Angling	5-19-86	David Leitten, Burnsville, MN
Ohrid Trout	6	6	Tofte Lake, Lake Co.	Angling	1-9-73	Jim Crigler, Babbitt, MN
Coho Salmon	10	6.5	Lake Superior, near Baptism River	Angling	11-7-70	Louis Rhode, Coon Rapids, MN
Chinook (King)	29	10.25	Cross River Cook Co.	Angling	9-20-85	Gary Bjerkness, Schroeder, MN
Kokanee Salmon	2	15	Caribou Lake, Itasca County	Angling	8-6-71	Lars Kindem, Bloomington, MN
Pink Salmon	3	14.1	Poplar River, near Lutsen, Cook Co.	Angling	9-13-83	Steven L. Ratte, Duluth, MN
Lake Sturgeon	92	4	Kettle River, Pine Co.	Angling	9-11-86	James DeOtis, Maple Grove, MN
Flathead Catfish	70		St. Croix River	Angling	1970	John L. Robert, Garden City, IA

The Story of Minnesota's Pike

It may come as a surprise that the muskellunge, better known as the "muskie", and the northern pike are the only two members of the pike family (Esocidae) in Minnesota. The other members of this family, the pickerels, are smaller fishes of more southern and eastern waters, but are not found in Minnesota.

The northern pike, known to most as the "northern", and the muskie are easily confused. They are found in similar environment and look much alike, both being very elongate with large heads shaped like a duck's bill. Irregular rows of light yellow spots on a dark background will usually tell you it's a northern. Muskies generally have dark, vertical bands on a light background.

But the surest way to distinguish between the two is to count the sensory pores (or tiny holes) under the lower jaw. If there are more than five pores on each side, chances are it's a muskie and if there are five or less, you most likely have a northern. Also, northerns have fully-scaled cheeks, whereas the cheeks of muskies are scaled only on the upper half.

Sometimes northerns do not have spots and such fish are called "silver pike". These silver pike are mutants of the northern and are not a separate species.

Also, during their first six to eight months of life, young northerns look quite different from adults. Immature northerns are usually lean and slender and older fish more chunky. This leads to the belief that there is a slender variety—a "snake pickerel"—and a chunky one, a true northern. The truth is that northerns are quite like people, when they get older, their stomachs tend to sag especially after a heavy meal.

The World of the Northern Pike

The adaptable northern pike lurks in nearly all types of Minnesota water including cold-water and warm-water lakes as well as slow-flowing rivers.

Northerns are primarily day-time feeders and rely on keen eye-sight to locate their food. They prey on nearly anything that moves within range of their vision and are especially fond of smaller fish such as suckers, minnows and perch.

When their hunger pangs are satisfied, northerns head for deeper water outside the weed beds where they spend the night.

Fishing for Northerns

The northern pike is one of our most reliable game fish and provides especially good fishing for the day-time angler. Morning is a good time as this is when they start their daily forage for food. They seem to be most active between 8 and 11 a.m. and again between 2 and 4 p.m.

Another consideration is water temperature. When water reaches about 65 degrees F., angling success lessens and summer catches usually diminish in late July and August. The most consistent catches are made along the edge of weed beds and patches of lily pads in water less than 15 feet deep.

One of the best times of the year to fish northerns is in mid-May or early June, a few weeks after they return from spring spawning runs. At this time, northerns are hungry and concentrate in shallow, weedy areas and in moderate to strong currents on the down-stream side of barriers or falls. Northerns can be caught in a variety of ways—trolling, casting and still fishing. Medium and shallow-running lures and large, lively minnows seems to be the most productive. The color and type of lure doesn't seem to make much difference to a northern pike.

The Yield - Northerns to Fishermen

In terms of total weight, northern pike out-rank all other game fish in the Minnesota angler's catch. To ensure equal fishing opportunities, to protect northerns during spawning and to protect them from being over-fished, daily limits and closed season regulations are enforced. In the inland waters, the fishing season for northerns is closed from mid-February to mid-May and the daily possession limit is three fish per angler. Catch limits vary somewhat in the waters bordering Minnesota and surrounding states.

Where Do Northerns Spawn?

Northerns spawn in submerged, marshy areas along lakes or streams. The best spawning areas are dry or nearly so in late summer, but flooded in the spring. Here ample food is produced for the young. Northerns are very prolific and one female may lay as many as 200,000 eggs. Northerns spawn in April or early May, about the time the ice breaks in our lakes when water in the spawning areas reaches about 40 degrees F.

To Insure Good Northern Pike Fishing

Each year the Department of Natural Resources Division of Game and Fish stocks about 7,500,000 northern pike from hatcheries, controlled and managed spawning and rearing areas and rescue operations. The primary emphasis however, is on preserving and developing spawning areas so northern pike populations can perpetuate themselves. On many lakes, these natural pike hatcheries are rapidly being eliminated by lake-shore residential developments. To save them, the Division of Game and Fish has acquired over 100 such areas on lakes where spawning sites are especially needed.

Spawning and hatching success and growth rates are checked periodically and the fingerlings removed at the proper time and transplanted to lakes where they are needed, or else allowed to drain into the adjacent lakes.

The Department of Natural Resources also has a large northern pike winter rescue program. Many of Minnesota's lakes are quite shallow and are subject to "winterkill". This is caused by a shortage of oxygen in the winter, which causes the fish to suffocate. By pumping aerated water through traps made from hardware cloth, the pike can be made to move into the traps when the oxygen becomes low in the lake water. In this way, each year several hundred thousand yearling northerns are rescued.

Minnesota's Muskie Waters

In Minnesota, muskies are not as widely distributed as northerns. About 60 lakes and many areas of the Mississippi and the Little Fork rivers have muskies. The best natural muskie waters are the Mississippi headwater lakes in north-central Minnesota and the river itself, especially between St. Cloud and Brainerd.

Cass and Winnibigoshish are famous Minnesota muskie lakes. But the most famous and widely publicized is Leech Lake. Here in 1955, an astonishing catch was made during a strange summer flurry.

During "mad muskie days," 140 muskies, some weighing up to 44 pounds, were taken in one week, July 19 to 25, and many more hooked and lost. The final tally was 163 fish in the 19 to 44-pound category taken in 5½ days. (In a normal entire year, about 150 muskies are caught at Leech Lake averaging 18 pounds.)

The muskie splurge remains a mystery, but it is known that the weather was hot, the humidity high and there was little wind for two weeks prior to the fabulous catch. These conditions lead to surfacing of tullibee and whitefish and such was the case that summer.

Fishing the Mighty Muskie

Weather conditions are said to play an important part in muskie fishing with some of the most productive angling occurring after a few days of extremely hot, humid weather when the water is glass calm. Remembering the conditions which prevailed before the muskie dilemma most Leech Lake enthusiasts look forward to a day following a period of 3 to 5 days of hot, humid weather during July and August. Some say the best time of the day is afternoon.

Where do Muskies Hide Out?

Muskies usually lurk in very dense weed beds in 6 to 15 feet of water, but in some lakes during hot weather, they are found at depths of 60 to 70 feet. Muskies prefer to lie in wait in weed beds which shelter and attract smaller fish, or near a place where other fish are apt to swim by such as near the mouth of feeder streams. They are also found under over-hanging tree trunks and frequent drop-offs at 6 to 30 feet or more depending on the season. In rivers, they are partial to quiet backwaters and sheltered places where there is a thick cover of vegetation. Flowages are especially good muskie waters.

You might expect a predatory fish like the muskie to snap at slow-moving baits as it lies in wait to ambush its food - yet it doesn't work this way. Nothing excites a muskie more than a lively lure teased along the water's surface. Top-water plugs are very effective. Next to plugs, large casting spinners with a bucktail trailer are preferred by many specialists. Others fish for them with a large sucker as bait. Muskies are solitary and will stay in one place unless driven out, so more than one cast in the same place may produce a strike.

Managing Minnesota's Muskies

More lakes suitable for muskies will be located and stocked as the Natural Resources Department's lake survey program progresses. Usually such lakes are those that contain few or no northerns.

The two species do not get along well particularly in smaller lakes. For one thing, both are fish-eaters and have about the same food habits. But most important, muskies spawn when the water temperature reaches about 47 to 48 degrees F., or two to four weeks after northerns spawn. Also, muskies mature more slowly reaching spawning age at five years, or one to three years after northerns. If the young of both kinds are present, the northerns will be larger and apt to feed on their smaller cousins.

To develop Minnesota's muskie program, about 20 lakes have been selected where muskies have been introduced to build up brood stock to obtain eggs for propagation.

Besides being two of Minnesota's most challenging and sporting game fishes, the northern pike and the muskie are both delectable dinner rewards. Through good management, they will continue to supply countless hours of pleasure both for those of us who live in Minnesota and to our out-of-state visitors.

How to Catch a Walleye

Walleyes are taken by a number of methods; still fishing with live minnows, trolling with live minnows, or with a number of different artificial lures—plugs, spoons, jigs—as well as frogs and nightcrawlers.

All in all, the old standby minnow, about 2½ to 3 inches, is still the most popular bait, but it must be lively and it must be fished deep! But don't forget the faithful nightcrawler.

Frogs, too, are popular. Use a plain hook or special frog harness. Frogs are especially effective in the fall when the shallow water begins to cool and the larger walleyes begin coming in-shore.

On our large expanses of prime walleye territory such as Lake of the Woods where launches with guides take numerous anglers, walleye fishing is usually done by trolling with minnows. An ordinary casting rod and reel are favored by many fishermen, but spin fishing equipment is also popular.

Walleyes are night-feeders and, when the sun goes down come in to shallow water on sand bars, reefs and drop-offs particularly those with gravel or rock bottoms where they feast primarily on young-of-the-year perch. These are the favorite hideouts of this fine piscatorian. Also, try the point where a stream enters the lake.

Early morning and late evening fishing are usually the most effective especially during the winter months. During the day, walleyes retreat to deeper holes. When day fishing, if deep trolling fails to score, still fishing just off the bottom of the deep places is apt to be the key to success.

An overcast sky and uncalm water seem to be the most productive conditions for walleye fishing. But this varies. Some fine stringers have been taken even when the water is calm and the day bright. And that's what makes fishing a challenge—any theory can be upset.

In the winter, live minnows fished nearly on the bottom are used almost exclusively.

Like other perch, walleyes travel in schools—a characteristic which adds to their popularity with the fishing fraternity. Once one is hooked, chances are there will be more.

Contour maps of lake bottoms have been prepared by the Department of Natural Resources and cover most of Minnesota's important walleye waters. These maps locate the bottom features - holes, reefs, drop-offs and deep areas - so important to walleye fishing. They are available from the Department of Administration, Documents Section, Room 140 Centennial Office Building, St. Paul, Minnesota 55101 at one dollar per map.

Minnesota Fishing Facts

There are 144 different species of fish in Minnesota living in 2.6 million acres of water. Of Minnesota's 12,054 lakes, 4,000 of them are considered fishable and 142 are reclaimed trout lakes. We have 15,000 miles of fishable streams, of which 1,600 miles are trout streams. There are 2 million anglers.

The annual fish harvest (angling) is 25 to 30 million pounds. 18 hatcheries raise and stock a total of 250 million fish. An annual stocking of walleye, northern pike, muskellunge, bass, panfish, catfish and trout in managed waters helps improve fishing. There are 222 walleye rearing ponds, 146 northern pike spawning areas, and 18 muskie rearing ponds.

The economic impact of sport fishing is $520 million or $260.00 average per angler. Commercial fisheries harvest 10 million pounds of fish annually at a value of one million dollars.

Fish

Fish species	144
Fishing waters	2,600,000 acres
Fishable lakes	4,000
Fishable streams	15,000 miles
Trout streams	1,600 miles
Trout lakes (reclaimed)	142
Number of anglers	2,000,000
Annual fish harvest— commercial	10,000,000 pounds
Annual fish harvest— anglers	25,000,000—30,000,000 pounds
Fish hatcheries	18 (5 trout, 3 muskie, 10 walleye)
Fish raised and stocked	250,000,000
Walleye rearing ponds	222
Northern Pike spawning areas	146
Muskie rearing ponds	18
Fish trapping and rescue sites	150
Annual economic impact —sport fishing	$520,000,000

Source: **Minnesota Department of Natural Resources, Fish and Wildlife Division.**

HUNTING IN MINNESOTA: AN OVERVIEW

Both the hunted and the hunter have fared well in Minnesota. The richness that was—the vast wilderness, sliced with waterways and secluded marshes, the transition line to the prairielands and the prairielands themselves—gave Minnesota a vast variety of animal and bird life.

It was so vast that a young nation, hellbent to cut and dam and control the land's wild forces somehow could not completely dominate Minnesota nor leave its boundaries irreparably harmed.

Of course there were some casualties—many well known. The buffalo that once roamed much of southern Minnesota was used as a pawn in the Indian Wars. And the big beast was destined to be harnessed within barbed wire, no longer free to roam in gigantic herds.

Elk was a prairie animal and once native to Minnesota. Caribou perhaps traveled the state's northern reaches. Antelope shared the prairies.

The prairie chicken—a colorful grassland dancer—was abundant. And as parts of the prairie were sliced by the pioneer's plows, the prairie chicken population exploded, enough to darken the sky. But as the plow bit into the earth and more farmers settled in Minnesota, the tide of the prairie chicken was turned. For with little prairie left, the bird was out of a home.

The forests of the north were plundered; the furbearers were trapped by the carloads; the predators, timber wolves and the like, were considered enemies and open warfare was declared by the early settlers.

But the thoughtless exploitation of Minnesota's natural resources began to slow as the young nation, disturbed by the havoc left in the eastern states, developed a conservation conscience.

Management of wildlife resources replaced senseless eradication. Hunting was controlled; lands for wildlife habitat were preserved: refuges were established.

The whitetail deer populations boomed in the young, rejuvenated forests and the moose started a long slow comeback. Potholes and marshes—invaluable habitats of waterfowl and numerous other wild critters—were maintained by both federal and state programs; of course not before millions of acres were drained and plowed.

Nevertheless, the conservation conscience made headway—slow though it was. The ringnecked pheasant replaced the prairie chicken—the pheasant more capable of surviving in intensely farmed land.

Man the hunter also evolved into man the sportsman. His hunting license money was used to propagate both hunted and non-hunted wildlife. Seasons and regulations controlled the harvest of wildlife to make sure that Minnesota's bounty would be self-sustaining yet provide hunting recreation, food and clothing.

So far the conservation ethic has been largely successful but not without setbacks.

The hunted and the hunter have fared well but many of the same problems which plagued wildlife a half century ago are still very real.

As Minnesota ages and develops, the land remaining for wildlife to live continues to disappear. The ringnecked pheasant, despite its hardy nature, cannot cope with a countryside that is becoming uniformly blackened by the plow.

The valuable timber wolf must have unsettled lands to thrive. The deer needs a young forest; the ruffed grouse prefers a forest of mixed-age trees.

The moose—now plentiful enough to support limited hunting—must also be given forest room to roam.

Ducks need marshes; muskrats, too. The redwings need the cattails; rabbits like brush patches.

It is not a question of if this wild life will continue to thrive in Minnesota.

They will if Minnesotans want them badly enough!

REMINDER

If outdoor users adhere strictly to the new trespass law by carefully avoiding dwellings, livestock areas and crops, a new attitude on the part of landowners toward use of their remaining lands for outdoor recreation should result. This would be of great benefit to everyone and it will happen if everyone considers the rights and needs of others. For those who are law abiding and considerate, the rewards can be greater outdoor opportunities. For the few who ignore the law, strengthened penalties will result in a loss of privileges.

Hunting Regulations for 1987-88

Hunting regulations for big game and small game is released every August. Information may be obtained from:

Minnesota Department of Natural Resources
Division of Fish and Wildlife
Centennial Building
St. Paul, MN 55155

Hunting Facts

Public hunting lands	11 million acres
Wildlife Management Areas	860
Wetlands (DNR Save- The-Wetlands Program)	460,000 acres
Wetlands (U.S. Fish & Wildlife Acquisition Program)	115,000 acres
Wetlands drained	13,000,000 acres
Licensed big game hunters	350,000
Licensed deer archery hunters	32,000
Deer harvest	65,000
Bear harvest	600
Licensed small game hunters	290,000
Small game harvest	3,081,500 (total)
Waterfowl	1,500,000
Ruffed Grouse	500,000
Squirrels	400,000
Pheasants	200,000
Rabbits	200,000
Sharp-tailed Grouse	30,000
Hungarian Partridge	35,000
Woodcock	40,000
Coots	100,000
Wilson's Snipe	25,000
Red Fox	50,000
Coyote	1,500
Licensed trappers	14,000
Value of fur harvest by trapping	$7 million

Source: Minnesota Department of Natural Resources Director of Fish and Wildlife.

The White-Tailed Deer

Fortunate is the person who happens upon a white-tailed deer during daylight hours.

With the scent of danger, the deer raises its tail in a flash of white. Then, with the "flag" waving, the deer is off—a streamlined, soaring, running, leaping, darting beauty whose movements typify the wild and free.

The whitetails of Minnesota are officially known as *"northern white-tailed deer"*.

The Whitetail's Minnesota History

The whitetail is Minnesota's most common big game animal. It is now found in every county of the state. Its major range is the forested area of the northern and northeastern one-third of Minnesota.

Before the lumberjack period, about 1900, deer were rather uncommon in the northern evergreen forests. However, logging and burning removed the mature timber and encouraged the succulent new growth of vegetation upon which deer feed. By 1920, deer were fairly common over much of the northeastern part of Minnesota.

During settlement of the southern counties of Minnesota, unregulated hunting reduced the herd to the extent that by 1880 deer had almost disappeared. At about the turn of the century, the enactment of more restrictive game laws prepared the way for natural restocking of the farmland country.

By the early 1940's, deer had exceeded the carrying capacity of the range in many northern areas and crop damage complaints were frequent in the south. As the herd increased and the food supply dwindled, winter starvation took a heavy toll in many localities.

In more recent times, sound game policies permitting consecutive annual hunting seasons, no restrictions as to the sex or age of the animal which may be taken, and zoning to distribute the kill over the state have kept Minnesota's deer herd in relative balance with the range.

The Deer's Family Life

The deer's life history may be divided into four periods which coincide with our four seasons of the year.

Spring—When the snow disappears from the fields and meadows, the deer disperse as smaller groups from their concentrated wintering areas. They are first attracted to the greens appearing in the clearings. By mid-May, the does seek seclusion as they enter the fawning season following a gestation period of close to seven months.

The fawning site may be almost anywhere—in field, marsh, or wood. Often twin fawns are born, particularly among healthy does from three to six years of age. By the time the beautiful four to eight-pound spotted fawns are born, the buck is off by himself somewhere. The new fawn may likely never see its sire, for the male deer is not a family man.

Within an hour after birth, the fawns are up and about although they remain a bit wobbly for several days. When not nursing, they remain nearly motionless, concealed by protective coloration among the vegetation, while the doe feeds and watches nearby.

A few weeks after birth, the fawns begin to supplement their milk diet with leafy greens, although they will continue to nurse for about four months.

Summer—Summer is the period of relative "plenty" for the deer. Food is abundant and the climate is mild. The deer now regain the weight lost during the winter.

Fall—As summer stretches into autumn, the adult deer exchange the red silky coat of summer for the heavier coarse grey coat of winter. The fawns, now weaned, are losing their white spots and assuming a coat similar to the adults. During October, the bucks once again begin to feel amorous. The fuzzy flesh covering or "velvet" has been rubbed from the antlers by sparring with the brush. The antlers are soon hardened and polished. The buck's neck becomes swollen, and clashed with other male deer are common. This period in which the buck enters the breeding season is also known as the "rutting season".

Generally, the peak of breeding activity in Minnesota occurs during the first half of November, coinciding with the firearms hunting season. Since the adult buck is particularly active at this time, he consistently makes up the greatest portion of the harvest. Normally, adult bucks comprise 40 per cent of the kill, adult females 30 per cent, and male and female fawns about equally making up the remainder of the harvest.

Winter—Following the breeding season, the crisp days of fall are replaced by winter. This is often a period of "want" for the deer herd and at times severe hardship occurs. Once again deer of both sexes and all ages congregate, as accumulated snow and low temperatures accompanied by cold winds, cause them to seek shelter.

Deer Hunting—From 1957 through 1965 the annual deer take increased from 67,000 to 127,000 animals. Throughout this period hunting success generally held above 40 per cent despite an increase of hunters from 180,000 in 1957 to 290,000 in 1965.

Although the number of hunters continued to climb, to a peak of 327,596 in 1975, the effects of several severe winters began to show in declining harvests and lower hunter success. The very bad winter of 1968-69 was reflected in the harvest of only 68,000 deer in the 1969 season. The 1970 season was reduced to two days to begin a restoration of the herd to a more desirable size. Another severe winter followed. In anticipation of poor reproduction, the 1971 season was closed and the 1976 season was restricted to bucks only to rebuild the herd.

Beginning in late December the buck sheds the antlers which he has carried for many months. These antlers have served their purpose, are now useless weight and often somewhat the worse for wear and tear. Antler growth will begin again the next May. Maximum antler development is normally attained when the bucks are in their prime, which occurs at about three to six years of age.

As the severity of the winter increases, the deer "yard" into smaller areas. If the winter is a long one the food supply, now consisting of the twigs and stems of various plants such as dogwood, mountain maple, ash, birch, hazel and willow, may become exhausted and a portion of the herd may be lost. In some years the losses are very great, rivaling the size of the hunter harvest. Even mild winters result in some weight loss among deer.

During periods of starvation, not only is the herd reduced by direct loss of animals, but the reproductive capacity is decreased. During the subsequent fawning period many does may not bear, while others will have a single fawn rather than twins.

With the coming of spring, the deer once again enter the period of recovery as they move out of the swamps where they had retreated to spend the more severe portion of the winter. Life will begin anew for the herd with the approaching fawning season and the pattern of season activity continues as before.

Deer Management

Deer management seeks maintenance of the deer population at a level high enough to make common the enjoyment of seeing deer, and high enough to produce a good crop for harvest by hunters annually. Hunting satisfaction can probably be attained with a somewhat lower population than it takes for the average person to see a deer on occasion.

Within the limits of the land to produce such levels, the size of the deer herd must also be a compromise between the maximum desired for sport and enjoyment, and the most that can be supported without undue damage to other interests such as farms and forest crops and automobile safety.

The principal means of maintaining a desired deer population level are (1) by hunting regulations that either increase or decrease the harvest of deer, and (2) by habitat improvements to increase the capacity of an area to support deer.

Winter food is not a problem in the agricultural areas. Here the deer feed primarily at the expense of the farmer. But there is a limit to how much of this can be allowed. Deer, if they are numerous, can be extremely damaging to crops, especially orchards.

Therefore, in agricultural areas we must maintain the deer herd at a size compatible with people and agriculture.

Setting Hunting Regulations

A number of factor enter into the selection of hunting regulations that will produce the desired effect in any one area. Determinations must be made regarding:

1. The extent to which the number of animals currently on hand is above or below the limit that can be supported by the food supply.
2. Whether it is easy or difficult for hunters to take the number that should be harvested.
3. The number of hunters that can be allowed in an area while maintaining safety for people and private property.

Deciding whether the deer population should be heavily or lightly harvested, or perhaps not hunted at all, depends largely upon management goals regarding the size of the herd that should be carried over from year to year. Unlike upland game birds deer can be "stockpiled". If the herd is to be held stable, about 25 per cent of the deer should be harvested each year. If the herd needs to be reduced, more liberal regulations can be set. If the deer population has declined and hunting has become poor, it may be necessary to reduce, or even stop the harvest to allow the herd to build up again.

A new approach to deer hunting began in 1972 following legislation establishing a deer season framework from November 1 through December 15. A season running the month of November was considered, with each hunter choosing any consecutive three days in which to hunt. Number of days allowed could be increased in the future as the deer herd increases. This type of season would actually reduce the deer harvest by dispersing hunting pressure. It would allow annual seasons while the herd rebuilds and greatly improve hunting quality.

However, there are factors other than hunting that reduce the number of deer. The variable effects of these must also be taken into account. In Minnesota, winter weather is one of the most important influences. A series of winter with relatively little snow will allow the deer to feed better and the resulting larger fawn crops will cause the population to increase despite hunting. This happened in the years 1957-64, making possible a deer harvest that increased each year and a hunting success that held above 40 per cent despite an increase of 60 per cent in the number of hunters from 1957 to 1965.

A winter with abnormally deep snow makes it difficult or impossible for deer to obtain adequate food. This causes the loss of many fawns, before or soon after birth, and the deer herd does not rebuild to the level of the previous hunting season. If several severe winters follow in close succession the population will be drastically reduced.

Deciding whether it is easy or difficult to take a deer in a particular area enters into setting regulations because in the agricultural and semi-agricultural areas of Minnesota deer must concentrate in shelterbelts, small woodlots or river valleys. Since the hunter has an advantage there, that he does not have in the heavily forested areas, the season must be shorter to avoid overshooting.

Maintaining safety for people and property during the hunting season requires regulations that will not create an undue concentration of hunters. This means that if deer numbers require that any part of the state be opened for hunting it is desirable to open the bulk of the deer range as well. In such a situation a very short season would achieve, to a large degree, any reduction of the harvest desired for the general range. A quota system would also control the concentration of hunters.

Habitat improvement, as well as proper hunting regulations, is necessary to maintain a satisfactory deer population in Minnesota. Large deer herds can be supported only where a large portion of the forest is in a brush, reproduction stage. Much of the northern forest is in a brush, reproduction stage. Much of the northern forest has now grown up to the "closed canopy" stage which shades out desirable food plants and shrubs in the understory.

In addition to a maturing forest, Minnesota is faced with natural plant succession toward a spruce-fir forest in many of the northern counties. Spruce-fir, the climax forest of this region, is poor habitat for deer. This natural succession toward evergreens is already far advanced in Cook, Lake, St. Louis, Koochiching, Itasca and Lake of the Woods counties.

To restore these areas as good deer habitat, many sites where balsam fir is invading aspen must be clear cut to set succession back to the aspen sprout stage which produces more deer food.

The goal of deer management in Minnesota is a sustained annual harvest of approximately 100,000 whitetails.

Hunting Tips
The best deer rifle, acceptable ammunition, appropriate clothing, and rights and wrongs of deer hunting are all important considerations in planning a deer hunt.

Scouting and learning the country is very important.

Every hunter should familiarize himself with the hunting regulations printed annually by the Minnesota Department of Natural Resources.

Deer move early in the morning. Movements dwindle by mid-morning then increase again shortly before dark. Trail sitting during these hours, reserving the middle of the day for resting, tracking, stalking or driving, is good strategy. Anticipate movements brought about by the presence of other hunters. Locate and study trails, feeding areas and places where tracks are found. The number of tracks, freshness, direction of prevailing travel are also important.

Whitetails eat leaves and ends of twigs, but normally only small amounts of grass. Important feeding areas are located where food is abundant in brushy or open stands where sunlight gets to the small trees and shrubs. Large stretches of grass with no shrubs are seldom used. Deer use thick stands of timber for bedding down and hiding, but not extensively for feeding. Wait on a runway near heavy cover where the whitetail may move or be driven from feeding places.

Snow greatly increases visibility and is extremely important to success. A hunter sitting motionless beside a well-used runway sees even the smallest movement and over a distance that would be impossible without snow.

Source: Department of Natural Rescources, Bureau of Information and Education.

SPORTSMEN ORGANIZATIONS

Minnesota sportsmen are famed throughout the nation for their enthusiasm and industry in the field of conservation. Not only are they known for their strict adherence to fishing and hunting regulations, but also for their work in improving the amount and quality of natural habitat for wild life.

Three of the more widely known such state groups:

Muskies, Inc.
A dream of St. Paulite Gil Hamm became a reality when 14 people signed the articles of an incorporation formed to further interest in and propagate the muskellunge, *esox masquinongy*, Minnesota's giant game fish.

Now over 2,000 strong, the society has raised and released almost 20,000 yearling having a nearly 100% survival rate in various state lakes.

Those who seek the "living log", as it's called by trophy fishermen, will want to know that the following lakes have been designated muskellunge lakes by the Dept. of Natural Resources: Deer, Little Moose, Pughole, Big Moose, North Star and Spider Lakes in Itasca County; Big Mantrap, Little Sand, Bad Ax, Big Sand, Spider, and Stocking in Hubbard; Baby and Howard in Cass; West Battle in Ottertail; Rush in Chisago, Sugar in Wright and Independence in Hennepin.

Further information may be obtained from Muskies, Inc., 1708 University Ave., St. Paul, MN. 55104

Ducks Unlimited

In a remarkable demonstration of "hands across the border" cooperation and dedication to a common cause, Ducks Unlimited was founded in the U.S. to solicit funds from private sources to provide waterfowl habitat in Canada, where 70% of all the feathered flyers on the North American continent originate.

Federal funds for the purpose cannot be spent on foreign soil, so duck and goose hunters have been donating the wherewithal to this end since 1937.

The Minnesota chapter of this national organization has been in the forefront of the movement to make available more than 3,000 reserve projects. (Two-hundred and twenty-three were completed in Canada in 1980.)

In 1980 alone, Minnesotans contributed $1.3 million for the work.

3.1 million acres of water are now being used for waterfowl protection and growth. Biologists estimate another 8 million acres of habitat will be needed to protect the program from the encroachment of agriculture, industry and urbanization. The Minnesota membership numbers 25,000 (as of 1980) in 95 chapters.

Minnesota Ducks Unlimited headquarters is at 2230 So. Hwy. 100, St. Louis Park, (612) 920-2225.

The Izaac Walton League

The League, named after Izaac Walton, an English writer who published *The Compleat Angler* in 1653, was organized in the U.S. on a national basis in 1922.

Among the society's accomplishments have been the preservation of some 300,000 acres of prime fish and wildlife habitat along the upper Mississippi, saving of western elk herds, and early work on water purity. As a result of their efforts, President Coolidge signed the first water pollution legislation in 1927.

Currently, the state organization has 2200 members and their efforts are devoted to preservation of the Boundary Waters Canoe Area, protection of wildlife habitat and wetland areas and maintenace of numerous nature centers in the state by their 33 chapters, 10 of which are in the Twin Cities and 23 outstate.

Information can be obtained from The Izaac Walton League, 3255 Hennepin Avenue, Minneapolis, MN, (612) 827-5361.

WILDLIFE
Minnesota's Mammals

Eighty different kinds of mammals have been recorded in the state, either living here now, or in the past. They range in size from the tiny **pigmy shrew,** weighing just a few ounces, to the mighty **moose,** over six feet tall and weighing over 1000 lbs. Listed here are the seven orders:

OPPOSSUM (*Order Marsupialia*) They have taken residency here in only recent years, coming northward from southern Minnesota. This is their northernmost range.

MOLES and SHREWS *(Order Insectivora)* In addition to the **pigmy**, the **least**, the shortest of all mammals, and the **water shrew**, so small and light-weight it can run on top of water. Occurring also here are the **cinerous, Richardson** and **shorttailed shrews.**

Unlike shrews, moles spend most of their time underground. There are two varieties of moles in Minnesota - the **star-nose** and the **common mole.**

THE BATS *(Order Chiroptera)* Seven of the nation's different kinds of bats are found in Minnesota—the **little brown-bat, Ken's little brown bat,** the **big brown bat, pipistrelle bat,** the **silver-haired bat, hoary bat** and the **red bat.**

RABBITS AND HARES *(Order Lagomorphia)* The **white-tailed jack rabbit** is the state's largest rabbit. This highly nocturnal animal lives in prairie country and has been timed for several miles running at speeds up to 25 miles per hour. **Snowshoe hares,** so called because the soles of their feet are furred, enabling them to get around in soft, deep snow, live the northern evergreen forests. Minnesota's smallest rabbit, the **cottontail,** lives in the hardwood forests and brush country of southern Minnesota.

THE RODENTS *(Order Rodentia)* This order has the largest number of varieties.

Squirrels and their relatives (Woodchucks, ground squirrels, chipmunks, tree squirrels and **flying squirrels).** The largest, the **woodchuck,** is also known as the **groundhog,** though no-one in Minnesota seems to observe its activities as a prophet about the end of winter.

Richardson's ground squirrel lives mostly on dry prairie.

The **Minnesota Gopher** is a striped ground squirrel with 13 lines alternating from light to dark. It is found throughout most of the state.

The **Franklin's ground squirrel,** or pocket gopher is found in brushy fields and rock piles. The **Eastern Chipmunk** lives off nuts and berries in the brushlands. **Least chipmunks** prefer the evergreen forests. **The Red Squirrel,** the smallest of our tree dwellers, is at his noisy and entertaining best in the northern forests. Bushy-tailed **Gray Squirrels** are common throughout the state, like the **Fox Squirrel,** the largest animal of this kind in the state. Sharp eyed observers may also spot two varities of flying squirrels.

Minnesota has two kinds of true gophers - the **Dakota** and the **Mississippi Valley pocket gophers.** Great diggers, they make burrows along the edges of roads. In a family all by itself is the **pocket mouse.**

The **beaver** is the largest of the rodents. Rare at the turn of the century when trappers had nearly wiped them out, they are now quite numerous. The fearless **porcupine** survives because of his barbed quills.

The largest group of rodents is mice and rats. There are the **harvest mouse, grasshopper mouse, prairie white-footed mouse, Canadian white-footed mouse, northern white-footed mouse, bog lemming, northern bog lemming, red-backed mouse, common meadow mouse, rock vole, prairie vole, pine mouse** and the **muskrat.**

Old world rats and mice occur throughout the world, and Minnesota is no exception. We have the **Norway** or **house rat** and the **house mouse.** The **meadow jumping mouse** and the rare **woodland jumping mouse** are the only jumping mice native to the state.

THE MEAT-EATERS *(Order Carnivora)* Minnesota's largest carnivore, the **black bear,** reaches 250 to 300 pounds, from a mere 12 ounces at birth. They are protected in certain areas but may be hunted during the deer season. Extinct as a wild animal in the state, the **grizzly bear** once lived in the Red River Valley where they followed herds of buffalo. The ring-tailed, black-masked **racoons** population is directly related to the availability of acorns - the more the merrier. Rarely seen are the tree-climbing **pine martens.** On the up-swing are the **fishers,** formerly quite abundant in the forests.

Minnesota has the **least weasel,** the world's smallest carnivore, the **long-tailed weasel,** and the **short-tailed weasel,** whose brown coat in winter turns to white except for the black-tipped tail in which phase they are known as ermines. **Mink** are the state's most valuable fur-bearers, with 50,000 pelts taken annually.

The largest of the weasel clan, the **wolverine** is extinct in the state. However, because of occasional sightings, it is not surprising that some will move down from Canada. The playful and frolicsome **otter,** though trapped to the point of extinction, is making a comeback in the north and is occasionally observed in southern Minnesota. Two versions of the 'pole-cat' or 'woodpussy' are the **striped skunk** or **civet cat.** To meet them is to know them. Except for the northeast, the **badger** digs his den throughout the state. Native to the state are the **red fox** and the **gray fox,** both nocturnal, the latter being most common in southeastern Minnesota.

Coyotes, looking like large-eared, medium-sized German Shepherd dogs, are to be found most anywhere in the state.

Timber, or **gray,** wolves are larger and more heavily bodied than coyotes and prefer the heavy cover of forests. Once found throughout the state, they are limited to the wildest of the north country and their population is estimated to be between 1,200 and 1,500. Their numbers have approximately doubled in the last 10 years.

The **Cougar,** or **mountain lion,** the largest member of the cat family, is the only long-tailed cat in Minnesota. Once roaming throughout the state, especially when deer herds were prolific, the cat was officially reported in Becker County in 1897, but recently has been reported. Though now quite rare, the **Canada lynx** is still taken in small numbers in the northern part of the state. **Bobcats** live in wooded areas of southern Minnesota, and have been seen recently in the northlands.

HOOVED ANIMALS *(Order Artiodactyla)* The **white-tailed deer** is Minnesota's most abundant big-game animal. It is found in all 87 counties, though its main range is in the north and northeast areas. Rare members of this family include the **mule deer** (rarely seen along the Red River) and the **elk,** last appearing in numbers in 1917 in the Lake of the Woods area. In spite of repeated attempts to increase the herds, the number of elk remains at about 10 to 30.

Before extensive lumbering in the 1800s, thousands of **moose** roamed northern Minnesota. The largest of our state deer, the herd had dwindled by 1922 to about 2500 animals. Recent conservation practices have brought the population to the point where the state legislature has authorized the taking of a limited number of moose on an experimental basis. The state's moose population is estimated now at between 6,000 and 7,000. Moose hunting is allowed every other year; there will be a season in 1981 with further information released by the Department of Natural Resources in July or August. Now extinct, the **woodland caribou** was last seen in the boggy area north of Red Lake. In 1967, a herd of four **pronghorn antelope** was seen in southwestern Minnesota. Conservation experts say they have never been regular visitors.

The mighty **buffalo** once were common in the southern two-thirds of the state. Indians stampeded them to their deaths over steep cliffs at what is now Blue Mounds State Park in Rock County and early records tell of 400 killed by LeSueur's party in the 1700's to use as winter food provisions near the present city of Mankato. The last account, in June 1880, reported four buffalo chased over the prairie by Indians in an area which is now the Carlos Avery Wildlife Management Area.

Source: Department of Natural Resources.

Steps to Extinction

Extinction

A species is extinct when it has vanished from the earth. There will never be any more animals of that species. The passenger pigeon is an example.

Extinction is an evolutionary process that was occurring long before man arrived. In 1600, there were about 4,226 species of mammals and 8,684 species of birds in the world. Since then, about 36 mammal and 94 bird species have become extinct.

Following is a breakdown of how these birds and mamals were lost forever:

• About one-fourth of the 130 extinct species disappeared because of the natural evolutionary process of extinction. These species, like dinosaurs and countless other species over the past three billion years, died out because they were unable to adapt to sweeping environmental changes or because of large-scale biological calamities.

• About 75 percent of our extinct species were lost because of the far-reaching activites of man.

From 15 to 17 percent died out because man introduced foreign or exotic species into their ranges.

From 4 to 6 percent were lost because foreign competitive species were introduced into their ranges.

Uncontrolled killing by man has wiped out 42 percent of birds and 33 percent of mammals. Some island species were killed off by sailors for food, fur, feathers, or oil. Some animals were considered pests and poisoned out. Others were killed by over-shooting in the days before hunting regulations were developed.

About 15 percent of birds and 19 percent of mammals disappeared because of habitat destruction—logging, wetland drainage, clearing land for agriculture, and the creation of reservoirs, building sites, and recreation areas.

(It should be emphasized that sport hunting, characterized by designated seasons, shooting hours, bag limits, and license requirements, has not caused the extinction of any bird or mammal species. Nor has regulated trapping of furbearers caused the extinction of any species.)

Extirpation

Many persons confuse the words "extinct" and "extirpated."

Extirpation means that a species has disappeared from part of its original range. For example, it is incorrect to say the trumpeter swan is extinct in Minnesota. If it were extinct, it would not be found anywhere in the world. The trumpeter swan **is**

American elk

Art by Dan Metz

extirpated as a wild species in Minnesota, but it still exist in the wild elsewhere. Moreover, it is neither a threatened nor endangered species when considering its worldwide population.

The gray (timber) wolf is extirpated from many states in its historical range. This fact played heavily in having it designated as an endangered species several years ago. When the gray wolf was classified as endangered, only its continental United States range was considered. However, its total North American range was ignored. Vast areas of Canada and Alaska have healthy wolf populations; likewise, Minnesota's northern forest has a sizeable population of gray wolves. These animals are not in danger of becoming extinct.

When a species becomes extirpated from an area it is sometimes feasible to reintroduce it.

Preventing Extinction

Since about three-fourths of the extinctions since 1600 were caused by man, threatened and endangered species conservation programs have been created at state and federal levels. These programs are designed to help review the status of extirpated species so they might be restored where they were lost.

If a species is in danger of extinction, it undergoes a legal process to become designated as "endangered" so state and federal money can be expended to save it. Recovery plans are drafted and implemented for each species.

If a species is likely to become endangered within the foreseeable future, it undergoes a similar legal listing process to be designated as "threatened." Then money can be allocated to help the species. Recovery plans are also implemented for threatened species.

It is not the goal of state and federal endangered species programs to keep species listed indefinitely. If a program is unsuccessful, a species may become extinct. Some species, like the whooping crane, may recover slowly and be endangered for several decades. Others, like the alligator, may be listed as endangered but after making a significant population recovery, be changed to threatened within a few years. If a recovery plan is successful, it will eventually lead to declassification of the species.

Threatened and endangered species programs will not prevent some species from becoming extinct in the future. But they can play a major role in preventing extinction that would otherwise be caused by human activities.

Species Classification

During the past 15 years, various terms for categorizing species based on rarity and possibilities for future survival have been devised and used by federal and state agencies and private organizations. None is entirely satisfactory. There are semantic difficulties—the words having different shades of meaning for different people. Also, species grouped under any one heading or placed in a single category vary considerably in abundance and prospects for survival.

The following explanatory symbols will be used to list species:

Endangered — En - Classified under federal regulations as endangered.

Threatened — Th - Classified under federal regulations as threatened in the United States. (The gray wolf, however, is not biologically threatened with becoming endangered in either Minnesota or in North America.)

Protected — Pr - Afforded some degree of protection under Minnesota laws, the amount and kind of protection varying with the species.

Unprotected — Un - Specifically "unprotected" under Minnesota laws.

Extinct — Ex - Totally disappeared from the earth.

Extirpated — Disappeared as a breeding species from Minnesota though it still breeds elsewhere.

Peripheral — Pl - Has a large range in North America but whose range includes only a portion of Minnesota.

Rare — Ra - Its range includes either all or much of Minnesota but is rare throughout its range.

Restricted — Re - Restricted to a small range in Minnesota, but not a peripheral range.

Passenger pigeons

Art by Dan Metz

UNOFFICIAL STATUS

The status assigned to each species is temporary and **unofficial.** It is based on the best information available. The state list is, by law, the same as the federal list for Minnesota. There are three federally-designated endangered species in the state: whooping crane, peregrine falcon, and Higgin's eye pearly mussel. Threatened species include the bald eagle and gray wolf.

Endangered Species
(Unofficial List)

Endangered Species. Species in danger of extinction, that are federally listed as endangered, or are extirpated or nearly extirpated as a breeding species in Minnesota.

Common Name	Scientific Name	Classification
Trumpeter swan	*Olor buccinator*	Pr, Re
American peregrine falcon	*Falco peregrinus*	*En, Pr, Et
Whooping crane	*Grus americanus*	*En, Pr, Et
Burrowing owl	*Speotyto cunicularia*	Pr, Et, Pl
Higgin's eye pearly mussel	*Lampsilis higginsii*	*En, Pr, Re
Federal Designation		

Threatened Species
(Unofficial List)

Species that could become endangered with extirpation in Minnesota in the forseeable future, but not necessarily throughout their entire natural range, or species that are federally listed as threatened though their status is secure in Minnesota.

Common Name	Scientific Name	Classification
Bald eagle	*Haliaeetus leucocephalus*	*Th, Pr
Bobwhite quail	*Colinus virginanus*	Pr, Pl
King rail	*Rallus elegans*	Pr, Ra
Piping plover	*Charadrius melodus*	Pr, Pl
Great Gray owl	*Strix nebulosa*	Pr, Pl
Gray (Timber) wolf	*Canis lupus*	*Th, Pr
Federal Designation		

MINNESOTA'S FLORA AND FAUNA

Minnesota is located at a biological crossroads of three great vegetation regions: the western plains and prairies, the northern coniferous forest, and the eastern hardwood forest.

Our North Star State, because of its unique location and climate, even features a touch of the Arctic in our cold northern muskegs, while some plants characteristic of the southern Appalachians are found in our southeastern counties. Then, there are countless lakes, streams and wetlands that provide a great variety of aquatic and marsh plants.

All of these habitat types, their developmental stages, environmental niches, and margins where habitat types merge (econtones), are the homes of many different kinds of plants and animals.

Each type of habitat favors certain kinds of plants and animals, and in turn, the habitat is modified by them.

If we add up the kinds (species) of plants and animals that thrive without care in Minnesota, such wildlings total approximately as follows: 69 Ferns and relatives; 13 Pines and relatives; 1,700 Flowering plants (1,500 of which are native to Minnesota; 80 Mammals; 240 Birds ("regular species"); 27 Reptiles; 18 Amphibians; and 144 Fish.

The above list is of "resident" species, in the sense that they reproduce in Minnesota. However, many of the birds that nest here winter elsewhere, and in this sense are "migratory." The American Eel is an exceptional case since it spends most of its adult life in inland waters, but spawns in the sea.

Most, but not all, of the wild plants are natives. About 200 of our wild flowering plants originally came from other places, especially Eurasia, and are accidental introductions or escaped cultivated plants. Many of these plants thrive in disturbed situations and soils. Some examples are the common dandelion, quack grass, catnip, curled pondweed and ox-eye daisy.

A smaller proportion of wild animals are non-natives. Among the mammals are the house mouse and Norway rat; the alien birds include the English sparrow, starling, common pigeon, ring-necked pheasant, Hungarian partridge, and quite recently, the cattle egret and monk parakeet; introduced fish include the German carp, rainbow trout, and brown trout.

Speed Skating Competition
Source: Courtesy of Minnesota Department of Economic Development

Sports

FROM THE legends of the Vikings to the present day arm wrestling and soccer, the state of Minnesota has had a rich tradition in the world of sports. No doubt the voyageurs raced their canoes as is done today and we know the early woodsmen had birling and tree climbing contests. Scandinavians were skiing cross country and downhill long before it became fashionable. The first ski club was organized in Red Wing and the first water skis were made in Minnesota. Snowmobiling, curling, ice fishing, skiing and ice boating are just not possible in most states but thousands of Minnesotans eagerly look forward to winter just to participate in these sports.

Football's Pudge Hefflefinger and baseball's Chief Bender were Minnesotans who had attained national fame by the turn of the century. Pudge is generally regarded as one of the eleven best football players of all time (along with Bronko Nagurski). The 'chief', a native of Brainerd, is a member of baseball's Hall of Fame.

Other Minnesotans who attained national fame were Bernie Bierman, an outstanding coach (and Bud Grant's mentor); Bronko Nagurski, who became a legend in his own time with the Gophers and the Chicago Bears; Bruce Smith, the only Gopher to win the Heisman trophy; Jeannie Arth who won the U.S. National Doubles championship twice and Wimbledon in 1959 (with Darlene Hard); Cindy Nelson of Lutsen won a bronze medal in the 1976 Olympics. Patty Berg won 83 National Womens Professional Golf Association titles and is a member of Golf's Hall of Fame. Hibbing's Roger Maris hit 61 home runs to break Babe Ruth's record.

From 1924 to 1927 Ole Haugsrud's Duluth Eskimos played in the National Football League with the famous Ernie Nevers on the team. When the NFL expanded in 1961, George Halas of Chicago saw that Ole retained his NFL franchise for Minnesota and Ole became an owner of the Vikings. Since the Eskimos a succession of major league teams have come and gone from the Minnesota scene. After WW II the Minneapolis Lakers came into being and brought national basketball championships to Minneapolis along with George Mikan, Vern Mikkelson and Jim Pollard. When attendance sagged they moved to Los Angeles but kept their name. Metropolitan stadium attracted the Washington Senators to Bloomington for the 1961 season as the Minnesota Twins.

Minnesota Vikings

VIKINGS FACTS

Name: Minnesota Vikings (nickname due to historical ties believed to exist between original Vikings and the area as well as Nordic and Scandinavian ancestry of many area residents).

Franchise Granted — January, 1960

First Season — 1961

Team Colors — Purple and White with Gold trim

Home Field — Metropolitan Stadium, Bloomington (capacity 48,446).

Affiliation — National Football League, National Football Conference, Central Division

Championships — Central Division 1968, 69, 70, 71, 73, 74, 75, 76, 77, 78, 80
NFL Western Division 1969
National Football League 1969
National Football Conference 1973, 74, 76

Club Record—199 wins, 167 losses, 9 ties (26 seasons)

JERRY BURNS
Head Coach

When Jerry Burns was named head coach of the Minnesota Vikings in 1986, Bud Grant passed the team's leadership to a man who had been providing direction since 1968.

Before Burns was selected as only the fourth head coach in Viking history, he had been the offensive coordinator, designing the offensive scheme and, for the most part, calling the plays. He had often been called an innovator and been credited with such things as originating the one-back offense and popularizing the short-passing game.

Thus, the head coaching responsibility was placed into the hands of a man familiar with the organization who possesses a wealth of experience. And it clearly shows. In just his first season as head coach of the Vikings, he led Minnesota to a 9-7 record, finishing second in the NFC Central Division and missing the playoffs by just one game. He is the first Viking coach to have a winning record in his initial season.

Burns has coached in a total of six Super Bowls. He guided the Viking offense during all four of Minnesota's appearances, and he was the defensive backfield coach on two winning Green Bay teams.

VIKINGS REGULAR-SEASON RESULTS

—1961—

37 Chicago (32,236)	13	
7 at Dallas (12,992)	21	
33 at Baltimore (54,259)	34	
0 Dallas (33,070)	28	
24 San Francisco (34,415)	38	
7 Green Bay (42,007)	33	
10 Green Bay (Mwk.—44,112)	28	

17 at Los Angeles (38,594) 31
28 Baltimore (38,010) 20
10 Detroit (32,296) 37
28 at San Francisco (43,905) 38
42 Los Angeles (30,068) 21
 7 at Detroit (42,655) 13
35 at Chicago (34,539) 52

WON 3   LOST 11   **POINTS—285   OPPONENTS—407**

—1962—

 7 at Green Bay (38,669) 34
 7 Baltimore (30,787) 34
 7 at San Francisco (38,407) 21
 0 Chicago (33,141) 13
21 Green Bay (41,475) 48
38 at Los Angeles (33,071) 14
31 Philadelphia (30,071) 21

31 at Pittsburgh (14,642) 39
30 at Chicago (46,984) 31
 6 Detroit (31,257) 17
24 Los Angeles (26,728) 24
12 San Francisco (33,076) 35
23 at Detroit (42,256) 37
14 at Baltimore (53,645) 42

WON 2   LOST 11   TIED 1   **POINTS—254   OPPONENTS—410**

—1963—

24 at San Francisco (30,781) 20
 7 Chicago (33,923) 28
45 San Francisco (28,567) 14
14 St. Louis (30,220) 56
28 Green Bay (42,567) 37
24 at Los Angeles (30,555) 27
10 at Detroit (44,509) 28

21 Los Angeles (33,567) 13
 7 at Green Bay (42,327) 28
34 Baltimore (33,136) 37
34 Detroit (28,763) 31
17 at Chicago (47,249) 17
10 at Baltimore (54,122) 41
34 at Philadelphia (54,403) 13

WON 5   LOST 8   TIED 1   **POINTS—309   OPPONENTS—390**

—1964—

34 Baltimore (35,563) 24
28 Chicago (41,387) 34
13 at Los Angeles (50,009) 22
24 at Green Bay (42,327) 23
20 Detroit (40,840) 24
30 Pittsburgh (39,873) 10
27 at San Francisco (31,845) 22

13 Green Bay (44,278) 42
24 San Francisco (40,408) 7
14 at Baltimore (60,213) 17
23 at Detroit (48,291) 23
34 Los Angeles (31,677) 13
30 at New York (62,802) 21
41 at Chicago (46,486) 14

WON 8   LOST 5   TIED 1   **POINTS—355   OPPONENTS—296**

—1965—

16 at Baltimore (56,562) 35
29 Detroit (46,826) 31
38 at Los Angeles (36,755) 35
40 New York (44,283) 14
37 Chicago (47,426) 45
42 at San Francisco (42,680) 41
27 at Cleveland (83,505) 17

24 Los Angeles (47,426) 13
21 Baltimore (47,426) 41
13 Green Bay (47,426) 38
24 San Francisco (40,306) 45
19 at Green Bay (50,852) 24
29 at Detroit (45,420) 7
24 at Chicago (46,604) 17

WON 7   LOST 7   **POINTS—383   OPPONENTS—403**

—1966—

20	at San Francisco (29,312)	20
23	Baltimore (47,426)	38
17	at Dallas (64,116)	28
10	Chicago (47,426)	13
35	Los Angeles (47,426)	7
17	at Baltimore (60,238)	20
28	San Francisco (45,077)	3

WON 4   LOST 9   TIED 1

20	at Green Bay (50,861)	17
31	Detroit (49,939)	32
6	at Los Angeles (38,775)	21
16	Green Bay (47,426)	28
13	Atlanta (37,117)	20
28	at Detroit (43,022)	16
28	at Chicago (45,191)	41

POINTS—292   OPPONENTS—304

—1967—

21	San Francisco (39,638)	27
3	at Los Angeles (52,255)	39
7	Chicago (44,868)	17
24	St. Louis (40,017)	34
10	at Green Bay (49,601)	7
20	Baltimore (47,693)	20
20	Atlanta (52,859)	21

WON 3   LOST 8   TIED 3

27	New York (44,960)	24
10	Detroit (40,032)	10
10	at Cleveland (68,431)	14
41	at Pittsburgh (23,773)	27
27	Green Bay (47,693)	30
10	at Chicago (40,110)	10
3	at Detroit (44,874)	14

POINTS—233   OPPONENTS—294

—1968—

47	Atlanta (45,563)	7
26	at Green Bay (49,346)	13
17	Chicago (47,644)	27
24	Detroit (44,289)	10
17	at New Orleans (71,105)	20
7	Dallas (47,644)	20
24	at Chicago (46,562)	26

WON 8   LOST 6   TIED 0

27	Washington (47,644)	14
14	Green Bay (47,644)	10
13	at Detroit (48,654)	6
9	at Baltimore (60,238)	21
3	Los Angeles (47,644)	31
30	at San Francisco (29,049)	20
24	at Philadelphia (54,530)	17

POINTS—282   OPPONENTS—242

—1969—

23	at New York Giants (62,900)	24
52	Baltimore (47,900)	14
19	Green Bay (60,740)	7
31	at Chicago (45,757)	0
27	at St. Louis (49,430)	10
24	Detroit (47,900)	10
31	Chicago (47,900)	14

WON 12   LOST 2   TIED 0

51	Cleveland (47,900)	3
9	at Green Bay (48,321)	7
52	Pittsburgh (47,202)	14
27	at Detroit (57,906)	0
20	at Los Angeles (80,430)	13
10	San Francisco (43,028)	7
3	at Atlanta (52,872)	10

POINTS—379   OPPONENTS—133

—1970—

27	Kansas City (47,900)	10
26	New Orleans (47,900)	0
10	at Green Bay (47,967)	13
24	at Chicago (45,485)	0
54	Dallas (47,900)	13
13	Los Angeles (47,900)	3
30	at Detroit (58,210)	17

WON 12   LOST 2   TIED 0

19	at Washington (50,415)	10
24	Detroit (47,900)	20
10	Green Bay (47,900)	3
10	at New York Jets (62,333)	20
16	Chicago (47,900)	13
35	at Boston (37,819)	14
37	at Atlanta (57,992)	7

POINTS—335   OPPONENTS—143

—1971—

16	at Detroit (54,418)	13	9	San Francisco (49,784)	13
17	Chicago (47,900)	20	3	Green Bay (49,784)	0
19	Buffalo (47,900)	0	23	at New Orleans (83,130)	10
13	at Philadelphia (65,358)	0	24	Atlanta (49,784)	7
24	at Green Bay (56,263)	13	14	at San Diego (54,505)	30
10	Baltimore (47,900)	3	29	Detroit (49,784)	10
17	at N.Y. Giants (62,829)	10	27	at Chicago (55,049)	10

WON 11   LOST 3   TIED 0   **POINTS—245   OPPONENTS—139**

—1972—

21	Washington (47,900)	24	37	New Orleans (49,784)	6
34	at Detroit (54,418)	10	16	Detroit (49,784)	14
14	Miami (47,900)	16	45	at Los Angeles (77,982)	41
17	St. Louis (49,784)	19	10	at Pittsburgh (50,348)	23
23	at Denver (51,656)	20	23	Chicago (49,784)	10
10	at Chicago (55,701)	13	7	Green Bay (49,784)	23
27	at Green Bay (56,263)	13	17	at San Francisco (61,214)	20

WON 7   LOST 7   TIED 0   **POINTS—301   OPPONENTS—252**

—1973—

24	Oakland (46,619)	16	26	Cleveland (48,503)	3
22			28	Detroit (48,503)	7
11	Green Bay (48,503)	3	14	at Atlanta (50,850)	20
23	at Detroit (54,418)	9	31	Chicago (48,503)	13
17	at San Francisco (59,359)	13	0	at Cincinnati (59,580)	27
28	Philadelphia (48,503)	21	31	at Green Bay (56,267)	7
10	Los Angeles (48,503)	9	31	Giants at New Haven (70,041)	7

WON 12   LOST 2   **POINTS—296   OPPONENTS—168**

—1974—

32	at Green Bay (56,312)	17	17	at Chicago (55,753)	0
7	at Detroit (49,703)	6	28	at St. Louis (51,392)	24
11	Chicago (46,619)	7	7	Green Bay (48,480)	19
23	at Dallas (60,817)	21	17	at Los Angeles (90,266)	20
51	Houston (48,490)	10	29	New Orleans (48,456)	9
16	Detroit (48,501)	20	23	Atlanta (48,480)	10
14	New England (48,497)	17	35	at Kansas City (72,474)	15

WON 10   LOST 4   **POINTS—310   OPPONENTS—195**

—1975—

27	San Francisco (48,418)	17	38	Atlanta (48,446)	0
42	at Cleveland (65,419)	10	20	at New Orleans (60,214)	7
28	Chicago (48,446)	3	28	San Diego (48,443)	13
29	New York Jets (48,444)	21	30	at Washington (54,311)	31
25	Detroit (48,446)	19	24	Green Bay (48,446)	3
13	at Chicago (56,302)	9	10	at Detroit (78,990)	17
28	at Green Bay (55,279)	17	35	at Buffalo (73,391)	13

WON 12   LOST 2   **POINTS—377   OPPONENTS—180**

Tommy Milton of St. Paul won the Indianapolis "500" in 1921 with an average speed of 89.62 mph, while driving a Frontenac. He also won the 1923 "500" averaging 90.95 mph.

—1976—

40	at New Orleans (58,156)	9
10	Los Angeles (47,310)	10(OT)
10	at Detroit (77,292)	9
17	Pittsburgh (47,809)	6
20	Chicago (47,948)	19
24	N.Y. Giants (47,156)	7
31	at Philadelphia (56,233)	12
13	at Chicago (56,602)	14
31	Detroit (46,735)	23
27	Seattle (45,087)	21
17	at Green Bay (53,104)	10
16	at San Francisco (56,775)	20
20	Green Bay (43,700)	9
29	at Miami (46,543)	7

WON 11   LOST 2   TIED 1   **POINTS—305   OPPONENTS—176**

—1977—

10	Dallas (47,678)	16(OT)
9	at Tampa Bay (66,272)	3
19	Green Bay (47,143)	7
14	Detroit (45,860)	7
22	Chicago (47,708)	16 (OT)
3	at Los Angeles (62,414)	35
14	at Atlanta (59,257)	7
7	St. Louis (47,066)	27
42	Cincinnati (47,371)	10
7	at Chicago (49,563)	10
13	at Green Bay (56,267)	6
28	San Francisco (40,745)	27
13	at Oakland (52,771)	35
30	at Detroit (78,572)	21

WON 9   LOST 5   **POINTS—231   OPPONENTS—227**

—1978—

24	at New Orleans (54,187)	31
12	Denver (46,508)	9 (OT)
10	Tampa Bay (46,152)	16
24	at Chicago (53,561)	20
24	at Tampa Bay (65,972)	7
28	at Seattle (62,031)	29
17	Los Angeles (46,551)	34
21	Green Bay (47,411)	7
21	at Dallas (61,848)	10
17	Detroit (46,008)	7
17	Chicago (43,286)	14
7	San Diego (38,859)	13
10	at Green Bay (51,737)	10 (OT)
28	Philadelphia (38,722)	27
14	at Detroit (78,685)	45
20	at Oakland (44,643)	27

WON 8   LOST 7   TIED 1   **POINTS—294   OPPONENTS—306**

—1979—

28	San Francisco (46,539)	22
7	at Chicago (53,231)	26
12	Miami (46,187)	27
27	Green Bay (45,524)	21 (OT)
13	at Detroit (75,295)	10
20	Dallas (47,572)	36
7	at N.Y. Jets (54,479)	14
30	Chicago (41,164)	27
10	Tampa Bay (46,906)	10
7	at St. Louis (47,213)	37
7	at Green Bay (52,706)	19
14	Detroit (43,650)	7
23	at Tampa Bay (70,039)	22
21	at Los Angeles (56,700)	27 (OT)
10	Buffalo (42,339)	3
23	at New England (54,710)	27

WON 7   LOST 9   TIED 0   **POINTS—259   OPPONENTS—337**

Bruce Smith of Fairibault was the only University of Minnesota player to win the Heisman Trophy. He won it in 1941.

—1980—

24	Atlanta	23
7	Philadelphia	42
34	at Chicago	14
7	at Detroit	27
17	Pittsburgh	23
13	Chicago	7
0	at Cincinnati	14
3	at Green Bay	16
39	at Washington	14
34	Detroit	0
38	Tampa Bay	30
13	Green Bay	25
23	at New Orleans	20
21	at Tampa Bay	10
28	Cleveland	23
16	at Houston	20

POINTS—317 OPPONENTS—308

WON 9   LOST 7

—1981—

13	at Tampa Bay	21
10	Oakland	36
26	Detroit	24
30	at Green Bay	13
24	Chicago	21
33	at San Diego	31
35	Philadelphia	23
17	at St. Louis	30
17	at Denver	19
25	Tampa Bay	10
20	New Orleans	10
30	at Atlanta	31
23	Green Bay	35
9	at Chicago	10
7	at Detroit	45
6	Kansas City	10

POINTS—325 OPPONENTS—369

WON 7   LOST 9

—1982—

17	Tampa Bay	10
22	at Buffalo	23
7	Green Bay at Milw.	26
35	Chicago	7
14	at Miami	22
13	Baltimore	10
34	at Detroit	31
14	New York Jets	42
31	Dallas	27

POINTS—187 OPPONENTS—198

WON 5   LOST 4

—1983—

27	at Cleveland	21
17	San Francisco	48
19	at Tampa Bay (OT)	16
20	Detroit	17
24	Dallas	37
23	at Chicago	14
34	Houston	14
20	at Green Bay (OT)	17
31	at St. Louis	41
12	Tampa Bay	17
21	Green Bay	29
17	at Pittsburgh	14
16	at New Orleans	17
2	at Detroit	13
13	Chicago	19
20	Cincinnati	14

POINTS—316 OPPONENTS—348

WON 8   LOST 8

—1984—

13	San Diego 42	17	at Green Bay (Milw.) 45
17	at Philadelphia 19	21	at Denver 42
27	Atlanta 20	3	Chicago 34
29	at Detroit 28	17	Washington 31
12	Seattle 20	7	at San Francisco 51
31	at Tampa Bay 35	14	Green Bay 38
20	at L.A. Raiders 23		
14	Detroit 16		**POINTS—276 OPPONENTS—484**
7	at Chicago 16		**WON 3 LOST 13**
27	Tampa Bay 24		

—1985—

28	San Francisco 21	21	at Detroit 41
31	at Tampa Bay 16	23	New Orleans 30
24	Chicago 33	28	at Philadelphia 23
27	at Buffalo 20	26	Tampa Bay 7
10	at L.A. Rams 13	13	at Atlanta 14
17	at Green Bay (Milw.) 20	35	Philadelphia 37
21	San Diego 17		
9	at Chicago 27		**POINTS—346 OPPONENTS—359**
16	Detroit 13		**WON 7 LOST 9**
17	Green Bay 27		

—1986—

10	Detroit 13	20	N.Y. Giants 22
23	at Tampa Bay 10	20	at Cincinnati 24
31	Pittsburgh 7	45	Tampa Bay 13
42	Green Bay 7	32	at Green Bay 6
0	at Chicago 23	10	at Houston 23
27	at San Francisco 24	33	New Orleans 17
23	Chicago 7		
20	Cleveland 23		**POINTS—398 OPPONENTS—273**
38	at Washington (OT) 44		**WON 9 LOST 7**
24	at Detroit 10		

Minnesota Twins

The Incredible Minnesota Twins did it. In seven games against the St. Louis Cardinals, the Twins became the World Champions of major league baseball.

In early 1987 baseball pundits suggested the Twins would probably do no better than 4th in the Western Division of the American League. Their inability to hold the lead in tight games was most often used as the strongest argument against the Twins showing significant improvement over their 1986 record.

The addition of Dan Gladden and Jeff Reardon were the two most highly acclaimed players added in the offseason. Reardon's somewhat shaky start didn't do much to add optimism to even the most optimistic fans. As a relief pitcher he was to "close-out" those games in which the Twins were hanging on to slim leads or to keep the Twins close in games where they could rally and win. Sometimes he was unable to do so.

Dan Gladden's performance and the performances of the other new players didn't always inspire confidence. It seemed as though there would be little improvement over the past.

Tom Kelly was also new at managing in the big leagues.

Liked and respected by the players, Kelly was the youngest manager in the majors. His inexperience was used as another argument against season long Twins success. He was a tad unorthodox too.

Sportswriters, managers and players from other teams, would often speculate about his decisions in game situations.

However, the Twins won. From the beginning of the season they showed potential to at least be an entertaining team to watch.

Solid hitting, anchored by the quartet of Gaetti, Puckett, Hrbek and Brunanski, who became known as the "Fab Four" consistently produced a half dozen runs per game.

Frank Viola began to show the kind of consistency as a starting pitcher the Twins needed. Bert Blyleven, the crafty veteran who had started his career with the Twins the last time they were in the playoffs, seemed to always come through in the must games. And the bullpen began to solidify. Especially, Berenguer in long relief and Reardon as the "stopper".

What also became apparent by mid-season was that this time was not being carried by one or two players.

Headlines in the sports pages heralded almost every one of the 24 man roster.

With one week to go in the season the Twins clinched a tie for the Western Division championship in the last home game of the season. The next day they won the title outright by beating the Rangers in Texas.

At the same time the Detroit Tigers were involved in a dogfight with Toronto, emerging narrowly as the champs in the east. And they moved into the playoffs as the heavy favorite to meet either St. Louis or San Francisco.

Detroit dropped the first two games in the Metrodome and lost two of three at home. Gary Gaetti was named the most valuable player.

It was during the playoffs that the Twins fans and the "homer hanky" became nationally known. Several weeks prior to the playoffs, homer hankys were distributed to fans as a give-away by the Star/Tribune newspaper. The hankys caught on with fans and along with cheering, which tested the limits of decible meters, the Twins players began talking about the 25th player in the stands.

The Cardinals came to town as the representative of the National League and the heavy favorites to win the series in "probably 5 or 6 games."

The first two games weren't even close. The Twins blasted the Cards in a 10-1 romp highlighted by a grand slam off the bat of Dan Gladden. The second game wasn't as close as the final score might indicate with the Twins winning 8-4.

The three games in St. Louis were won by the Cardinals, with some less than usual pitching, hitting, and defense in evidence.

Returning to the Metrodome, the Twins evened the series at three games apiece with Kent Hrbek hitting the series second grand slam over the center field wall.

The final game had all the drama any fan would ever want. Three Twins were thrown out at home plate. The winning run was scored on an infield hit by Greg Gagne. Viola pitched 8 masterful innings with the only runs scored against him coming in the second inning. And, as had happened so many times during the year, Reardon shut down the Cards in the ninth with the final out coming on McGee's ground ball to Gary Gaetti.

Two days later more than 300,000 fans lined the streets in Minneapolis and St. Paul and the Capitol Grounds to celebrate Minnesota's first major league baseball world championship.

Through it all the Twins coaches and manager Tom Kelly talked about "teamwork", and the players talked about the fans. . .the 25th player.

On October 29th, 1987 in the White House Rode Garden, President Reagan honored the Twins, and invited the former Calvin Griffith franchise to return to Washington D.C. . . . . . ."if you ever want to leave the beautiful state of Minnesota and its marvelous fans."

WORLD SERIES COMPOSITE BOXSCORE

Minnesota wins series 4-3
Batting

St. Louis	ab	r	h	2b	3b	hr	rbi	avg		Minnesota	ab	r	h	2b	3b	hr	rbi	avg
e-Pendleton dh	7	2	3	0	0	0	1	.429		bhnt-Smalley ph	2	0	1	1	0	0	0	.500
Pena c	22	2	9	1	0	0	4	.409		Lombardozzi 2b	17	3	7	1	0	1	4	.412
McGee cf	27	2	10	2	0	0	4	.370		jp-Baylor dh	13	3	5	0	0	1	3	.385
q-Lindeman 1b-rf	15	3	5	1	0	0	2	.333		Puckett cf	28	5	10	1	1	0	3	.357
Lake c	3	0	1	0	0	0	1	.333		Laudner c	22	4	7	1	0	1	4	.318
v-Ford rf	13	1	4	0	0	0	2	.308		Gladden lf	31	3	9	2	1	1	7	.290
Herr 2b	28	2	7	0	0	1	1	.250		Gaetti 3b	27	4	7	2	1	1	4	.259
Oquendo rf-3b	24	2	6	0	0	0	2	.250		Hrbek 1b	24	4	5	0	0	1	6	.208
r-Pagnozzi dh	4	0	1	0	0	0	0	.250		Gagne ss	30	5	6	1	0	1	3	.200
Driessen 1b	13	3	3	2	0	0	1	.231		Brunansky rf	25	5	5	0	0	0	2	.200
Smith ss	28	3	6	0	0	0	2	.214		cmu-Newman 2b	5	0	1	0	0	0	0	.200
Coleman lf	28	5	4	2	0	0	2	.143		fos-Bush dh	6	1	1	1	0	0	2	.167
Lawless 3b	10	1	1	0	0	1	3	.100		adgk-Larkin 1b	3	1	0	0	0	0	0	.000
Cox p	2	0	0	0	0	0	0	.000		Straker p	2	0	0	0	0	0	0	.000
Forsch p	2	0	0	0	0	0	0	.000		Blyleven p	1	0	0	0	0	0	0	.000
Morris rf	2	0	0	0	0	0	0	.000		i-Davidson rf	1	0	0	0	0	0	0	.000
Tudor p	2	0	0	0	0	0	0	.000		Viola p	1	0	0	0	0	0	0	.000
Dayley p	1	0	0	0	0	0	0	.000		Atherton p	0	0	0	0	0	0	0	.000
Mathews p	1	0	0	0	0	0	0	.000		Berenguer p	0	0	0	0	0	0	0	.000
Horton p	0	0	0	0	0	0	0	.000		Frazier p	0	0	0	0	0	0	0	.000
l-Johnson pr	0	0	0	0	0	0	0	.000		Niekro p	0	0	0	0	0	0	0	.000
Magrane p	0	0	0	0	0	0	0	.000		Reardon p	0	0	0	0	0	0	0	.000
Tunnell p	0	0	0	0	0	0	0	.000		Schatzeder p	0	0	0	0	0	0	0	.000
Worrell p	0	0	0	0	0	0	0	.000										
Totals	232	26	60	8	0	2	25	.259		**Totals**	238	38	64	10	3	7	38	.269

Pitching

St. Louis	g	ip	h	r	er	bb	so	era
Worrell	4	7	6	1	1	4	3	1.29
Dayley	4	4¾	2	1	1	0	3	1.93
Tunnell	2	4⅓	4	2	1	2	1	2.08
Mathews	1	3⅔	2	1	1	2	3	2.46
Tudor 1-1	2	11	15	7	7	3	8	5.73
Horton	2	3	5	2	2	0	1	6.00
Cox 1-2	3	11⅔	13	10	10	8	9	7.71
Magrane 0-1	2	7⅓	9	7	7	5	3	8.59
Forsch 1-0	3	6⅓	8	7	7	5	3	9.95
Totals	7	59	64	38	37	29	36	5.64

Saves — Worrell 2, Dayley.

Minnesota	g	ip	h	r	er	bb	so	era
Reardon	4	4⅔	5	0	0	0	3	0.00
Frazier	1	2	1	0	0	0	2	0.00
Niekro	1	2	1	0	0	1	1	0.00
Blyleven 1-1	2	13	13	5	4	2	12	2.77
Viola 2-1	3	19⅓	17	8	8	3	16	3.72
Straker	2	9	9	4	4	3	6	4.00
Schatzeder 1-0	3	4⅓	4	3	3	3	3	6.23
Atherton	2	1⅓	0	1	1	1	0	6.75
Berenguer 0-1	3	4⅓	10	5	5	0	1	10.39
Totals	7	60	60	26	25	13	44	3.75

Save — Reardon.

St. Louis . . . . 141 823 520—26
Minnesota . . . . 221 (13)87 140—38

Fielding

St. Louis	po	a	e
Pendleton	0	0	0
Pena	32	1	1
McGee	21	1	1
Lindeman	28	2	3
Lake	8	1	0
Ford	5	0	0
Herr	23	17	1
Oquendo	8	10	0
Pagnozzi	0	0	0

Minnesota	po	a	e
Smalley	0	0	0
Lombardozzi	9	24	0
Baylor	0	0	0
Puckett	15	1	1
Laudner	46	2	0
Gladden	12	0	0
Gaetti	6	15	0
Hrbek	68	2	0
Gagne	6	20	2

	po	a	e		po	a	e
Driessen	27	1	0	Brunansky	14	0	0
Smith	7	19	0	Newman	1	2	0
Coleman	10	2	0	Bush	0	0	0
Lawless	3	6	1	Larkin	1	0	0
Cox	1	1	0	Straker	1	0	0
Forsch	1	0	0	Blyleven	0	1	0
Morris	2	0	0	Davidson	0	0	0
Tudor	0	4	0	Viola	1	5	0
Dayley	0	0	0	Atherton	0	0	0
Mathews	0	1	0	Berenguer	0	0	0
Horton	0	1	0	Frazier	0	1	0
Johnson	0	0	0	Niekro	0	1	0
Magrane	1	1	0	Reardon	0	0	0
Tunnell	0	1	0	Schatzeder	0	0	0
Worrell	0	0	0				
Totals	177	69	6	Totals	180	74	3

Source: St. Paul Pioneer Press Dispatch

TWINS' ALL-STAR GAME PLAYERS

ALLISON, Bob, of, 1b 1963-64
BATTEY, Earl, c 1962-62-63-65-66
BLYLEVEN, Bert, p 1973-85
BRUNANSKY, Tom, of 1971
CARDENAS, Leo, ss 1971
CAREW, Rod, 2b, 1b 1967-68-69-70-71-72-73-74-75-76-77-78
CHANCE, Dean, p 1967
CORBETT, Doug, p 1981
ENGLE, Dave, c 1984
GRANT, Jim, p 1965
HALL, Jimmie, of 1964-65
HISLE, Larry, of 1977
HRBEK, Kent, 1b 1982
KAAT, Jim, p 1962-66
KILLEBREW, Harmon, 3b, 1b, of 1961-61-63-64-65-66-67-68-69-70-71
LANDREAUX, Ken, of 1980
OLIVA, Tony, of 1964-65-66-67-68-69-70-71
PASCUAL, Camilo, p 1961-62-62-64
PERRY, Jim, p 1970-71
PUCKETT, Kirby, of 1986-87
ROLLINS, Rich, 3b 1962-62
ROSEBORO, John, c 1969
SMALLEY, Roy, ss 1979
VERSALLES, Zoilo, ss 1963-65
WARD, Gary, of 1983
WYNEGAR, Butch, c 1976-77

World Series History

1903/Boston (AL) def. Pittsburgh (NL), 5-3.
1904/No series.
1905/N.Y. (NL) def. Philadelphia (AL),4-1
1906/Chicago (AL) def. Chicago (NL),4-2
1907/Chicago (NL) def. Detroit (AL),4-0-1
1908/Chicago (NL) def. Detroit (AL),4-1
1909/Pittsburgh (NL) def. Detroit (AL),4-3
1910/Philadelphia (AL) def. Chicago (NL),4-1
1911/Philadelphia (AL) def. N.Y. (NL),4-2
1912/Boston (AL) def. N.Y. (NL),4-3-1
1913/Philadelphia (AL) def. N.Y. (NL),4-1
1914/Boston (NL) def. Philadelphia (AL),4-0
1915/Boston (AL) def. Philadelphia (NL),4-1
1916/Boston (AL) def. Brooklyn (NL),4-1
1917/Chicago (AL) def. N.Y. (NL),4-2
1918/Boston (AL) def. Chicago (NL),4-2
1919/Cincinnati (NL) def. Chicago (AL),5-3
1920/Cleveland (AL) def. Brooklyn (NL),5-2
1921/N.Y. (NL) def. N.Y. (AL),5-3
1922/N.Y. (NL) def. N.Y. (AL),4-0-1
1923/N.Y. (AL) def. N.Y. (NL),4-2
1924/Washington (AL) def. N.Y. (NL),4-3
1925/Pitt. (NL) def. Washington (AL),4-3
1926/St. Louis (NL) def. N.Y. (AL),4-3
1927/N.Y. (AL) def. Pittsburgh (NL),4-0
1928/N.Y. (AL) def. St. Louis (NL),4-0
1929/Philadelphia (AL) def. Chicago (NL),4-1
1930/Philadelphia (AL) def. St. Louis(NL),4-2
1931/St. Louis (NL) def. Philadelphia(AL),4-3
1932/N.Y. (AL) def. Chicago (NL),4-0
1933/N.Y. (NL) def. Washington (AL),4-1
1934/St. Louis (NL) def. Detroit (AL),4-3
1935/Detroit (AL) def. Chicago (NL),4-2
1936/N.Y. (AL) def. N.Y. (NL),4-2
1937/N.Y. (AL) def. N.Y. (NL),4-1
1938/N.Y. (AL) def. Chicago (NL),4-0
1939/N.Y. (AL) def. Cincinnati (NL),4-0
1940/Cincinnati (NL) def. Detroit (AL), 4-3
1941/N.Y. (AL) def. Brooklyn (NL),4-1
1942/St. Louis (NL) def. N.Y. (AL),4-1
1943/N.Y. (AL) def. St. Louis (NL),4-1
1944/St. Louis (NL) def. St. Louis (AL),4-2
1945/Detroit (AL) def. Chicago (NL),4-3

1946/St. Louis (NL) def. Boston (AL),4-3
1947/N.Y. (AL) def. Brooklyn (NL),4-3
1948/Cleveland (AL) def. Boston (NL),4-2
1949/N.Y. (AL) def. Brooklyn (NL),4-1
1950/N.Y. (AL) def. Philadelphia (NL),4-0
1951/N.Y. (AL) def. N.Y. (NL),4-2
1952/N.Y. (AL) def. Brooklyn (NL),4-3
1953/N.Y. (AL) def. Brooklyn (NL),4-2
1954/N.Y. (NL) def. Cleveland (AL), 4-0
1955/Brooklyn (NL) def. N.Y. (AL),4-3
1956/N.Y. (AL) def. Brooklyn (NL),4-3
1957/Milwaukee (NL) def. N.Y. (AL),4-3
1958/N.Y. (AL) def. Milwaukee (NL),4-3
1959/L.A. (NL) def. Chicago (AL),4-2
1960/Pittsburgh (NL) def. N.Y. (AL),4-3
1961/N.Y. (AL) def. Cincinnati (NL),4-1
1962/N.Y. (AL) def. San Fran. (NL),4-3
1963/L.A. (NL) def. N.Y. (AL),4-0
1964/St. Louis (NL) def. N.Y. (AL),4-3
1965/L.A. (NL) def. Minnesota (AL),4-3
1966/Baltimore (AL) def. L.A. (NL),4-0
1967/St. Louis (NL) def. Boston (AL),4-3
1968/Detroit (AL) def. St. Louis (NL),4-3
1969/N.Y. (NL) def. Baltimore (AL),4-1
1970/Baltimore (AL) def. Cincinnati (NL),4-1
1971/Pittsburgh (NL) def. Baltimore (AL),4-3
1972/Oakland (AL) def. Cincinnati (NL),4-3
1973/Oakland (AL) def. N.Y. (NL),4-3
1974/Oakland (AL) def. L.A. (NL),4-1
1975/Cincinnati (NL) def. Boston (AL),4-3
1976/Cincinnati (NL) def. N.Y. (AL),4-0
1977/N.Y. (AL) def. L.A. (NL),4-2
1978/N.Y. (AL) def. L.A. (NL),4-2
1979/Pittsburgh (NL) def. Baltimore (AL),4-3
1980/Philadelphia (NL) def. K.C. (AL),4-2
1981/L.A. (NL) def. N.Y. (AL),4-2
1982/St. Louis (NL) def. Milwaukee (AL),4-3
1983/Baltimore (AL) def. Phil. (NL),4-1
1984/Detroit (AL) def. San Diego (NL),4-1
1985/Kansas City (AL) def. St. Louis(NL),4-3
1986/N.Y. (NL) def. Boston (AL),4-3
1987/Minnesota (AL) def. St. Louis (NL),4-3

Twins' Yearly Batting Leaders

Average	Homeruns	Runs-Batted-In
1961-Battey 302	Killebrew 46	Killebrew 122
1962-Rollins 298	Killebrew 48*	Killebrew 126*
1963-Rollins 307	Killebrew 45*	Killebrew 96
1964-Oliva 323*	Killebrew 49*	Killebrew 111
1965-Oliva 321*	Killebrew 25	Oliva 98
1966-Oliva 307	Killebrew 39	Killebrew 110
1967-Carew 292	Killebrew . . . . 44 +	Killebrew 113
1968-Oliva 289	Alison 22	Oliva 68
1969-Carew 332*	Killebrew 49*	Killebrew 140*
1970-Oliva 325	Killebrew 41	Killebrew 113
1971-Carew 337*	Killebrew 28	Killebrew 119*
1972-Carew 318*	Killebrew 26	Darwin 80
1973-Carew 350*	Darwin 18	Oliva 91
1974-Carew 364*	Darwin 25	Darwin 94
1975-Carew 359*	Ford 15	Carew 80
1976-Carew 330	Ford 20	Hisle 96
1977-Carew 388*	Hisle 28	Hisle 119*
1978-Carew 333*	Smalley 19	Ford 82
1979-Landreaux . . .305	Smalley 24	Smalley 95
1980-Castino 302	Castino 13	Castino 64
1981-Castino 268	Smalley 7	Hatcher 37
1982-Hrbek 301	Ward 28	Hrbek 92
1983-Hrbek 297	Brunansky 28	Ward 88
1984-Hrbek 311	Brunansky 32	Hrbek 107
1985-Puckett 288	Brunansky 27	Hrbek 93
1986-Puckett 328	Gaetti 34	Gaetti 108
1987-Puckett 332	Hrbek 34	Gaetti 109

(*-Denotes league-leadership;   + -Denotes tie for leadership.)

TOBACCO CHEWING CURE

An exchanger says a man who chewed 20ᶜ worth of tobacco a week concluded to try the tobacco cure. In 2 weeks he ate up $1.50 worth of the cure and for the next 2 weeks he used 10ᶜ worth of candy, 5ᶜ of chewing gum, 5ᶜ worth of peanuts, 5ᶜ worth of cough drops per day. And during these 2 weeks he also consumed 2 large rubber erasers, ate the rubber tips from 14 lead pencils, chewed up a dozen penholders and browsed off his mustache as high as he could reach. He is now chewing tobacco again in the interest of economy.

"Spectator" June, 1895 St. Hilaire, Minnesota

Standing of Twins
Year-By-Year

Year	Won	Lost	Pct.	Pos.	Manager	Home Attend.
1961 70	90	.438	7	Lavagetto-Mele	1,256,722
1962 91	71	.562	2	Mele	1,433,116
1963 91	70	.565	3	Mele	1,406,652
1964 79	83	.488	*6	Mele	1,207,514
1965 102	60	.630	1	Mele	1,463,268
1966 89	73	.549	2	Mele	1,259,374
1967 91	71	.562	**2	Mele-Ermer	1,483,547
1968 79	83	.488	7	Ermer	1,143,257
1969 97	65	.599	1	Martin	1,349,327
1970 98	64	.605	1	Rigney	1,261,887
1971 74	86	.463	5	Rigney	940,858
1972 77	77	.500	3	Rigney-Quilici	797,901
1973 81	81	.500	3	Quilici	907,499
1974 82	80	.506	3	Quilici	662,401
1975 76	83	.478	4	Quilici	737,156
1976 85	77	.525	3	Mauch	715,394
1977 84	77	.522	4	Mauch	1,162,727
1978 73	89	.451	4	Mauch	787,878
1979 82	80	.506	4	Mauch	1,070,521
1980 77	84	.478	3	Mauch-Goryl	769,206
1981 . . .1st . . .17	39	.304	7	Goryl-Gardner	469,090
2nd 24	29	.453	4	Gardner	
1982 60	102	.370	7	Gardner	921,186
1983 70	92	.432	*5	Gardner	858,939
1984 81	81	.500	*2	Gardner	1,598,692
1985 77	85	.475	*4	Gardner-Miller	1,651,814
1986 71	91	.438	6	Miller-Kelly	1,255,453
1987 85	77	.525	1	Kelly	2,081,000
Totals	2163	2140	.503			30,652,371

* *Denotes Tie*

MINNESOTA NORTH STARS HISTORY

The Minnesota North Stars have experienced both the ecstasy of triumph and the throes of defeat during the course of their 20-season existence, but their indomitable spirit has made them a noted and respected team in the NHL.

On March 11, 1965 NHL President Clarence Campbell announced that the six-team league would expand. Hearing this news, a group of nine Twin City businessmen joined in a partnership to support a NHL franchise. On February 9, 1966 they learned Minnesota would become one of the six new teams in the NHL's West Division.

Plans were swiftly put into motion and ground was broken for a $7 million Met Center on October 3, 1966. The structure was erected in just more than 12 months, in time for the North Stars' maiden season in the league.

Wren Blair was named the team's first general manager (later first coach) and masterminded the selection of 20 players at a cost of $2 million in the NHL's Expansion Draft on June 6, 1967.

Plunging into their first season, the North Stars became a Cinderella success story finishing just four points out of first in the West Division, winning their quarter-final series, and battling St. Louis to the finish in the semifinals, falling just short in their seventh game.

After missing the playoffs in 1968-69, the team advanced to post-season play the next four years in succession, one under the coaching of Charlie Burns, the latter three under the guidance of Jack Gordon. The North Stars carried eventual Stanley Cup champion Montreal to six games in the 1971 semifinals and became the first post 1967 team ever to win a playoff game from one of the original six clubs.

Gordon replaced Blair as general manager after the 1973-74 season. The club missed the playoffs until the 1976-77 season when Ted Harris coached the club to a preliminary round berth against Buffalo.

Lou Nanne was named general manager in February of 1978 and also acted as coach during the remainder of the season. Despite finishing last overall in 1977-78, the floundering Stars' revival had been set in motion.

Further transformation of the club took place later that summer when George Gund III and Gordon Gund assumed complete control of the team, replacing the nine owners of the Stars. George and Gordon Gund are co-chairmen of the board. John Karr is president. Lou Nanne stayed on as general manager and began to meld together a team from the merger.

The Stars' finishing dead last in the Smythe Division at the conclusion of the 1977-78 season may have been a blessing in disguise, for they were rewarded with Bobby Smith, the number one draft choice overall. In his rookie season, the lanky center earned himself 74 points. This impressive finish also earned him the Calder Trophy.

Through further intuitive draft picks and the combined talents of the merged teams, the North Stars rose from the cellar to sixth overall in 1979-80, advancing to the semifinals against Philadelphia, after ousting Montreal in the quarterfinals.

The Stars' success was due in part to the man behind the bench, coach Glen Sonmor. When Sonmor came to the Stars in 1978 from Birmingham, he faced quite a task, but Glen utilized his vast reservior of hockey knowledge to put the North Stars back on a winning trail.

The North Stars reached their pinnacle of success in 1981 as they surged through three rounds of playoffs, reaching the acme when they attempted to topple the reigning Stanley Cup Champions, the New York Islanders, from their perch.

The Minnesotans found new heights to conquer during the 1981-82 season. The club won the first divisional championship in the team's history, finishing atop the Norris Division. The North Stars made their ninth appearance in the playoffs, but were eliminated by the Chicago Black Hawks in four games in the first round.

The North Stars amassed 96 points (most in the team's history) while finishing second in the Norris Division during the 1982-83 season. The Minnesotans beat Toronto in the first round of the playoffs, but lost to Chicago in the division final.

After the season, the team signed long time Canadian college coach Bill Mahoney to lead the North Stars from the bench. The North Stars enjoyed success in Mahoney's first season, winning the Norris Division title and advancing to the third round of the playoffs before being eliminated by eventual champion Edmonton. However, the North Stars' slow start (3-8-2) in the 1984-85 season resulted in the return of Sonmor to the bench. Even with Sonmor, Minnesota slumped to its worst finish (62 points) in eight seasons. During the off-season, ex-N.Y. Islander player and assistant coach Lorne Henning became the North Stars' 13th head coach.

Although Henning led the North Stars to within one point of the Norris Division in 1985-86, the North Stars missed the playoffs for the first time in eight seasons in 1986-87. Lorne Henning was fired as head coach, opening the door for Herb Brooks to become the 14th coach of the North Stars on April 23, 1987.

Over the 20 seasons that the North Stars have played in the NHL, they have attracted more than 10 million spectators. The North Stars have built a team with strength, depth and a promising future which keeps hockey fans coming back for more.

ALL-TIME HOME/ROAD RECORD

Season	IN MINNESOTA							ON ROAD						
	GP	W	L	T	GF	GA	PTS	GP	W	L	T	GF	GA	PTS
1967-68	37	17	12	8	103	88	42	37	10	20	7	88	138	27
1968-69	38	11	21	6	98	115	28	38	7	22	9	91	155	23
1969-70	38	11	16	11	120	131	33	38	8	19	11	104	126	27
1970-71	39	16	15	8	104	107	39	39	12	19	8	87	116	32
1971-72	39	22	11	6	120	83	50	39	15	18	6	92	108	36
1972-73	39	26	8	5	154	95	57	39	11	22	6	100	135	28
1973-74	39	18	15	6	144	123	42	39	5	23	11	91	152	21
1974-75	40	17	20	3	133	161	37	40	6	30	4	88	180	16
1975-76	40	15	22	3	121	151	33	40	5	31	4	74	152	14
1976-77	40	17	14	9	134	138	43	40	6	25	9	106	170	21
1977-78	40	12	24	4	123	151	28	40	6	29	5	95	174	17
1978-79	40	19	15	6	143	116	44	40	9	25	6	114	173	24
1979-80	40	25	8	7	180	102	57	40	11	20	9	131	151	31
1980-81	40	23	10	7	166	120	53	40	12	18	10	125	143	34
1981-82	40	21	7	12	202	142	54	40	16	16	8	144	146	40
1982-83	40	23	6	11	170	128	57	40	17	18	5	151	162	39
1983-84	40	22	14	4	179	160	48	40	17	17	6	166	184	40
1984-85	40	14	19	7	147	153	35	40	11	24	5	121	168	27
1985-86	40	21	15	4	161	137	46	40	17	18	5	166	168	39
1986-87	40	17	20	3	150	143	37	40	13	20	7	146	171	33

The University of Minnesota Athletic program has been dominated over the years by football, basketball, hockey and baseball. On the following pages is a statistical representation of the history of these sports at the University.

Further information about these sports or any of the men's or women's intercollegiate athletic programs can be obtained by contacting the University of Minnesota Sports Information Office, Room #208, 516 15th Ave. S.E., University of Minnesota, Minneapolis, Minnesota 55455.

University of Minnesota: Football

The Big Ten Conference

The Big Ten Conference was born on January 11, 1895 when President James H. Smart of Purdue University called a meeting of the presidents of seven midwestern universities at Chicago for the purpose of considering regulation and control of intercollegiate athletics.

Just over a year later, representatives from the University of Chicago, the University of Illinois, the University of Michigan, the University of Minnesota, Northwestern University, Purdue University and the University of Wisconsin met at the Palmer House in Chicago to establish standards and machinery for the regulation and administration of intercollegiate athletics.

ALL-TIME MINNESOTA FOOTBALL COACHING RECORDS

Coach	Seasons	Years	Won	Lost	Tied	Pct
Thomas Pebbles	1	1883	1	2	0	.333
Fred Jones	4	1886-89	6	4	0	.667
Tom Eck	1	1890	5	1	1	.833
Ed Moulton	1	1891	3	1	1	.750
Wallie Winter	1	1893	6	0	0	1,000
Tom Cochrane Jr.	1	1894	3	1	0	.750
Walter Heffelfinger	1	1895	7	3	0	.700
Alex Jerrems	2	1896-97	12	6	0	.667
Jack Minds	1	1898	4	5	0	.444
John Harrison & Bill Leary	1	1899	6	3	2	.682
Dr. Henry L. Williams	22	1900-21	140	33	11	.791
William Spaulding	3	1922-24	11	7	4	.611
Dr. Clarence Spears	5	1925-29	28	9	3	.757
Fritz Crisler	2	1930-31	10	7	1	.588
Bernie Bierman	16	1932-41 & 45-50	93	35	6	.727
George Hauser	3	1942-44	15	11	1	.577
Wes Fesler	3	1951-53	10	13	4	.435
Murray Warmath	18	1954-71	86	78	7	.528
Cal Stoll	7	1972-78	39	39	0	.500
Joe Salem	5	1979-83	19	35	1	.352
Lou Holtz	2	1984-85	10	12	0	.455
John Gutekunst	1+	1986	7	6	0	.538

MINNESOTA ALL-TIME FOOTBALL RECORDS
from 1946

Individual Records
CAREER

Total Offense:
Most Pass-Rush Plays: 999 — Tony Dungy (1973-76)
Most Yards Gained: 5,118 — Rickey Foggie (1984-86).
  1,447 rush, 3,671 pass
Best Avg. Yards Per Play: 6.2 — Rickey Foggie (1984-86)

Rushing:
Most Rushes: 656 — Marion Barber (1977-80)
Most Net Yards Gained: 3,087 — Marion Barber (1977-80)

Passing:
Most Attempts: 722 — Mike Hohensee (1981-82)
Most Completions: 392 — Mike Hohensee (1981-82)
Most Yards Gained: 4,792 — Mike Hohensee (1981-82)
Most HAD Intercepted: 39 — Paul Giel (1951-53)
Most TD Passes: 33 — Mike Hohensee (1981-82)
Best Average Gain: 16.2 — Sandy Stephens (1959-61)
Best Completion Pct.: .571 — Mark Carlson (1977-79, 255 of
  447)

Pass Receiving:
Most Receptions: 95 — Dwayne McMullen (1982-84)
Most Yards Gained: 1627 — Dwayne McMullen (1982-84)
Most TD Receptions: 15 — Dwayne McMullen (1982-85)

Punting:
Most Punts: Frank Mosko (1973-75)
Best Average: 43.5 — Adam Kelly (1983-85)

Pass Interceptions:
Most Intercepted: 12 - Jeff Wright (1968-70)
Most Yards Returned: 255 - Walter Bowser (1968-70)

Punt Returns:
Most Returns: 69 — Mel Anderson (1983-85)
Most Yards Returned: 1,427 — Mel Anderson (1983-85)
Best Avg. Return: 24.9 — Bobby Weber (1974-77)

Kickoff Returns:
Most Returns: 91 — Mel Anderson (1983-86)
Most Yards Returned: 1,965 — Mel Anderson
Best Avg. Return: 24.9 — Bobby Weber (1974-77)

Field Goals:
Most Made: 44 — Paul Rogind (1976-79)
Longest Made: 62 — Chip Lohmiller vs. Iowa 11/22/86

Scoring:
Most Points: 217 — Paul Rogind (1976-79)
Most TDs: 35 — Marion Barber (1977-80)
Most PATs: 94 — Jim Gallery (1980-83)
Most Consecutive PATs: 56 — Paul Rogind (1976-79)

Single Season
Total Offense:
Most Pass-Rush Plays: 427 — Mike Hohensee (1981) 65 rush, 362 pass
Most Net Yards Gained: 2,437 — Mike Hohensee (1981) 11 games

Rushing:
Most Rushes: 247 — Marion Barber (1978)
Most Gross Yards Gained: 1,264 — Darrell Thompson (1986)
Most Yards Lost: 217 — John Hankinson (1965)
Most Net Yards Gained: 1,240 — Darrell Thompson (1986)

Passing:
Most Attempts: 362 — Mike Hohensee (1981)
Most Completions: 210 — Mike Hohensee (1982)
Most Yards Gained: 2-412 — Mike Hohensee (1981)
Most TD Passes: 20 - Mike Hohensee (1981)
Most HAD Intercepted: 19 — Paul Giel (1951) and Mike Hohensee (1982)

Pass Receiving:
Most Receptions: 58 — Chester Cooper (1981)
Most Yards Gained: 1,012 — Chester Cooper (1981)
Most TD Receptions: 7 — Elmer Bailey (1979)

Pass Interceptions:
Most Intercepted: 7 — Jeff Wright (1970)
Most Yards Returned: 203 — Walter Bowser (1970)

Punting:
Most Punts: 77 — Frank Mosko (1973)
Best Average: 46.2 — Adam Kelly (1984) 59 Punts

Punt Returns:
Most Returned: 29 — Terrance Henderson (1982)
Most Yards Returned: 305 — Rick Upchurch (1973)

Kickoff Returns:
Most Returns: 27 — Mel Anderson (1984)
Most Yards Returned: 603 — Mel Anderson (1984)
Best Avg. Return (Min. 10): 27.4 — Bobby Weber (1977)

Scoring:
Most Points: 78 — Jim Perkins (1976)
Most Touchdowns: 13 — Jim Perkins (1976)
Most Field Goals: 18 — Paul Rogind (1977)
Most PATs: 31 — Paul Rogind (1979)

MINNESOTA'S SINGLE SEASON LEADERS

Rushing

Year	Player					Yards
1960	Sandy Stephens	52	20	2	2	305
1961	Sandy Stephens	142	47	13	9	794
1962	Duane Blaska	154	71	11	8	862
1963	Bob Sadek	128	58	6	2	647
1964	John Hankinson	178	86	6	8	1084
1965	John Hankinson	214	111	16	8	1477
1966	Larry Carlson	108	56	5	5	599
1967	Curtis Wilson	76	33	8	6	543
1968	Phil Hagen	157	75	8	4	771
1969	Phil Hagen	208	109	9	6	1266
1970	Craig Curry	228	103	12	6	1315
1971	Craig Curry	266	118	10	9	1691
1972	Bob Morgan	89	32	10	2	475
1973	John Lawing	48	23	6	3	276
1974	Tony Dungy	94	39	7	5	612
1975	Tony Dungy	225	123	14	15	1515
1976	Tony Dungy	234	104	12	4	1291
1977	Wendell Avery	76	33	4	3	461
1978	Mark Carlson	113	64	9	3	736
1979	Mark Carlson	300	177	10	11	2188
1980	Tim Salem	170	81	13	2	887
1981	Mike Hohensee	362	182	12	20	2412
1982	Mike Hohensee	360	210	19	13	2380
1983	Greg Murphy	242	115	16	6	1410
1984	Rickey Foggie	121	57	9	10	1036
1985	Rickey Foggie	141	65	4	7	1370
1986	Rickey Foggie	191	87	7	8	1265

Basketball: U. of Minn.

RECORDS

Year	Conference W	L	Place	All Games W	L	T
1950-51	7	7	4th-T	13	9	
1951-52	10	4	3rd	15	7	
1952-53	11	7	3rd-T	14	8	
1953-54	10	4	3rd-T	17	5	
1954-55	10	4	2nd-T	15	7	
1955-56	6	8	6th-T	11	11	
1956-57	9	5	3rd-T	14	8	
1957-58	5	9	8th-T	9	12	
1958-59	5	9	9th	8	14	
1959-60	8	6	3rd-T	12	12	
1960-61	8	6	4th-T	10	13	
1961-62	6	8	7th	10	14	
1962-63	8	6	4th-T	12	12	
1963-64	10	4	3rd	17	7	
1964-65	11	3	2nd	19	5	
1965-66	7	7	5th-T	14	10	
1966-67	5	9	9th	9	15	
1967-68	4	10	9th-T	7	17	
1968-69	6	8	5th-T	12	12	
1969-70	7	7	5th	13	11	
1970-71	5	9	5th-T	11	13	
1971-72	11	3	1st	18	7	
1972-73	10	4	2nd	21	5	
1973-74	6	8	6th	12	12	
1974-75	11	7	3rd-T	18	8	
1975-76	8	10	6th	16	10	
1976-77*	15	3	2nd	24	3	
1977-78	12	6	2nd-T	17	10	
1978-79	6	12	8th-T	11	16	
1979-80	10	8	4th-T	21	11	
1980-81	9	9	5th-T	19	11	
1981-82	14	4	1st	23	6	
1982-83	9	9	6th-T	18	11	
1983-84	6	12	7th-T	15	13	
1984-85	6	12	8th	13	15	
1985-86	5	13	8th	15	16	

*NCAA declared season forfeited to 0-27

U. of Minn. Baseball

A tradition that began in 1948 remains intact at the University of Minnesota. The tradition. . .that baseball is indeed a full-time program at the major University of the great upper midwest.

Started when the late Dick "Chief" Siebert took the baseball reigns following an outstanding professional career, the same traditions are now being carried on'.

GOPHERS IN THE PROS
(includes signing years, draft or free agent)

Pete Bauer	1986	Mets	Tim Grice	1973	Yankees
Tim McIntosh	1986	Brewers	Ken Schultz	1972	Twins
Bryan Hickerson	1986	Twins	Tom Epperly	1971	Twins
Mike Clarkin	1985	Red Sox	Steve Chapman	1971	Red Sox
Dan VanDehey	1985	Twins	Bruce Erickson	1971	Twins
Jack Schlichting	1984	Dodgers	Dave Carey	1971	Espos
Bill Cutshall	1984	Espos	Phil Flodin	1970	Twins
Doug Kampsen	1984	Reds	Bob Nelson	1970	Yankees
Jim Francour	1984	Dodgers	Al Kaminski	1970	Tigers
Bill Piwinica	1983	Brewers	Mike Walseth	1969	Braves
Terry Steinbach	1983	Athletics	Russ Rolandson	1968	Twins
Tom Steinbach	1983	Mariners	Mike Sadek	1967	Giants
Barry Wohler	1983	Dodgers	Jerry Wickman	1967	Yankees
Greg Olson	1982	Mets	Bob Fenwick	1967	Houston
Ron VanKrevelen	1982	Twins	Neil Weber	1967	Dodgers
Tom Jaremko	1981	Twins	Steve Schneider	1966	Angels
Doug Fregin	1981	Twins	Gary Hoffman	1966	Twins
Tom Smith	1980	Cubs	Ron Roalstad	1966	Twins
Ed Rech	1980	Mets	Jerry Fuchs	1966	Twins
Tarry Boelter	1978	Twins	Frank Brosseau	1966	Pirates
Joe Lentsch	1978	Angels	Bill Davis	1964	Indians
George Dierberger	1978	Twins	Al Druskin	1964	Twins
Bob Blake	1978	Twins	Dewey Marcus	1964	Cubs
Brad Barclay	1978	Twins	Ron Wojciak	1964	Twins
Brian Denman	1978	Red Sox	Dick Mielke	1964	Orioles
Jerry Ujdur	1978	Tigers	Jon Andresen	1963	Twins
Tim Loberg	1977	Twins	Steve Wally	1963	Senators
Paul Molitor	1977	Brewers	John Oster	1963	Twins
Tom Mee, Jr.	1977	Braves	John Stephens	1963	Orioles
Chuck Viscocil	1977	Rangers	Wayne Haefner	1962	Senators
Dan Morgan	1977	Espos	Bruce Evans	1962	Tigers
Steve Comer	1976	Rangers	Wayne Knapp	1962	Senators
Joe Kordosky	1975	Twins	John Erickson	1960	Senators
Mike Fitzenberger	1974	Twins	Jim Rantz	1960	Senators
Jim Moldenhauer	1974	Athletics	Fred Bruckbauer	1959	Senators
Bruce Gustafson	1974	Mets	George Thomas	1957	Tigers
Dave Winfield	1973	Padres	Jerry Thomas	1956	Tigers
John Holm	1973	Angels	Jerry Kindall	1956	Cubs
Tom Buettner	1973	Royals	Paul Giel	1954	Giants
Chris Brown	1973	Rangers			

U. of Minn. Hockey

MINNESOTA HOCKEY ALL-AMERICANS

Year	Name	Position
1940	John Mariucci	Defense
1940	Harold "Babe" Paulson	Forward
1951	Gordon Watters	Center
1952	Larry Ross	Goalie
1954	Ken Yackel	Defense
1954	Jim Mattson	Goalie
1954	Dick Dougherty	Wing
1954-55	John Mayasich	Center
1958	Jack McCartan	Goalie
1958	Dick Burg	Wing
1958	Mike Pearson	Center
1959	Murray Williamson	Wing
1963	Louis Nanne	Defense
1964	Craig Falkman	Wing
1965	Doug Woog	Center
1968	Gary Gambucci	Center
1970	Murray McLachlan	Goalie
1970	Wally Olds	Defense
1975	Les Auge	Defense
1975	Mike Polich	Center
1979	Bill Baker	Defense
1980	Tim Harrer	Wing
1981	Neal Broten	Center
1981	Steve Ulseth	Wing
1985	Pat Micheletti	Wing

HIGH SCHOOL ATHLETICS

The Minnesota State High School League

The Minnesota State High School League was first organized in 1916 as the State High School Athletic Association. Its primary purposes were (1) to promote amateur sports, and (2) to establish uniform eligibility rules for interscholastic athletic contests.

In 1929 it broadened its scope by including all interscholastic athletic activities and added speech and debate. At that time the name was changed to the Minnesota State High School League. Music was added in 1965 and Girls' Athletics in 1969.

The opportunities provided through League-sponsored activities has grown from the original program of football, basketball, track and baseball to include 13 athletic activities for boys; 10 athletic activities for girls.

The League has existed as a non-profit, voluntary association of the public high schools since its inception. In 1960 it was officially incorporated under the laws of the State of Minnesota as a non-profit corporation.

Four hundred and eighty one (481) public and non-public schools in Minnesota belong to the Minnesota State High School League.

REORGANIZATION AND REASSIGNMENT OF SCHOOLS

On April 17, 1975 the member schools of the Minnesota State High School League approved amendments that provided the changes necessary to implement reorganization for two class competition.

The new plan provided that district, region and state competition be conducted in two classes, "A" and "AA", in each of those activities that have more than 50% of the member schools participating in that activity. The largest 128 schools by enrollment will be in the large school or "AA" classification. All other member schools would be in the "A" Class. The "AA" schools were organized into eight regions of sixteen schools each. The "A" schools membership was reassigned into eight regions, each containing four districts, or a total of 32 districts.

Source: All information on high school athletics is from the Minnesota State High School League *Yearbook, 1986-87* and the League's monthly *Bulletin*.

Peter Arness won the 120 yard high hurdle state high school title in 1943 and 1944. He is better known as Peter Graves, star of the television series "Mission Impossible."

STATE BOYS BASKETBALL TOURNAMENT
ALL-TIME RECORDS

Team Records/Tournament—3 Games

Most Points . . . . 250, Minneapolis Roosevelt-1956
Most Field Goals Made . . . . 98, St. Paul Highland Park-1968
Most Rebounds 131, Glencoe-1977

Team Records/Single Game

Most Points . . . . 107, Moorhead (vs. St. Paul Highland Park)-1968
Most Field Goals Made . . . . . 41, Mpls. Roosevelt-1956 and South St. Paul-1970
Most Field Goal Attempts . . . . 81, Granite Falls (vs. Hayfield)-1968
Most Rebounds . . . . 65, Glencoe (vs. Twin Valley)-1977

Individual Records/Tournament—3 Games

Most Points . . . . 113, Randy Breuer, (Lake City)-1979
Most Field Goals . . . . 50, Randy Breuer, (Lake City)-1979
Best Field Goal Percentage . . . . .794 (27-34) Kevin McHale, Hibbing-1976
Best Free Throw Percentage . . . . 1,000 minimum 20 attempts.
(20-20) Mark Nelson, (Stillwater)-1979
Most Rebounds . . . . 69, Bob Laney, (Proctor)-1964
Most Personal Fouls . . . . 15, Jim Rust, (Alexander Ramsey)-1969

Individual Records/Single Game

Most Points . . . . 50, Jimmy Jensen, Bemidji (vs. Woodbury)-1978
Most Field Goals Made . . . . . . 20, Jimmy Jensen, Bemidji (vs. Woodbury)-1978
Best Field Goal Percentage . . . . John Wilson, St. Anthony Village
1,000 (10-10) vs. Winona Cotter-1984
Best Free Throw Percentage . . . . 1,000, minimum 12 attempts
Tom Bock (N. St. Paul)-1971 (13-13)

State Girls Basketball Tournament All-Time Records

Team Records/Tournament—3 Games

Most Points	203, New York Mills-1978
Most Field Goals Made	90, New York Mills-1978
Most Rebounds	146, Albany-1980

Team Records/Single Game

Most Points	88, Eden Valley-Watkins (vs. Cass Lake)-1984
Most Field Goals Made	39, New York Mills (vs. Fertile-Beltrami)-1978
Most Field Goal Attempts	91, Eden Valley-Watkins (vs. Cass Lake)-1984
Most Rebounds	67, Archbishop Brady (vs. Redwood Falls)-1979

Individual Records/3—Games

Most Points	102, Kelly Skalicky, Albany-1981
Most Field Goals Made	47, Kelly Skalicky, Albany-1981
Best Field Goal Percentage	750, (18-24) Kristi Wolhowe, Staples-1985
Best Free Throw Percentage	1,000 (22-22), Laura Gardner Bloomington Jefferson-1978
Most Rebounds:	64, Janice Streit, Eden Valley-Watkins-1983

Individual Records/Single Game

Most Points	45, Kelly Skalicky, Albany (vs. Bagley)-1981
Most Field Goals Made	21, Kelly Skalicky, Albany-1981
Best Field Goal Percentage	900 (9-10), Melanie Moore, Marshall-University (vs. Esko)-1976
Best Free Throw Percentage	1,000 (10-10), Laura Gardner, Bloomington Jefferson-1978 and Tess Rizzardi, Hill-Murray-1978

STATE FOOTBALL PLAYOFF
CHAMPIONSHIP GAMES
1983-1986

1983

Class	Champions	Runners-up	Score
AA	Coon Rapids	Bloomington Jefferson	34-31
A	Hutchinson	Park Rapids	36-14
B	Jordan	Breckenridge	27-0
C	Southland (Adams)	Bird Island-Lake Lillian	28-0
9-Man	Silver Lake	Norman County West/Climax	27-12

1984

Class	Champions	Runners-up	Score
AA	Stillwater	Burnsville	36-33
A	Hutchinson	Centennial	32-7
B	Granite Falls	Breckenridge	13-7
C	Harmony	Glyndon-Felton	20-14
9-Man	Norman Co. West	Silver Lake	37-20

1985

Class	Champions	Runners-up	Score
AA	Burnsville	Appley Valley	27-21
A	New Prague	Mora	16-12
B	Jackson	Mahnomen	26-20
C	Glyndon-Felton	Zumbrota	38-14
9-Man	Westbrook	Norman Co. West	45-18

1986

Class	Champions	Runners-up	Score
AA	Apple Valley	Osseo	35-6
A	Cambridge	Stewartville	24-0
B	Watertown-Mayer	Granite Falls	29-6
C	Minneota	Sherburn-Dunnell	52-19
9-Man	Argyle	Silver Lake	32-7

PREP BOWL RECORDS

Individual Records

Most Yards Rushing . . . . 170, Tom Moll, Glyndon-Felton-1985
Best Rushing Average (15 + att.) . . 10.2, Chris SanAgustin, Apple Valley-1985
Most Touchdowns Rushing . . . . 3, Bruce Bates, Owatonna-1982
Paul Lenz, Hutchinson-1983
Brett Storsved, Norman Co. West-1984
Tommy Durand, Argyle-1986
Longest Run from Scrimmage . . . . 71 yds, Frank Burdick, Mahnomen-1985
Most Yards Passing . . . . 259, Chris Meidt, Minneota-1986
Most Passes Completed . . . . 25, Chris Meidt, Minneota-1986
Most Passes Caught . . . . 7, Bob DeSutter, Minneota-1986
Most Touchdowns Passing . . . . 3, Chris Meidt, Minneota-1986
Most Touchdowns (Rushing/Receiving/Passing) . . . . 4 (2/2/0), Kermit Klefsaas
Brooklyn Center-1982
Most Offensive Yards (Passing/Rushing) . . . . 273 (259/14), Chris Meidt
Minneota-1986

Team Records

Most Points (One Team) 52, Minneota-1986
Most First Downs 24, Minneota-1986
Most Yards Rushing 346, Hutchinson-1983
Most Passes Completed 27, Minneota-1986
Most Passes Intercepted 5, Cambridge-1986
Most Total Offensive Net Yards . . . . 440, Apple Valley-1986

STATE HOCKEY TOURNAMENT WINNERS
1978-1987

Year	CHAMPION	RUNNER-UP	SCORE
1978	Edina East (25-1)	Grand Rapids	5-4**
1979	Edina East (22-4)	Roch. John Marshall	4-3*
1980	Grand Rapids (21-5)	Hill-Murray	2-1
1981	Bloomington Jefferson (17-8-1)	Irondale	3-2
1982	Edina (22-4)	White Bear Lake	6-0
1983	Hill-Murray (28-0)	Burnsville	4-3
1984	Edina (21-4-1)	Bloomington Kennedy	4-2
1985	Burnsville (24-1-1)	Hill-Murray	4-3
1986	Burnsville (20-5-1)	Hill-Murray	4-1
1987	Bloomington Kennedy (25-1-0)	Burnsville	4-1

* Overtime game   **Double Overtime game

MINNESOTA HIGH SCHOOL STATE HOCKEY TOURNAMENT ALL-TIME INDIVIDUAL RECORDS
1945-1987

Most All-Time Total Goals . . . . 36—John Mayasich, Eveleth (1948-51)
Most Goals One Tournament . . . . 15—John Mayasich, Eveleth (1951)
Most Goals One Game . . . . 7—John Mayasich, Eveleth (1951)
Most Points One Period . . . . 5—John Mayasich, Eveleth (1951)
Most Goals One Period . . . . 4—John Mayasich, Eveleth (1951)
Most All-Time Hat Tricks . . . . 7—John Mayasich, Eveleth (1948-51)
Most Stops One Game . . . . 61—Doug Loug, St. Paul Johnson (1970)

STATE WRESTLING TOURNAMENT TEAM CHAMPIONS 1978-1987

Year	School	Region
1978	Anoka (Class AA)	4AA
	Staples (Class A)	6A
1979	Fridley (Class AA)	5AA
	Canby (Class A)	3A
1980	Bloomington Kennedy (Class AA)	6AA
	Goodhue and Staples (Class A)	1A and 6A
1981	Albert Lea (Class AA)	1AA
	Staples (Class A)	6A
1982	Brainerd (Class AA)	8AA
	Staples (Class A)	6A
1983	Apple Valley (Class AA)	1AA
	Staples (Class A)	6A
1984	Bloomington Kennedy (Class AA)	6AA
	Staples (Class A)	6A
1985	Apple Valley (Class AA)	1AA
	Staples (Class A)	6A
1986	Apple Valley (Class AA)	1AA
	Canby (Class A)	3A
1987	Simley (Class AA)	3AA
	Paynesville (Class A)	5A

STATE BOYS TRACK AND FIELD

The Sixty-fifth Annual MSHSL State Boys Track and Field Meet was conducted for a third year at Carl Tonn Field in Osseo on Friday and Saturday, June 5 and 6, 1987, under a format which brought together qualifying participants from Class "AA" and Class "A" in conjunction with participants in the Sixteenth Annual MSHSL State Girls Class "AA" and Class "A" Track and Field Meet.

Class "AA"

Moorhead won its fourth state boys track and field team championship when out-pointing Roseville Area High, 38-34. Mounds View finished in third place for a second straight year with 33 counters. Fifty-two teams scored points.

The title for the Spuds was the school's first in track since 1973. Other championships were won in 1967 and 1968. Moorhead had one state champion, triple jumper Jamie Hagness, who captured the event with a jump of 46'9½".

There was one record set in the boys "AA" competition. Minneapolis North senior Dan Banister set an all-time record in the 300 meter intermediate hurdles event with a time of :36.97 in Friday's preliminaries. Banister also captured a first in the 110 meter high hurdles.

Another double winner in the meet was Roseville Area junior Rod Smith. He won both the 100 and 200 meter dash events.

Class "A"

Elgin-Millville High School won its first ever state team championship in track when amassing 48 points to easily triumph over runner-up Minneapolis DeLaSalle, who had 36 counters in the Class "A" competition.

Elgin-Millville's Donovan Bergstrom set a Class "A" record en route to winning the 1,600 meter run event. He had a time of 4:16.63.

Other Class "A" record holders were Mike Yonkey, a senior from Wells-Easton; Ed Hegland, a senior from Appleton/Milan; and Ross Thompson, a senior from Esko.

Yonkey was a double winner, capturing firsts in the shot put (60'8½) and discus (192'7"), which is an all-time meet record. Hegland, too, set an all-time record with a triple jump (48'8½"), while Thompson now has the "A" pole vault record (14'9").

STATE GIRLS TRACK AND FIELD

Class "AA"

Rocori High in Cold Spring won its first state championship in track with a 48-42 point margin over runner-up Rosemount. Forest Lake was in third place with 34 counters.

The state title for the Central Minnesota school was the school's first in any sport since joining the MSHSL during the 1974-75 school year.

Kristie Oleen of Blaine was the lone "AA" participant to set an all-time record. Other records included Kim Kauls, a senior from Forest Lake, and Kristi Dean, a junior from Fridley. Kauls set the 1,600 meter run mark with a time of 4:56.46, while Dean established a new record in the 300 meter low hurdles event with a :43.82 clocking.

Class "A"

Windom, led by triple winner Heather Van Norman, won the Class "A" track title for the first time when outpointing runner-up Plainview, 30-28.

Van Norman, a junior, scored all of Windom's 30 points in capturing first place finishes in the 100, 200, and 400 meter runs. Her time of :24.58 in the 200 was an all-time state record.

Van Norman has now won each of those three events the past three years for a total of nine gold medals earned.

Other records broken this year in addition to the one established by Van Norman were by Liesa Brateng, a junior from Roseau who set an all-time mark of :42.62 in the 300 meter low hurdles, and by the Norwood-Young America 4 x 100 meter relay team who had a :49.38 time in that event for an "A" record. Members of that team were Cathy Oelfke, Brigitte Stuewe, Julie Glaeser, and Sheila Stuewe.

Myth, Humor and Comedy

Two firm-jawed women stare from the cover of John Louis Anderson's book, "Scandinavian Humor & Other Myths."

That the women are not smiling - in fact, they look positively grim - is the point of the joke. Minnesotans know very well the women may be guffawing inside, but they're certainly not going to let it show.

Anderson, a Minneapolis free-lance writer and photographer, has sold more than 100,000 copies of his self-published book. In it he's caught the spirit of this state's humor with his pictures of Convolu, the God of Sullen Depression; Lefse, the Goddess of Unseasoned Food and Comatose, God of Fishing. He warns non-Minnesotans never to confuse **hot dish** which is the thing you eat, with **casserole** the thing in which you put the hot dish.

Howard Mohr, a free-lance writer from southwestern Minnesota, explains the rituals of the state's social life in his book, "How to Talk Minnesotan."

He gravely takes the reader through "The Long Goodbye," in which a couple takes several hours to depart after a visit, and offers the uninitiated a way to respond to the invitation to have "a little lunch." His list of the 15 opening gambits in Minnesota conversation begins with "The heat's not bad if you don't move around."

Mohr honed his craft as a writer from Garrison Keillor's A Prairie Home Companion, the public radio show for which the Anoka-born Keillor invented Lake Wobegon, the mythical little Minnesota town "that time forgot."

Keillor ended the show in the summer of 1987, but for more than 10 years PHC had entertained some three million Americans with nostalgic tales of life in Lake Wobegon sponsored by Bertha's Kitty Boutique and the Fearmonger's Shoppe. Keillor's book, "Lake Wobegon Days," was a national best-seller.

Keillor, Mohr and Anderson illustrate the elements of Minnesota's unique sense of humor.

It is low key, going for grins rather than guffaws. It pokes gentle fun at the state's inhabitants. It focuses on the little pleasures of life, like nice weather and potluck suppers. It shows its immigrant roots by celebrating family, friends and church doings. And it is **clean**.

Whether or not Minnesotans have a sense of humor, and what makes them laugh, was probably a matter of supreme indifference to the rest of the country until Walter Mondale, who is Norwegian, ran for President of the United States in 1984.

Mondale's campaign was covered by political reporters from other states who just didn't understand the Minnesota psyche. One nationally-syndicated scribe allowed as how he couldn't always tell when Fritz was awake, much less when he was enjoying himself.

Molly Ivins, who was a journalist in the Twin Cities for three years, tried to explain Minnesotans to readers of her column in the **Dallas Times Herald** newspaper.

"Like other Midwestern tribes," Ivins wrote, "Minnesotans are almost terminally sensible; another deep cultural trait of the Minnesotans is reticence. They do not believe in putting themselves forward; they consider it unseemly."

Ivins ended her affectionate essay by saying, "It's utterly hopeless to criticize Mondale for being dull: in Minnesota, excitement is frowned upon."

Not that famous Minnesotans haven't been chided before for lacking a sense of humor.

Charles A. Lindbergh, the state's most celebrated aviator, was noted for having almost never said anything funny. Someone is supposed to have explained that by saying: "Well, did you ever try to tell a joke in Minneapolis?"

When the first white settlers began building towns in Minnesota in about the 1840's, there wasn't much to joke about. These immigrants from Scandinavian countries, Germany and, later, from Ireland, were fleeing harsh social and political times in their homelands and faced a difficult and untamed land when they arrived.

These pioneers liked strong words. They liked action even better.

James M. Goodhue, editor of the **Minnesota Pioneer**, typified the kind of journalism the settlers approved. When Territorial Secretary Charles K. Smith was hounded from office in 1851, Goodhue recalled with satisfaction his prediction two years earlier that "Secretary Smith had stolen **into** the Territory, and stolen **in** the Territory and would in the end steal **out** of the Territory, with whatever plunder he could abstract from it."

Goodhue was a wit, too. In a notice concerning a well-known local vagrant, he even anticipated a line that would later be used to good effect by Mark Twain, who was still a small boy in Hannibal, Mo., at the time: "Bob Hughes, who it was feared was drowned, requests us to say that the report of his death is undoubtedly premature and greatly exaggerated."

History, folklore and humor come together in Minnesota's most famous character—Paul Bunyan.

It's been assumed that Paul is a true American myth, a character spun out of whole cloth by lumberjacks telling tall tales around the stove during long winter nights.

It's not that simple. Paul Bunyan himself was very likely a genuine folk character, with French-Canadian roots. The first published Paul Bunyan story appeared in 1910 in a Detroit newspaper. It concerned the Round River drive, a long drive which took place on a river that seemed to go on forever until the loggers realized that it was a circular stream; they were passing the same point over and over.

In 1914 the **American Lumberman**, a journal published by Minnesota's Red River Company, printed a Paul Bunyan poem. The company also issued a booklet that same year entitled, "Introducing Mr. Paul Bunyan of Westwood, California."

Why Westwood, California? Because Red River had just opened a new mill there,

Scandinavian Humor

JOHN LOUIS ANDERSON'S

OTHER & MYTHS

and wanted to expand its market for California pine.

The author of these works was William B. Laughead (yes, that was his real name), who insisted that he had heard Paul Bunyan stories in the lumber camps well before 1910. Laughead, however, took sole credit for creating Babe the Blue Ox, Johnny Inkslinger and the rest of Paul's supporting cast.

Laughead wrote Paul Bunyan stories for the company until its sale in the 1940's. Scholars think most of the tales we know today were Laughead's creations and not real lumberjack yarns at all.

Minnesota has authentic lumberjack heroes. One was Otto Walta, whom the Finns of St. Louis county in northern Minnesota speak of with pride.

Walta was born in Finland in 1875 and died in 1959. He came to America in 1898, but never learned to speak English. Even in his old age, they say, he could rip trees from the ground, carry boulders, and bend a three-inch steel bar into a fishhook shape. He was alleged to have once ripped up an 800-pound piece of the railroad to use for prying up stumps on his farm.

Minnesota's Swedes also have a lumberjack hero, the trickster Ola Varmlanning, who achieved immortality when he moved to the Twin Cities during the 1880's and became a regular at various bars, singing and playing the accordion for drinks.

They tell how Ola once took offense at a rookie Irish policeman who was trying to arrest him. So Ola took away the young man's badge, club and revolver, locked him to a call box (from which policemen phoned in reports to the station) and proceeded to the nearest station house. There he turned in the hardware and asked to be arrested in a more courteous manner. He was, and "sentenced to 90 days" became a Swedish-American saying.

Today, Scandinavian humor still provides a bedrock for many of the jokes that make Minnesotans smile. (Or at least twitch their mouths.)

Scandinavian jokes, which have now spread into the general population, can be roughly divided into three groups. But anyone reading humor about immigrants should remember that the immigrants themselves may never have told some of these jokes; rather, the jokes were told to ridicule the newcomers. A staff member at St. Paul's Irish American Institute said this is especially true of "Pat and Mike" jokes that were told about the Irish but are offensive to them.

The first kind of Scandinavian-derived joke is all-purpose, in that it can be told on any ethnic group:

Ole and Yon were shingling a roof. Yon noticed that Ole was studying his nails carefully and discarding many of them. He asked why. Ole said, "Dose are no gude—da heads are on da wrong end."

"Ya lunkhead, Ole," Yon replied. "Dose nails are left-handed nails vich ve use ven ve are vorking on de odder side of dis roof."

Then there's the dialect joke, as in, "Ya know, ven ay kom to America saz years ago, ay couldn't even speak 'Enyinear'—an now, by golly, ay are vun."

Some Scandinavian humor revolved around rivalries and antagonisms among the immigrants from various nations.

The Danes tell this one: A Swede came home drunk one night and collapsed in a pigsty. He woke the next morning and felt a warm body next to him. He asked the obvious question, "Er de Svensk? (Are you Swedish?)" The pig replied, grunting, "Norsk, Norsk."

The third kind of Scandinavian humor is a little harder to describe. It reflects the stern, uncompromising conditions the immigrants left in Scandinavia, conditions which produced a humor that scorned petty considerations like a punchline.

A good example is the comic strip "Han Ola og Han Per," which appeared in the Norwegian-American newspaper, **Decorah Posten**, from 1918 to 1942.

Dr. Johan Buckley, professor of English at Concordia College, Moorhead, has researched and co-edited a book about Ola and Per.

Buckley says the comic strip is significant today because it "illustrates the traditional primary values of humor: as entertainment; as literary and graphic artistry; and as history, with predominant folklore elements that mainly reflect an immigrant society's pains and difficulties of adapting to mainstream America with its rapidly changing customs and attitudes."

Created by Peter Julius Rosendahl, a farmer-artist from Spring Grove, Minn., who died in 1942, the Ola and Per strips were in Norwegian. Buckley explains that the main humorous theme is the tension between the dream world and the real world of the immigrants.

In one strip Per complains he never has a chance with the young girls. Ola advises him that the problem is simply that he cannot speak "Yeinki." Following Ola's advice the next time Per meets a young girl, he lifts his hat and greets her, "Hello, Pie Faes." Per lands in the gutter, where he comforts himself with the favorite sentimental song of Norwegians in America, "Kan de glemme Norge?" (Can You Forget Old Norway?)

"The comic strip is a unique document of the times that span the coming of not only the immigrant but also the machine age to the American farm," Buckley says. "As the human being struggles to bridge the Old and New worlds, the comic strip gives ample humorous evidence that the individual endures."

In the 1920's and 30's Minnesota, somewhat surprisingly, became a sort of "blue humor" capitol of the nation, because it was from Robbinsdale that Wilford Fawcett published a magazine called **Captain Billy's Whiz-Bang**, which filled the niche in its time that **National Lampoon** fills in ours, with just a touch of the **National Enquirer** thrown in.

One veteran of **Captain Billy's Whiz-Bang** was Cedric Adams. As a news reporter for WCCO radio and columnist for the **Minneapolis Star** and **Sunday Tribune**, Adams dispensed folksy, friendly information and advice from the 20's through the 50's.

His typically Minnesota humor was subtle, producing good feelings more than guffaws.

Another Minnesota humorist who gained wide respect was Clelland Card, best known for his Scandinavian-dialect character, Axel Torgerson, whom he portrayed on radio and television in the late 40's and 50's.

The tradition of radio humor started by Adams and Card continued in the 60's and 70's with WCCO's Charlie Boone and Roger Erickson, the irreverent pair who have made the Worst Jokes a kind of institution. The pair celebrated their 25th year on the air in August, 1984, and Steve Cannon, who does WCCO's drive-time shows, has invented a whole cast of bizarre characters, including the folksy Ma Linger, Morgan Mundane and Backlash LaRue.

Charles Schulz, whose Peanuts cartoon strip runs in hundreds of newspapers, started drawing Charlie Brown and his friends while he worked at the **St. Paul Pioneer Press**. Unfortunately, Schulz was told by an editor that nobody wanted to look at pictures of "a round-headed little kid." Said editor kept a Schulz drawing in his office for years, as a constant humbling reminder of his ability to make mistakes.

More quirky (some say indefinable) humor enlivened the Twin Cities when cartoonist Dick Guindon worked for the **Minneapolis Tribune**.

Guindon, who has moved to Detroit, was tuned into every nuance of Minnesota living. From his drawing board leaped well-dressed, upwardly mobile little kids from Wayzata, ice fishermen wearing flap-eared caps sitting motionless by their holes in the ice, and the two ladies in what had to be polyester dresses commenting on the world at large. Guindon's cartoons about carp could only be appreciated in Minnesota. In fact, there are now Guindon-inspired carp T-shirts and there are even carp festivals in the state.

In the late 1970's and early 80's, a new source of laughter came onto the scene as Minnesota began to produce stand-up comedians who are making names for themselves nationally.

Jeff Gerbino, Louis Anderson, Joel Hodgson and Jeff Cesario are all young comics who started in Minneapolis clubs and moved to Los Angeles. Hodgson has appeared on Saturday Night Live and the David Letterman television shows and rotund Louis Anderson has signed a six-figure contract to appear as Fatty Arbuckle in a movie about the late comedian's life.

Both Anderson and Hodgson have said they are glad they began their careers in the Twin Cities, where they could experiment with various styles.

Minnesota audiences, Anderson said, made him work hard and forced him to keep his act clean. "They force you to use material rather than just swearing," he said.

Hansen says the Twin Cities is a good area for comedy because there are so many clubs and colleges to play. He takes his own act to Los Angeles and New York, and is in a good position to talk about contemporary Minnesota humor.

"Minnesota audiences will give the benefit of the doubt," he said. "They're polite, they'll take political humor during elections; otherwise, forget it. They like to be lampooned."

Hansen does jokes about deer hunting, ice fishing and the weather—traditional sources of Minnesota humor, as well as jokes about the St. Paul-Minneapolis rivalry.

But Hansen does not do ethnic jokes, nor do any of the other comics he knows. Then he pauses and admits, "Well, sometimes I add a Norwegian accent when I'm doing ice fishing jokes."

But what, a non-Minnesotan might ask, could be funny about ice fishing in the first place? Why does it, and other code words, automatically draw smiles?

Ice fishing is funny because so many people love it even though it's a form of slow torture in cold weather.

Lutefisk is funny because, even though it smells awful and doesn't even taste very good, kids are still being subjected to it during the holidays by their Scandinavian grandmothers.

"Uff dah" is funny because, even though the immigrants may never have said it, it now means anything from rage to embarrassment.

Even Minnesotans who leave the state cling to their roots, as shown in a **Minneapolis Tribune** letter to the editor from a woman who now lives in Casper, Wyo.

She wrote, "My 5-year-old son came home from kindergarten and reported an extremely amusing incident. "It was so funny I almost laughed," she explained gravely. "I was a proud mother that day. The Norwegian taboo against ever looking like you're having fun had been thoroughly internalized."

INDEX

NOTES

NOTES

NOTES

NOTES

NOTES

NOTES

NOTES

NOTES

A Visit to
CHRISTMASLAND

A Visit to
CHRISTMASLAND

ARMAND EISEN

Illustrated by Victoria Lisi

Background illustrations by Julio Lisi

Ariel Books

Andrews and McMeel

Kansas City

This book is dedicated to Emily Egan.

—AE

Library of Congress Catalog Card Number: 93-70497

ISBN: 0-8362-4506-7

Design: Diane Stevenson / Snap-Haus Graphics

A Visit to
CHRISTMASLAND

Dear Santa,

I live in a house and my name is Emily.
You live in Christmasland, a place I would love to see.

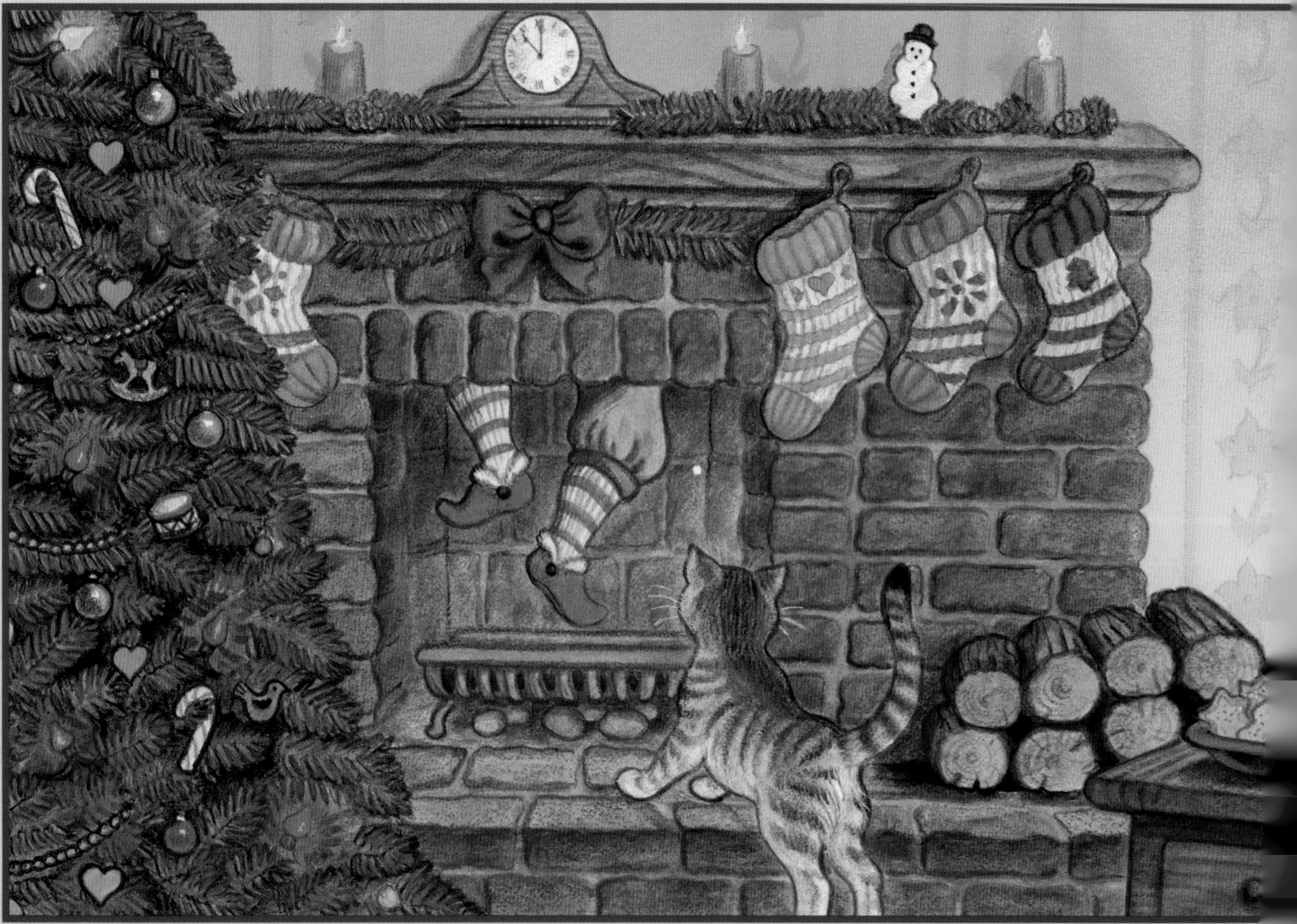

While Emily took her nap by the big Christmas tree,
One of Santa's elves slid down the chimney.

"Wake up, Emily," a little voice said.
"Really! This is no time for bed!
Santa sent me. So please take my hand.
And we will both fly away to Christmasland!"

"That's where we're going to have lots of fun.
Soon you'll meet Santa, the elves, and everyone."

"Welcome to Christmasland! Ho! Ho! Ho! Ho!
Have a good time on your visit. Now off you go!"

"This is Santa's Workshop where we make all the toys.
Pretty dolls for girls and soldiers for boys."

"Meet Dasher and Dancer,
And there are Comet and Prancer!
Each year on Christmas Eve up, up they will fly,
Pulling Santa's sleigh into the sky!"

"These gifts are for children who've been good all year.
Each box holds a toy and lots of Christmas cheer."

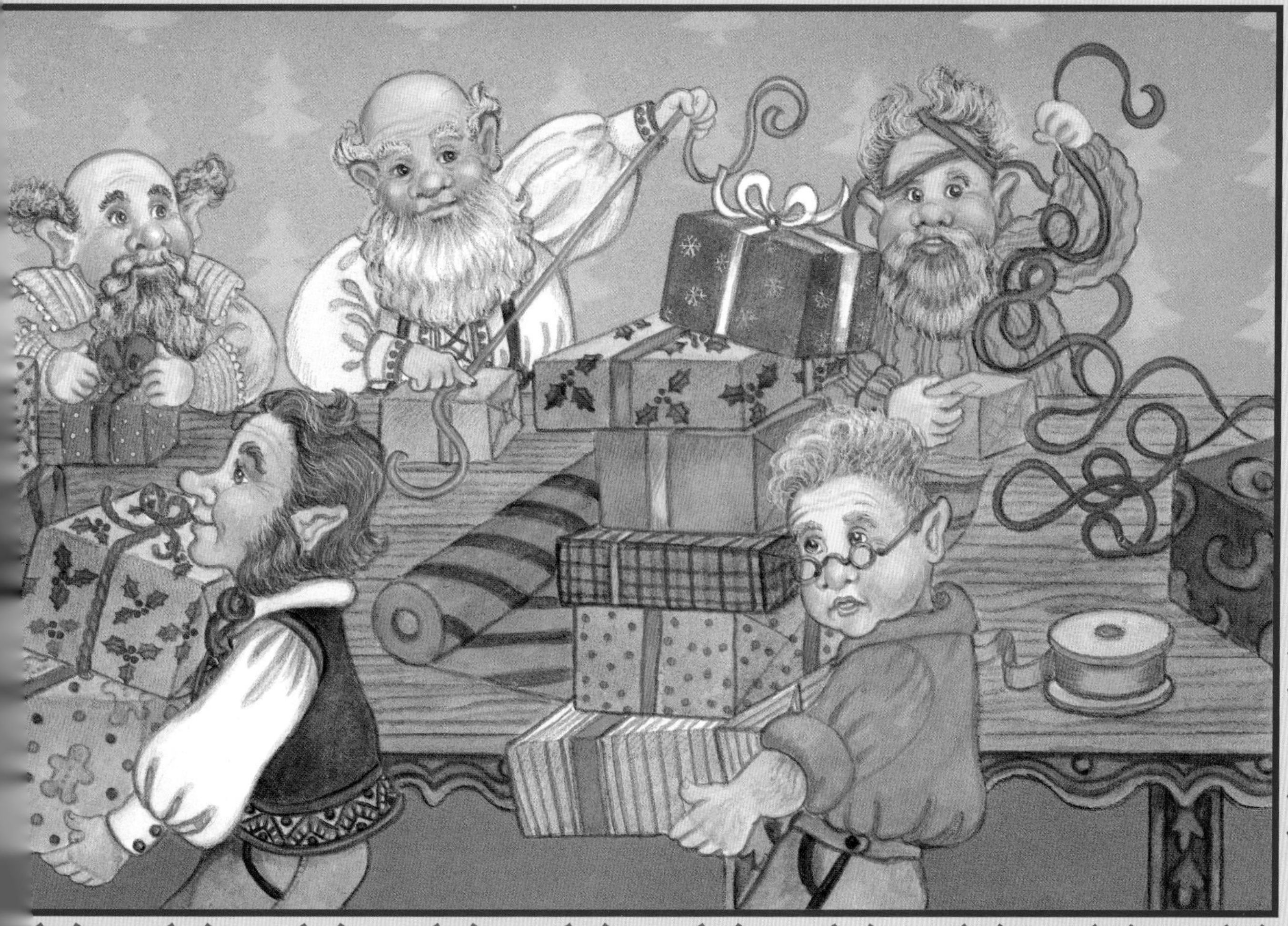

"Shall we visit Santa's baby animals, too?
I see Snowflake the Bear has taken a liking to you."

"Cookies, candy, and cake all taste so yummy!
But if you eat too much, you'll get sick to your tummy!"

"Here's a bracelet I made. Slip it over your hand.
It will make you think of Santa and of Christmasland."

"Goodbye, everybody! My bracelet ... oh, no!
I'll never see it again. It will be lost in the snow!"